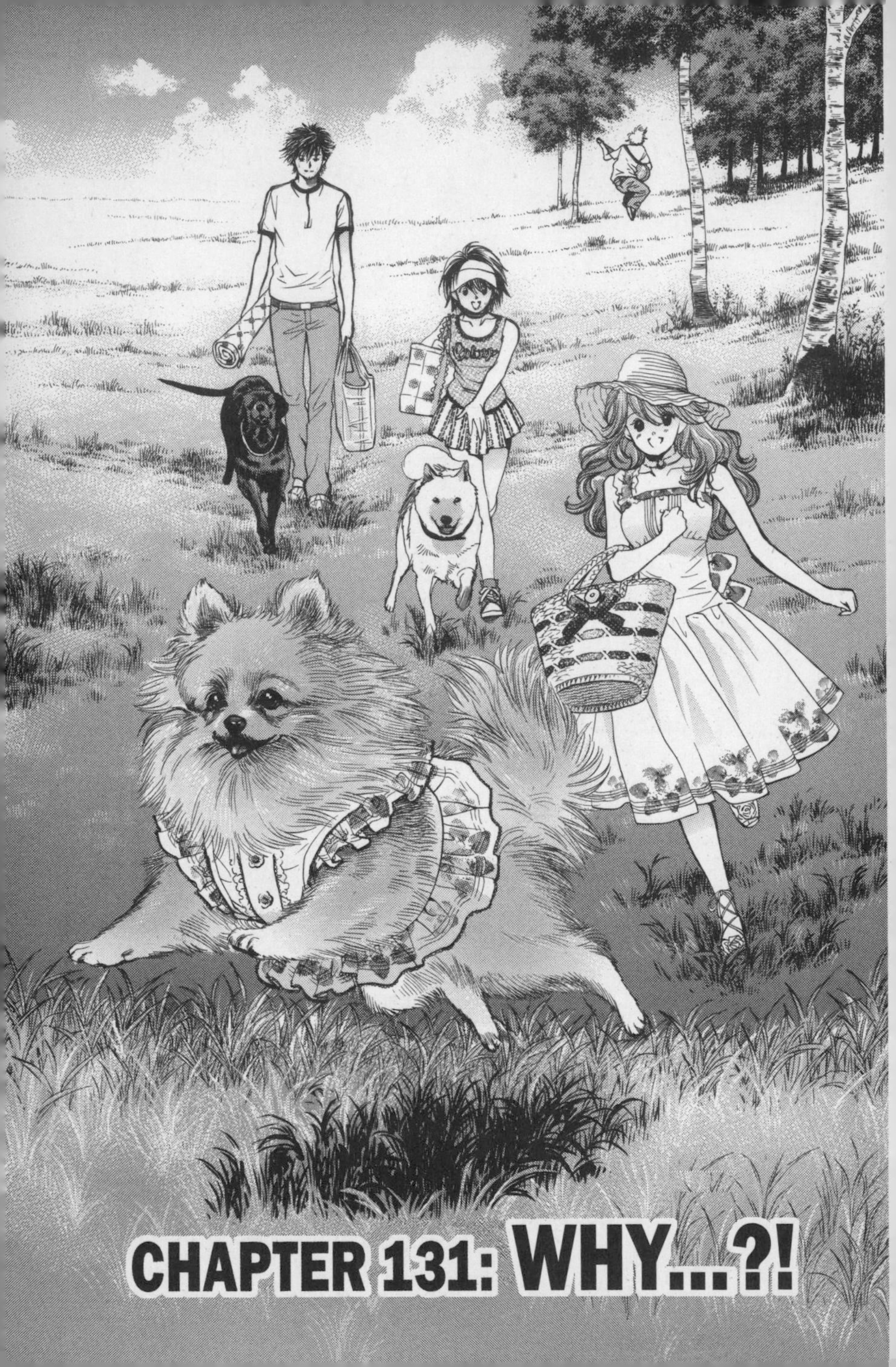

CHAPTER 131: WHY...?!

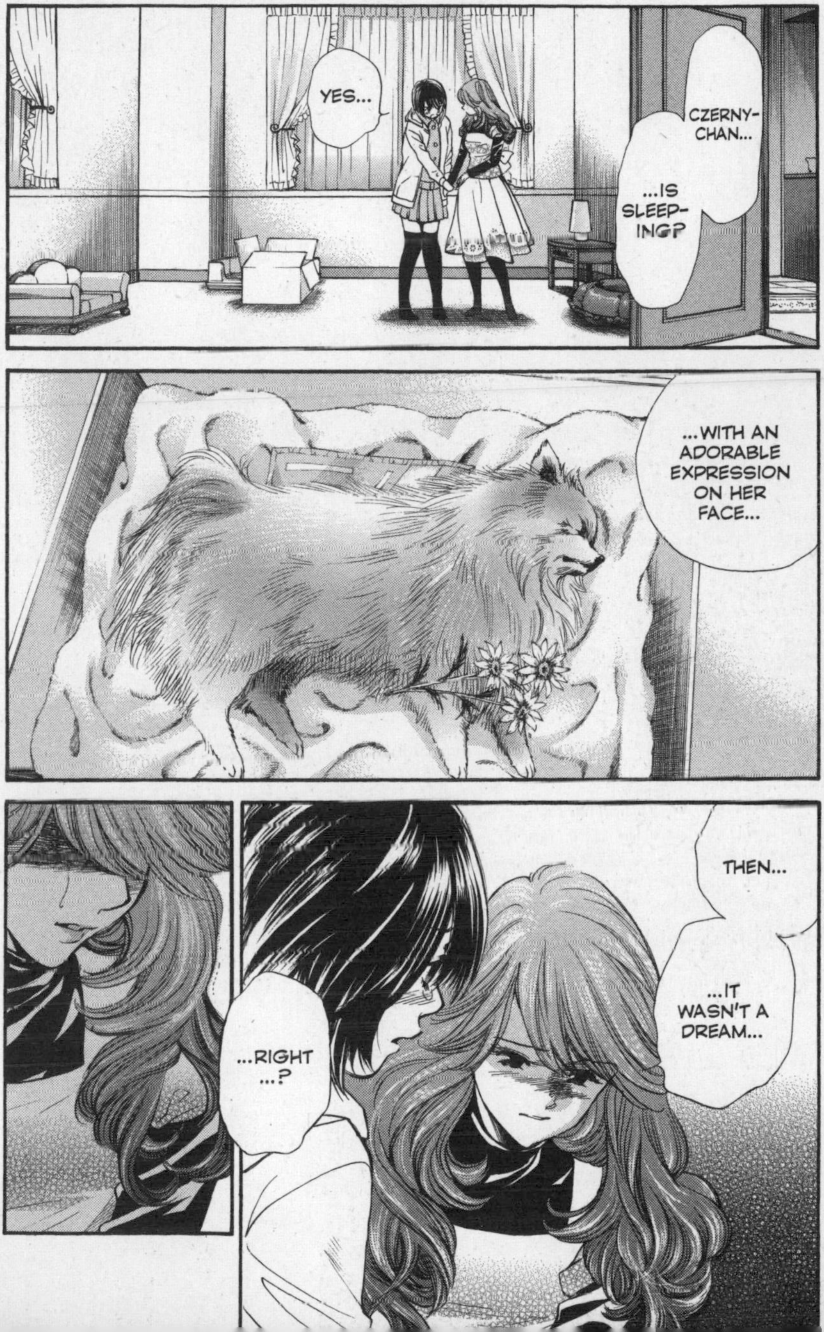
CZERNY-CHAN...
...IS SLEEPING?
YES...
...WITH AN ADORABLE EXPRESSION ON HER FACE...
THEN...
...IT WASN'T A DREAM...
...RIGHT ...?

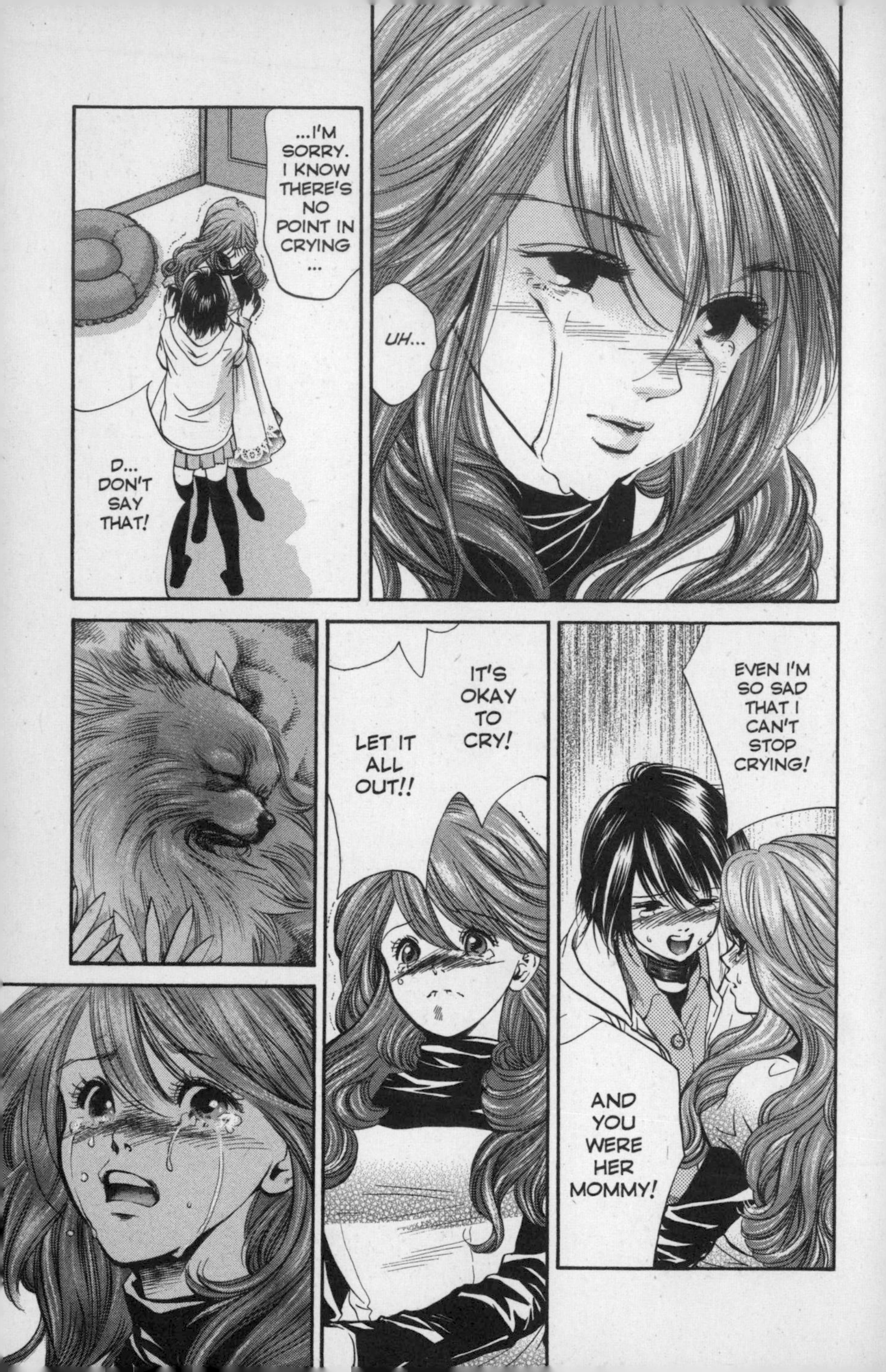
UH...
...I'M SORRY. I KNOW THERE'S NO POINT IN CRYING ...
D... DON'T SAY THAT!
EVEN I'M SO SAD THAT I CAN'T STOP CRYING!
AND YOU WERE HER MOMMY!
IT'S OKAY TO CRY!
LET IT ALL OUT!!

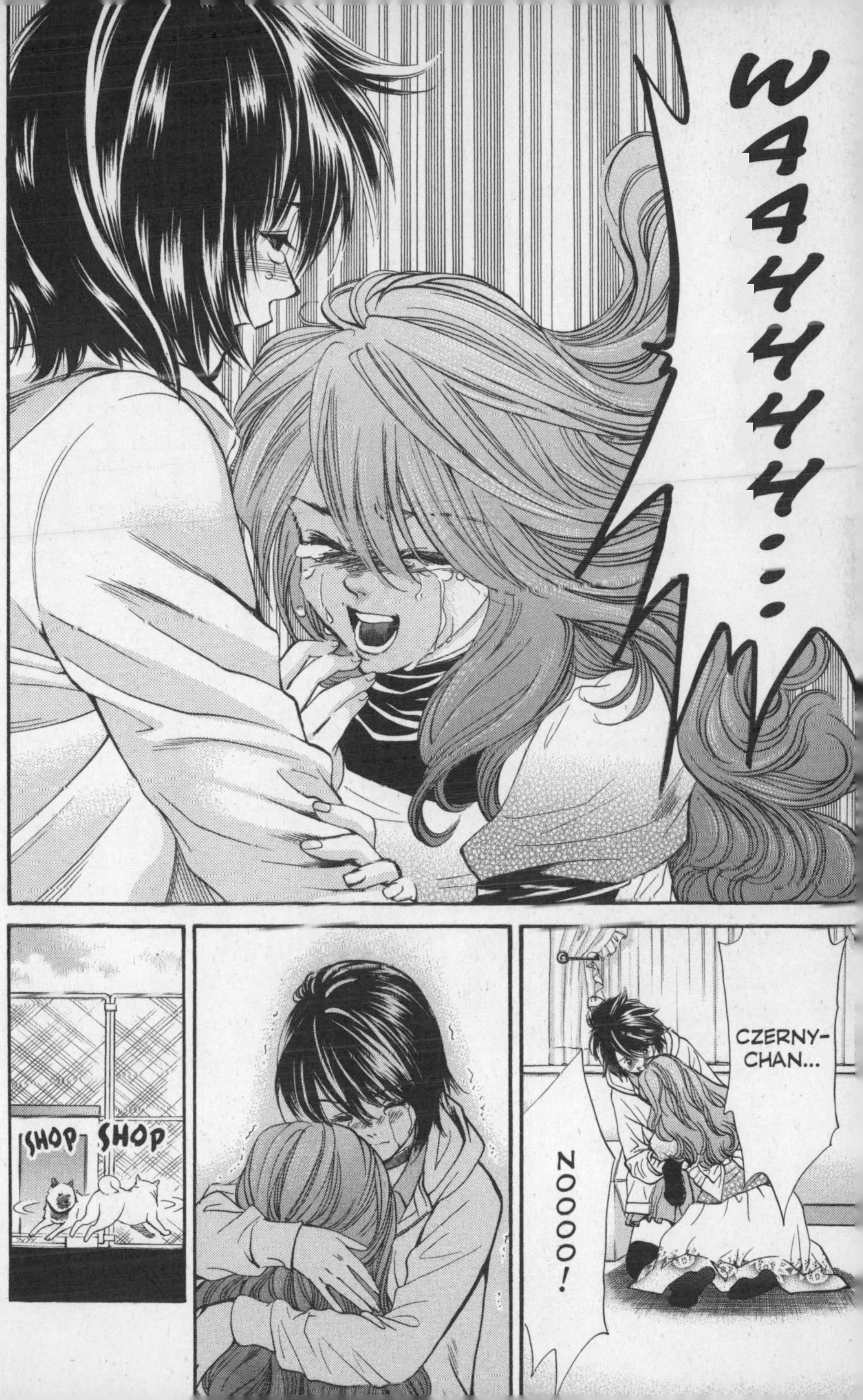
WAAHHHH...
CZERNY-CHAN...
NOOOOO!
SHOP SHOP

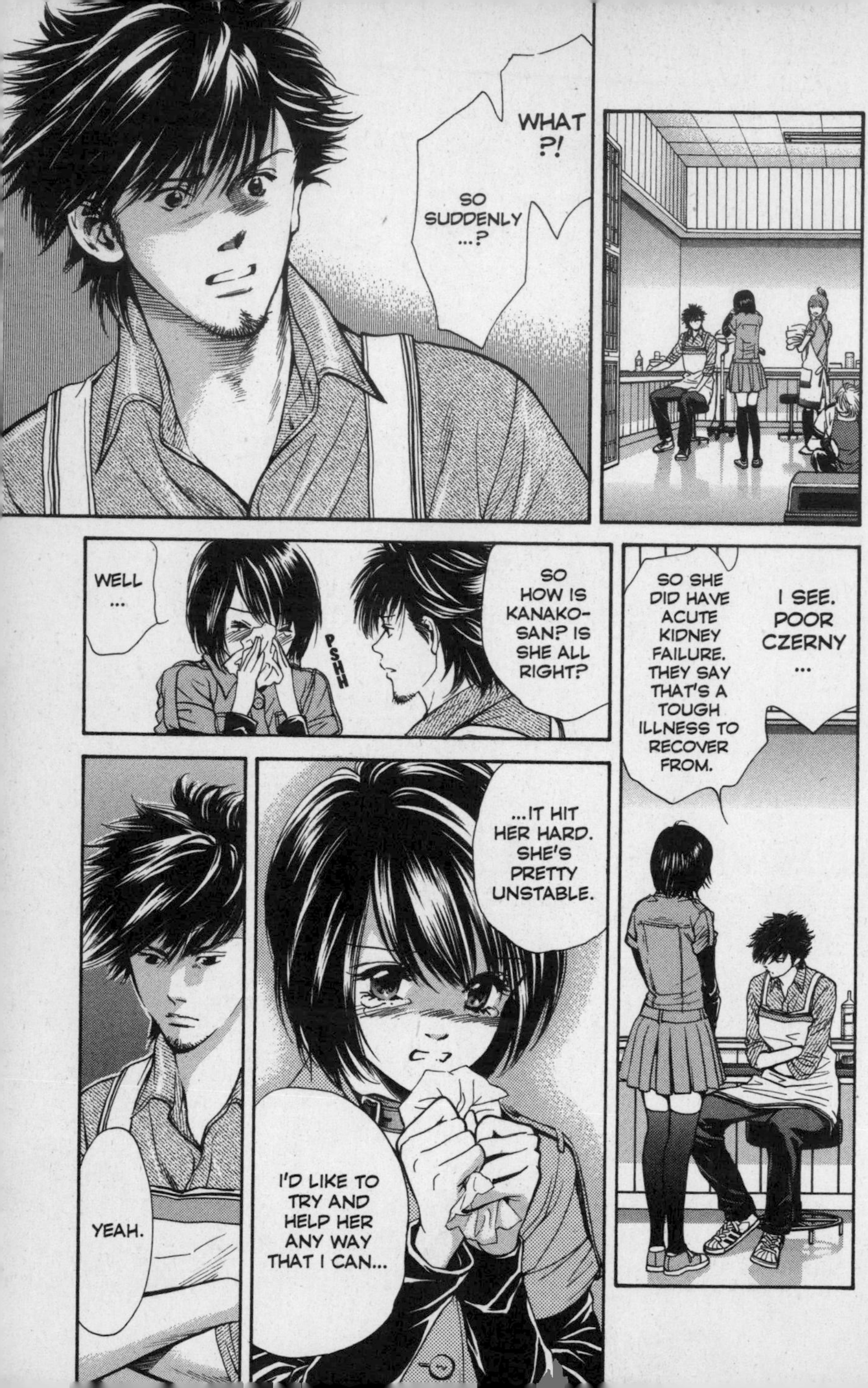

WHAT ?!
SO SUDDENLY ...?
I SEE. POOR CZERNY ...
SO SHE DID HAVE ACUTE KIDNEY FAILURE. THEY SAY THAT'S A TOUGH ILLNESS TO RECOVER FROM.
SO HOW IS KANAKO-SAN? IS SHE ALL RIGHT?
PSHH
WELL ...
...IT HIT HER HARD. SHE'S PRETTY UNSTABLE.
I'D LIKE TO TRY AND HELP HER ANY WAY THAT I CAN...
YEAH.

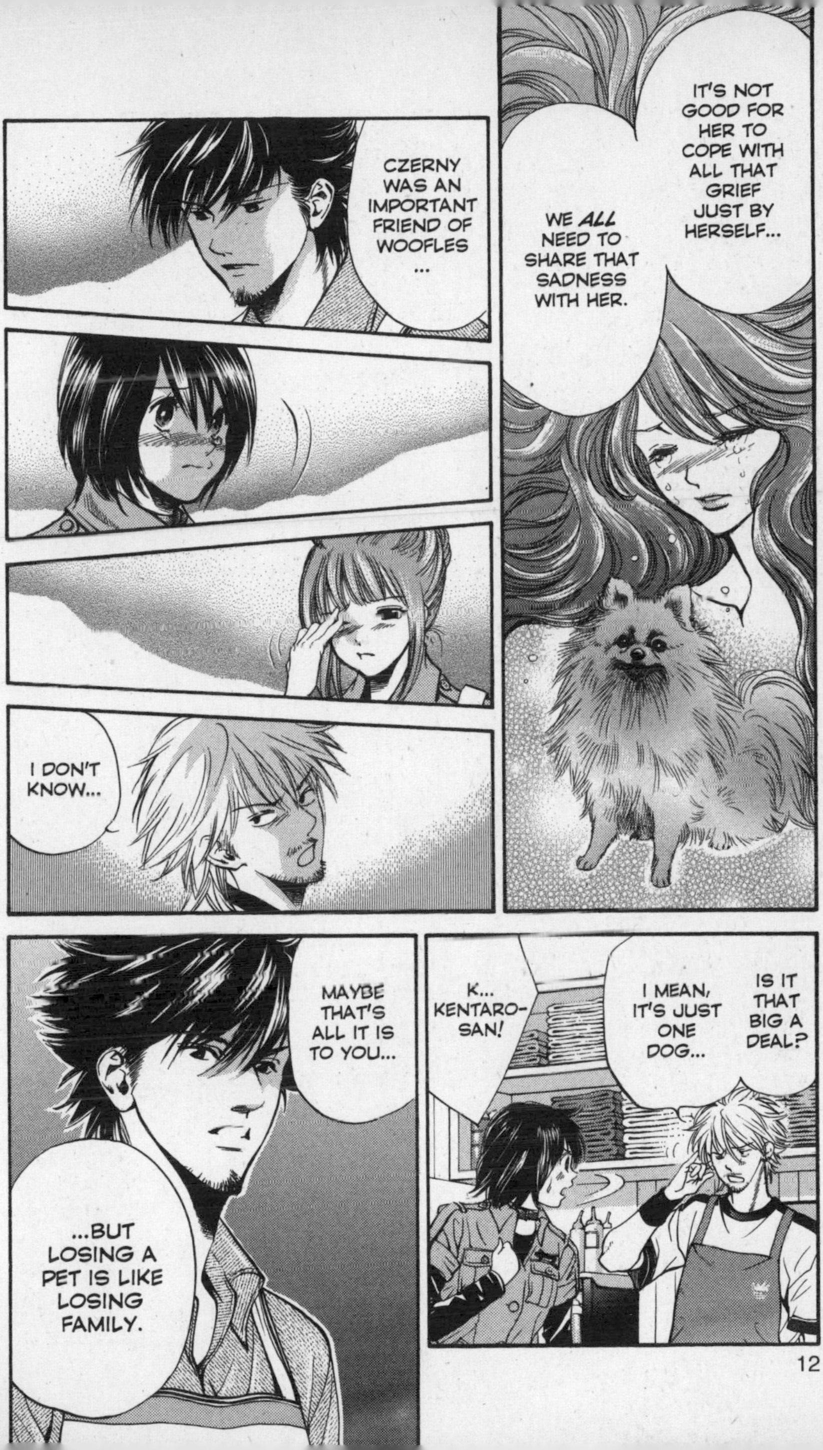
IT'S NOT GOOD FOR HER TO COPE WITH ALL THAT GRIEF JUST BY HERSELF...
WE *ALL* NEED TO SHARE THAT SADNESS WITH HER.
CZERNY WAS AN IMPORTANT FRIEND OF WOOFLES ...
I DON'T KNOW...
IS IT THAT BIG A DEAL?
I MEAN, IT'S JUST ONE DOG...
K... KENTARO-SAN!
MAYBE THAT'S ALL IT IS TO YOU...
...BUT LOSING A PET IS LIKE LOSING FAMILY.

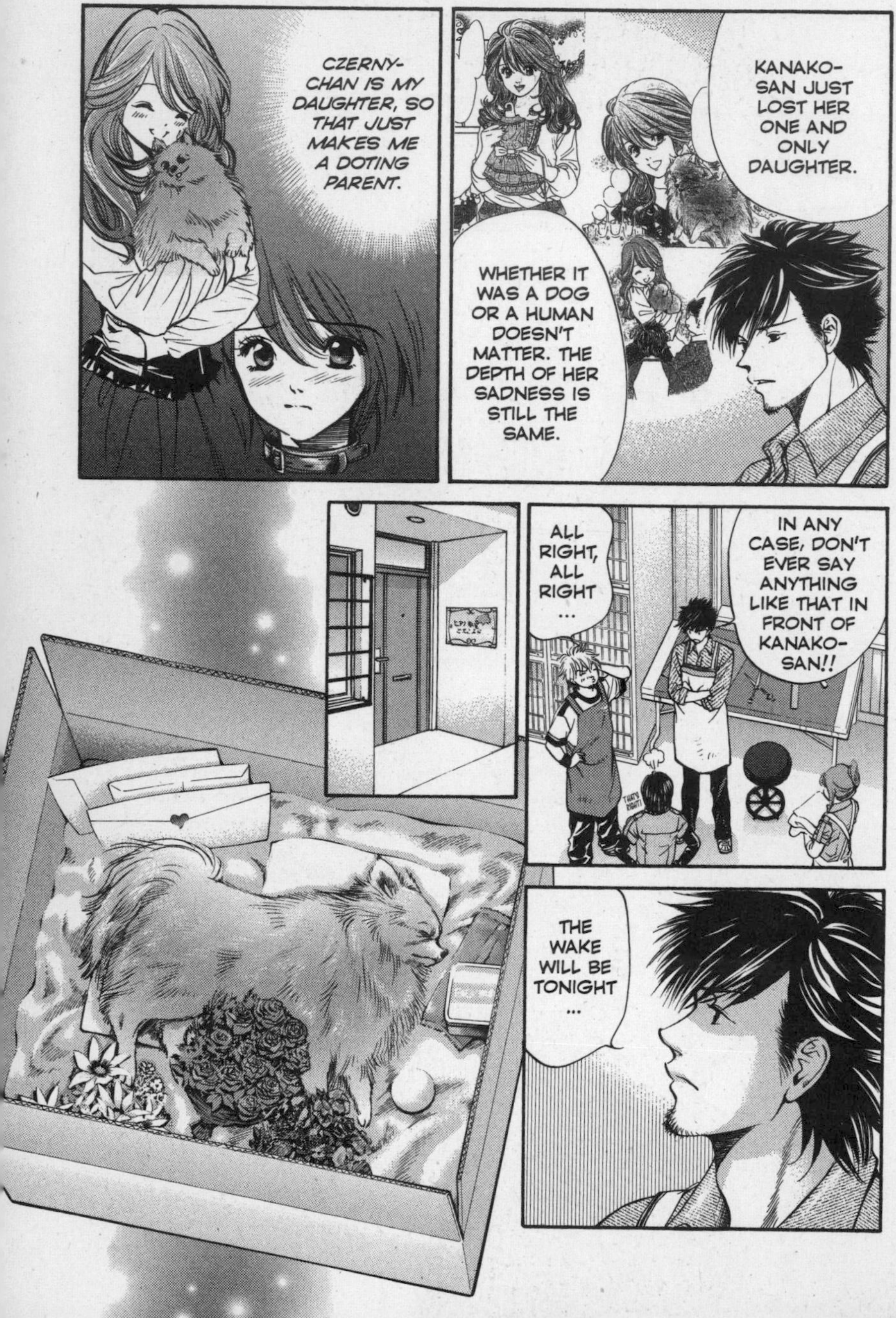
KANAKO-SAN JUST LOST HER ONE AND ONLY DAUGHTER.
WHETHER IT WAS A DOG OR A HUMAN DOESN'T MATTER. THE DEPTH OF HER SADNESS IS STILL THE SAME.
CZERNY-CHAN IS MY DAUGHTER, SO THAT JUST MAKES ME A DOTING PARENT.
IN ANY CASE, DON'T EVER SAY ANYTHING LIKE THAT IN FRONT OF KANAKO-SAN!!
ALL RIGHT, ALL RIGHT ...
THE WAKE WILL BE TONIGHT ...

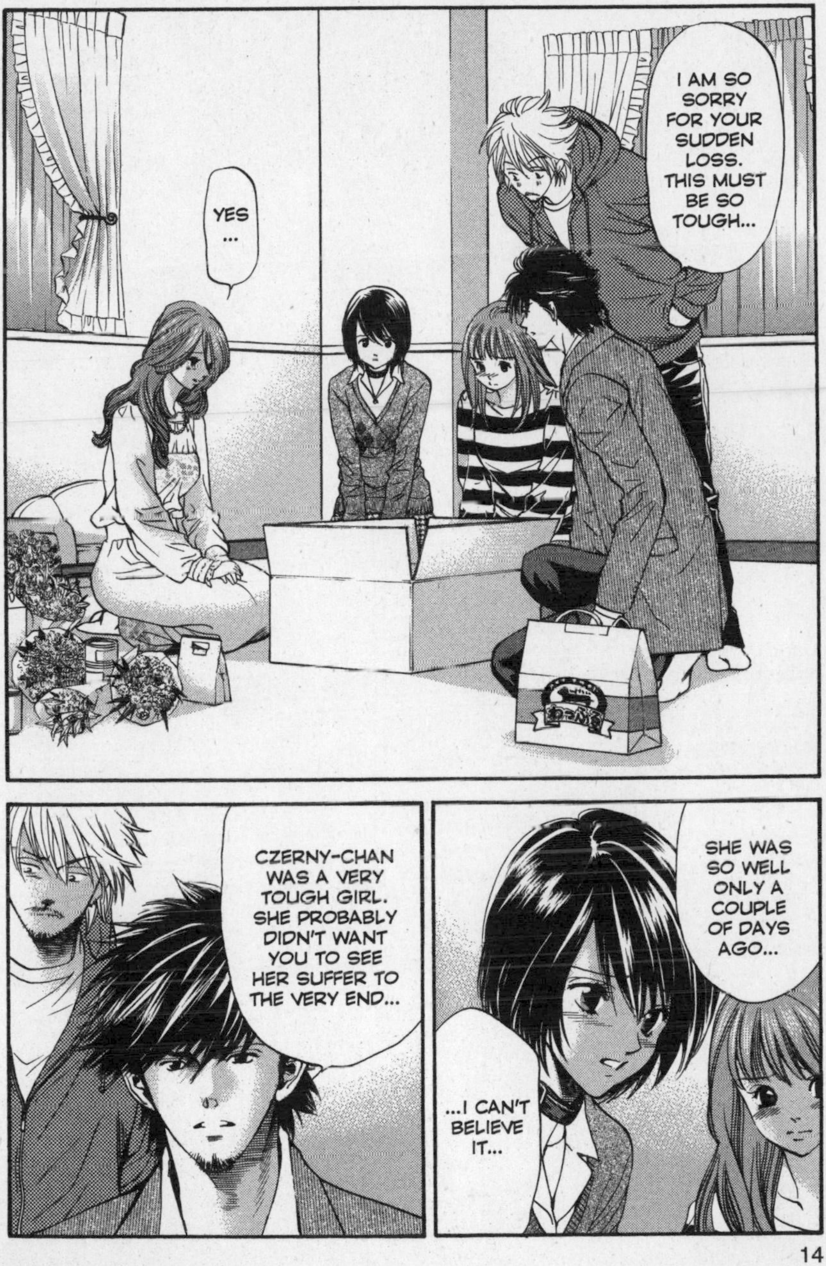
I AM SO SORRY FOR YOUR SUDDEN LOSS. THIS MUST BE SO TOUGH...
YES ...
SHE WAS SO WELL ONLY A COUPLE OF DAYS AGO...
...I CAN'T BELIEVE IT...
CZERNY-CHAN WAS A VERY TOUGH GIRL. SHE PROBABLY DIDN'T WANT YOU TO SEE HER SUFFER TO THE VERY END...

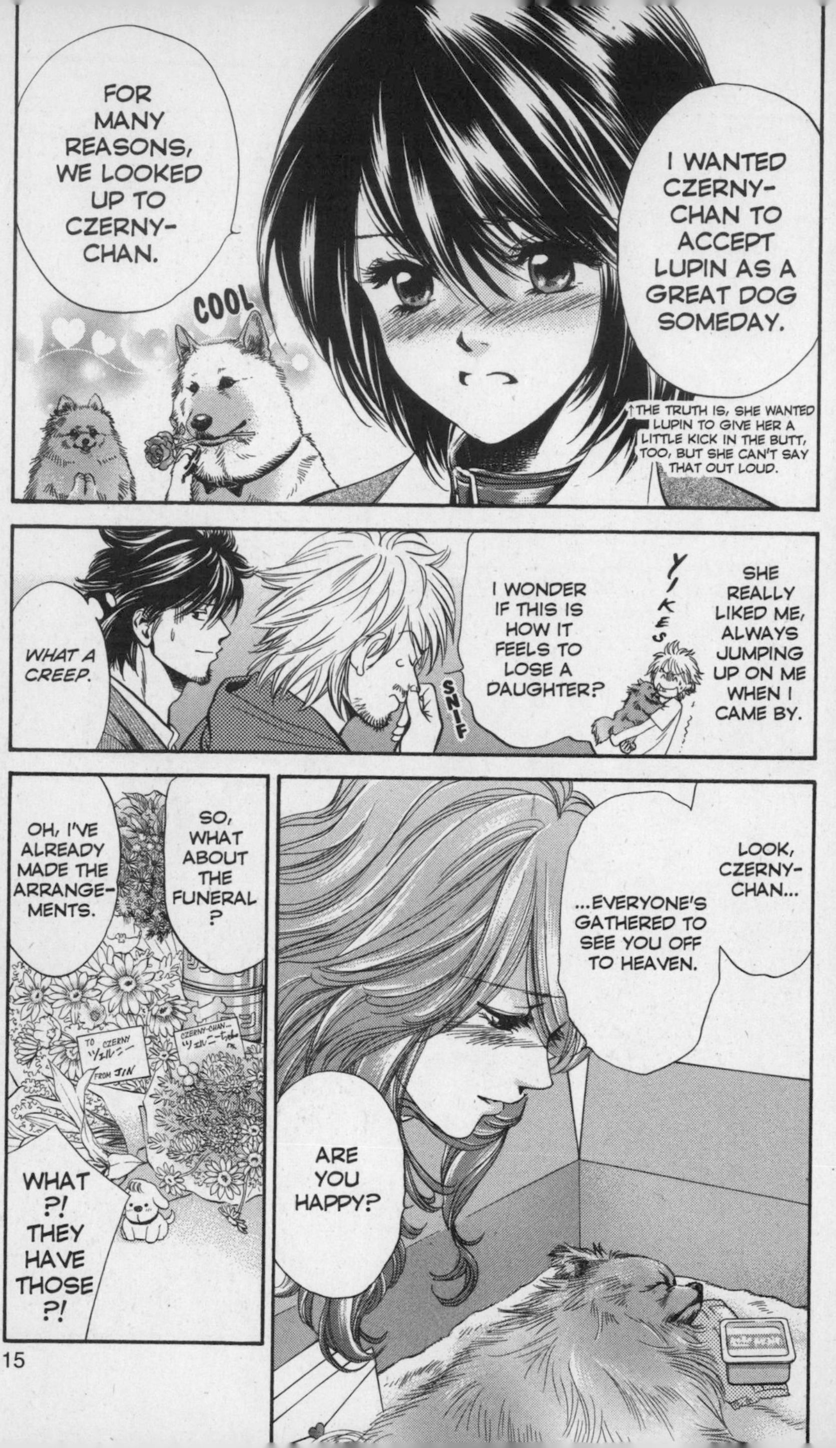
I WANTED CZERNY-CHAN TO ACCEPT LUPIN AS A GREAT DOG SOMEDAY.
FOR MANY REASONS, WE LOOKED UP TO CZERNY-CHAN.
COOL
↑THE TRUTH IS, SHE WANTED LUPIN TO GIVE HER A LITTLE KICK IN THE BUTT, TOO, BUT SHE CAN'T SAY THAT OUT LOUD.
SHE REALLY LIKED ME, ALWAYS JUMPING UP ON ME WHEN I CAME BY.
YIKES
I WONDER IF THIS IS HOW IT FEELS TO LOSE A DAUGHTER?
SNIF
WHAT A CREEP.
LOOK, CZERNY-CHAN...
...EVERYONE'S GATHERED TO SEE YOU OFF TO HEAVEN.
ARE YOU HAPPY?
SO, WHAT ABOUT THE FUNERAL?
OH, I'VE ALREADY MADE THE ARRANGEMENTS.
TO CZERNY
FROM JIN
WHAT?! THEY HAVE THOSE?!

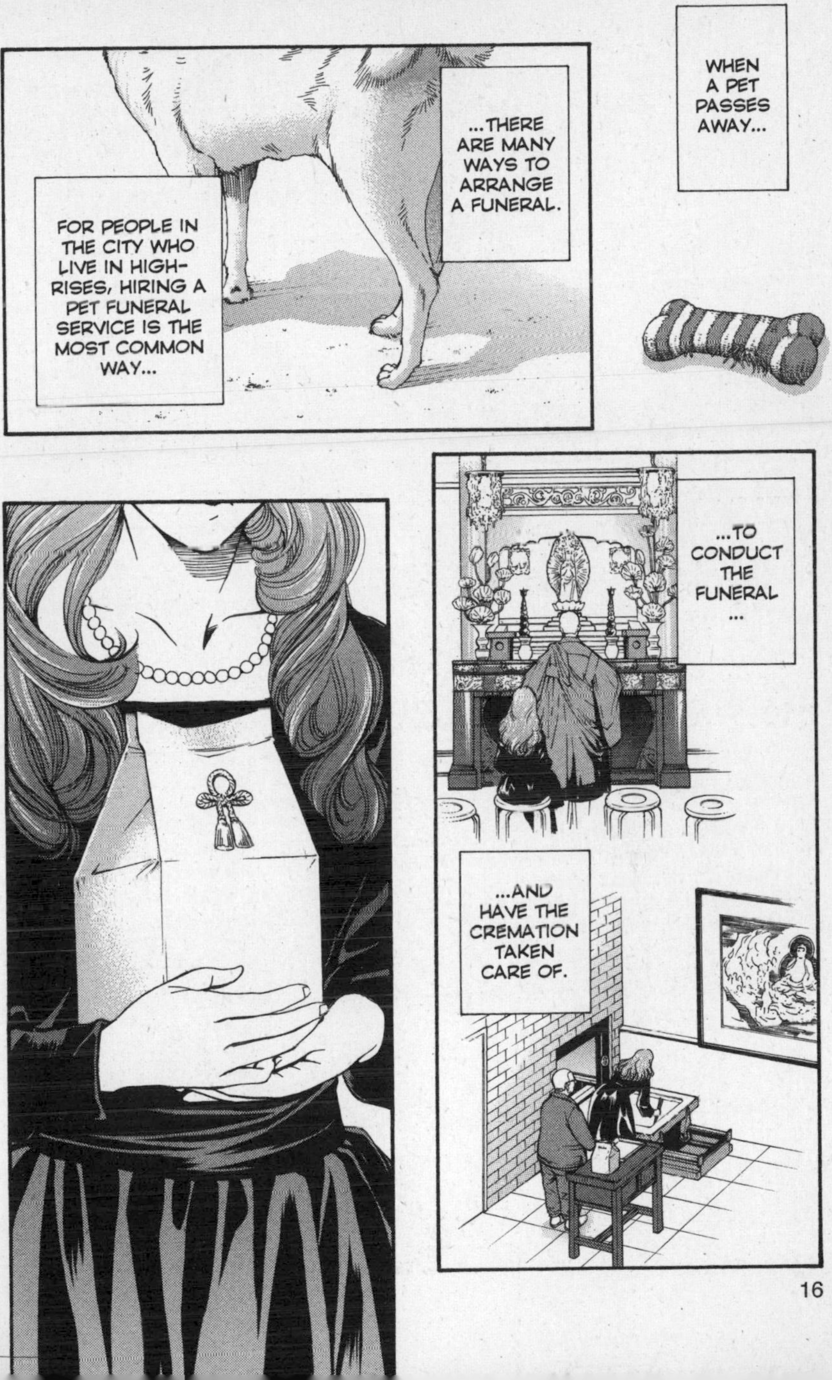
WHEN A PET PASSES AWAY...
...THERE ARE MANY WAYS TO ARRANGE A FUNERAL.
FOR PEOPLE IN THE CITY WHO LIVE IN HIGH-RISES, HIRING A PET FUNERAL SERVICE IS THE MOST COMMON WAY...
...TO CONDUCT THE FUNERAL ...
...AND HAVE THE CREMATION TAKEN CARE OF.

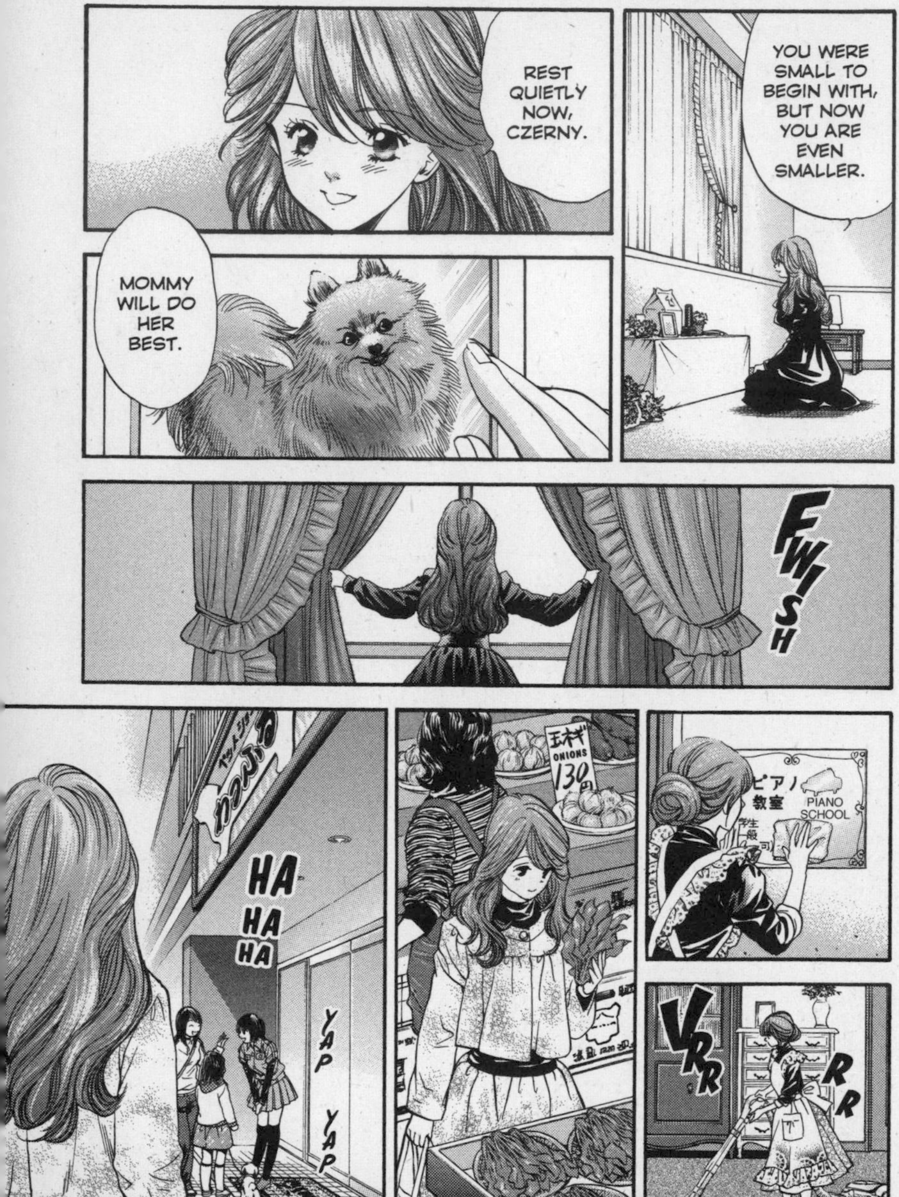
YOU WERE SMALL TO BEGIN WITH, BUT NOW YOU ARE EVEN SMALLER.
REST QUIETLY NOW, CZERNY.
MOMMY WILL DO HER BEST.
FWISH
ピアノ教室
PIANO SCHOOL
VRR
RR
玉ネギ
ONIONS
130円
HA HA HA
YAP YAP

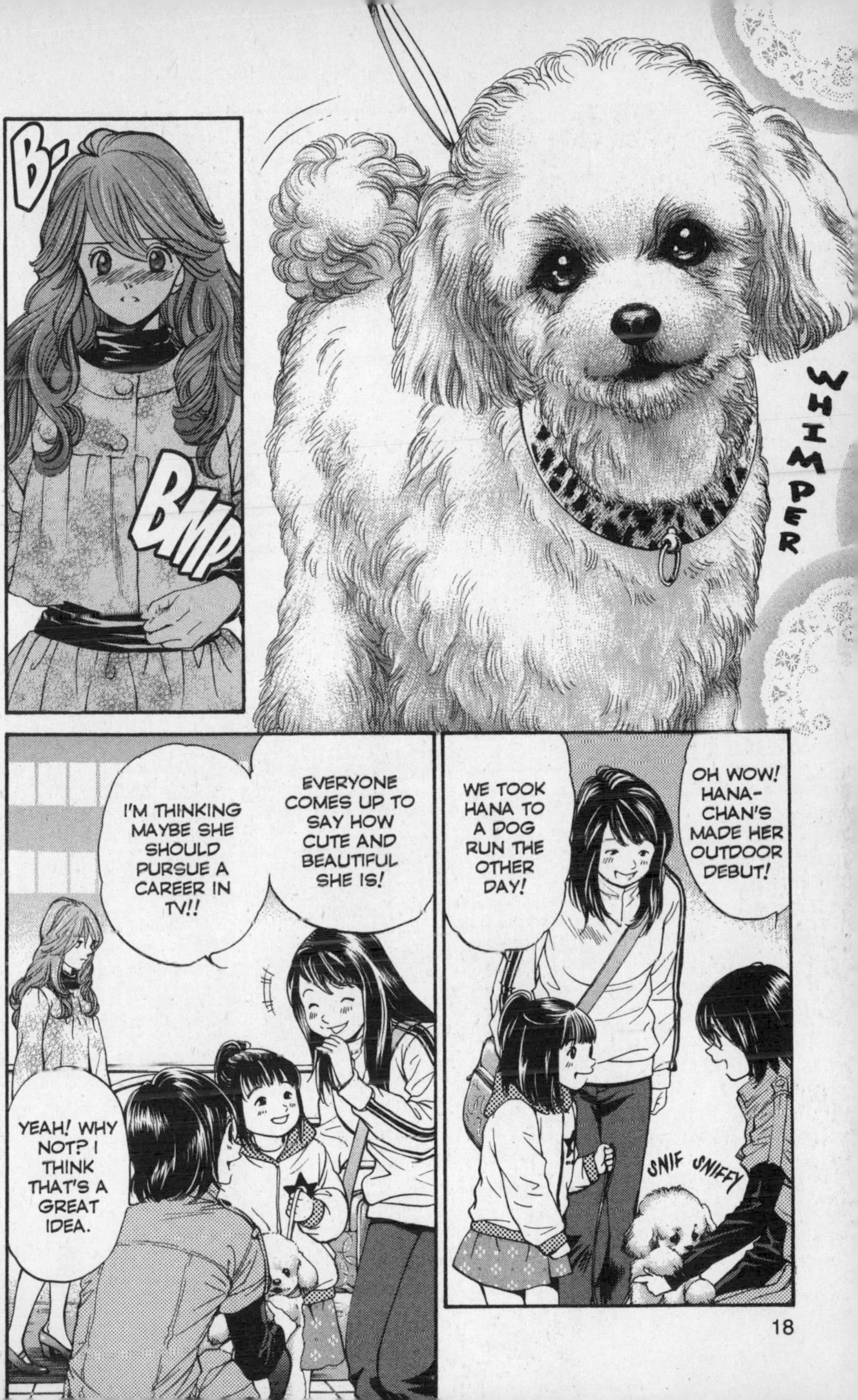
WHIMPER
B-
BMP
OH WOW! HANA-CHAN'S MADE HER OUTDOOR DEBUT!
WE TOOK HANA TO A DOG RUN THE OTHER DAY!
EVERYONE COMES UP TO SAY HOW CUTE AND BEAUTIFUL SHE IS!
SNIF SNIFFY
I'M THINKING MAYBE SHE SHOULD PURSUE A CAREER IN TV!!
YEAH! WHY NOT? I THINK THAT'S A GREAT IDEA.

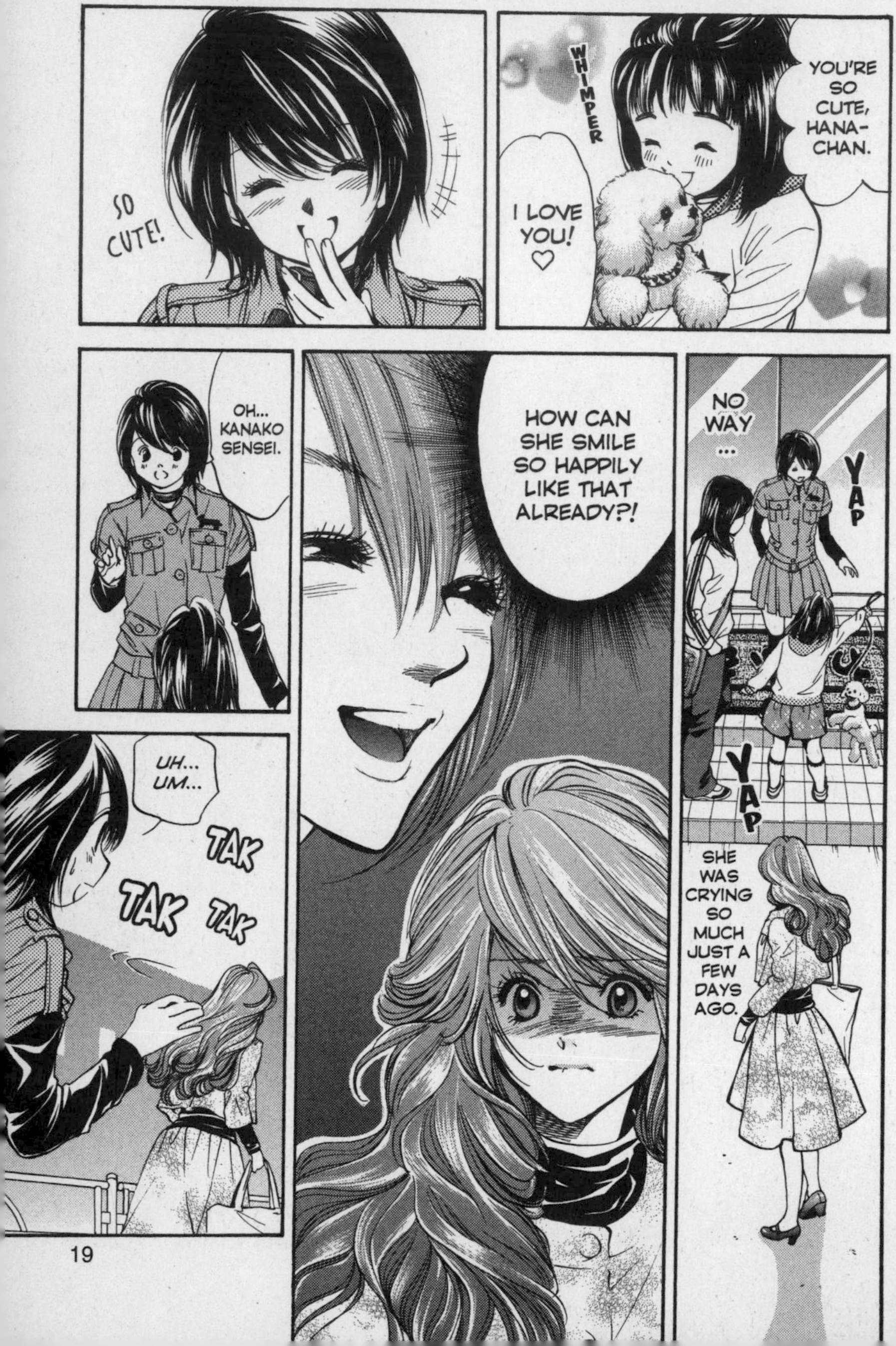
YOU'RE SO CUTE, HANA-CHAN.
WHIMPER
I LOVE YOU! ♡
SO CUTE!
NO WAY...
YAP
YAP YAP
SHE WAS CRYING SO MUCH JUST A FEW DAYS AGO.
HOW CAN SHE SMILE SO HAPPILY LIKE THAT ALREADY?!
OH... KANAKO SENSEI.
UH... UM...
TAK
TAK TAK

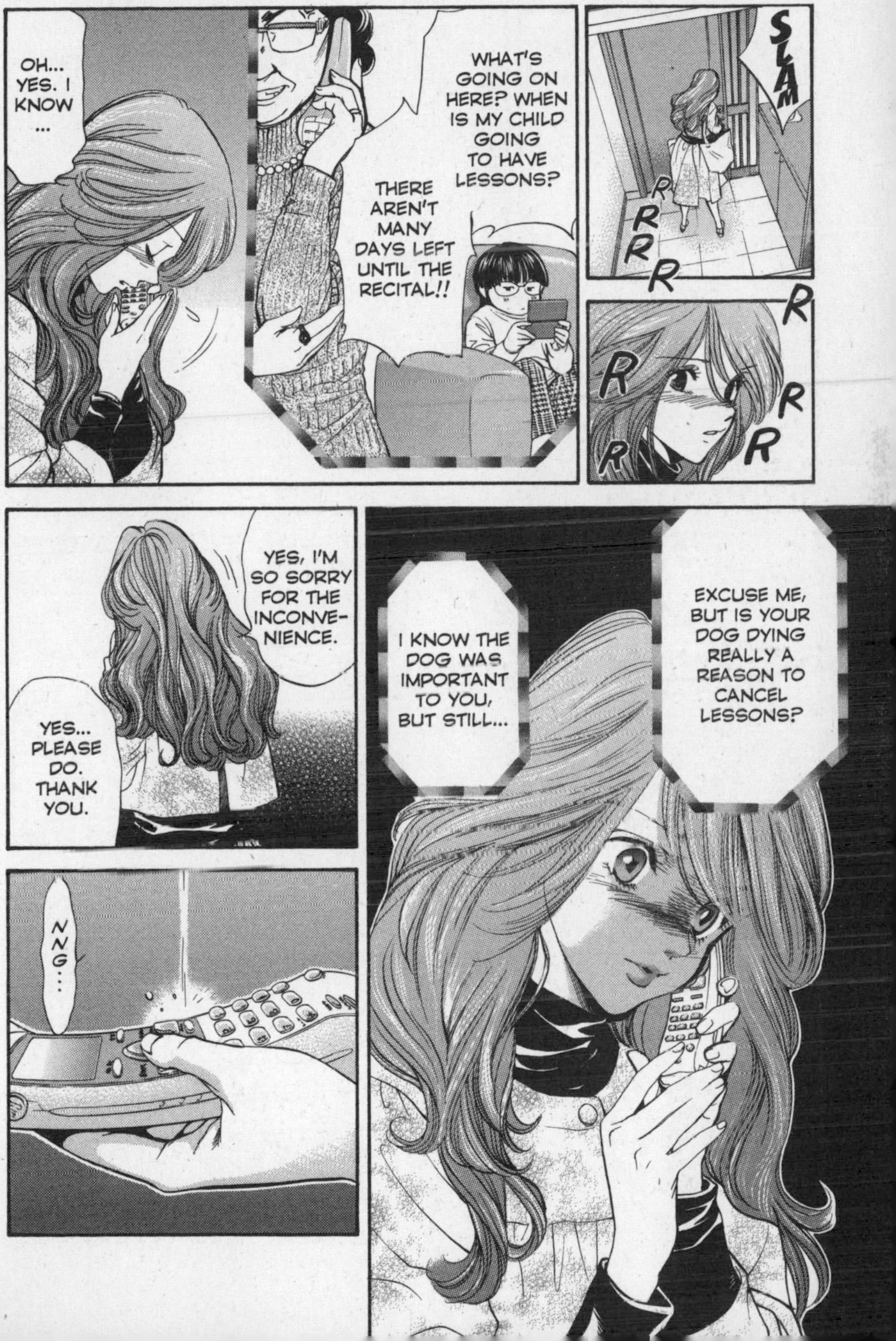
SLAM
RRRR
RRRRR
WHAT'S GOING ON HERE? WHEN IS MY CHILD GOING TO HAVE LESSONS?
THERE AREN'T MANY DAYS LEFT UNTIL THE RECITAL!!
OH... YES. I KNOW ...
EXCUSE ME, BUT IS YOUR DOG DYING REALLY A REASON TO CANCEL LESSONS?
I KNOW THE DOG WAS IMPORTANT TO YOU, BUT STILL...
YES, I'M SO SORRY FOR THE INCONVENIENCE.
YES... PLEASE DO. THANK YOU.
NNG...

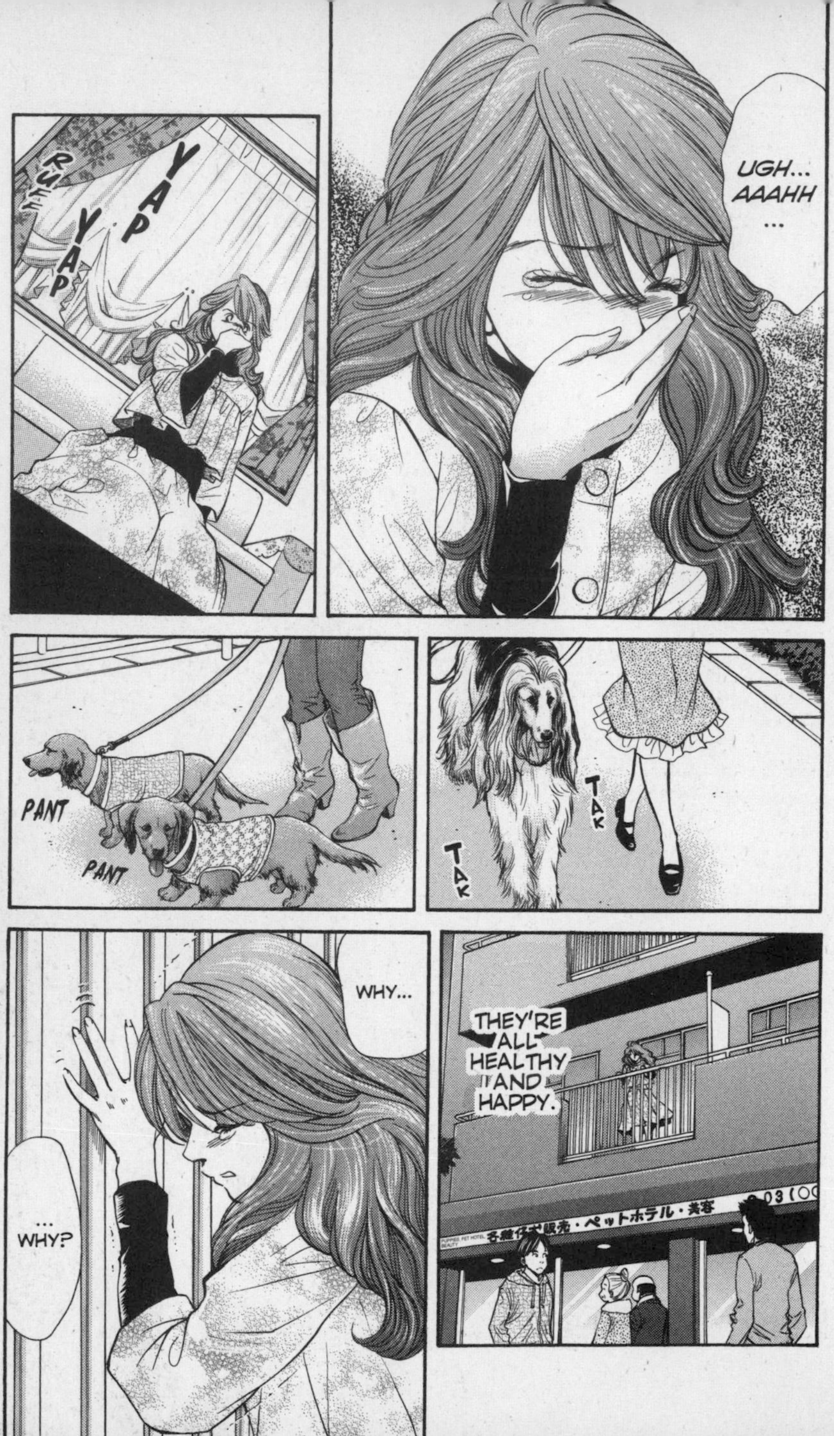

UGH... AAAHH ...
YAP
YAP
YAP
RUFF
TAK
TAK
PANT
PANT
THEY'RE ALL HEALTHY AND HAPPY.
WHY...
... WHY?

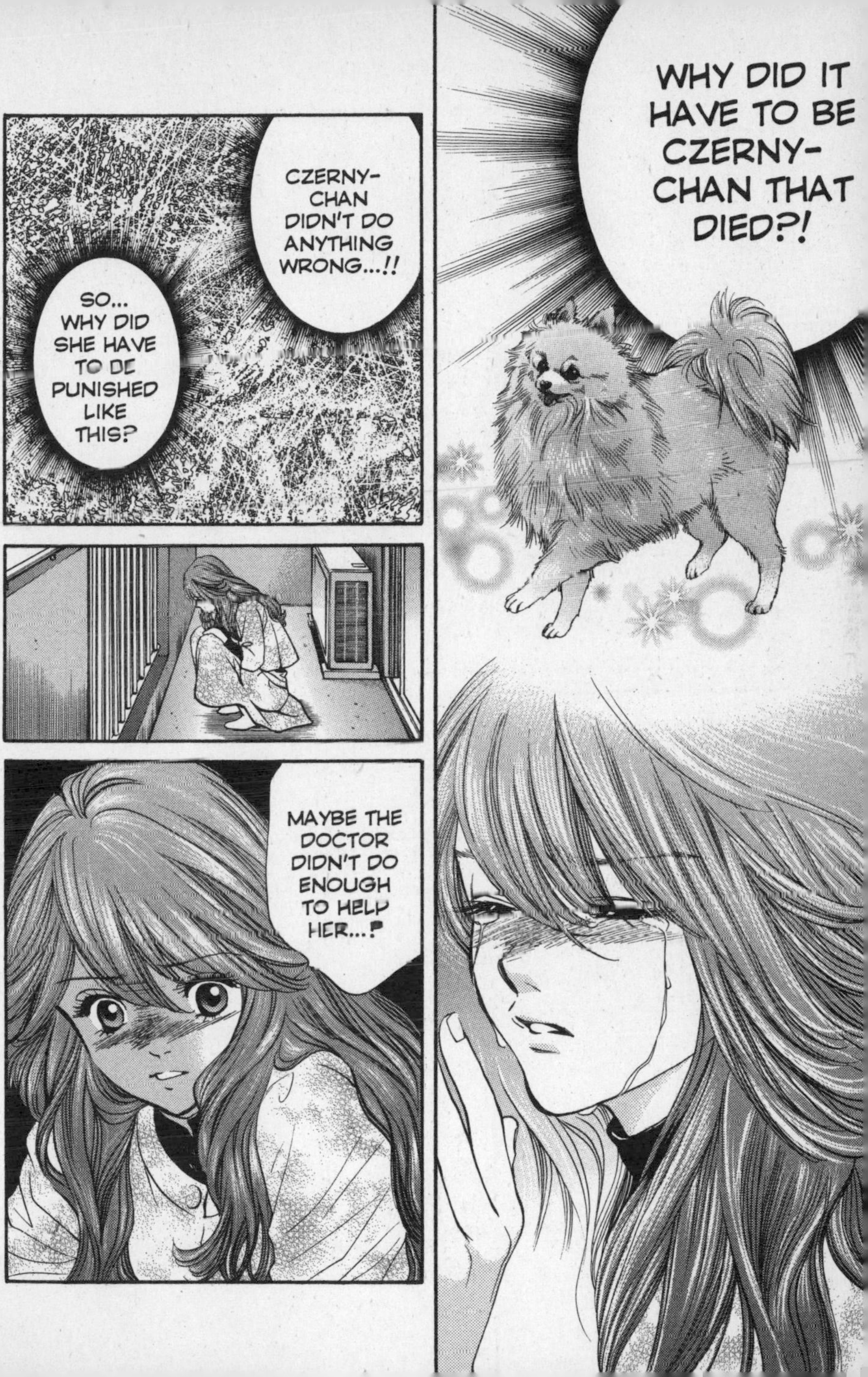
WHY DID IT HAVE TO BE CZERNY-CHAN THAT DIED?!
CZERNY-CHAN DIDN'T DO ANYTHING WRONG...!!
SO... WHY DID SHE HAVE TO BE PUNISHED LIKE THIS?
MAYBE THE DOCTOR DIDN'T DO ENOUGH TO HELP HER...!?

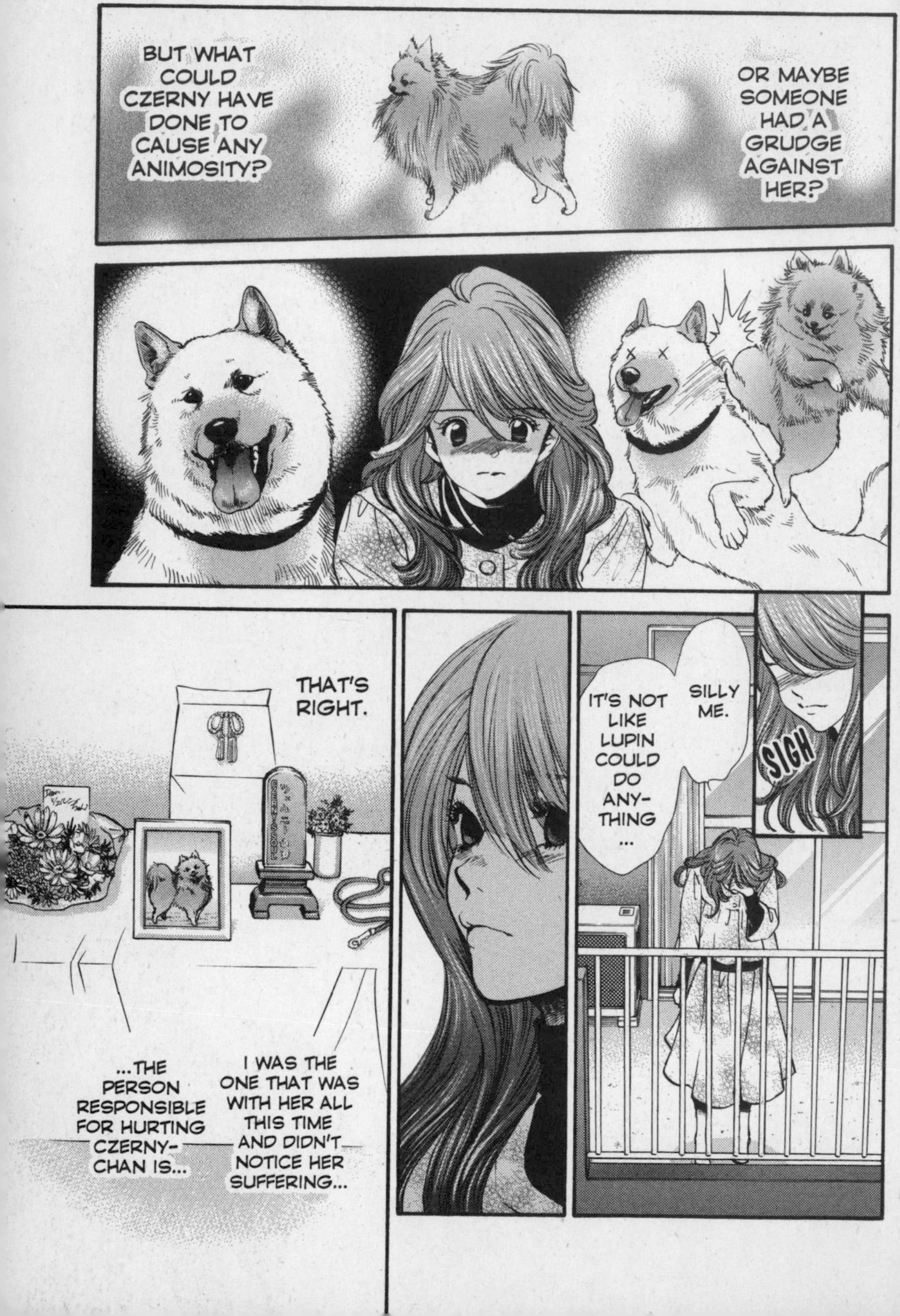
OR MAYBE SOMEONE HAD A GRUDGE AGAINST HER?
BUT WHAT COULD CZERNY HAVE DONE TO CAUSE ANY ANIMOSITY?
SIGH
SILLY ME.
IT'S NOT LIKE LUPIN COULD DO ANYTHING...
THAT'S RIGHT.
I WAS THE ONE THAT WAS WITH HER ALL THIS TIME AND DIDN'T NOTICE HER SUFFERING...
...THE PERSON RESPONSIBLE FOR HURTING CZERNY-CHAN IS...

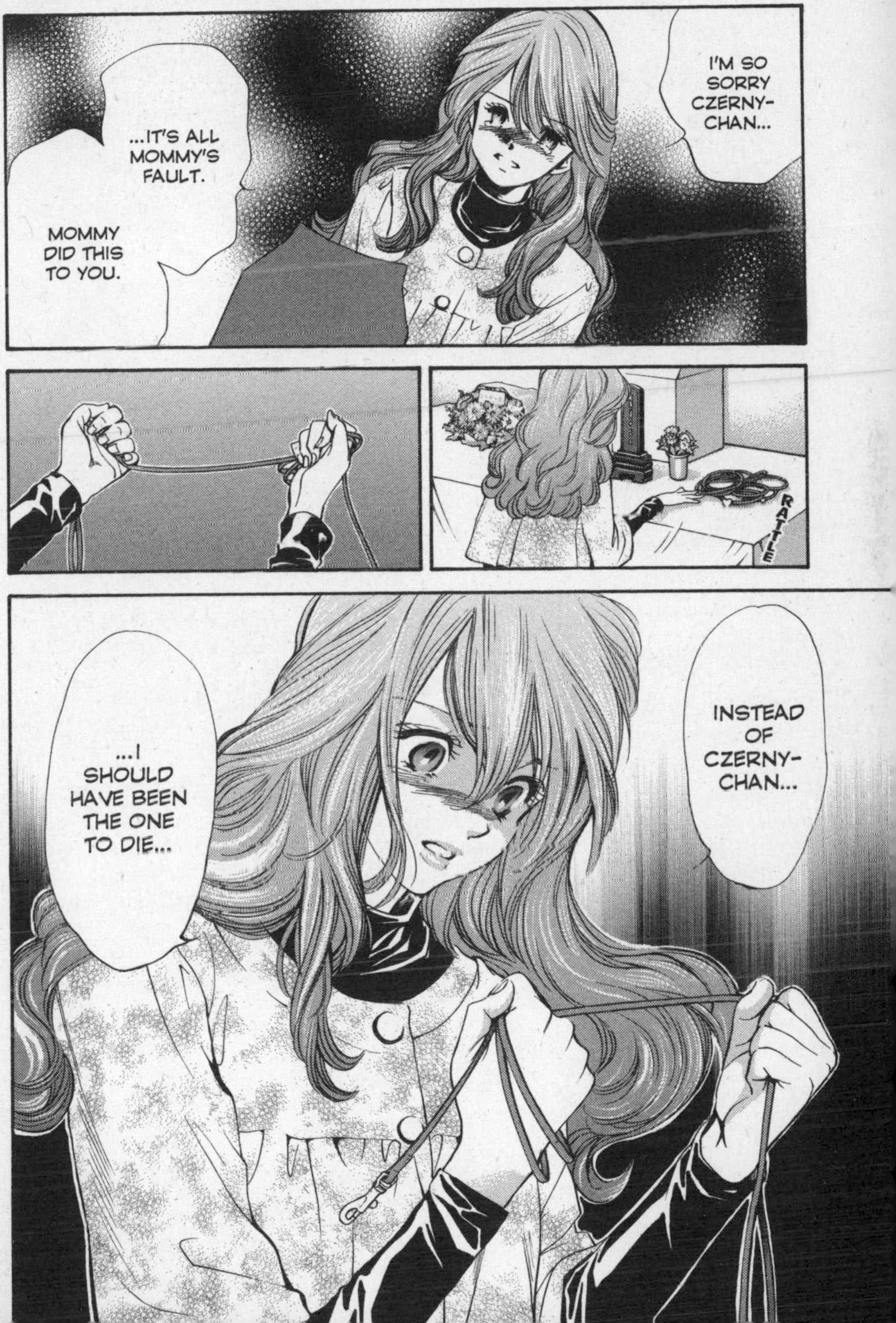
I'M SO SORRY CZERNY-CHAN...
...IT'S ALL MOMMY'S FAULT.
MOMMY DID THIS TO YOU.
RATTLE
INSTEAD OF CZERNY-CHAN...
...I SHOULD HAVE BEEN THE ONE TO DIE...

CHAPTER 132: PET LOSS

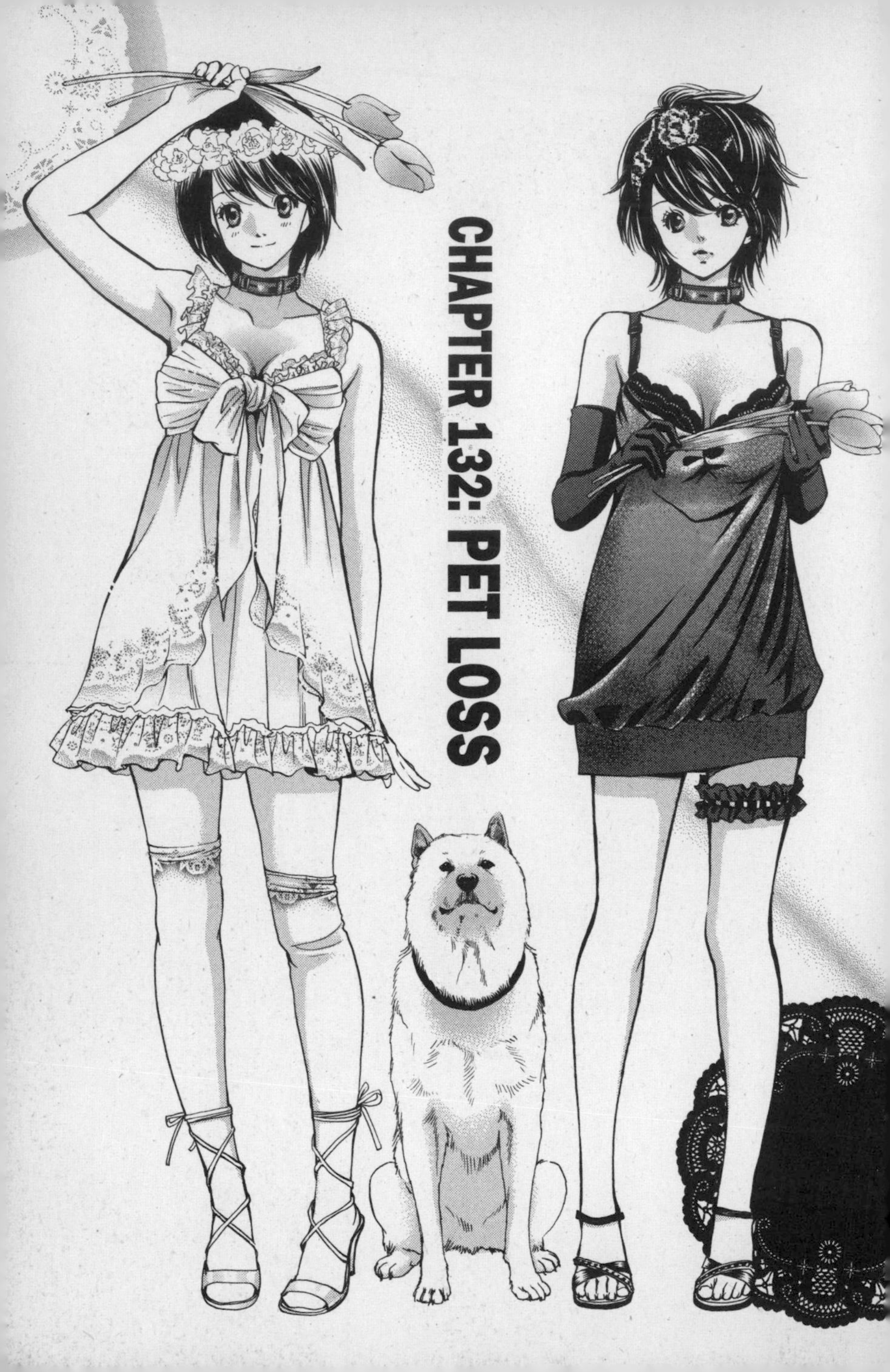

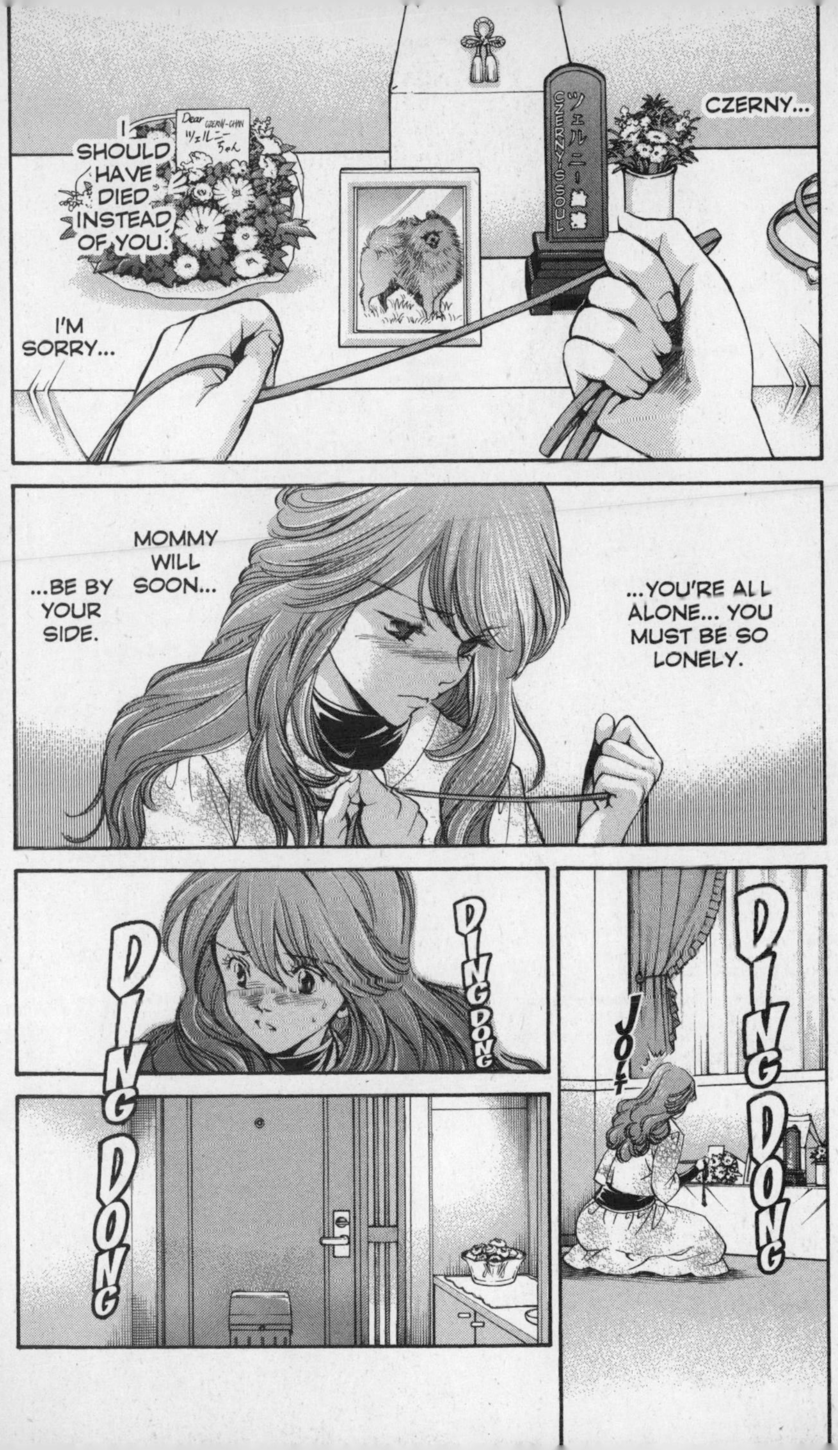
CZERNY...
CZERNY'S SOUL
Dear CZERN-CHAN ツェルニーちゃん
I SHOULD HAVE DIED INSTEAD OF YOU.
I'M SORRY...
...YOU'RE ALL ALONE... YOU MUST BE SO LONELY.
MOMMY WILL SOON...
...BE BY YOUR SIDE.
DING DONG
JOLT
DING DONG
DING DONG
DING DONG

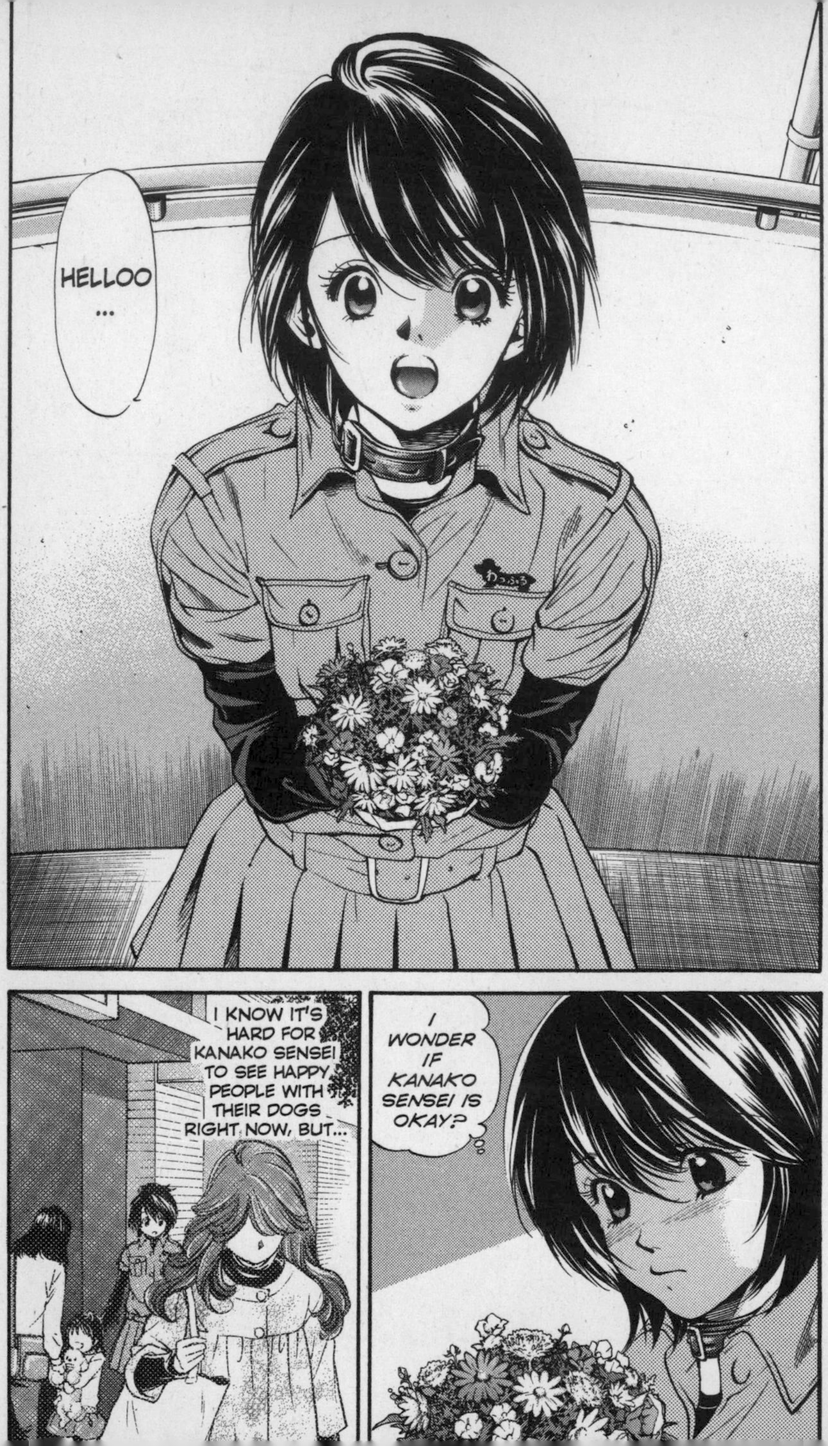
HELLOO ...
I WONDER IF KANAKO SENSEI IS OKAY?
I KNOW IT'S HARD FOR KANAKO SENSEI TO SEE HAPPY PEOPLE WITH THEIR DOGS RIGHT NOW, BUT...

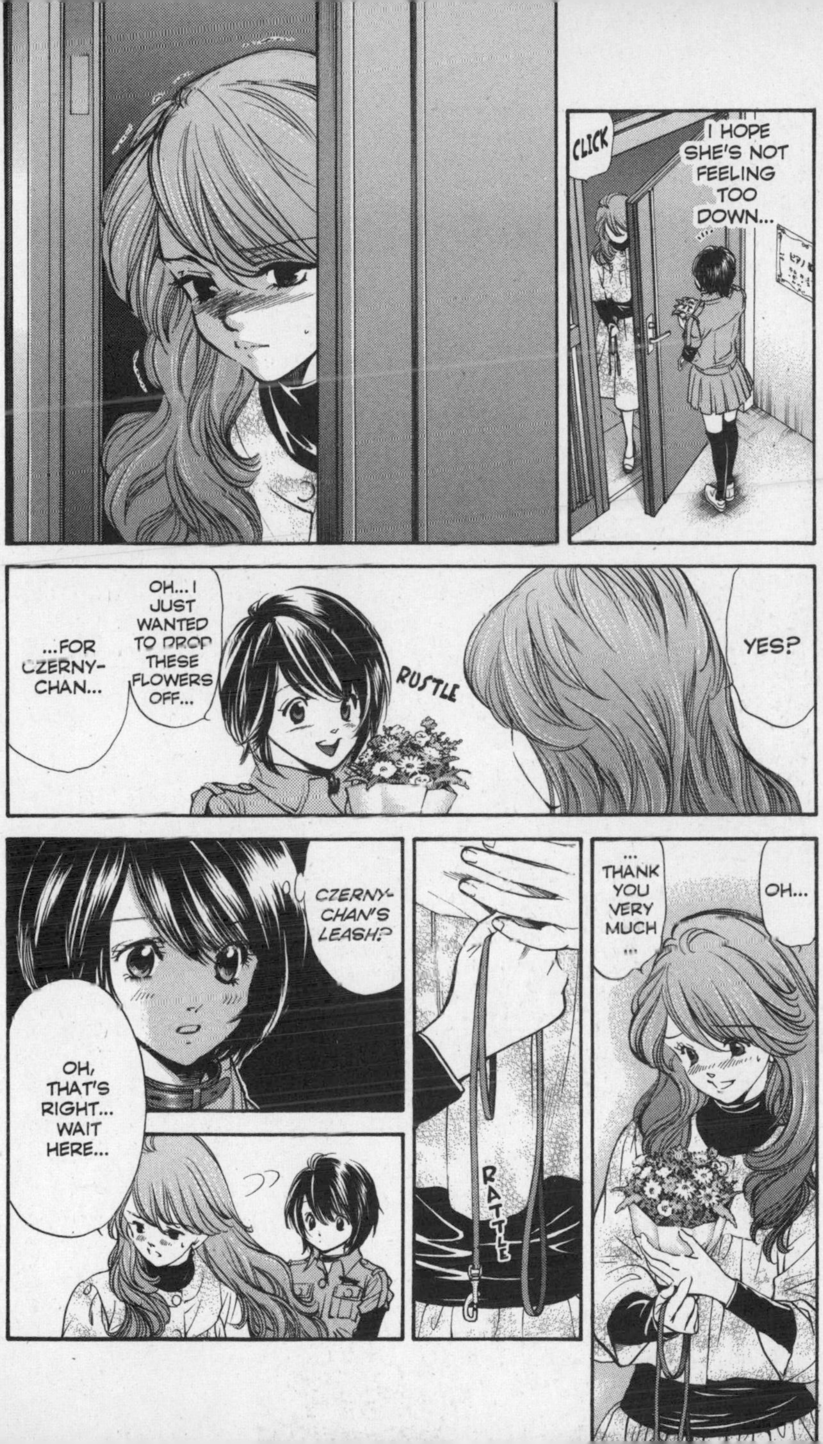

CLICK
I HOPE SHE'S NOT FEELING TOO DOWN...
YES?
OH... I JUST WANTED TO DROP THESE FLOWERS OFF...
RUSTLE
...FOR CZERNY-CHAN...
OH...
... THANK YOU VERY MUCH ...
RATTLE
CZERNY-CHAN'S LEASH?
OH, THAT'S RIGHT... WAIT HERE...

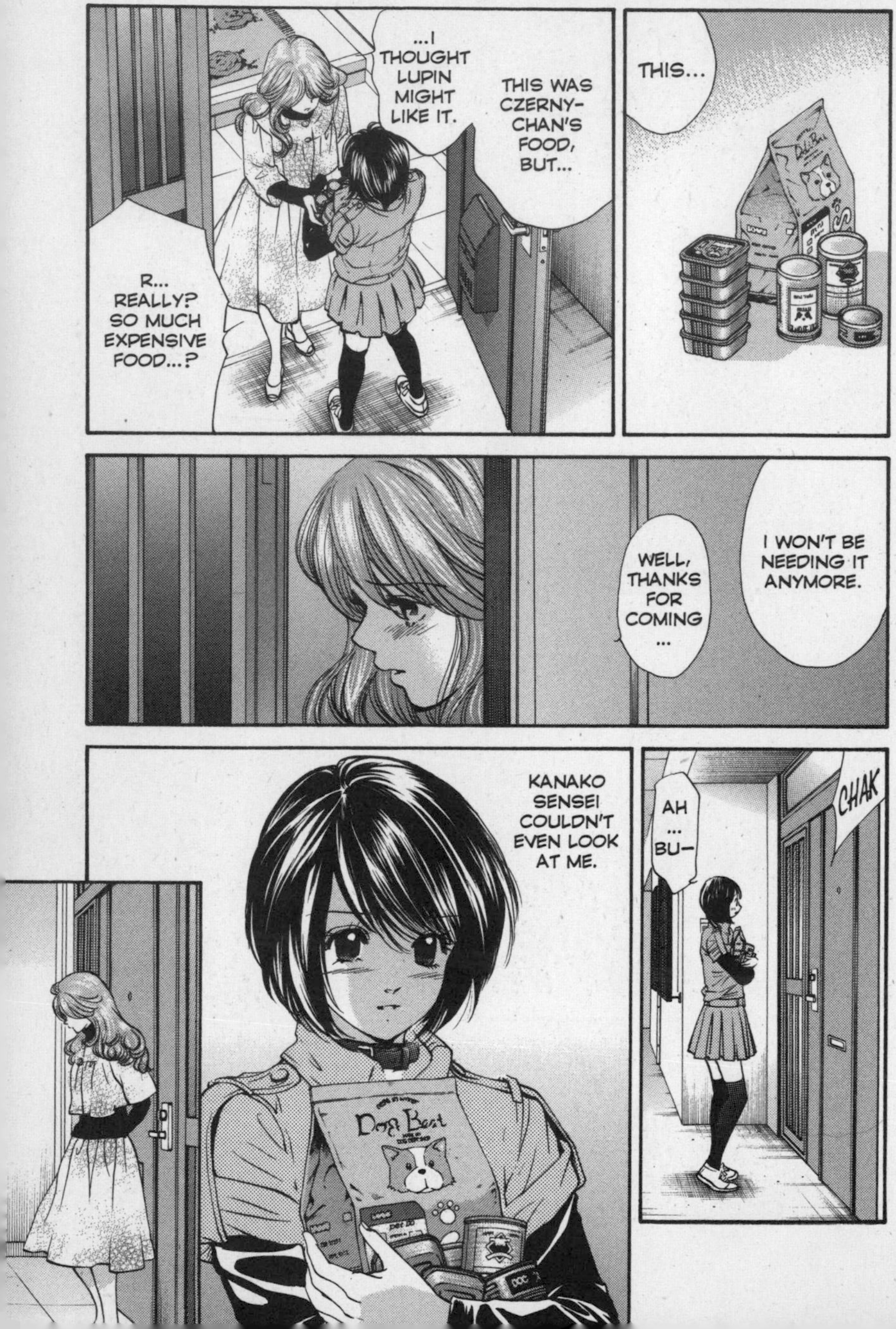

THIS...
THIS WAS CZERNY-CHAN'S FOOD, BUT...
...I THOUGHT LUPIN MIGHT LIKE IT.
R... REALLY? SO MUCH EXPENSIVE FOOD...?
I WON'T BE NEEDING IT ANYMORE.
WELL, THANKS FOR COMING...
CHAK
AH... BU—
KANAKO SENSEI COULDN'T EVEN LOOK AT ME.

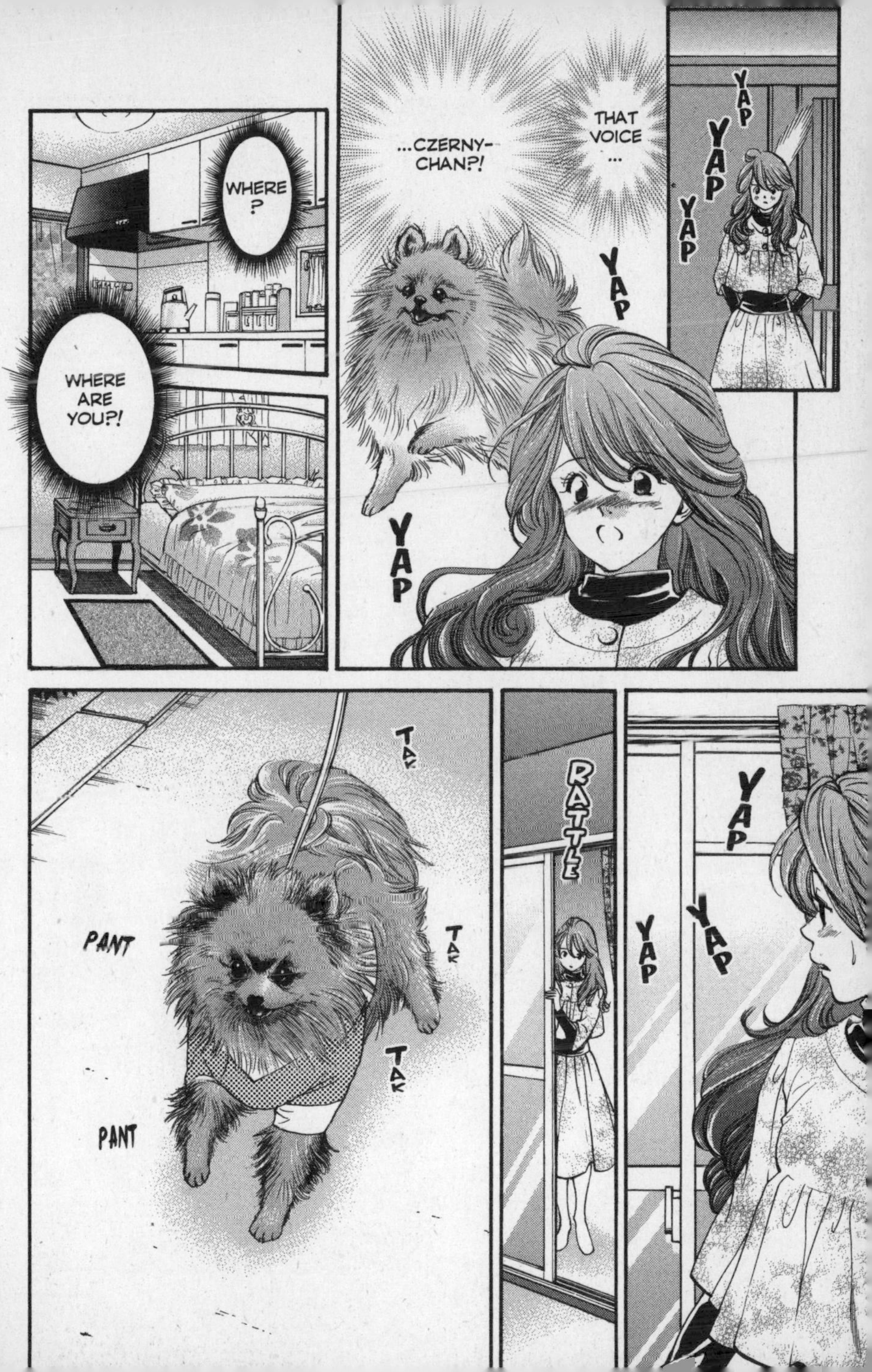
YAP
YAP
YAP
YAP
THAT VOICE ...
...CZERNY-CHAN?!
YAP
YAP
WHERE?
WHERE ARE YOU?!
YAP
YAP
YAP
YAP
RATTLE
TAK
TAK
TAK
PANT
PANT

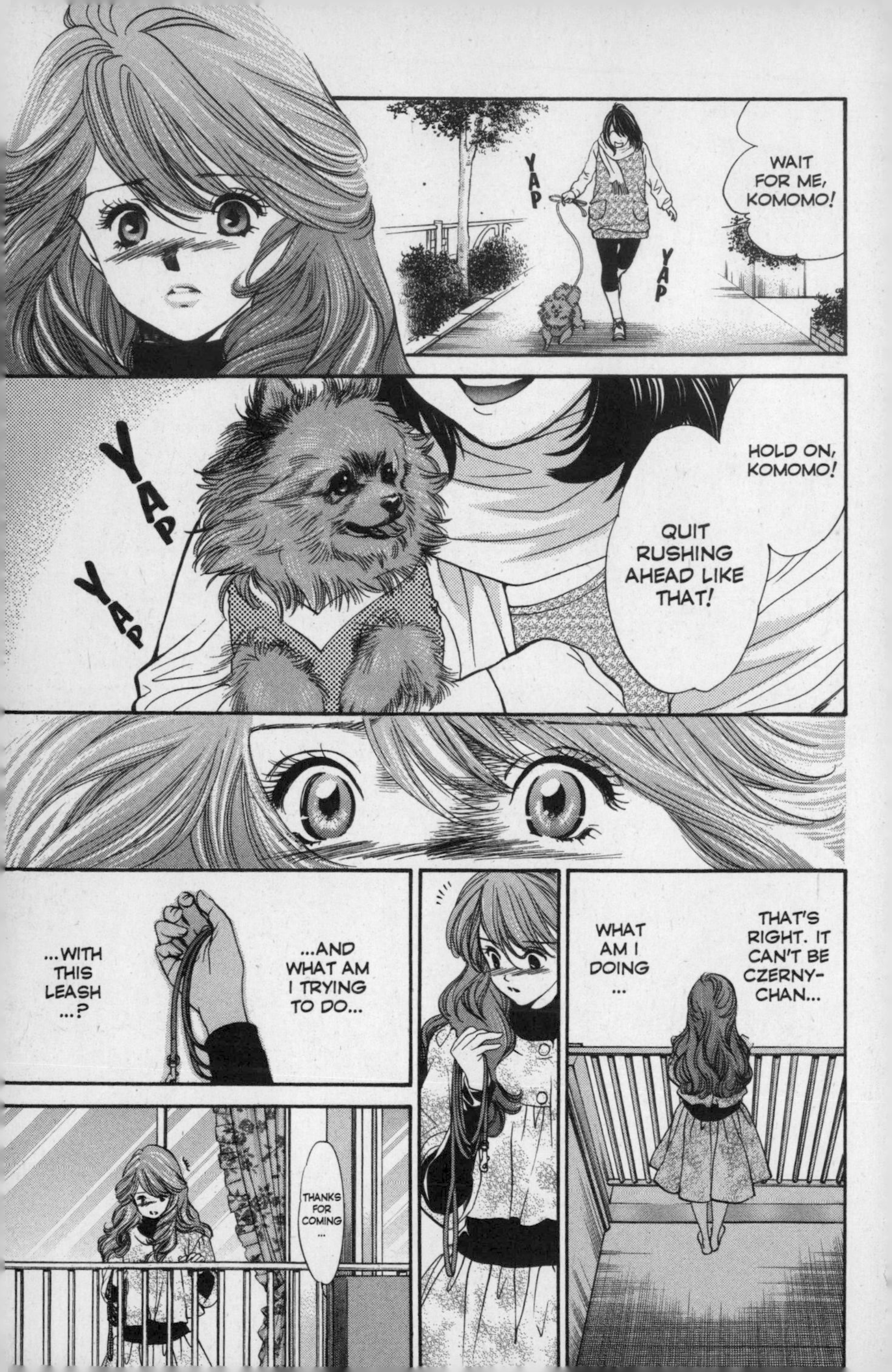

WAIT FOR ME, KOMOMO!
YAP
YAP
HOLD ON, KOMOMO!
QUIT RUSHING AHEAD LIKE THAT!
YAP
YAP
THAT'S RIGHT. IT CAN'T BE CZERNY-CHAN...
WHAT AM I DOING ...
...AND WHAT AM I TRYING TO DO...
...WITH THIS LEASH ...?
THANKS FOR COMING ...

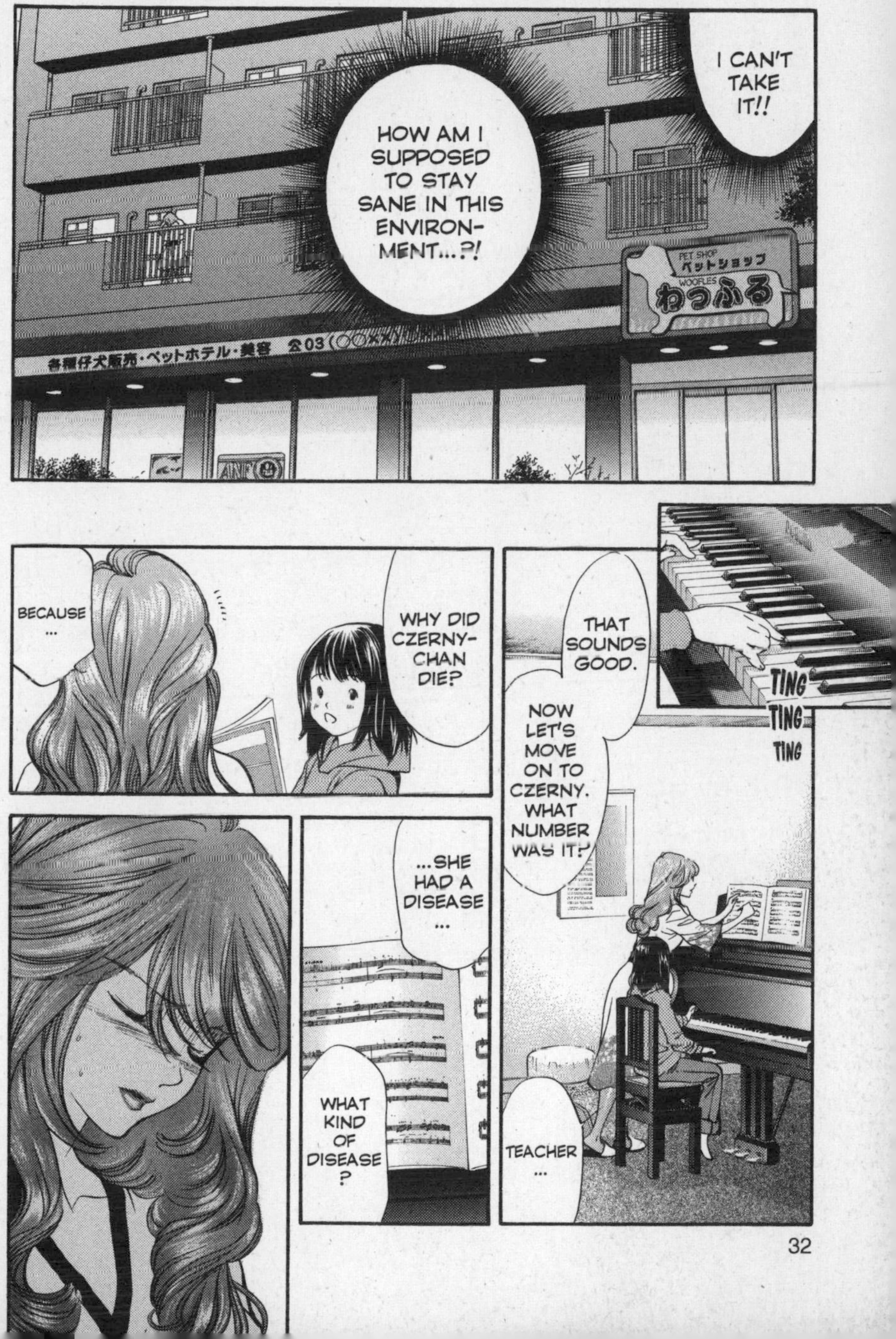
I CAN'T TAKE IT!!
HOW AM I SUPPOSED TO STAY SANE IN THIS ENVIRON-MENT...?!
PET SHOP ペットショップ
WOOFLES わっふる
各種仔犬販売・ペットホテル・美容
TING TING TING
THAT SOUNDS GOOD.
NOW LET'S MOVE ON TO CZERNY. WHAT NUMBER WAS IT?
TEACHER ...
WHY DID CZERNY-CHAN DIE?
BECAUSE ...
...SHE HAD A DISEASE ...
WHAT KIND OF DISEASE ?

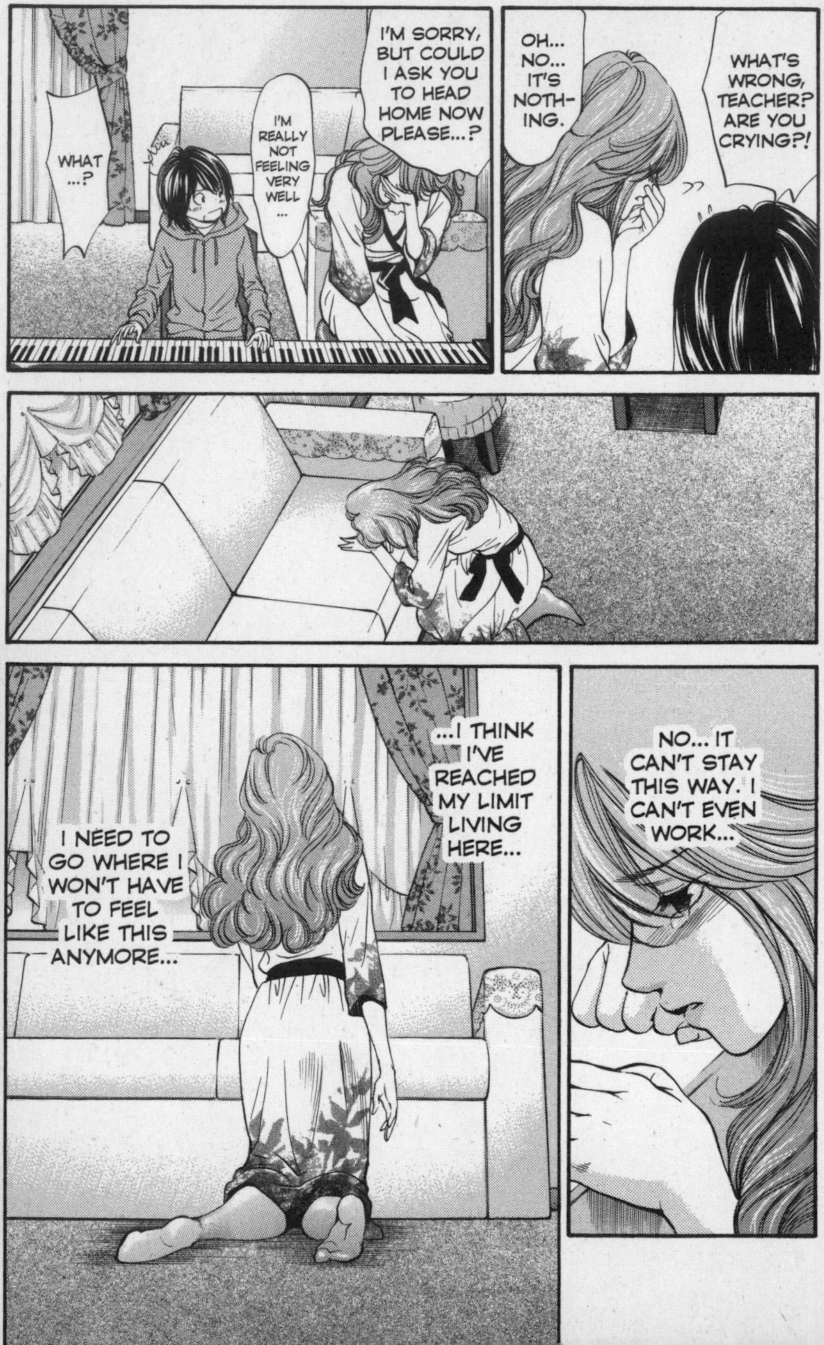
WHAT'S WRONG, TEACHER? ARE YOU CRYING?!
OH... NO... IT'S NOTHING.
I'M SORRY, BUT COULD I ASK YOU TO HEAD HOME NOW PLEASE...?
I'M REALLY NOT FEELING VERY WELL...
WHAT...?
NO... IT CAN'T STAY THIS WAY. I CAN'T EVEN WORK...
...I THINK I'VE REACHED MY LIMIT LIVING HERE...
I NEED TO GO WHERE I WON'T HAVE TO FEEL LIKE THIS ANYMORE...

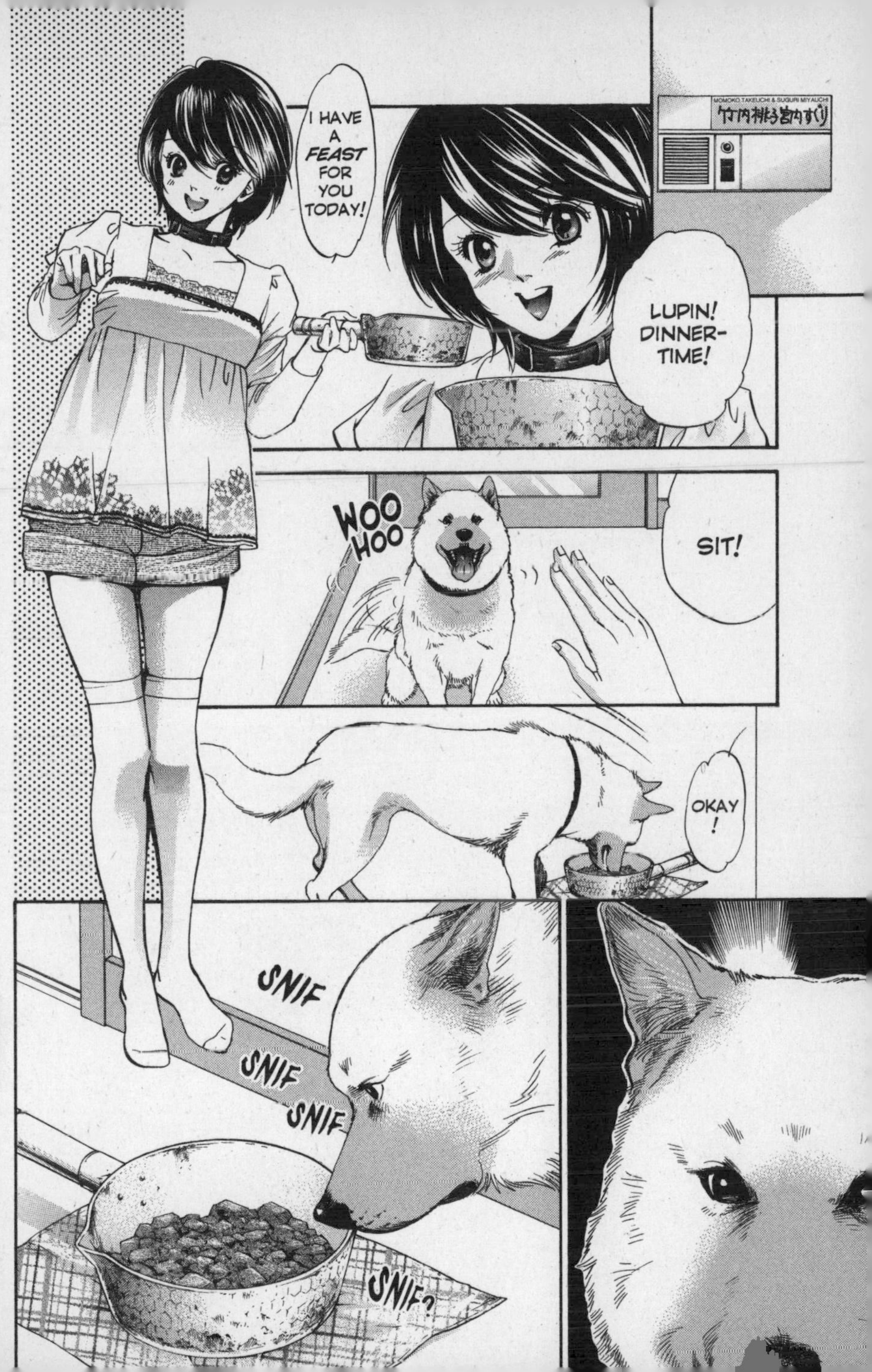
MOMOKO TAKEUCHI & SUGURI MIYAUCHI
竹内桃子 宮内すぐり
LUPIN! DINNER-TIME!
WOO HOO
SIT!
OKAY!
I HAVE A FEAST FOR YOU TODAY!
SNIF
SNIF
SNIF
SNIF?

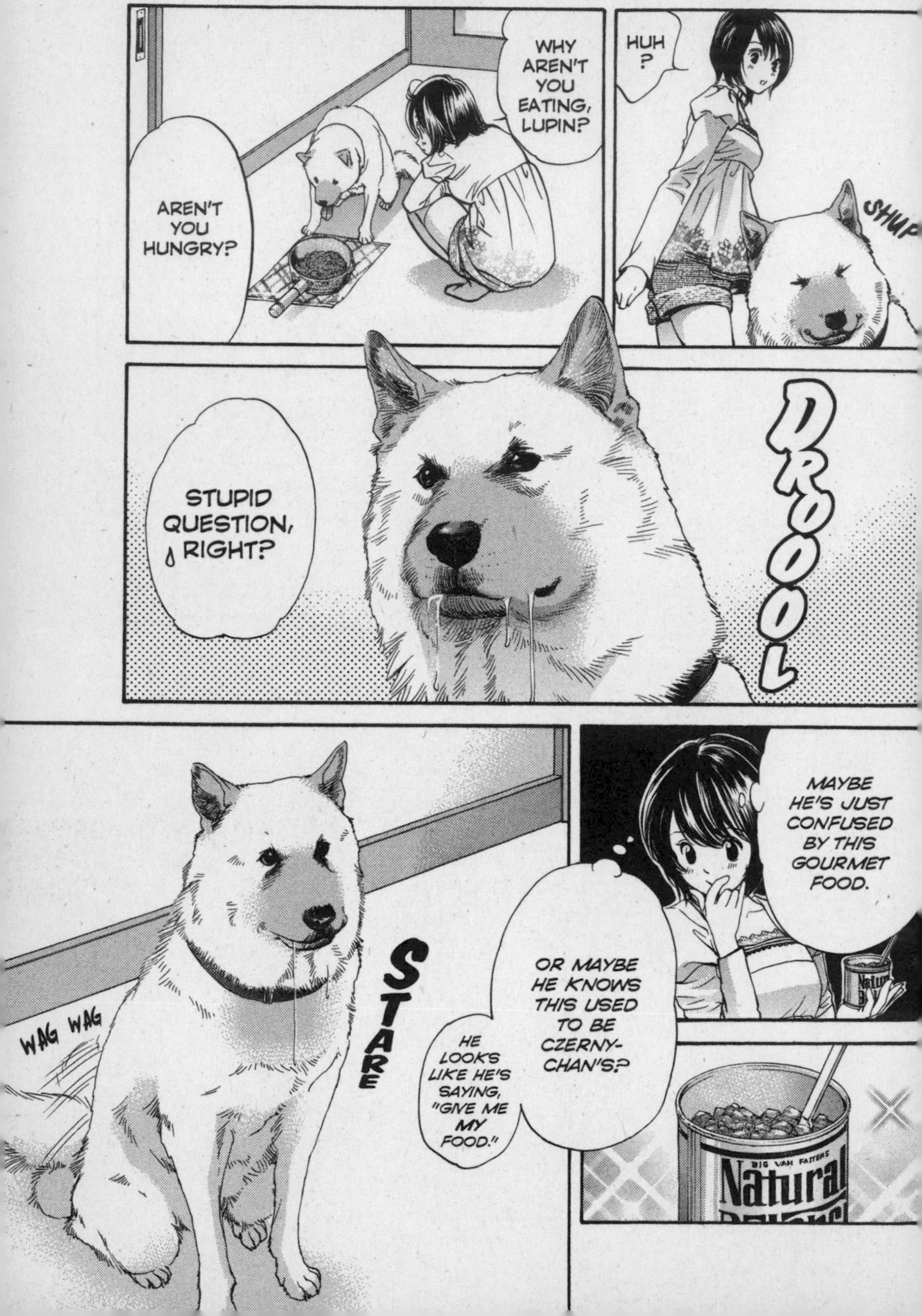
HUH ?
SHUP
WHY AREN'T YOU EATING, LUPIN?
AREN'T YOU HUNGRY?
DROOOL
STUPID QUESTION, RIGHT?
MAYBE HE'S JUST CONFUSED BY THIS GOURMET FOOD.
OR MAYBE HE KNOWS THIS USED TO BE CZERNY-CHAN'S?
Natural
STARE
HE LOOKS LIKE HE'S SAYING, "GIVE ME MY FOOD."
WAG WAG

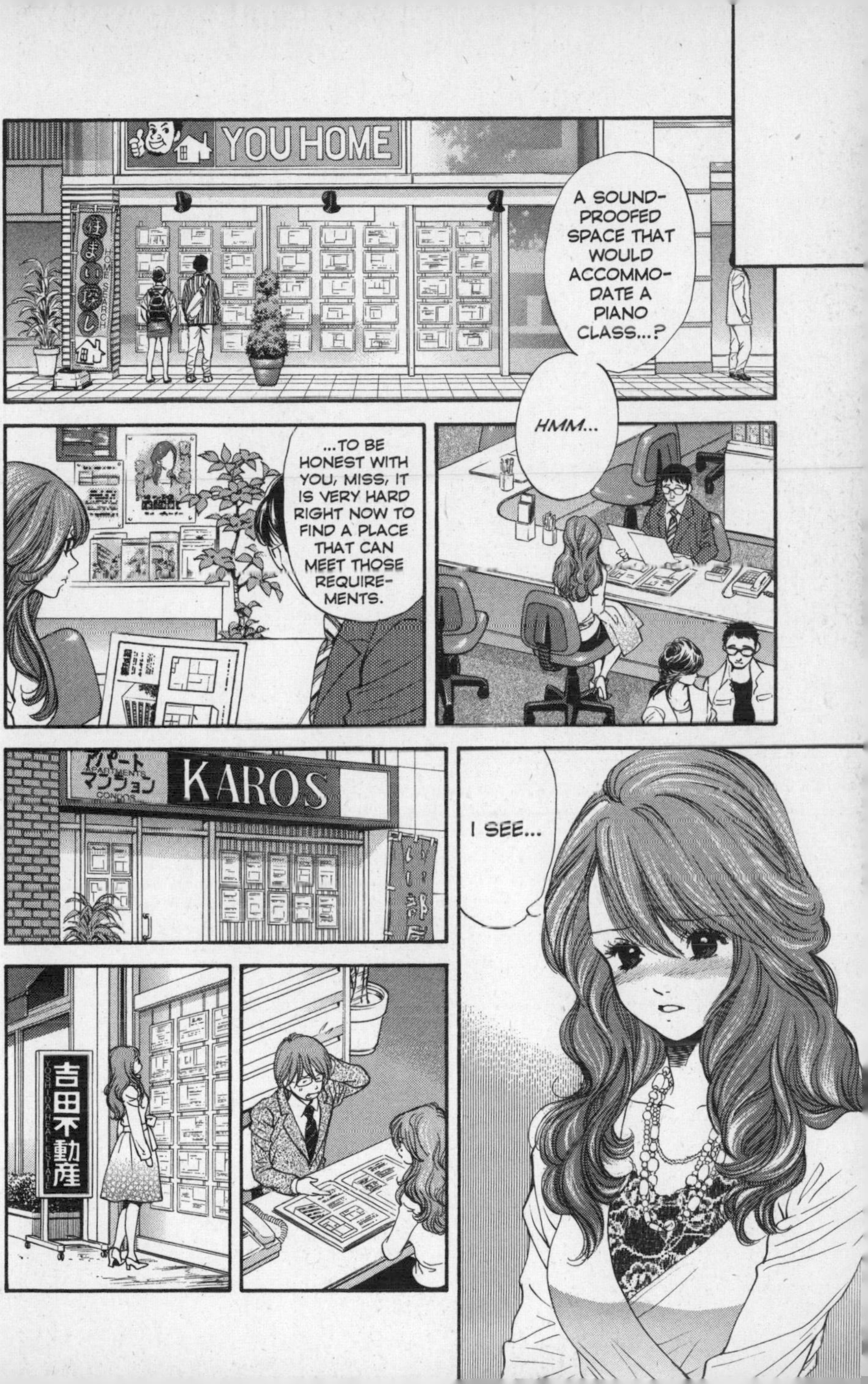
YOU HOME
A SOUND-PROOFED SPACE THAT WOULD ACCOMMODATE A PIANO CLASS...?
HMM...
...TO BE HONEST WITH YOU, MISS, IT IS VERY HARD RIGHT NOW TO FIND A PLACE THAT CAN MEET THOSE REQUIREMENTS.
I SEE...
アパート マンション
KAROS
吉田不動産

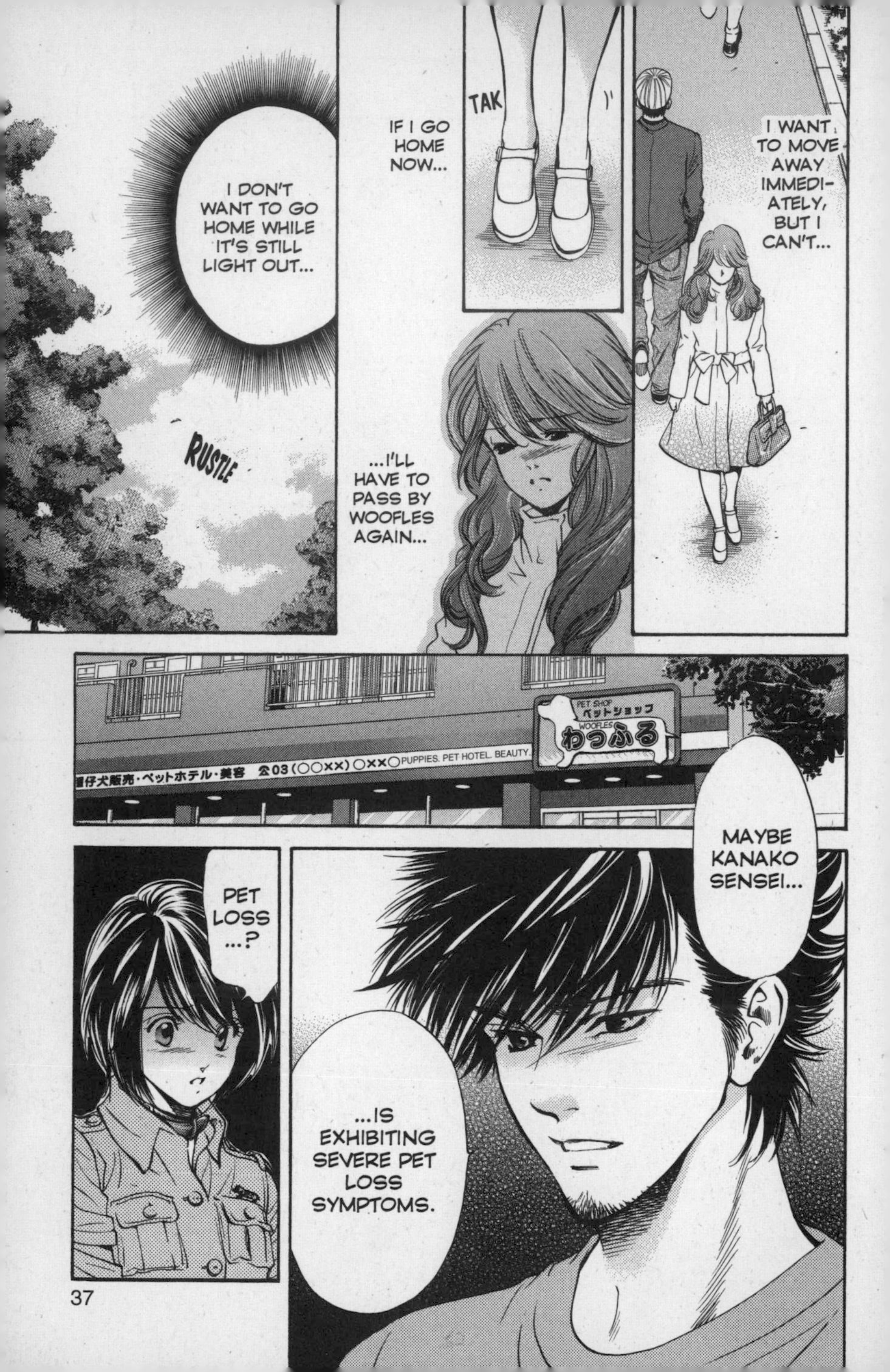
I WANT TO MOVE AWAY IMMEDI-ATELY, BUT I CAN'T...
TAK
IF I GO HOME NOW...
...I'LL HAVE TO PASS BY WOOFLES AGAIN...
I DON'T WANT TO GO HOME WHILE IT'S STILL LIGHT OUT...
RUSTLE
PET SHOP ペットショップ
WOOFLES わっふる
仔犬販売・ペットホテル・美容 ☎03(○○××)○××○ PUPPIES. PET HOTEL. BEAUTY.
MAYBE KANAKO SENSEI...
...IS EXHIBITING SEVERE PET LOSS SYMPTOMS.
PET LOSS ...?

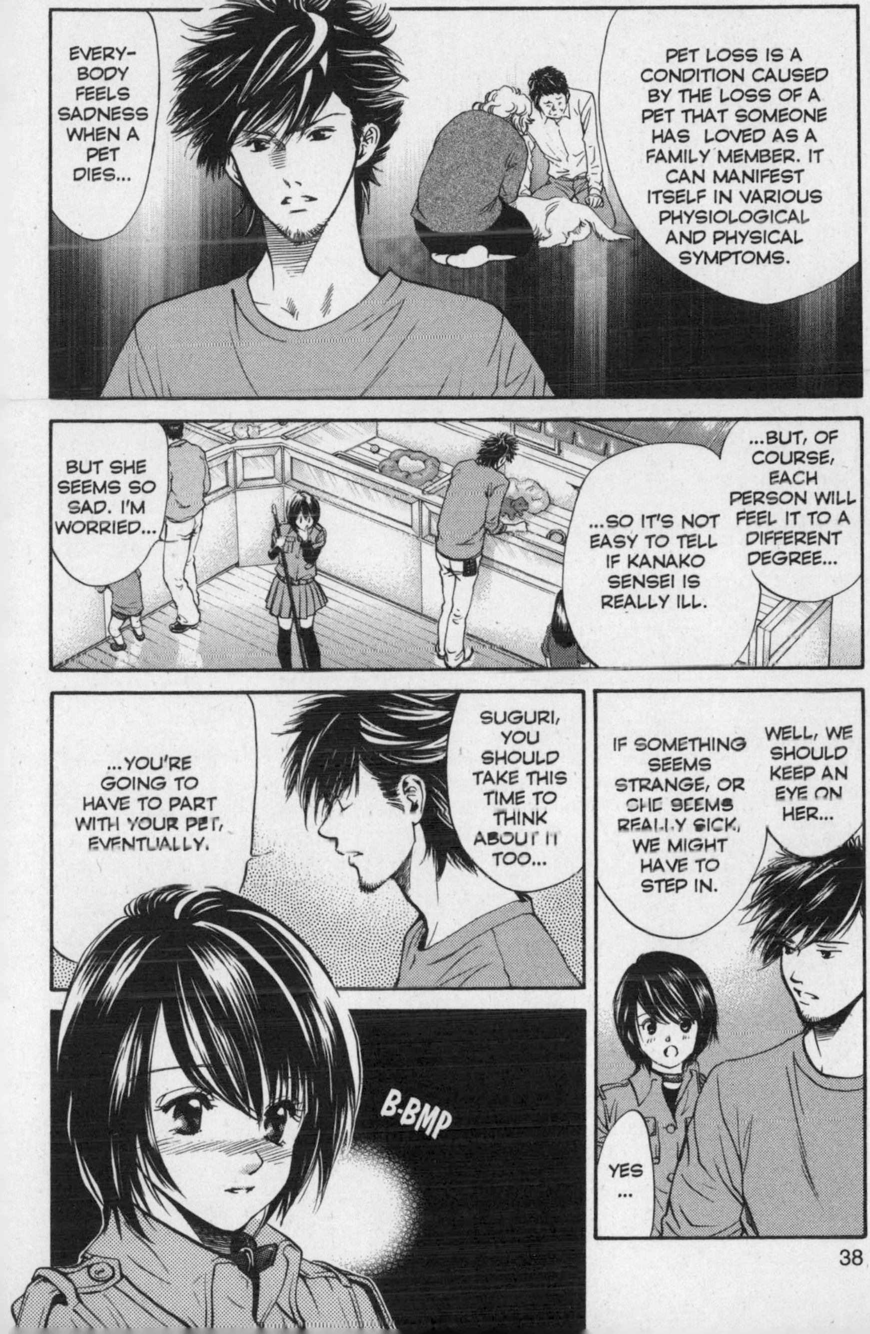
PET LOSS IS A CONDITION CAUSED BY THE LOSS OF A PET THAT SOMEONE HAS LOVED AS A FAMILY MEMBER. IT CAN MANIFEST ITSELF IN VARIOUS PHYSIOLOGICAL AND PHYSICAL SYMPTOMS.
EVERY-BODY FEELS SADNESS WHEN A PET DIES...
...BUT, OF COURSE, EACH PERSON WILL FEEL IT TO A DIFFERENT DEGREE...
...SO IT'S NOT EASY TO TELL IF KANAKO SENSEI IS REALLY ILL.
BUT SHE SEEMS SO SAD. I'M WORRIED...
WELL, WE SHOULD KEEP AN EYE ON HER...
IF SOMETHING SEEMS STRANGE, OR SHE SEEMS REALLY SICK, WE MIGHT HAVE TO STEP IN.
YES ...
SUGURI, YOU SHOULD TAKE THIS TIME TO THINK ABOUT IT TOO...
...YOU'RE GOING TO HAVE TO PART WITH YOUR PET, EVENTUALLY.
B-BMP

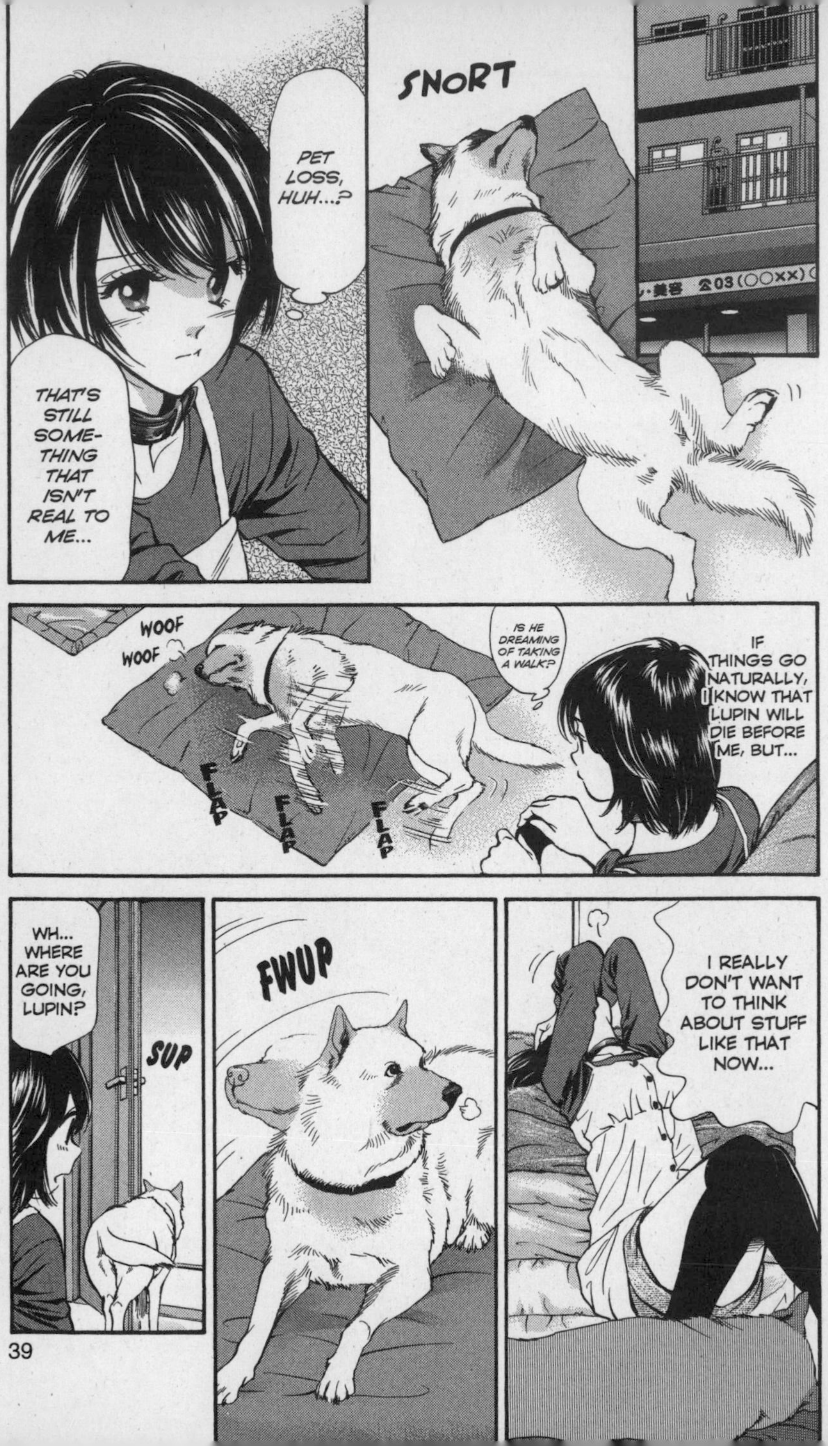
SNORT
PET LOSS, HUH...?
THAT'S STILL SOME-THING THAT ISN'T REAL TO ME...
IF THINGS GO NATURALLY, I KNOW THAT LUPIN WILL DIE BEFORE ME, BUT...
IS HE DREAMING OF TAKING A WALK?
WOOF WOOF
FLAP FLAP FLAP
I REALLY DON'T WANT TO THINK ABOUT STUFF LIKE THAT NOW...
FWUP
WH... WHERE ARE YOU GOING, LUPIN?
SUP

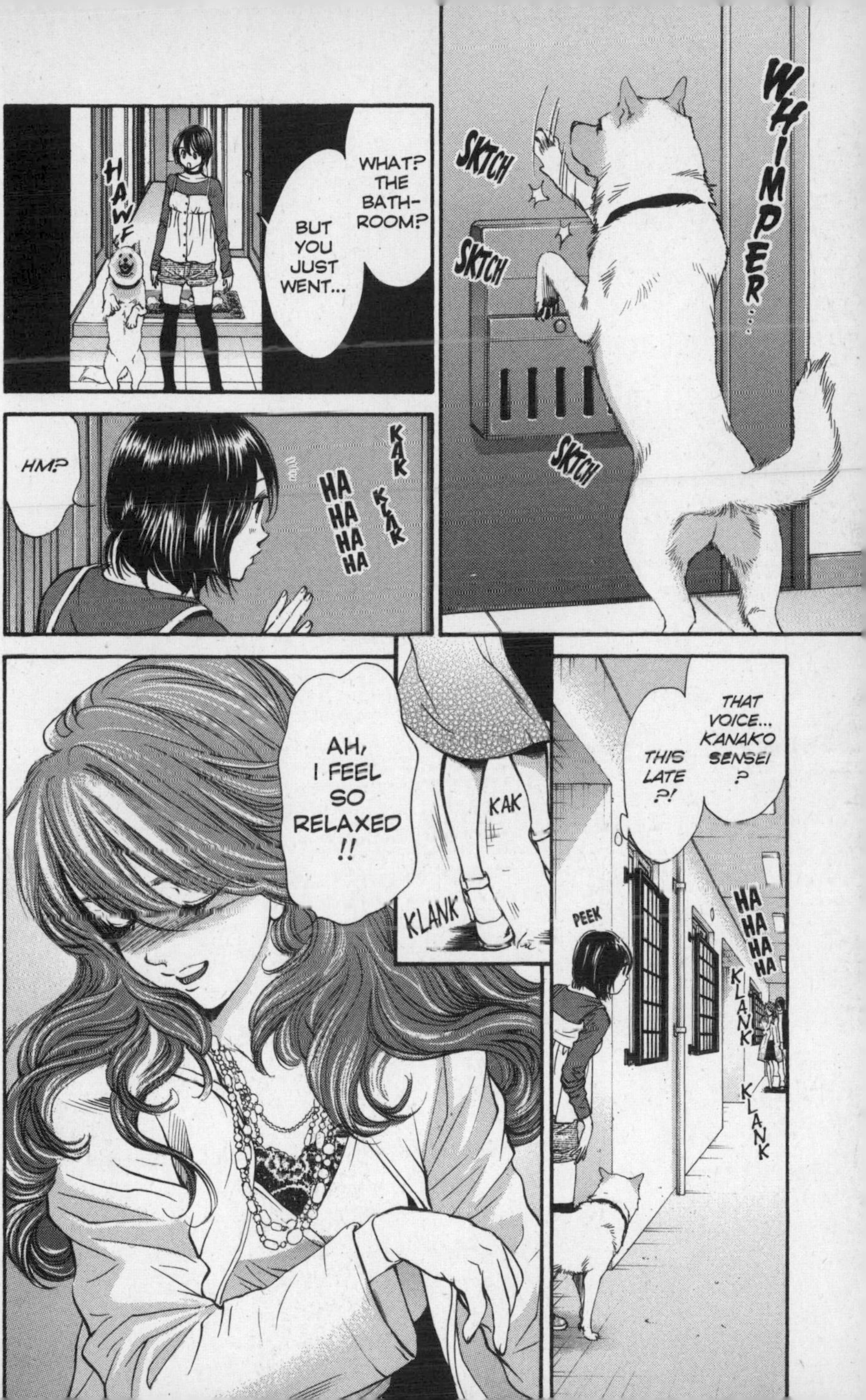
SKTCH
SKTCH
SKTCH
WHIMPER...
WHAT? THE BATH-ROOM?
BUT YOU JUST WENT...
HAWF
KAK KLAK
HAHAHAHA
HM?
THAT VOICE... KANAKO SENSEI?
THIS LATE?!
HAHAHAHA
KLANK KLANK
PEEK
KAK
KLANK
AH, I FEEL SO RELAXED!!

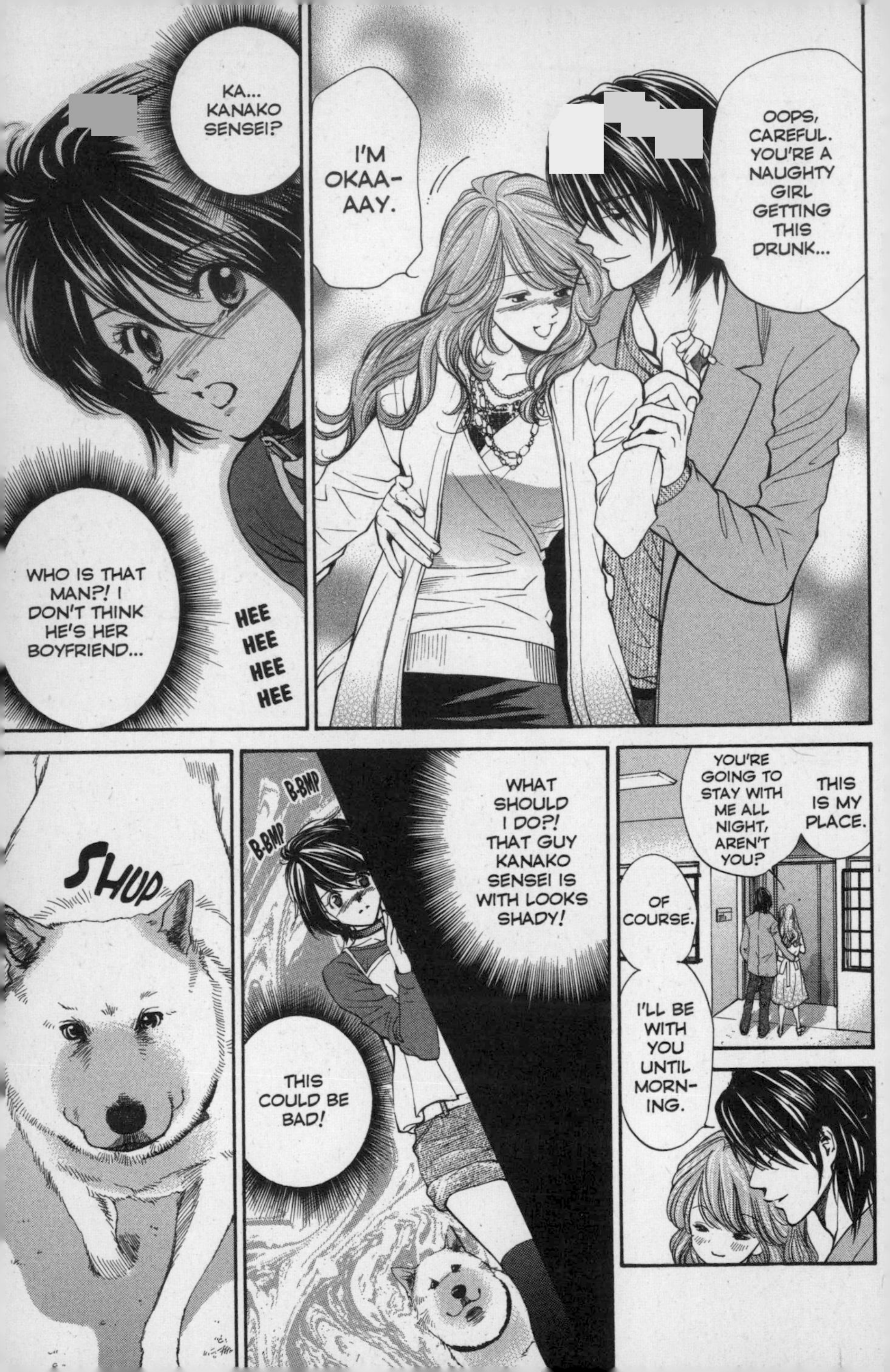
OOPS, CAREFUL. YOU'RE A NAUGHTY GIRL GETTING THIS DRUNK...
I'M OKAAA-AAY.
KA... KANAKO SENSEI?
HEE HEE HEE HEE
WHO IS THAT MAN?! I DON'T THINK HE'S HER BOYFRIEND...
THIS IS MY PLACE.
YOU'RE GOING TO STAY WITH ME ALL NIGHT, AREN'T YOU?
OF COURSE.
I'LL BE WITH YOU UNTIL MORN-ING.
WHAT SHOULD I DO?! THAT GUY KANAKO SENSEI IS WITH LOOKS SHADY!
B-BMP
B-BMP
THIS COULD BE BAD!
SHUP

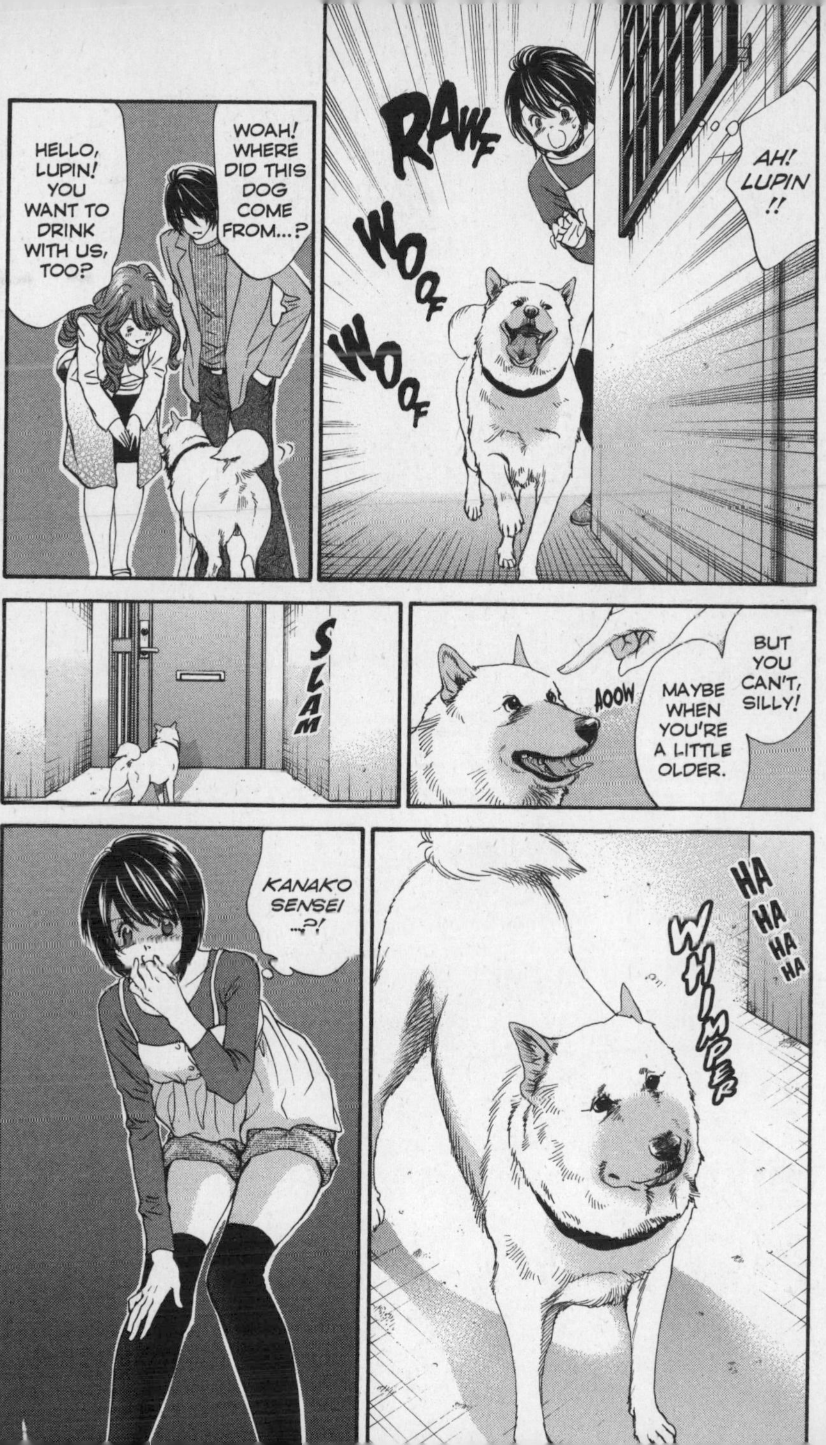

RAWF
WOOF
WOOF
AH! LUPIN!!
WOAH! WHERE DID THIS DOG COME FROM...?
HELLO, LUPIN! YOU WANT TO DRINK WITH US, TOO?
BUT YOU CAN'T, SILLY!
MAYBE WHEN YOU'RE A LITTLE OLDER.
AOOW
SLAM
HA HA HA HA HA
WHIMPER
KANAKO SENSEI ...?!

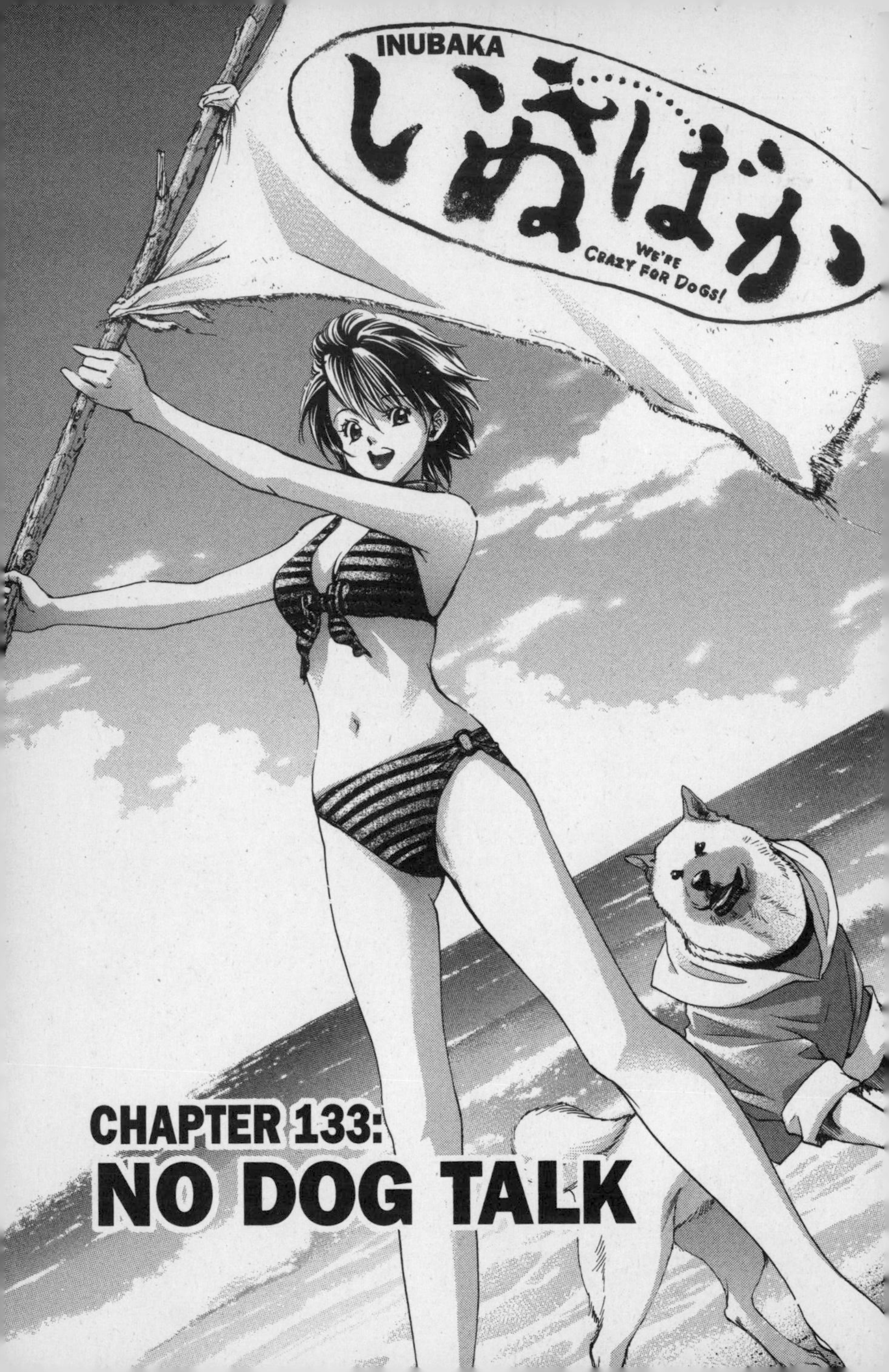
INUBAKA
いぬばか
WE'RE CRAZY FOR DOGS!
CHAPTER 133:
NO DOG TALK

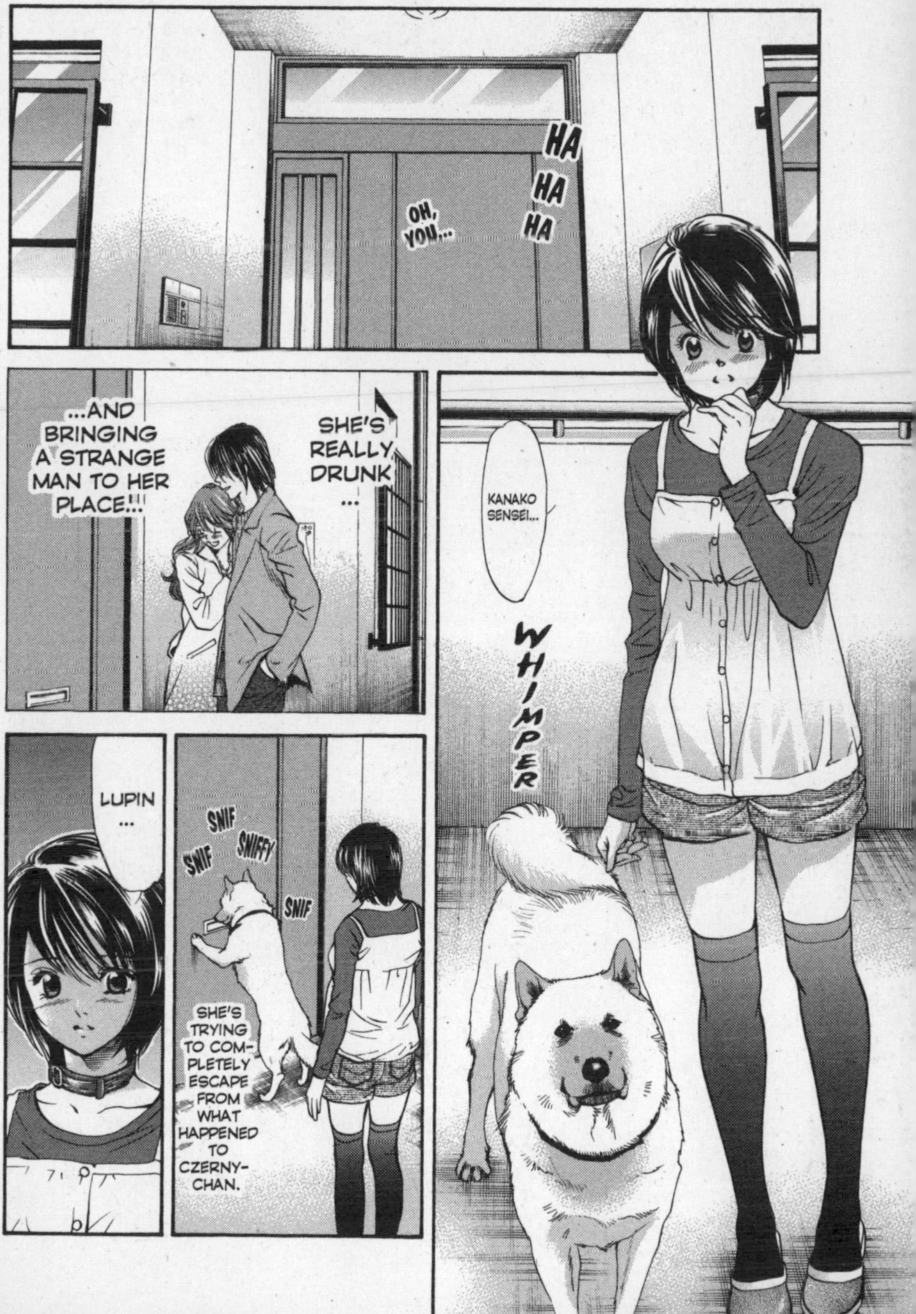
HA
HA
HA
OH, YOU...
KANAKO SENSEI...
WHIMPER
SHE'S REALLY DRUNK ...
...AND BRINGING A STRANGE MAN TO HER PLACE!...
SNIF
SNIFFY
SNIF
SNIF
SHE'S TRYING TO COM-PLETELY ESCAPE FROM WHAT HAPPENED TO CZERNY-CHAN.
LUPIN ...

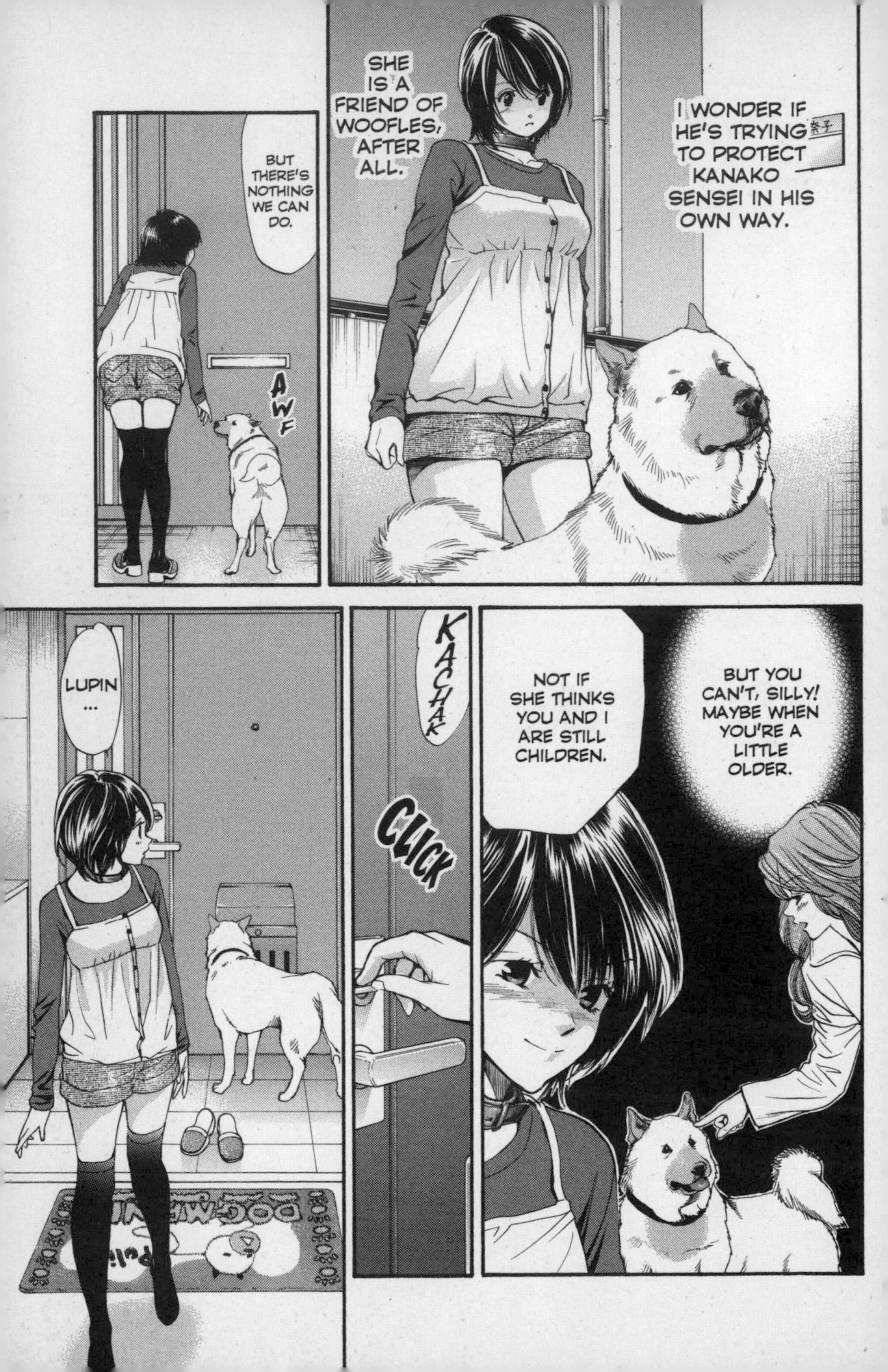
I WONDER IF HE'S TRYING TO PROTECT KANAKO SENSEI IN HIS OWN WAY.
SHE IS A FRIEND OF WOOFLES, AFTER ALL.
BUT THERE'S NOTHING WE CAN DO.
AWF
BUT YOU CAN'T, SILLY! MAYBE WHEN YOU'RE A LITTLE OLDER.
NOT IF SHE THINKS YOU AND I ARE STILL CHILDREN.
KACHAK
CLICK
LUPIN ...

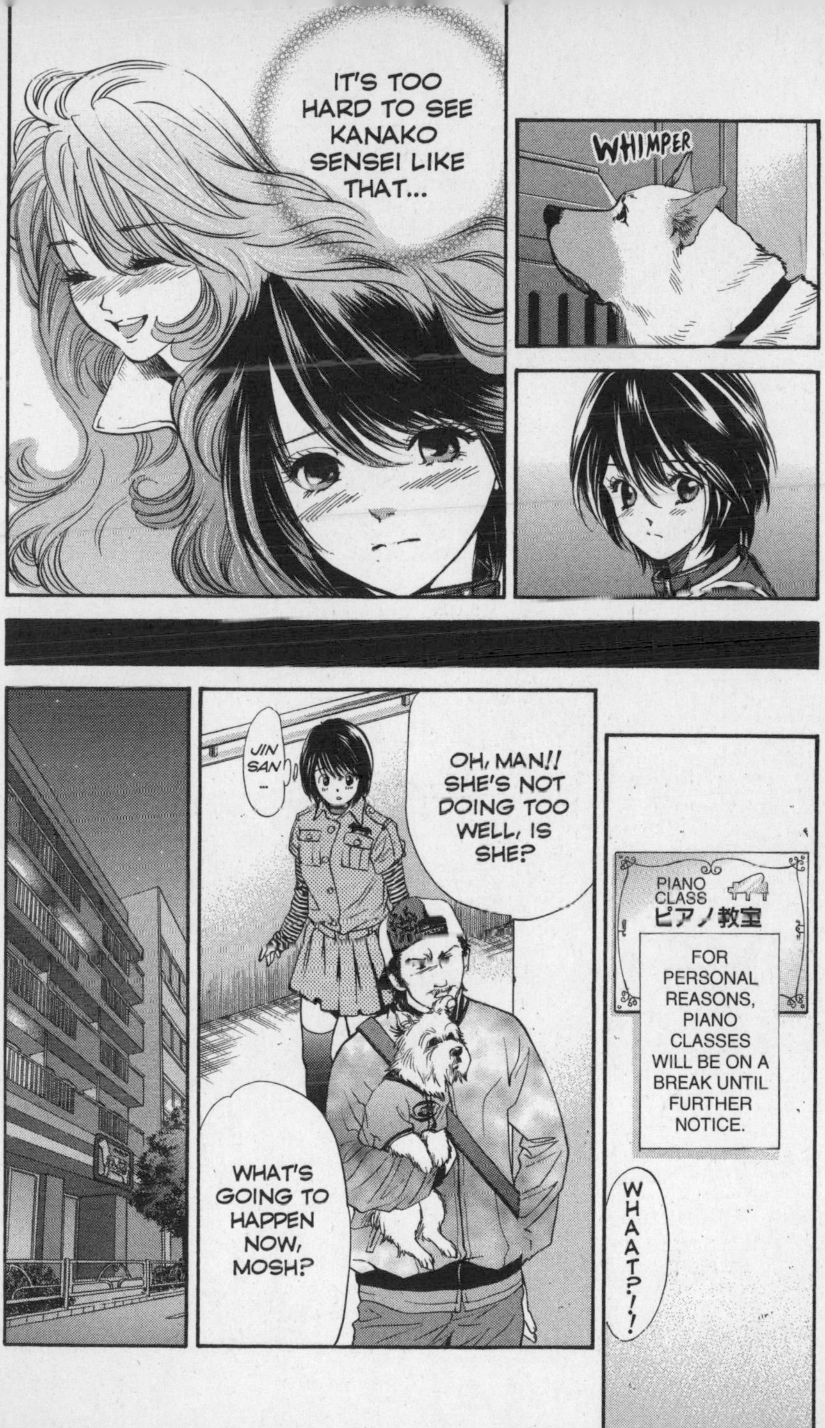
WHIMPER
IT'S TOO HARD TO SEE KANAKO SENSEI LIKE THAT...
PIANO CLASS
ピアノ教室
FOR PERSONAL REASONS, PIANO CLASSES WILL BE ON A BREAK UNTIL FURTHER NOTICE.
WHAAT?!!
JIN SAN...
OH, MAN!! SHE'S NOT DOING TOO WELL, IS SHE?
WHAT'S GOING TO HAPPEN NOW, MOSH?

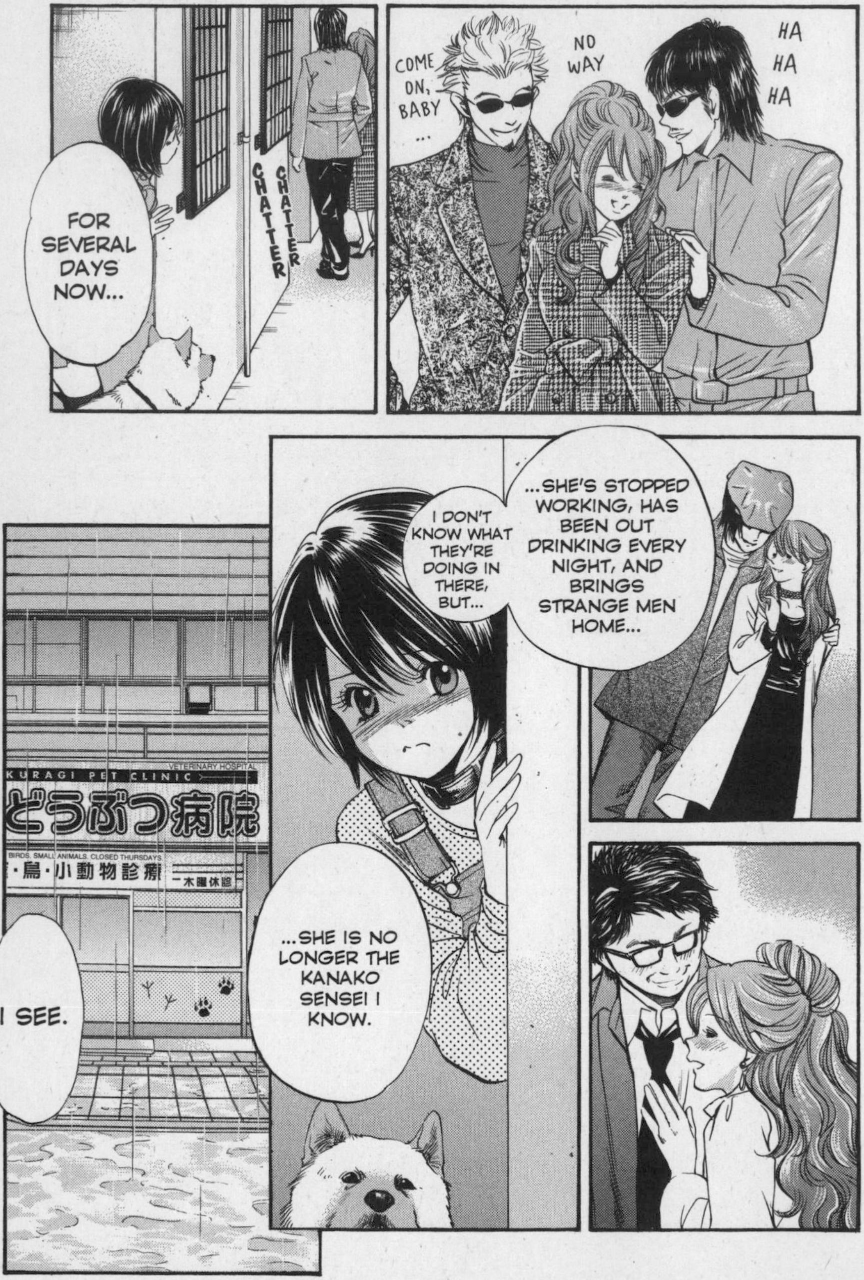
HA HA HA
NO WAY
COME ON, BABY ...
CHATTER CHATTER
FOR SEVERAL DAYS NOW...
...SHE'S STOPPED WORKING, HAS BEEN OUT DRINKING EVERY NIGHT, AND BRINGS STRANGE MEN HOME...
I DON'T KNOW WHAT THEY'RE DOING IN THERE, BUT...
...SHE IS NO LONGER THE KANAKO SENSEI I KNOW.
VETERINARY HOSPITAL
KURAGI PET CLINIC
どうぶつ病院
BIRDS. SMALL ANIMALS. CLOSED THURSDAYS.
・鳥・小動物診療
木曜休診
I SEE.

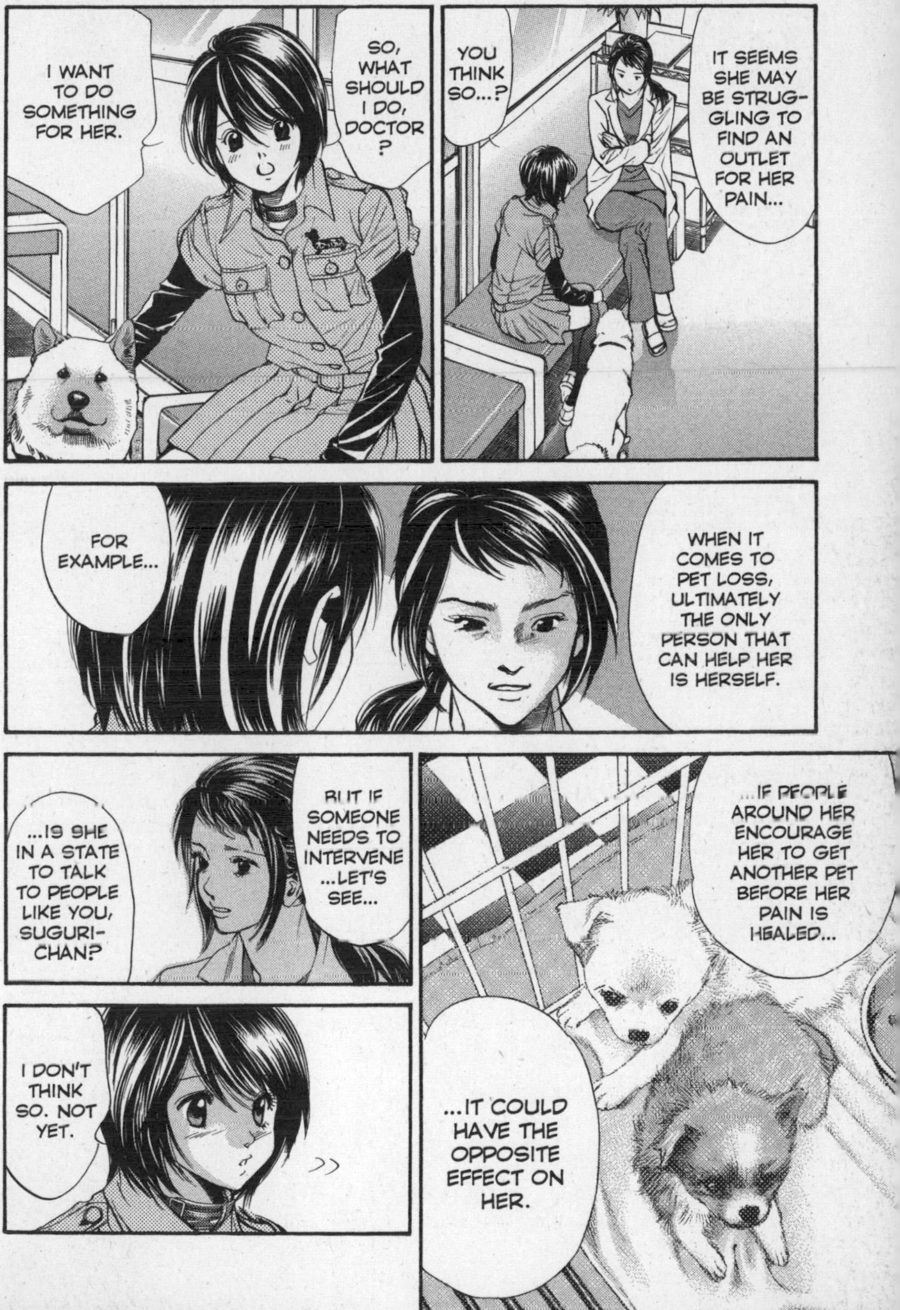
IT SEEMS SHE MAY BE STRUG-GLING TO FIND AN OUTLET FOR HER PAIN...
YOU THINK SO...?
SO, WHAT SHOULD I DO, DOCTOR?
I WANT TO DO SOMETHING FOR HER.
WHEN IT COMES TO PET LOSS, ULTIMATELY THE ONLY PERSON THAT CAN HELP HER IS HERSELF.
FOR EXAMPLE...
...IF PEOPLE AROUND HER ENCOURAGE HER TO GET ANOTHER PET BEFORE HER PAIN IS HEALED...
...IT COULD HAVE THE OPPOSITE EFFECT ON HER.
BUT IF SOMEONE NEEDS TO INTERVENE ...LET'S SEE...
...IS SHE IN A STATE TO TALK TO PEOPLE LIKE YOU, SUGURI-CHAN?
I DON'T THINK SO. NOT YET.

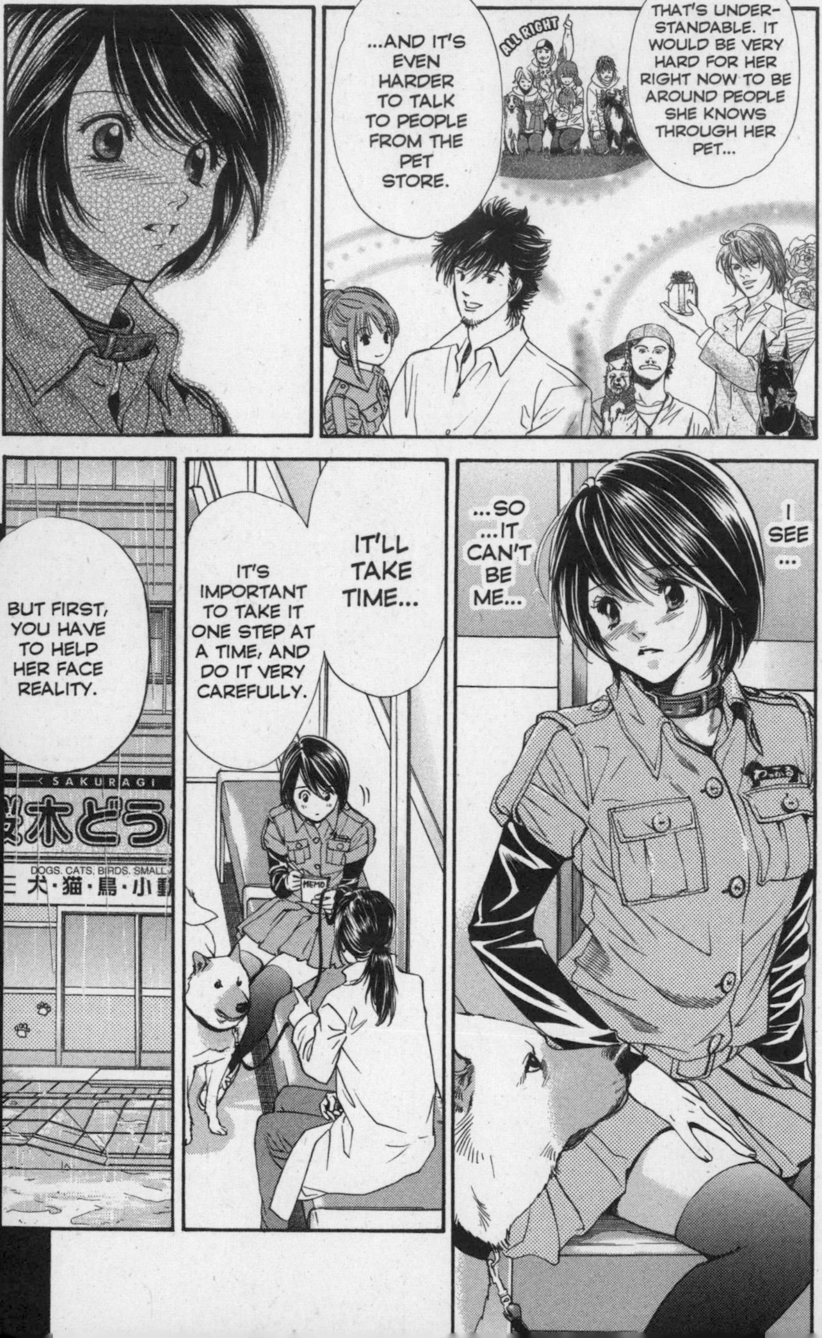
THAT'S UNDER-STANDABLE. IT WOULD BE VERY HARD FOR HER RIGHT NOW TO BE AROUND PEOPLE SHE KNOWS THROUGH HER PET...
...AND IT'S EVEN HARDER TO TALK TO PEOPLE FROM THE PET STORE.
ALL RIGHT
I SEE ...
...SO ...IT CAN'T BE ME...
IT'LL TAKE TIME...
IT'S IMPORTANT TO TAKE IT ONE STEP AT A TIME, AND DO IT VERY CAREFULLY.
MEMO
BUT FIRST, YOU HAVE TO HELP HER FACE REALITY.
SAKURAGI
DOGS. CATS. BIRDS. SMALL
犬・猫・鳥・小

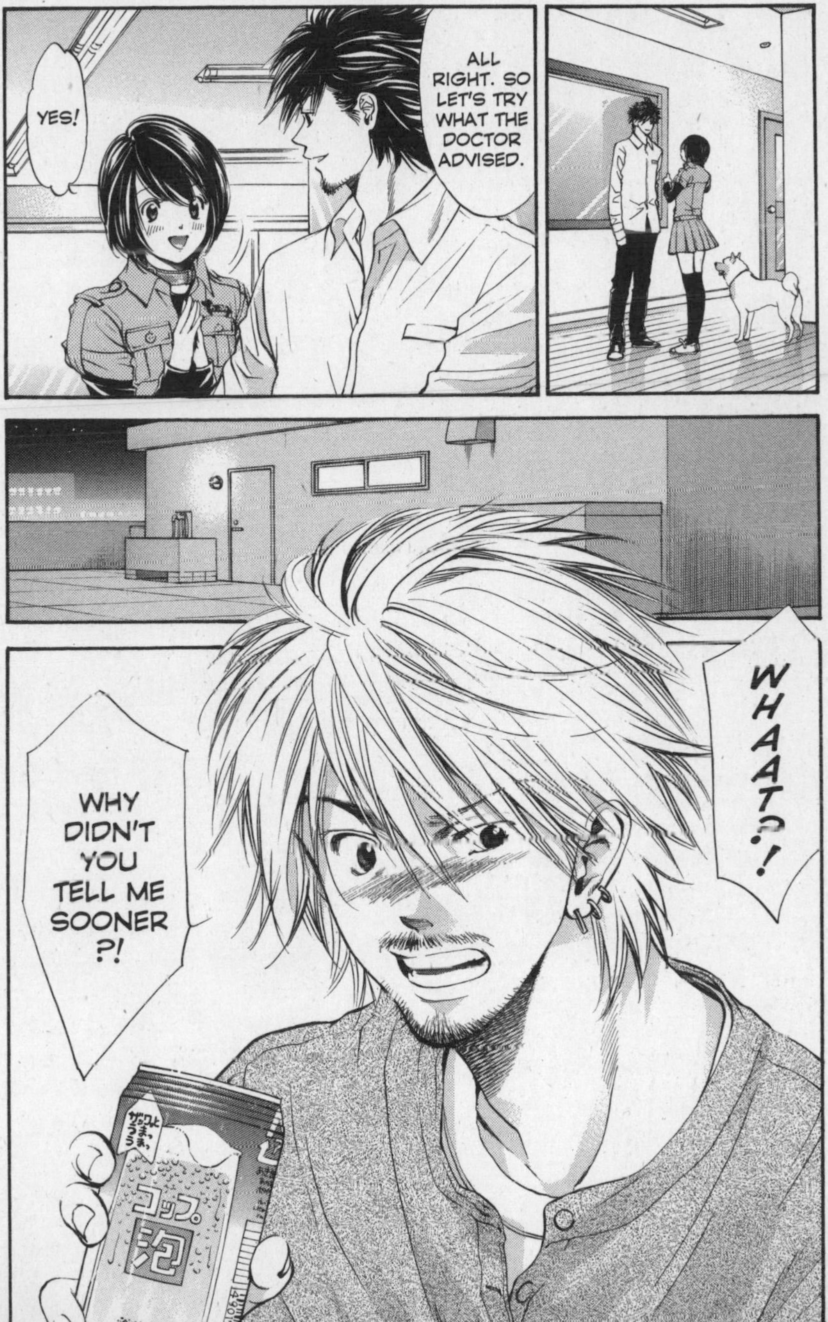
ALL RIGHT. SO LET'S TRY WHAT THE DOCTOR ADVISED.
YES!
WHAAT?!
WHY DIDN'T YOU TELL ME SOONER?!

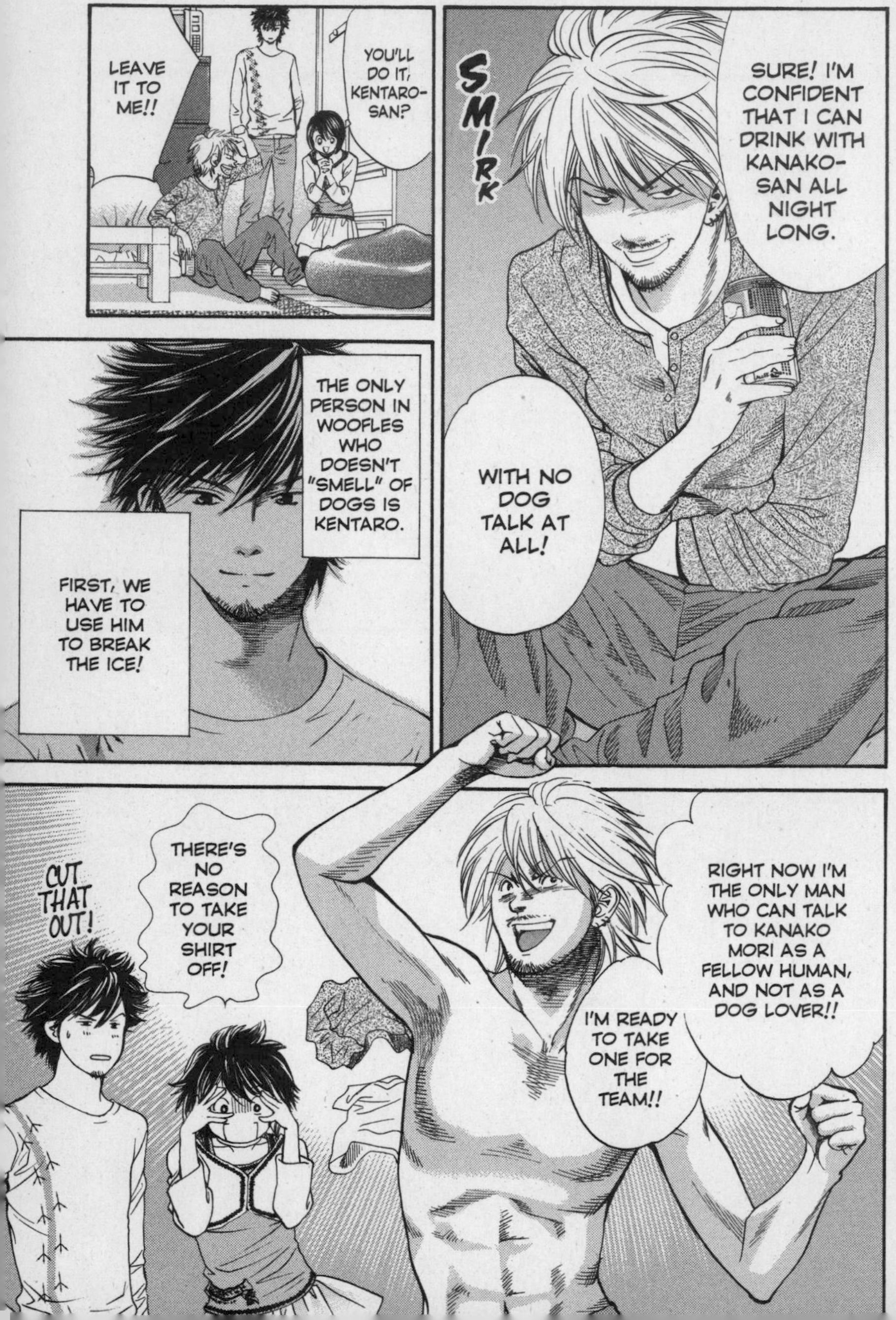
SMIRK
SURE! I'M CONFIDENT THAT I CAN DRINK WITH KANAKO-SAN ALL NIGHT LONG.
WITH NO DOG TALK AT ALL!
YOU'LL DO IT, KENTARO-SAN?
LEAVE IT TO ME!!
THE ONLY PERSON IN WOOFLES WHO DOESN'T "SMELL" OF DOGS IS KENTARO.
FIRST, WE HAVE TO USE HIM TO BREAK THE ICE!
RIGHT NOW I'M THE ONLY MAN WHO CAN TALK TO KANAKO MORI AS A FELLOW HUMAN, AND NOT AS A DOG LOVER!!
I'M READY TO TAKE ONE FOR THE TEAM!!
THERE'S NO REASON TO TAKE YOUR SHIRT OFF!
CUT THAT OUT!

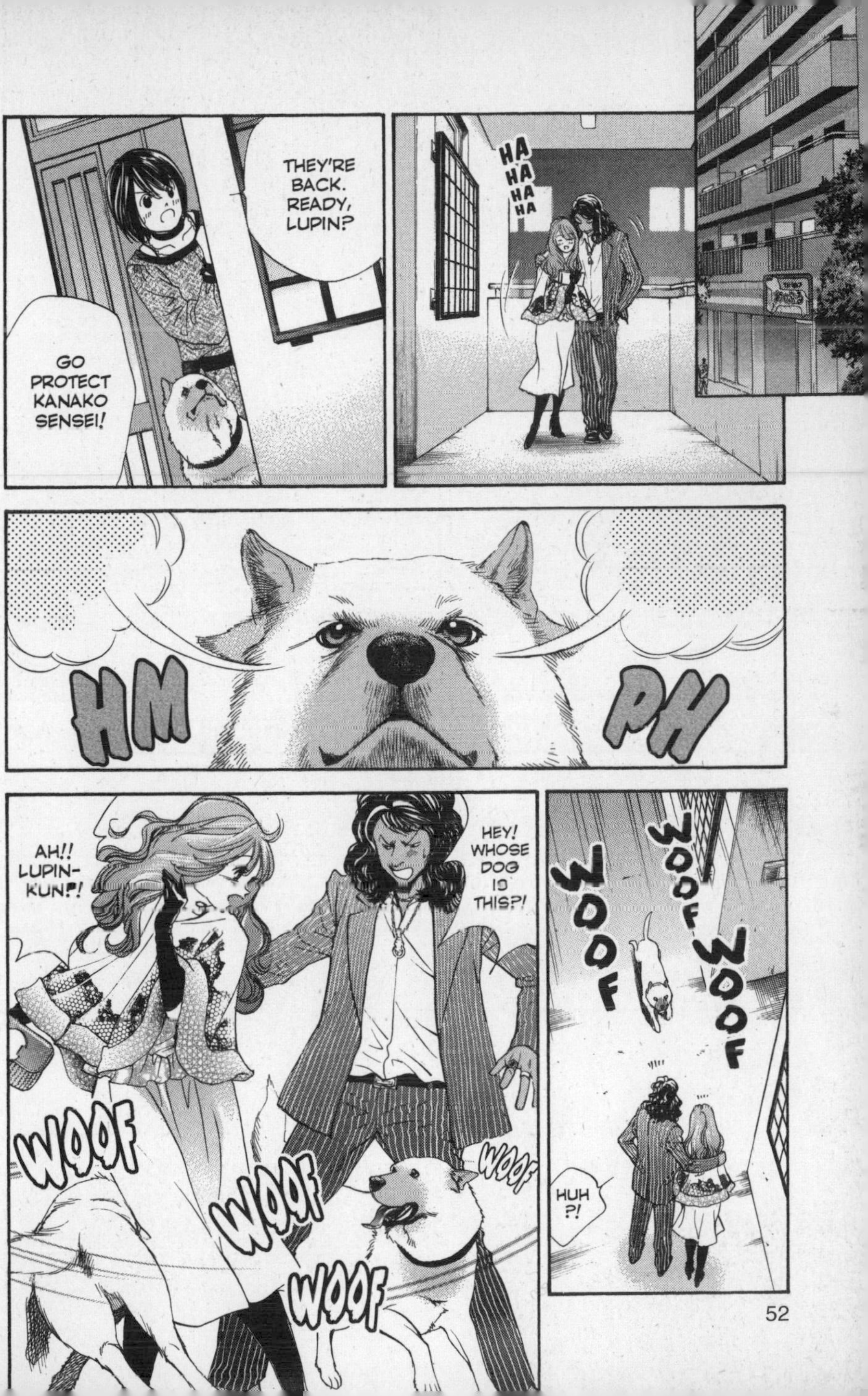
HA HA HA HA
THEY'RE BACK. READY, LUPIN?
GO PROTECT KANAKO SENSEI!
HM PH
WOOF WOOF
WOOF WOOF
WOOF
WOOF
HUH ?!
HEY! WHOSE DOG IS THIS?!
AH!! LUPIN-KUN?!
WOOF
WOOF
WOOF
WOOF

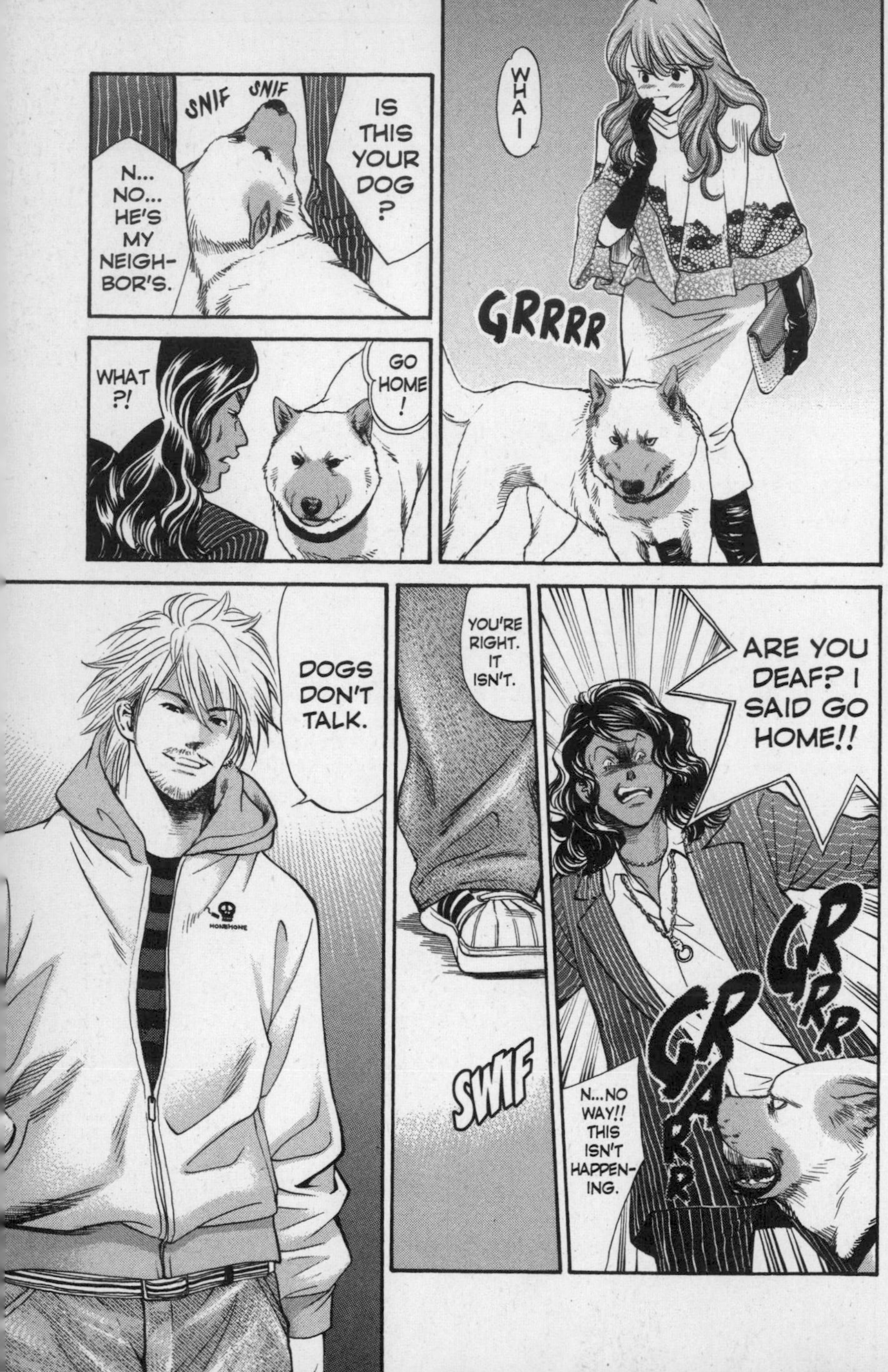
WHA I
GRRRR
SNIF SNIF
IS THIS YOUR DOG?
N... NO... HE'S MY NEIGH-BOR'S.
GO HOME!
WHAT?!
ARE YOU DEAF? I SAID GO HOME!!
GRRR
GRARR
N...NO WAY!! THIS ISN'T HAPPEN-ING.
YOU'RE RIGHT. IT ISN'T.
SWIF
DOGS DON'T TALK.

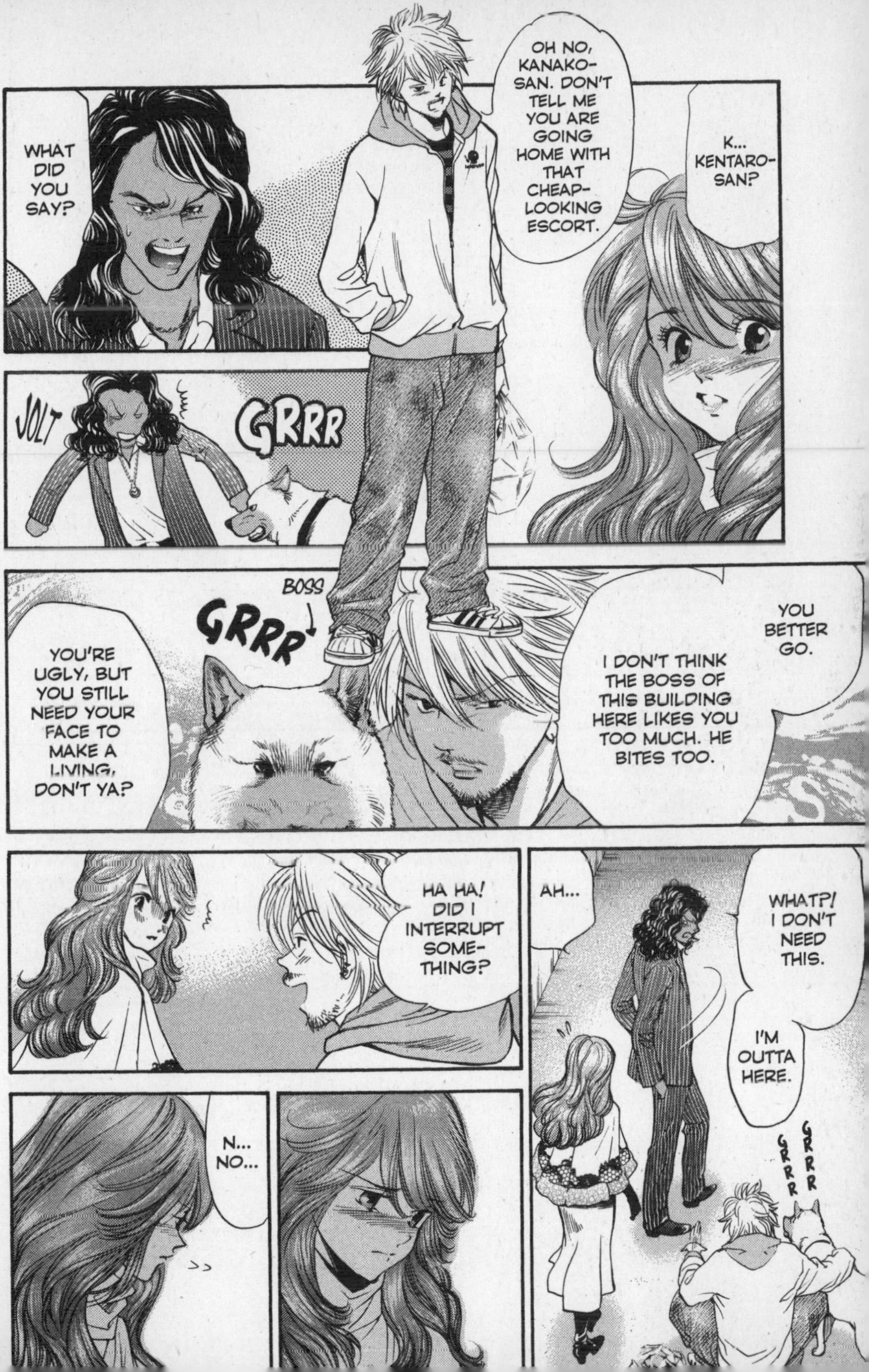
K... KENTARO-SAN?
OH NO, KANAKO-SAN. DON'T TELL ME YOU ARE GOING HOME WITH THAT CHEAP-LOOKING ESCORT.
WHAT DID YOU SAY?
GRRR
JOLT
YOU BETTER GO.
I DON'T THINK THE BOSS OF THIS BUILDING HERE LIKES YOU TOO MUCH. HE BITES TOO.
BOSS
GRRR
YOU'RE UGLY, BUT YOU STILL NEED YOUR FACE TO MAKE A LIVING, DON'T YA?
WHAT?! I DON'T NEED THIS.
AH...
I'M OUTTA HERE.
GRRR
GRRR
HA HA! DID I INTERRUPT SOME-THING?
N... NO...

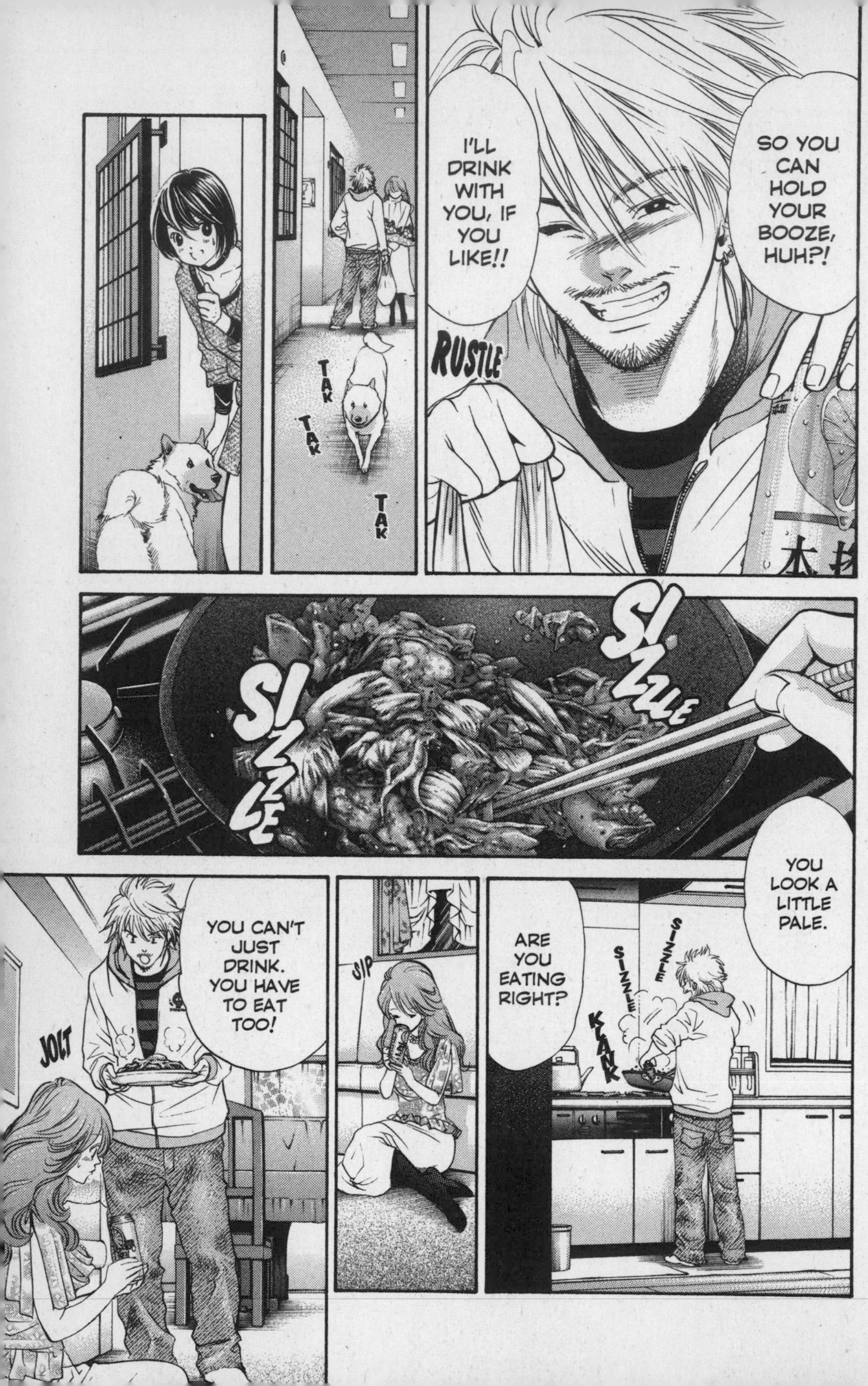
SO YOU CAN HOLD YOUR BOOZE, HUH?!
I'LL DRINK WITH YOU, IF YOU LIKE!!
RUSTLE
TAK
TAK
TAK
SIZZLE
SIZZLE
YOU LOOK A LITTLE PALE.
ARE YOU EATING RIGHT?
SIZZLE
SIZZLE
KLANK
SIP
YOU CAN'T JUST DRINK. YOU HAVE TO EAT TOO!
JOLT

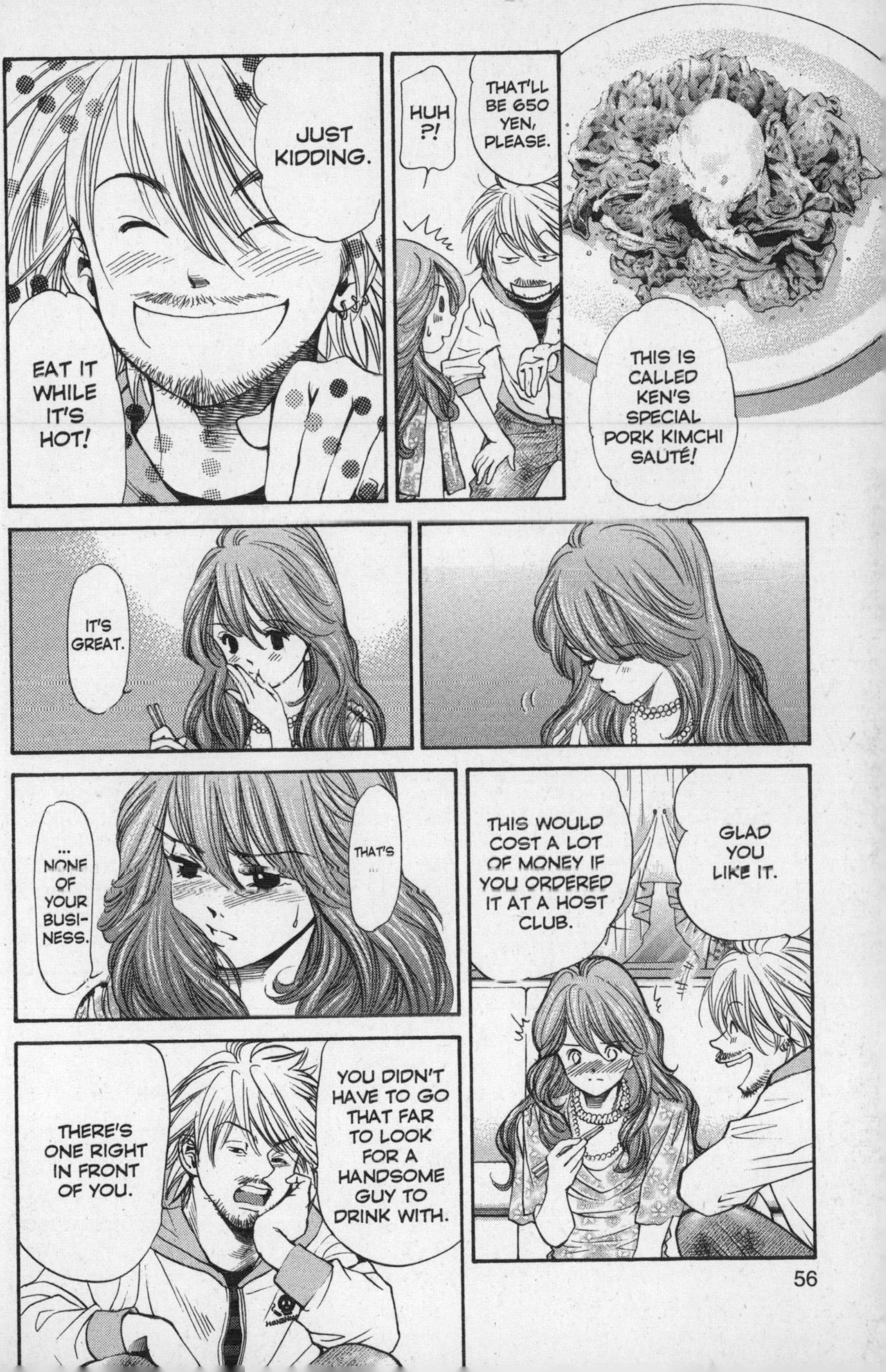
THIS IS CALLED KEN'S SPECIAL PORK KIMCHI SAUTÉ!
THAT'LL BE 650 YEN, PLEASE.
HUH ?!
JUST KIDDING.
EAT IT WHILE IT'S HOT!
IT'S GREAT.
GLAD YOU LIKE IT.
THIS WOULD COST A LOT OF MONEY IF YOU ORDERED IT AT A HOST CLUB.
THAT'S ...
... NONE OF YOUR BUSI- NESS.
YOU DIDN'T HAVE TO GO THAT FAR TO LOOK FOR A HANDSOME GUY TO DRINK WITH.
THERE'S ONE RIGHT IN FRONT OF YOU.

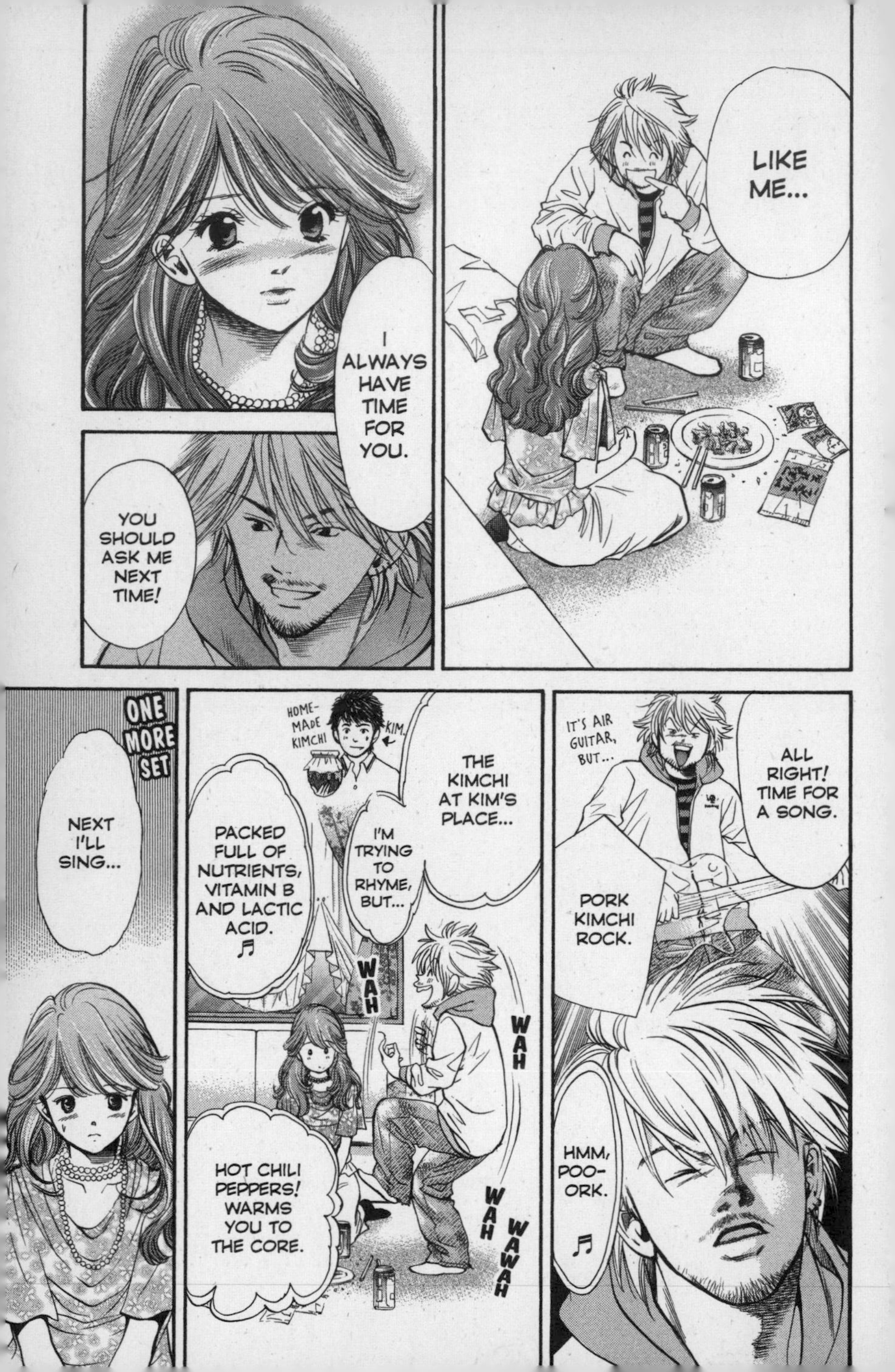
LIKE ME...
I ALWAYS HAVE TIME FOR YOU.
YOU SHOULD ASK ME NEXT TIME!
ALL RIGHT! TIME FOR A SONG.
IT'S AIR GUITAR, BUT...
PORK KIMCHI ROCK.
HMM, POO-ORK. ♬
THE KIMCHI AT KIM'S PLACE...
KIM.
HOME-MADE KIMCHI
I'M TRYING TO RHYME, BUT...
PACKED FULL OF NUTRIENTS, VITAMIN B AND LACTIC ACID. ♬
WAH
WAH
WAH
WAWAH
HOT CHILI PEPPERS! WARMS YOU TO THE CORE.
ONE MORE SET
NEXT I'LL SING...

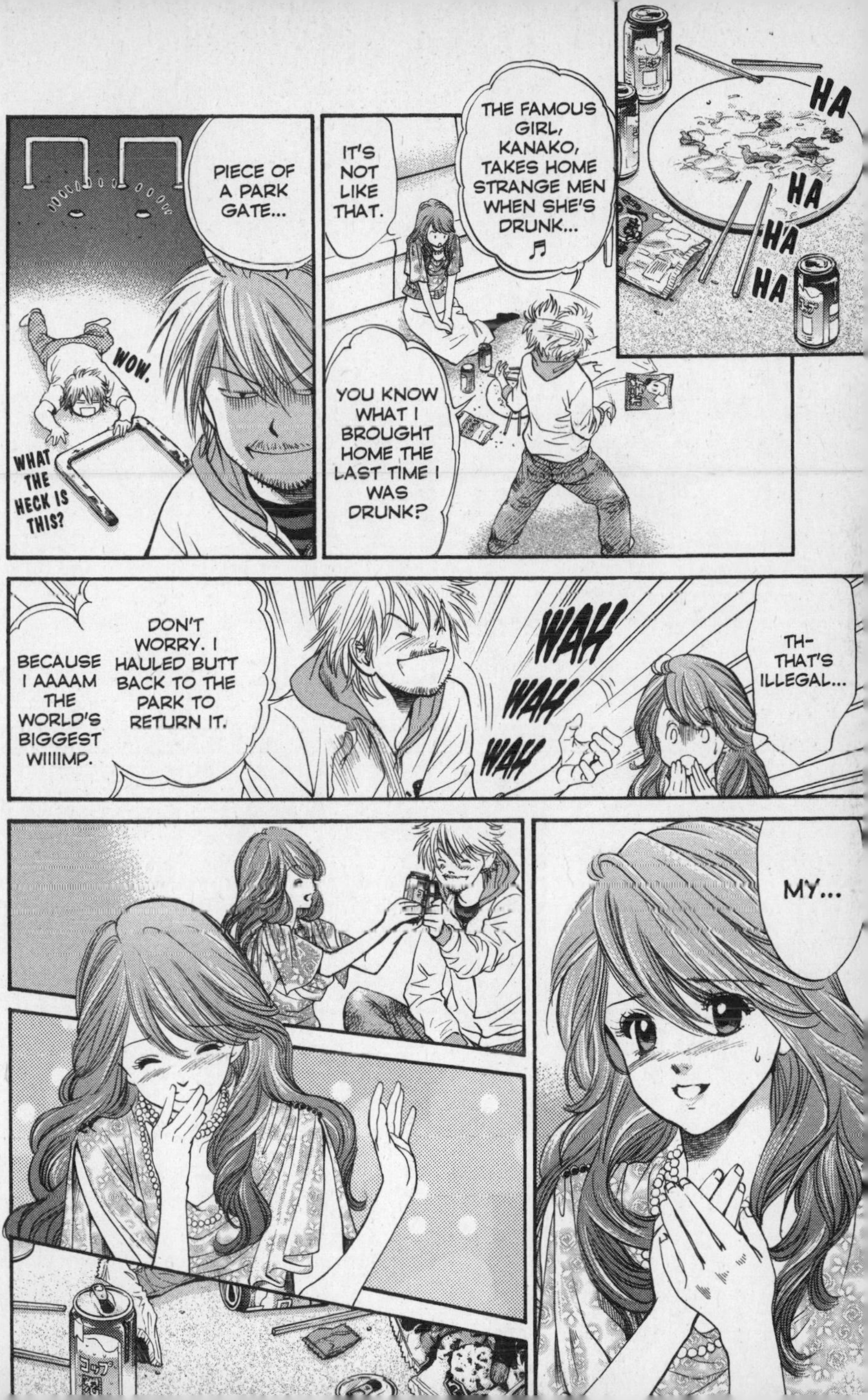
HA
HA
HA
HA
THE FAMOUS GIRL, KANAKO, TAKES HOME STRANGE MEN WHEN SHE'S DRUNK... ♬
IT'S NOT LIKE THAT.
YOU KNOW WHAT I BROUGHT HOME THE LAST TIME I WAS DRUNK?
PIECE OF A PARK GATE...
WOW.
WHAT THE HECK IS THIS?
TH- THAT'S ILLEGAL...
WAH
WAH
WAH
DON'T WORRY. I HAULED BUTT BACK TO THE PARK TO RETURN IT.
BECAUSE I AAAAM THE WORLD'S BIGGEST WIIIIMP.
MY...

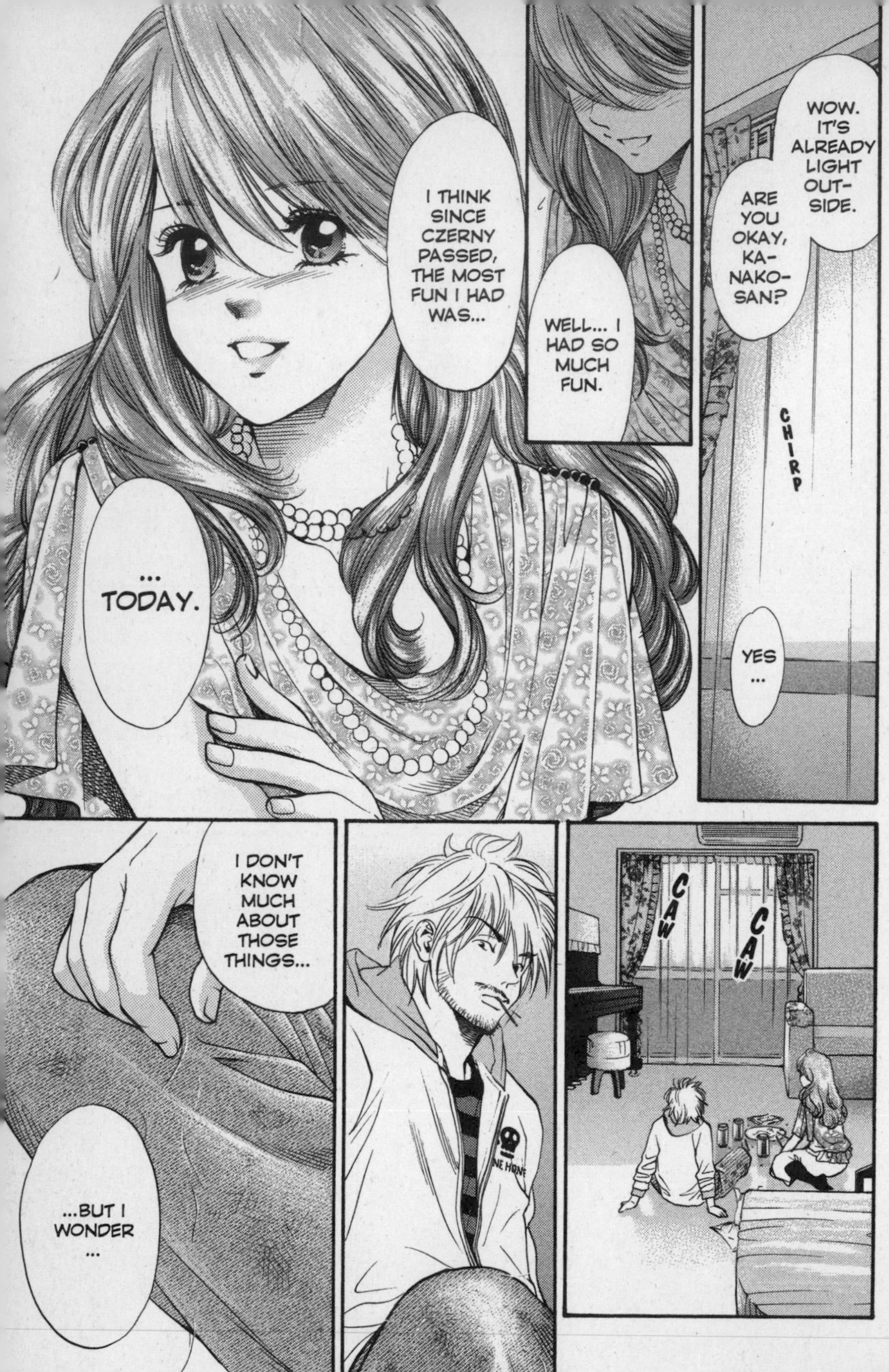
WOW. IT'S ALREADY LIGHT OUT-SIDE.
ARE YOU OKAY, KA-NAKO-SAN?
CHIRP
YES ...
WELL... I HAD SO MUCH FUN.
I THINK SINCE CZERNY PASSED, THE MOST FUN I HAD WAS...
... TODAY.
CAW
CAW
I DON'T KNOW MUCH ABOUT THOSE THINGS...
...BUT I WONDER ...

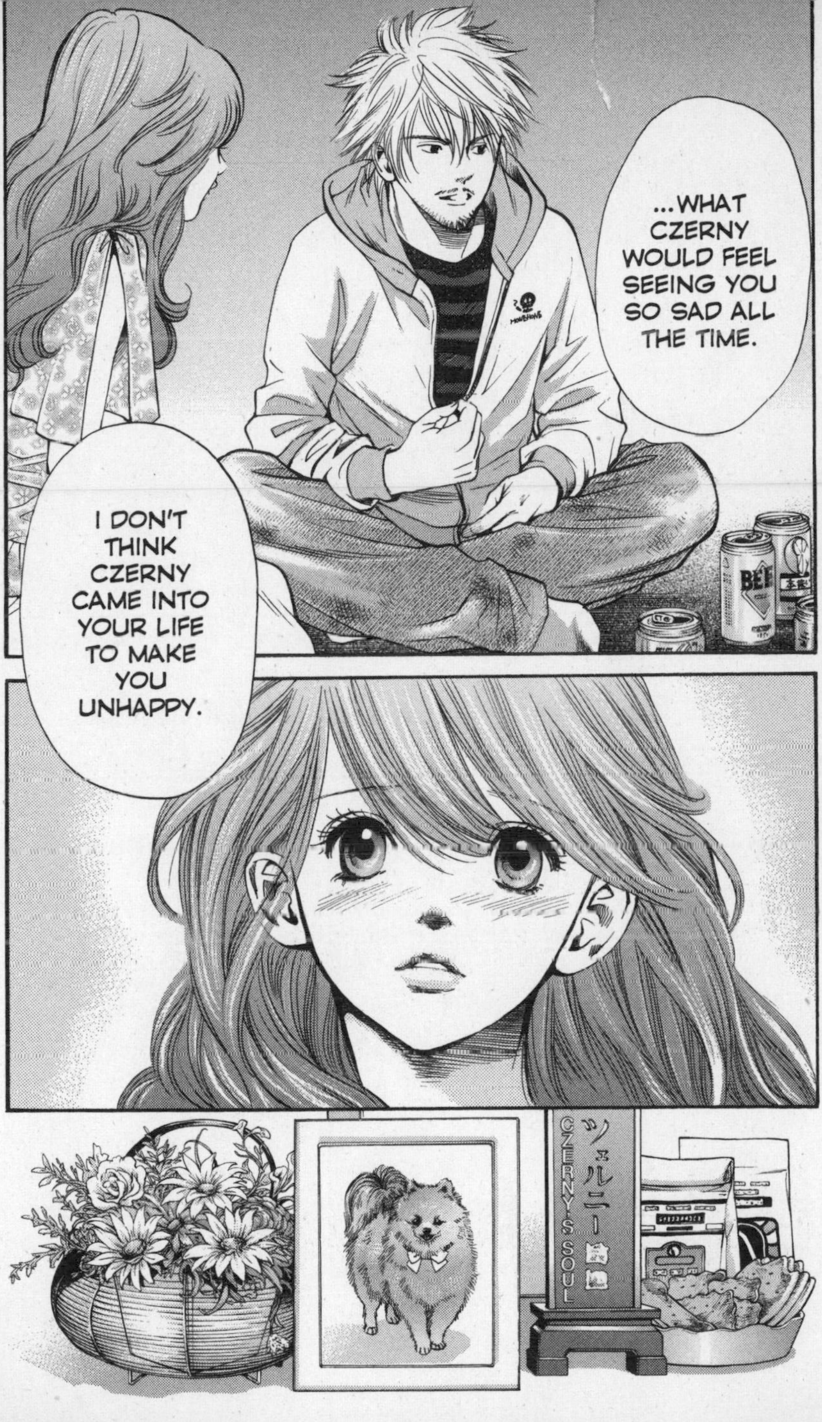
...WHAT CZERNY WOULD FEEL SEEING YOU SO SAD ALL THE TIME.
I DON'T THINK CZERNY CAME INTO YOUR LIFE TO MAKE YOU UNHAPPY.
ツェルニー
CZERNY'S SOUL

INUBAKA

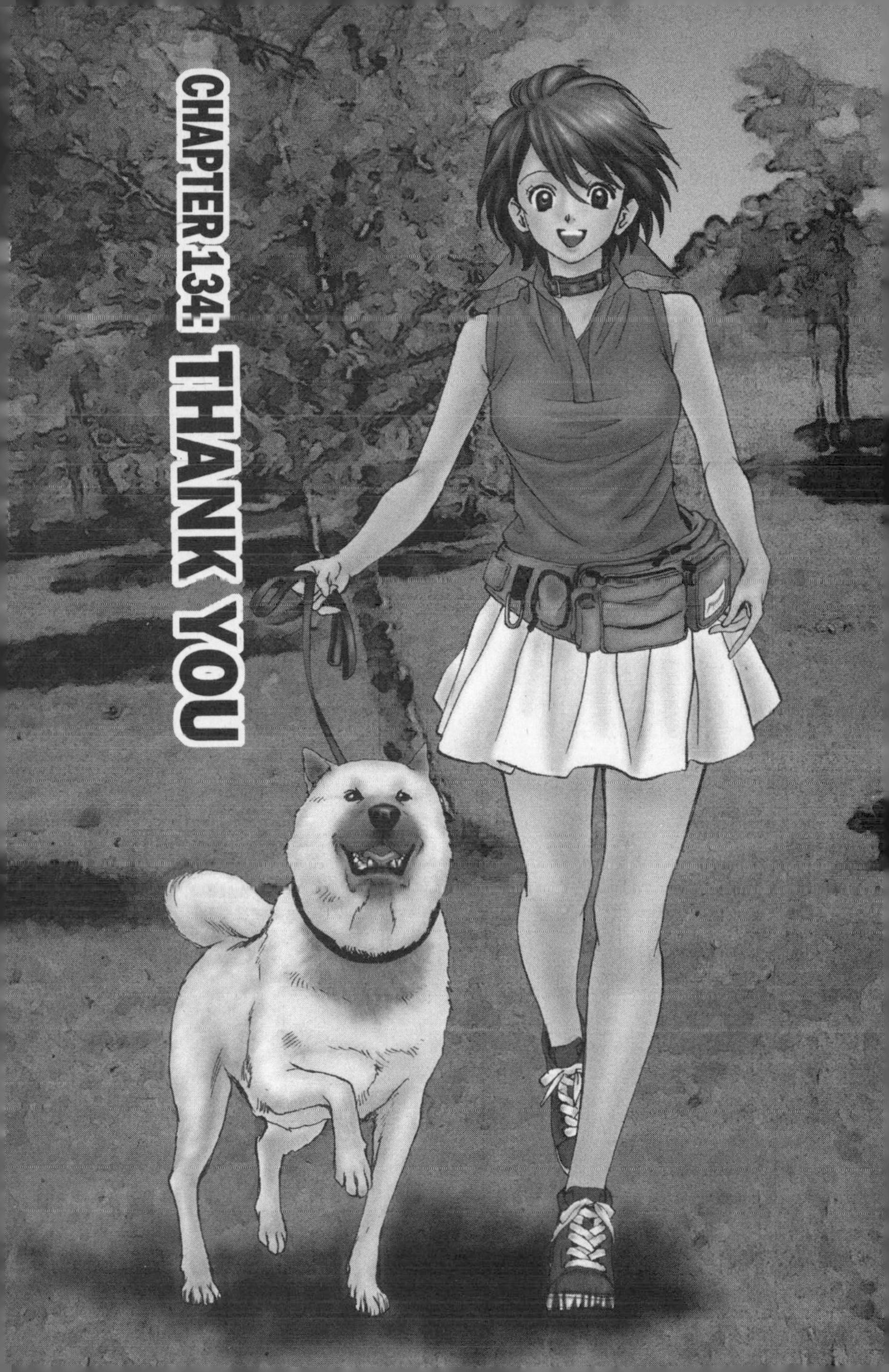
CHAPTER 134: THANK YOU

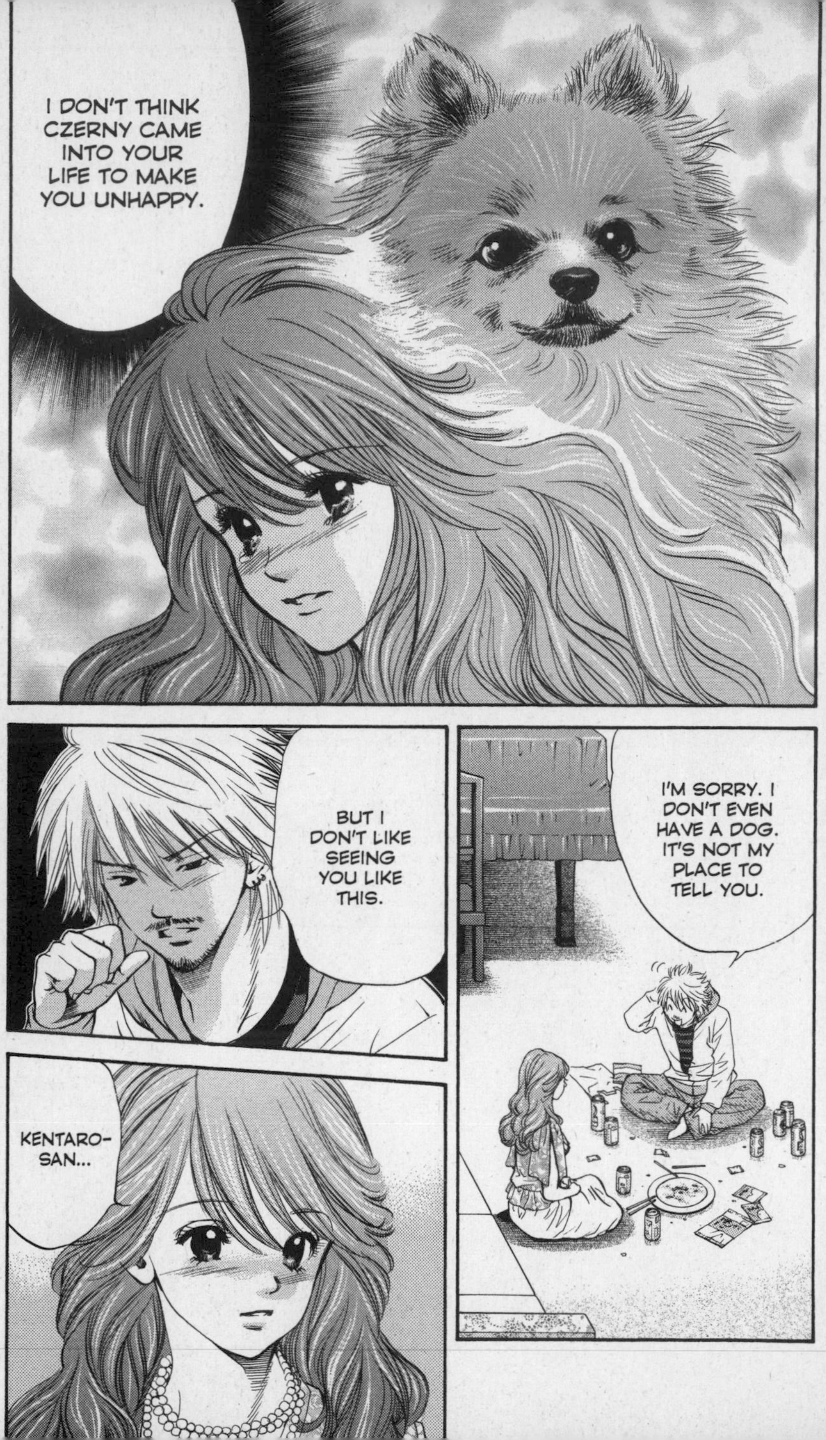
I DON'T THINK CZERNY CAME INTO YOUR LIFE TO MAKE YOU UNHAPPY.
I'M SORRY. I DON'T EVEN HAVE A DOG. IT'S NOT MY PLACE TO TELL YOU.
BUT I DON'T LIKE SEEING YOU LIKE THIS.
KENTARO-SAN...

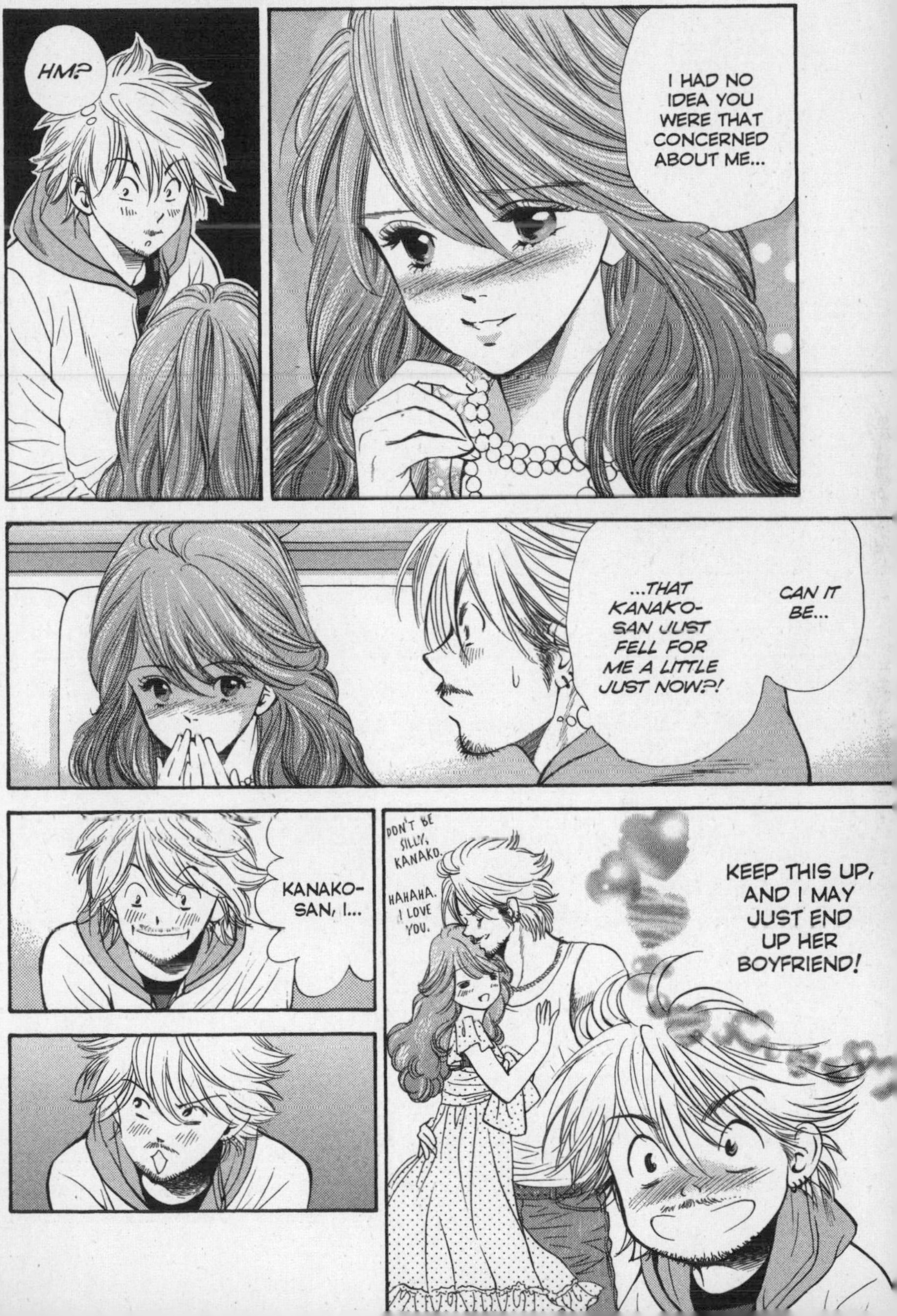
I HAD NO IDEA YOU WERE THAT CONCERNED ABOUT ME...
HM?
CAN IT BE...
...THAT KANAKO-SAN JUST FELL FOR ME A LITTLE JUST NOW?!
KEEP THIS UP, AND I MAY JUST END UP HER BOYFRIEND!
DON'T BE SILLY, KANAKO.
HAHAHA. I LOVE YOU.
KANAKO-SAN, I...

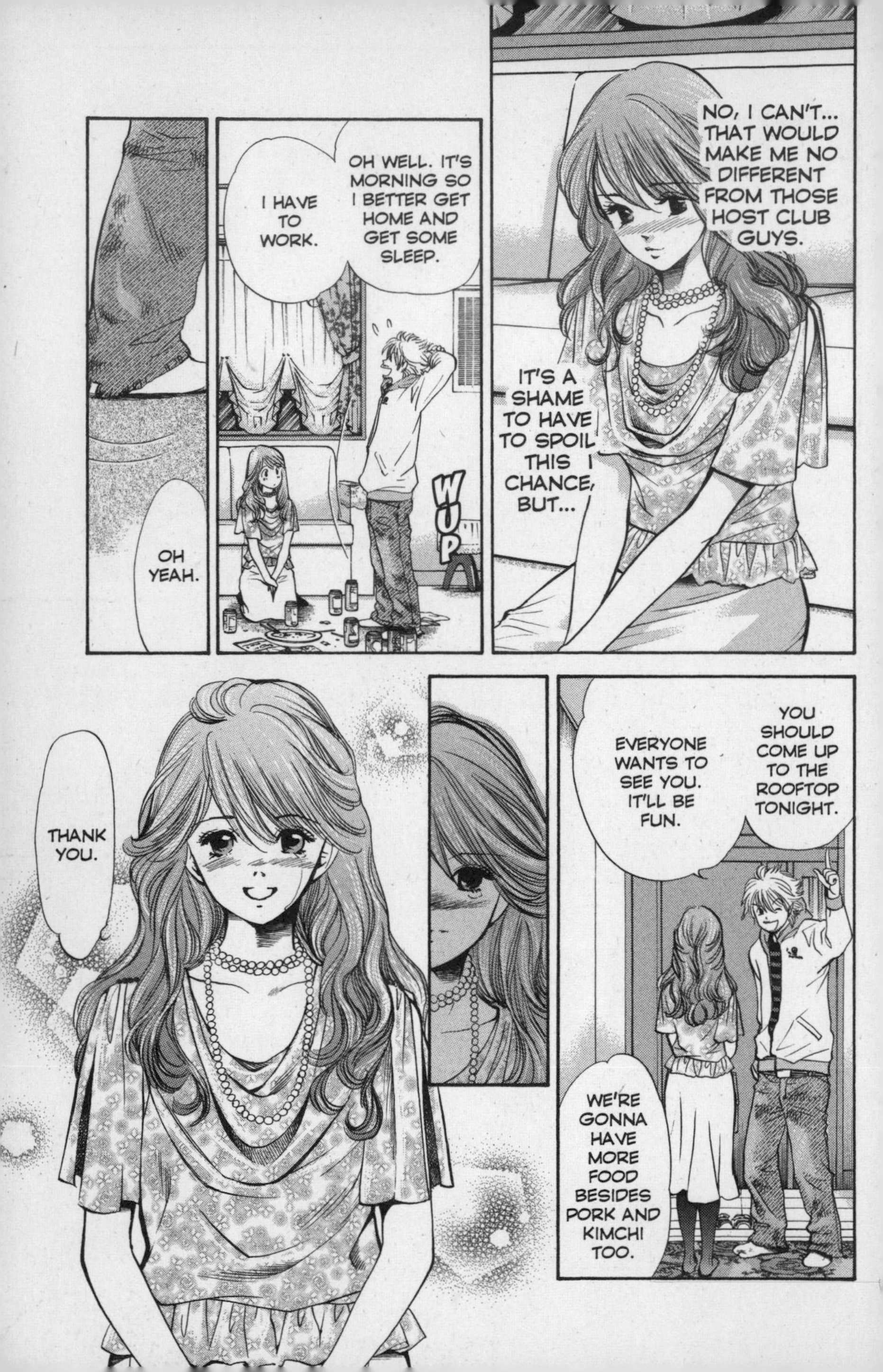
NO, I CAN'T... THAT WOULD MAKE ME NO DIFFERENT FROM THOSE HOST CLUB GUYS.
IT'S A SHAME TO HAVE TO SPOIL THIS CHANCE, BUT...
OH WELL. IT'S MORNING SO I BETTER GET HOME AND GET SOME SLEEP.
I HAVE TO WORK.
WUP
OH YEAH.
YOU SHOULD COME UP TO THE ROOFTOP TONIGHT.
EVERYONE WANTS TO SEE YOU. IT'LL BE FUN.
WE'RE GONNA HAVE MORE FOOD BESIDES PORK AND KIMCHI TOO.
THANK YOU.

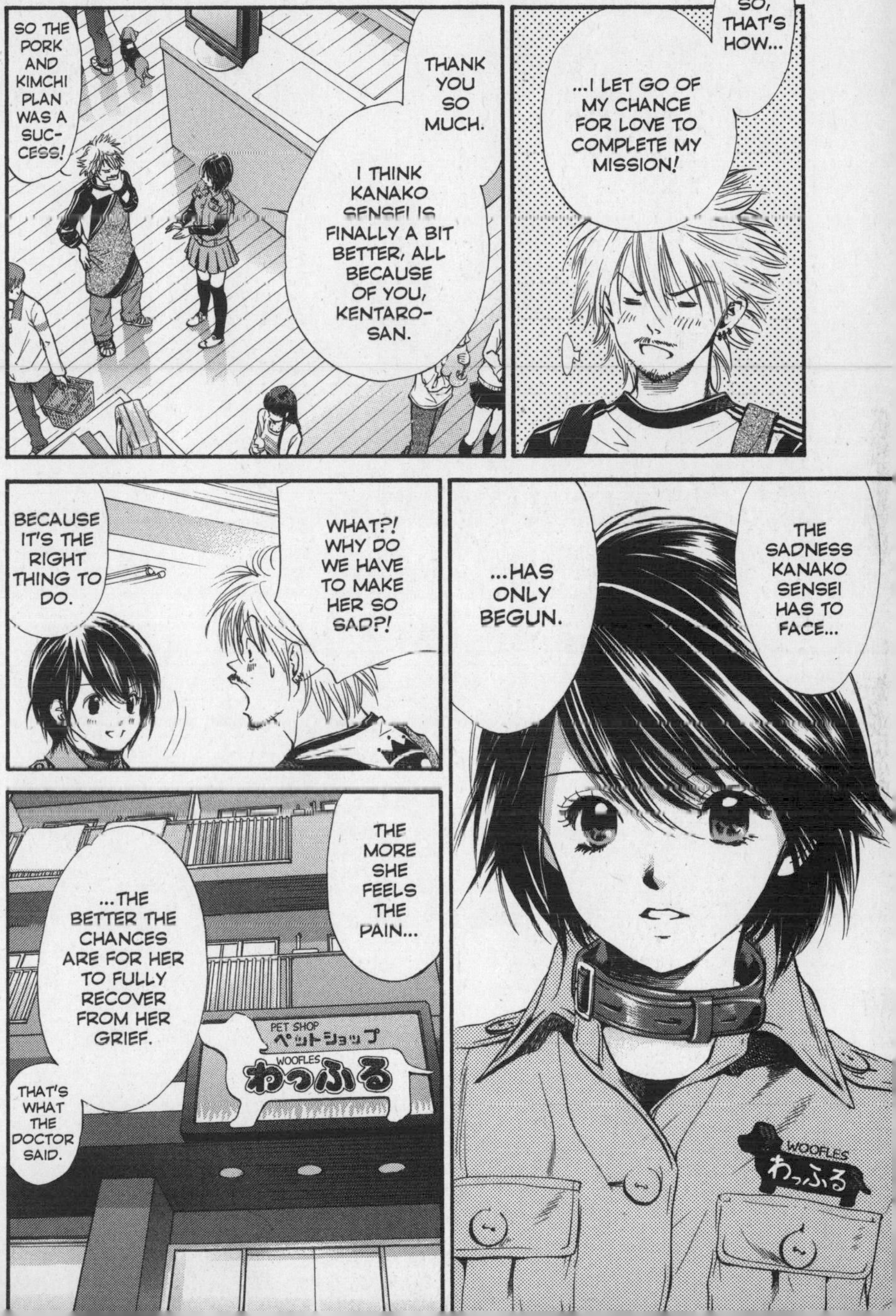
SO, THAT'S HOW...
...I LET GO OF MY CHANCE FOR LOVE TO COMPLETE MY MISSION!
THANK YOU SO MUCH.
I THINK KANAKO SENSEI IS FINALLY A BIT BETTER, ALL BECAUSE OF YOU, KENTARO-SAN.
SO THE PORK AND KIMCHI PLAN WAS A SUCCESS!
THE SADNESS KANAKO SENSEI HAS TO FACE...
...HAS ONLY BEGUN.
WOOFLES
わっふる
WHAT?! WHY DO WE HAVE TO MAKE HER SO SAD?!
BECAUSE IT'S THE RIGHT THING TO DO.
THE MORE SHE FEELS THE PAIN...
...THE BETTER THE CHANCES ARE FOR HER TO FULLY RECOVER FROM HER GRIEF.
PET SHOP
ペットショップ
WOOFLES
わっふる
THAT'S WHAT THE DOCTOR SAID.

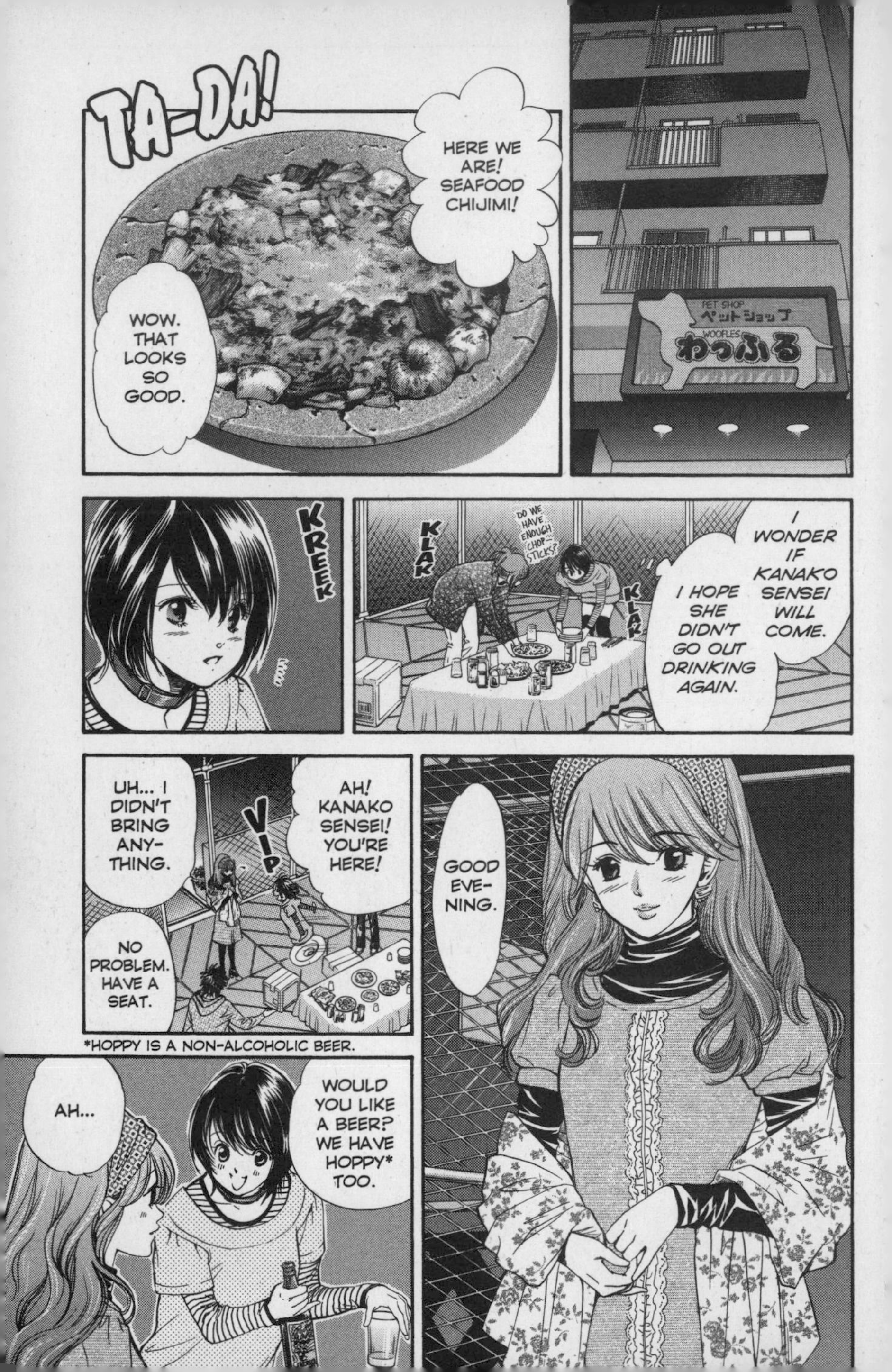
PET SHOP
ペットショップ
WOOFLES
わっふる
TA-DA!
HERE WE ARE! SEAFOOD CHIJIMI!
WOW. THAT LOOKS SO GOOD.
KLAK
KLAK
DO WE HAVE ENOUGH CHOP-STICKS?
I WONDER IF KANAKO SENSEI WILL COME.
I HOPE SHE DIDN'T GO OUT DRINKING AGAIN.
KREEK
GOOD EVE-NING.
VIP
AH! KANAKO SENSEI! YOU'RE HERE!
UH... I DIDN'T BRING ANY-THING.
NO PROBLEM. HAVE A SEAT.
WOULD YOU LIKE A BEER? WE HAVE HOPPY* TOO.
AH...
*HOPPY IS A NON-ALCOHOLIC BEER.

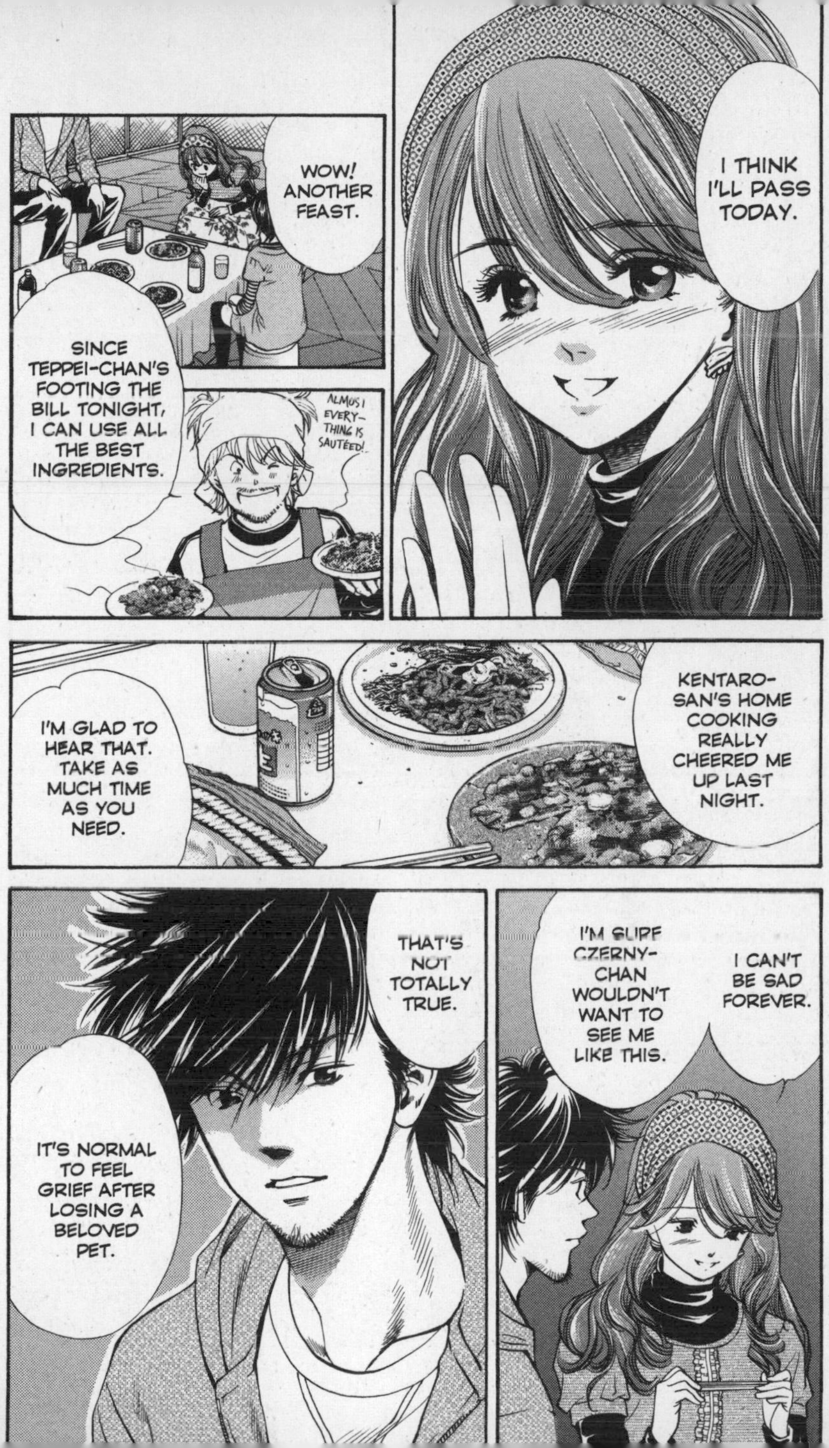
I THINK I'LL PASS TODAY.
WOW! ANOTHER FEAST.
SINCE TEPPEI-CHAN'S FOOTING THE BILL TONIGHT, I CAN USE ALL THE BEST INGREDIENTS.
ALMOST EVERYTHING IS SAUTÉED!
KENTARO-SAN'S HOME COOKING REALLY CHEERED ME UP LAST NIGHT.
I'M GLAD TO HEAR THAT. TAKE AS MUCH TIME AS YOU NEED.
I CAN'T BE SAD FOREVER.
I'M SURE CZERNY-CHAN WOULDN'T WANT TO SEE ME LIKE THIS.
THAT'S NOT TOTALLY TRUE.
IT'S NORMAL TO FEEL GRIEF AFTER LOSING A BELOVED PET.

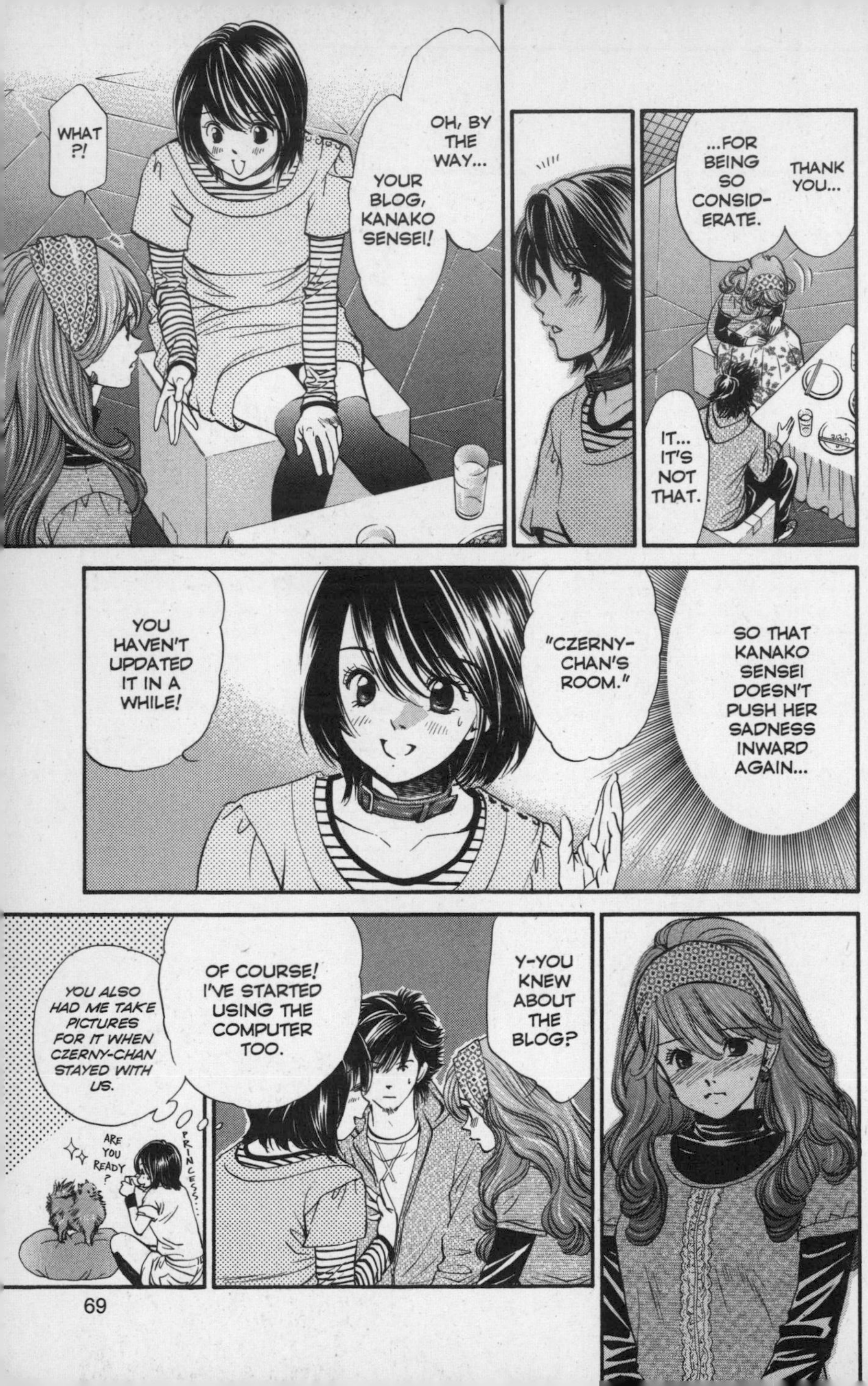
THANK YOU...
...FOR BEING SO CONSID-ERATE.
IT... IT'S NOT THAT.
OH, BY THE WAY...
YOUR BLOG, KANAKO SENSEI!
WHAT?!
SO THAT KANAKO SENSEI DOESN'T PUSH HER SADNESS INWARD AGAIN...
"CZERNY-CHAN'S ROOM."
YOU HAVEN'T UPDATED IT IN A WHILE!
Y-YOU KNEW ABOUT THE BLOG?
OF COURSE! I'VE STARTED USING THE COMPUTER TOO.
YOU ALSO HAD ME TAKE PICTURES FOR IT WHEN CZERNY-CHAN STAYED WITH US.
PRINCESS...
ARE YOU READY?

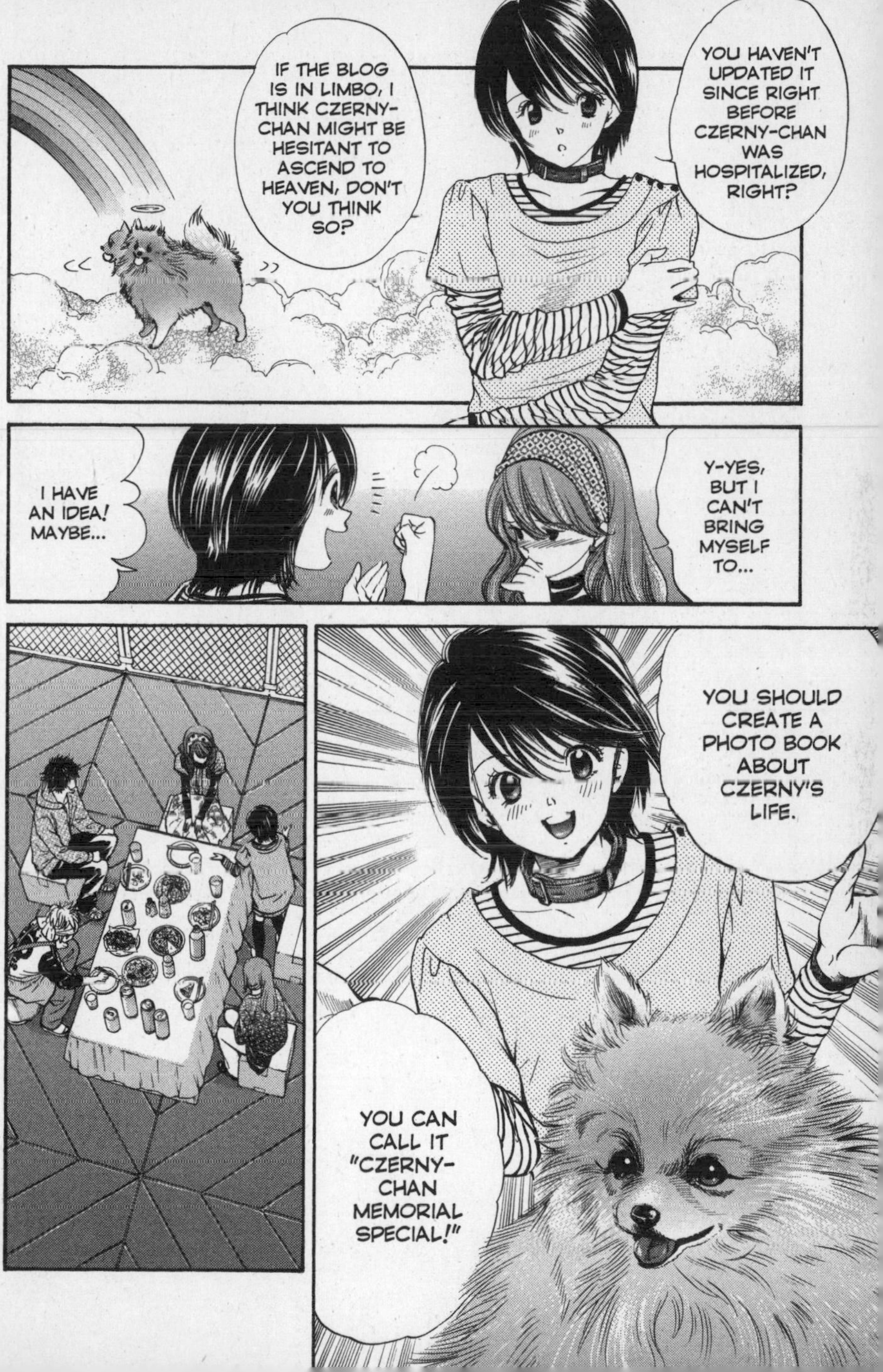
YOU HAVEN'T UPDATED IT SINCE RIGHT BEFORE CZERNY-CHAN WAS HOSPITALIZED, RIGHT?
IF THE BLOG IS IN LIMBO, I THINK CZERNY-CHAN MIGHT BE HESITANT TO ASCEND TO HEAVEN, DON'T YOU THINK SO?
Y-YES, BUT I CAN'T BRING MYSELF TO...
I HAVE AN IDEA! MAYBE...
YOU SHOULD CREATE A PHOTO BOOK ABOUT CZERNY'S LIFE.
YOU CAN CALL IT "CZERNY-CHAN MEMORIAL SPECIAL!"

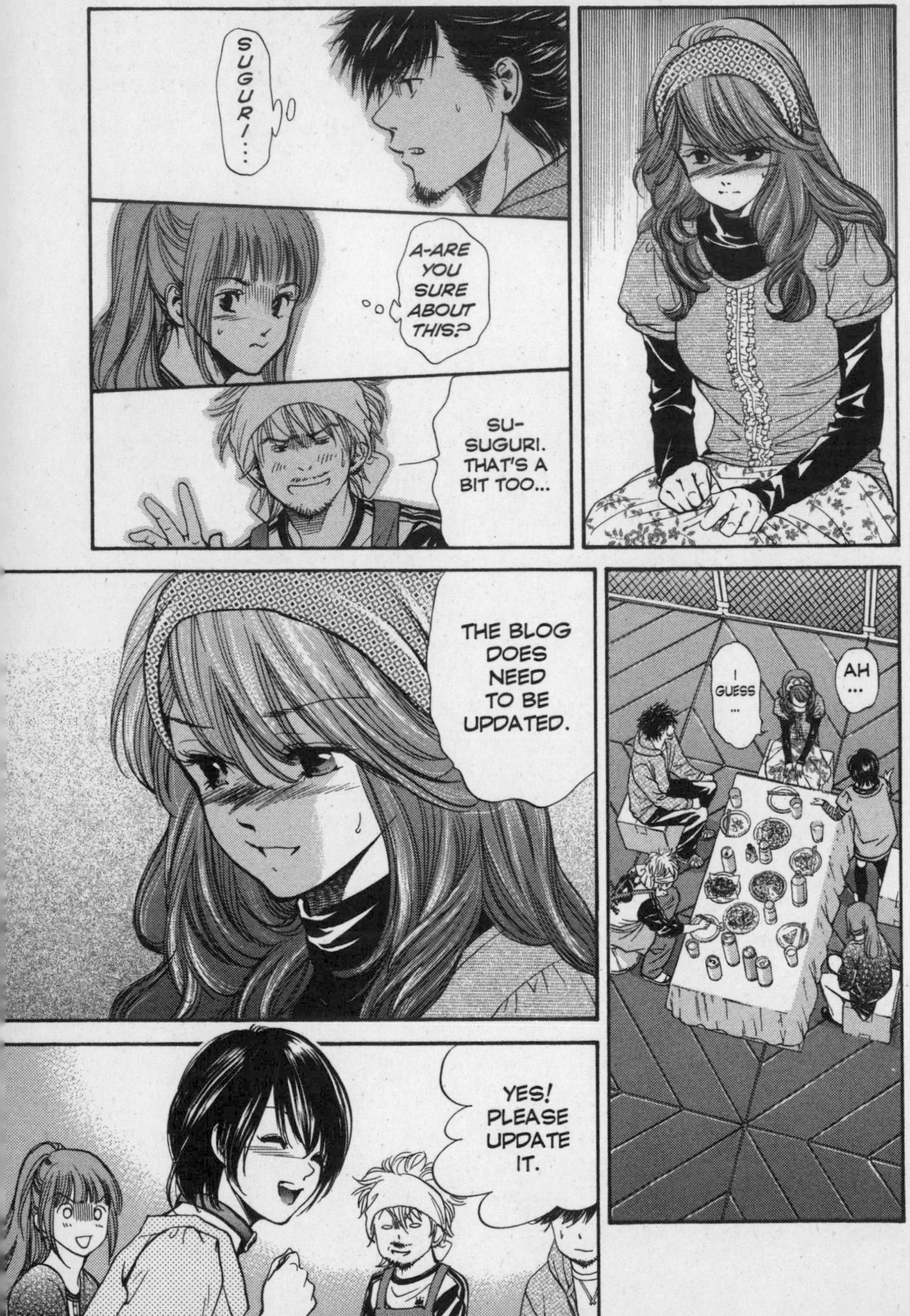
SUGURI...
A-ARE YOU SURE ABOUT THIS?
SU-SUGURI. THAT'S A BIT TOO...
AH...
I GUESS...
THE BLOG DOES NEED TO BE UPDATED.
YES! PLEASE UPDATE IT.

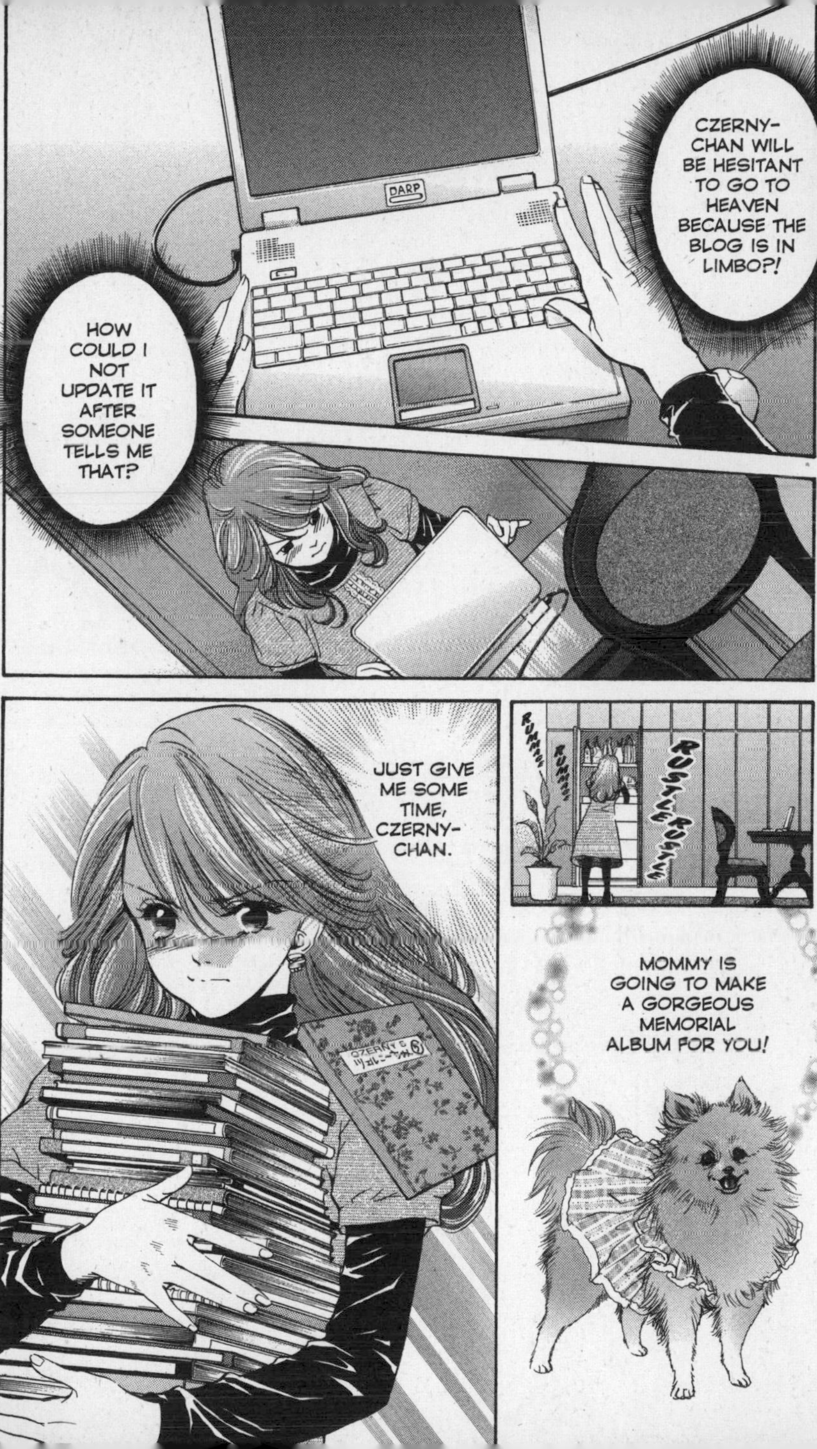
CZERNY-CHAN WILL BE HESITANT TO GO TO HEAVEN BECAUSE THE BLOG IS IN LIMBO?!
HOW COULD I NOT UPDATE IT AFTER SOMEONE TELLS ME THAT?
RUSTLE RUSTLE
RUMMAGE
RUMMAGE
MOMMY IS GOING TO MAKE A GORGEOUS MEMORIAL ALBUM FOR YOU!
JUST GIVE ME SOME TIME, CZERNY-CHAN.

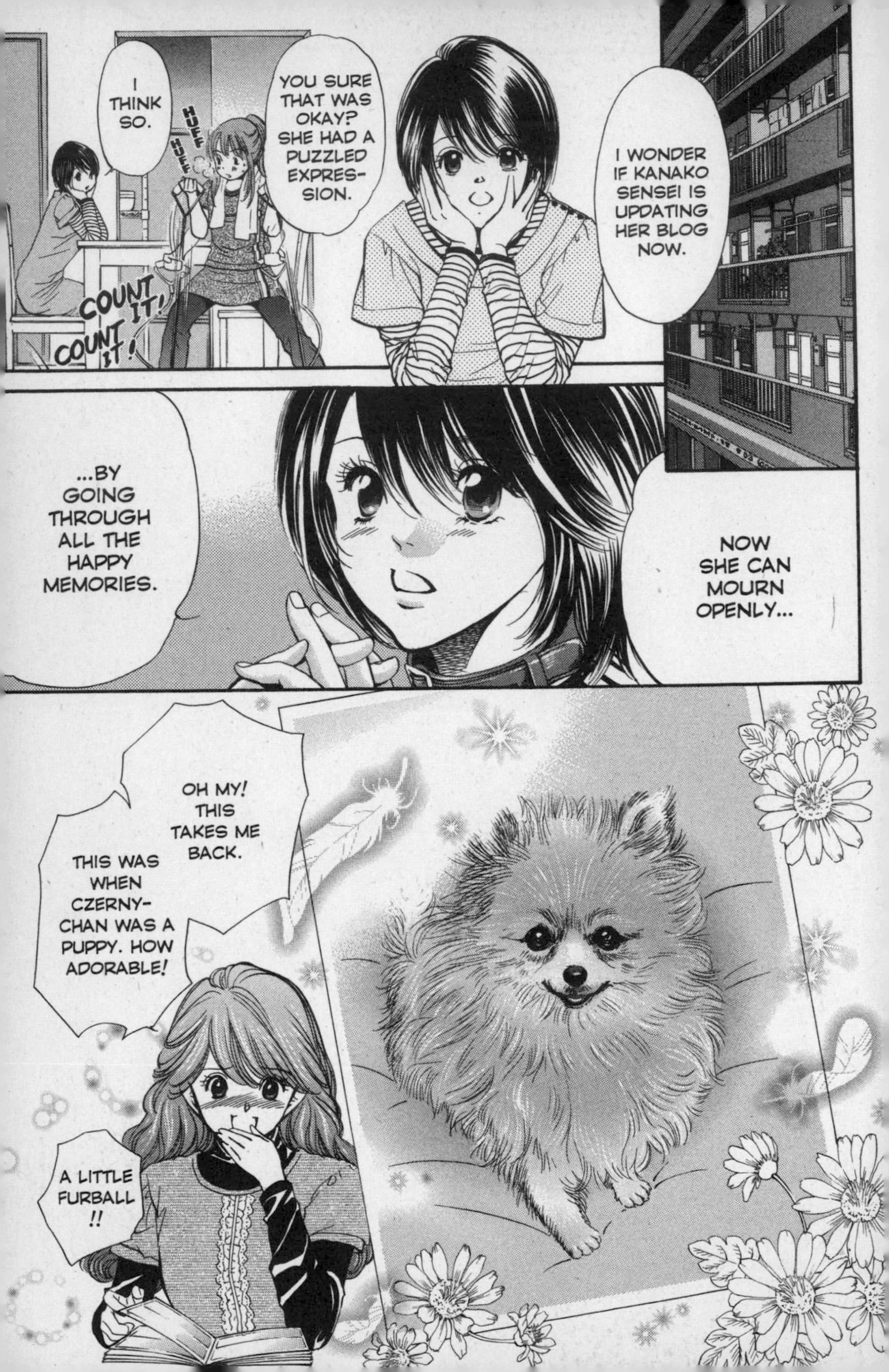

I WONDER IF KANAKO SENSEI IS UPDATING HER BLOG NOW.
YOU SURE THAT WAS OKAY? SHE HAD A PUZZLED EXPRESSION.
I THINK SO.
HUFF HUFF
COUNT IT! COUNT IT!
NOW SHE CAN MOURN OPENLY...
...BY GOING THROUGH ALL THE HAPPY MEMORIES.
OH MY! THIS TAKES ME BACK.
THIS WAS WHEN CZERNY-CHAN WAS A PUPPY. HOW ADORABLE!
A LITTLE FURBALL !!

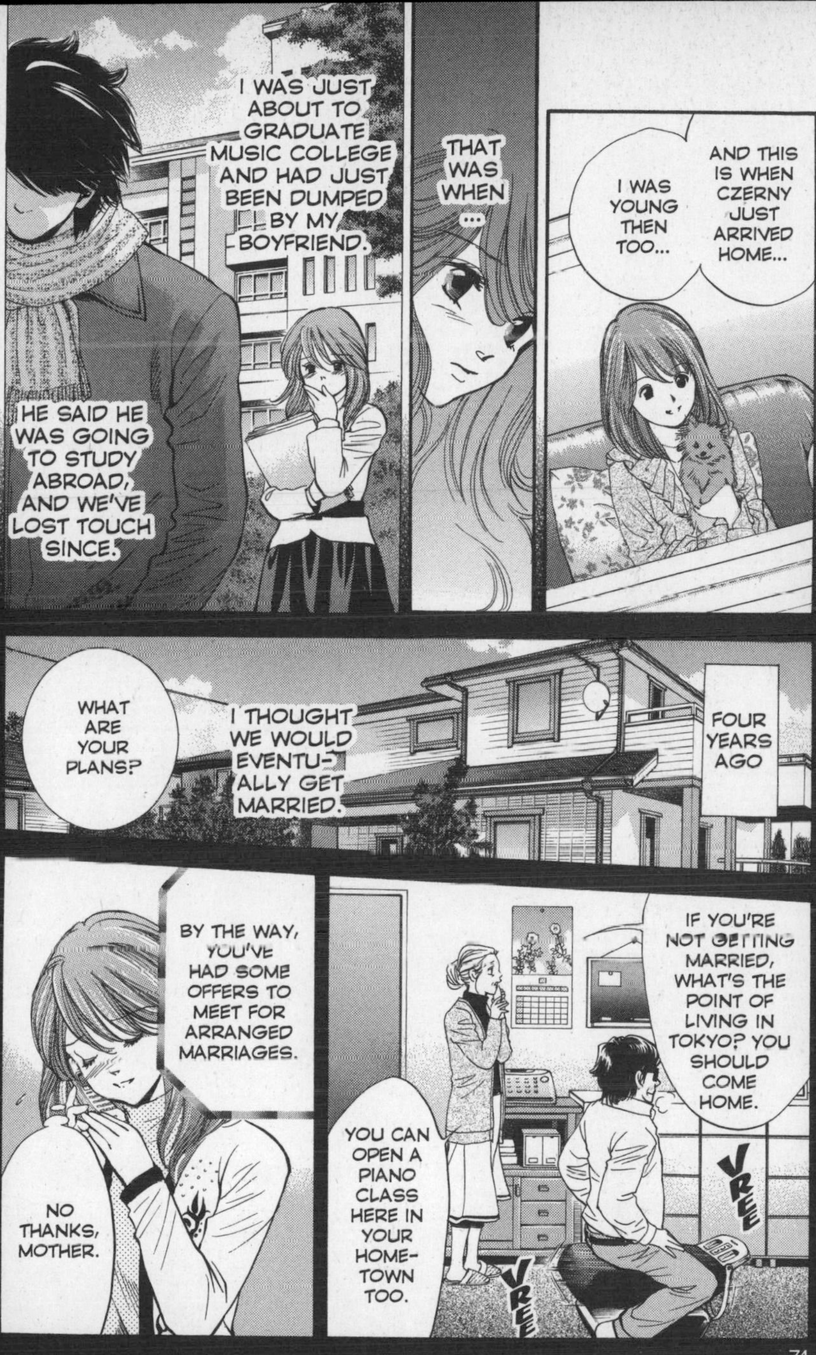
AND THIS IS WHEN CZERNY JUST ARRIVED HOME...
I WAS YOUNG THEN TOO...
THAT WAS WHEN ...
I WAS JUST ABOUT TO GRADUATE MUSIC COLLEGE AND HAD JUST BEEN DUMPED BY MY BOYFRIEND.
HE SAID HE WAS GOING TO STUDY ABROAD, AND WE'VE LOST TOUCH SINCE.
FOUR YEARS AGO
I THOUGHT WE WOULD EVENTU-ALLY GET MARRIED.
WHAT ARE YOUR PLANS?
IF YOU'RE NOT GETTING MARRIED, WHAT'S THE POINT OF LIVING IN TOKYO? YOU SHOULD COME HOME.
VREE
YOU CAN OPEN A PIANO CLASS HERE IN YOUR HOME-TOWN TOO.
VREE
BY THE WAY, YOU'VE HAD SOME OFFERS TO MEET FOR ARRANGED MARRIAGES.
NO THANKS, MOTHER.

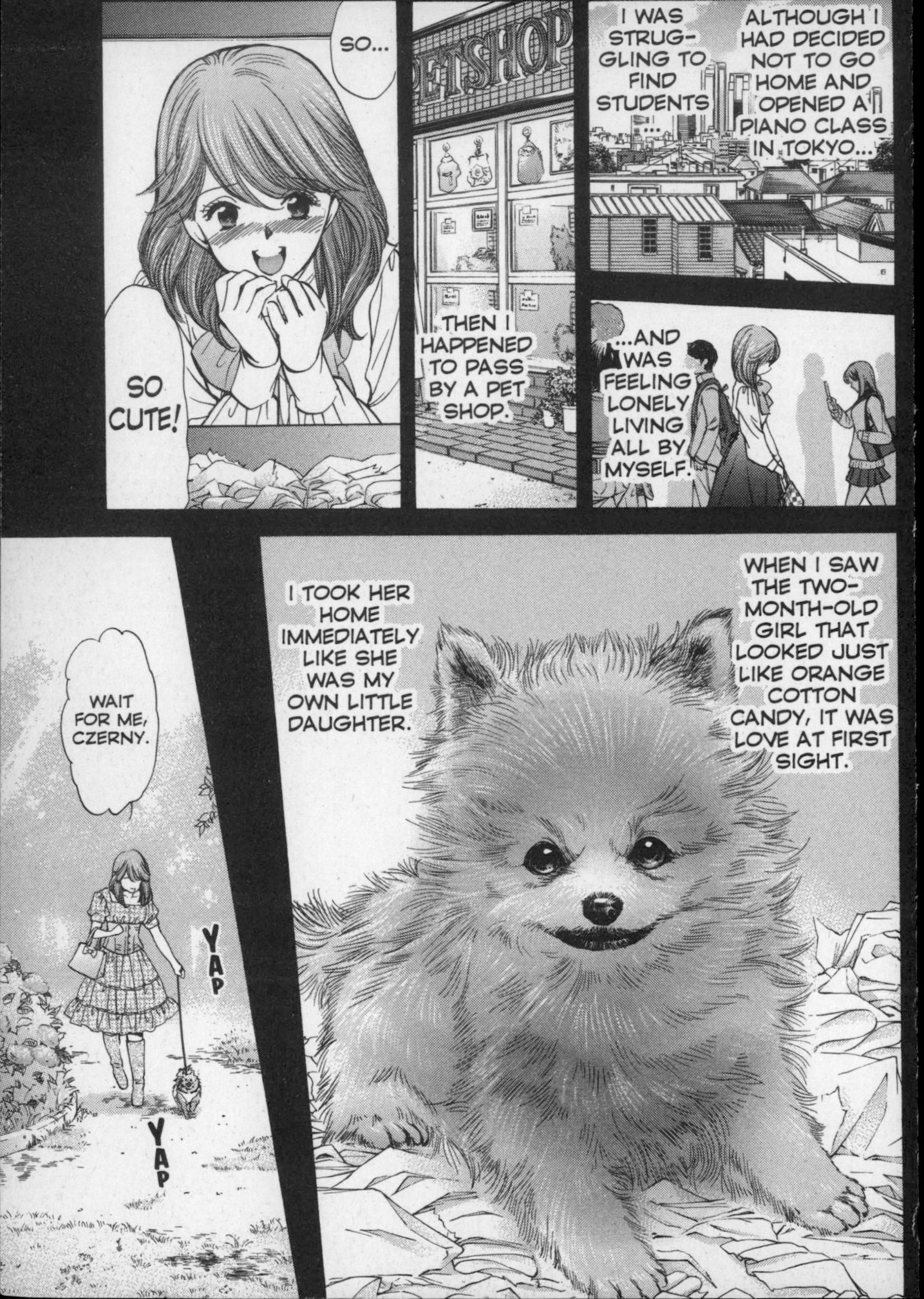
ALTHOUGH I HAD DECIDED NOT TO GO HOME AND OPENED A PIANO CLASS IN TOKYO...
I WAS STRUGGLING TO FIND STUDENTS...
...AND WAS FEELING LONELY LIVING ALL BY MYSELF.
THEN I HAPPENED TO PASS BY A PET SHOP.
PETSHOP
SO...
SO CUTE!
WHEN I SAW THE TWO-MONTH-OLD GIRL THAT LOOKED JUST LIKE ORANGE COTTON CANDY, IT WAS LOVE AT FIRST SIGHT.
I TOOK HER HOME IMMEDIATELY LIKE SHE WAS MY OWN LITTLE DAUGHTER.
WAIT FOR ME, CZERNY.
YAP
YAP

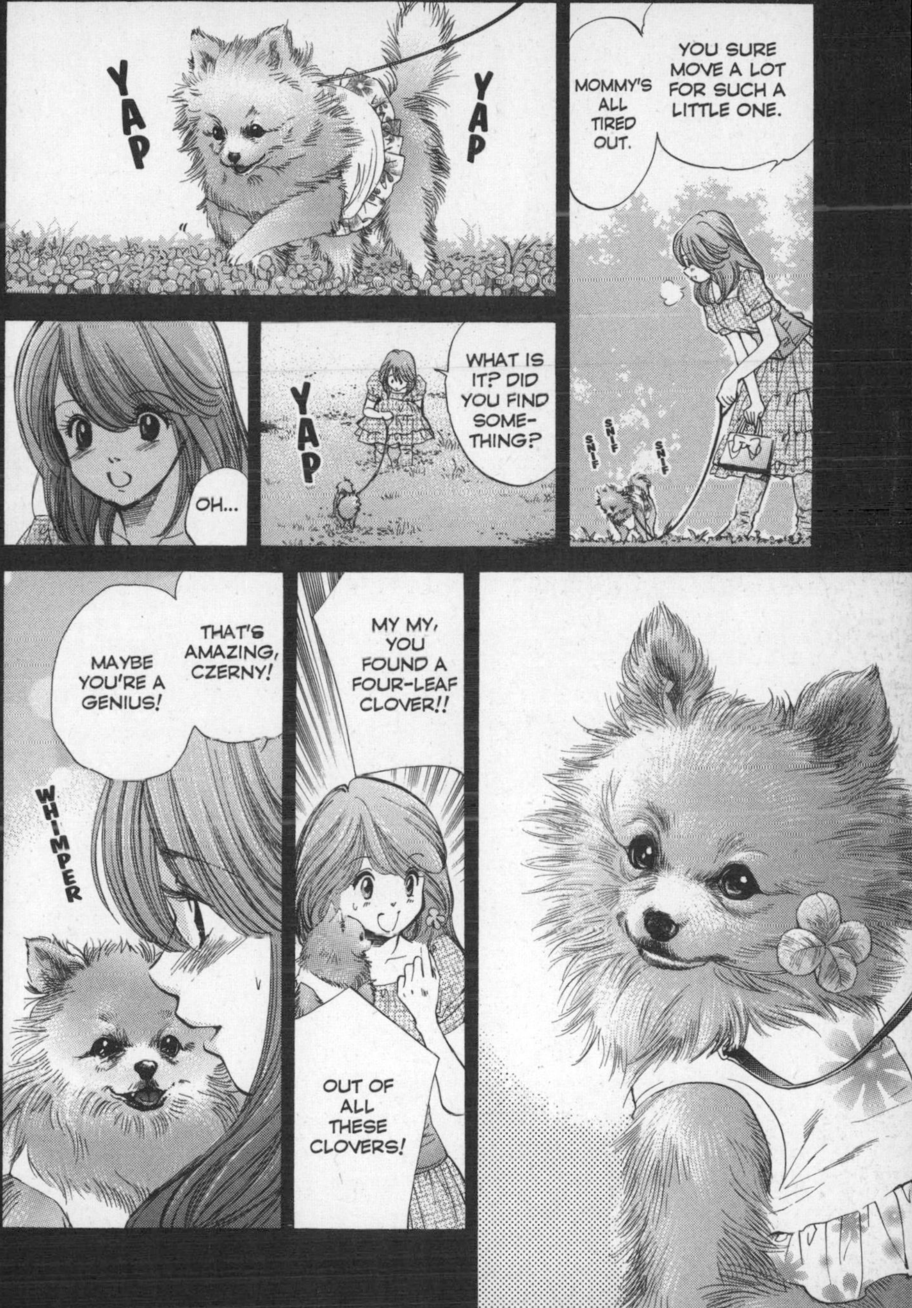
YOU SURE MOVE A LOT FOR SUCH A LITTLE ONE.
MOMMY'S ALL TIRED OUT.
SNIF SNIF SNIF
YAP YAP
WHAT IS IT? DID YOU FIND SOME-THING?
YAP YAP
OH...
MY MY, YOU FOUND A FOUR-LEAF CLOVER!!
OUT OF ALL THESE CLOVERS!
THAT'S AMAZING, CZERNY!
MAYBE YOU'RE A GENIUS!
WHIMPER

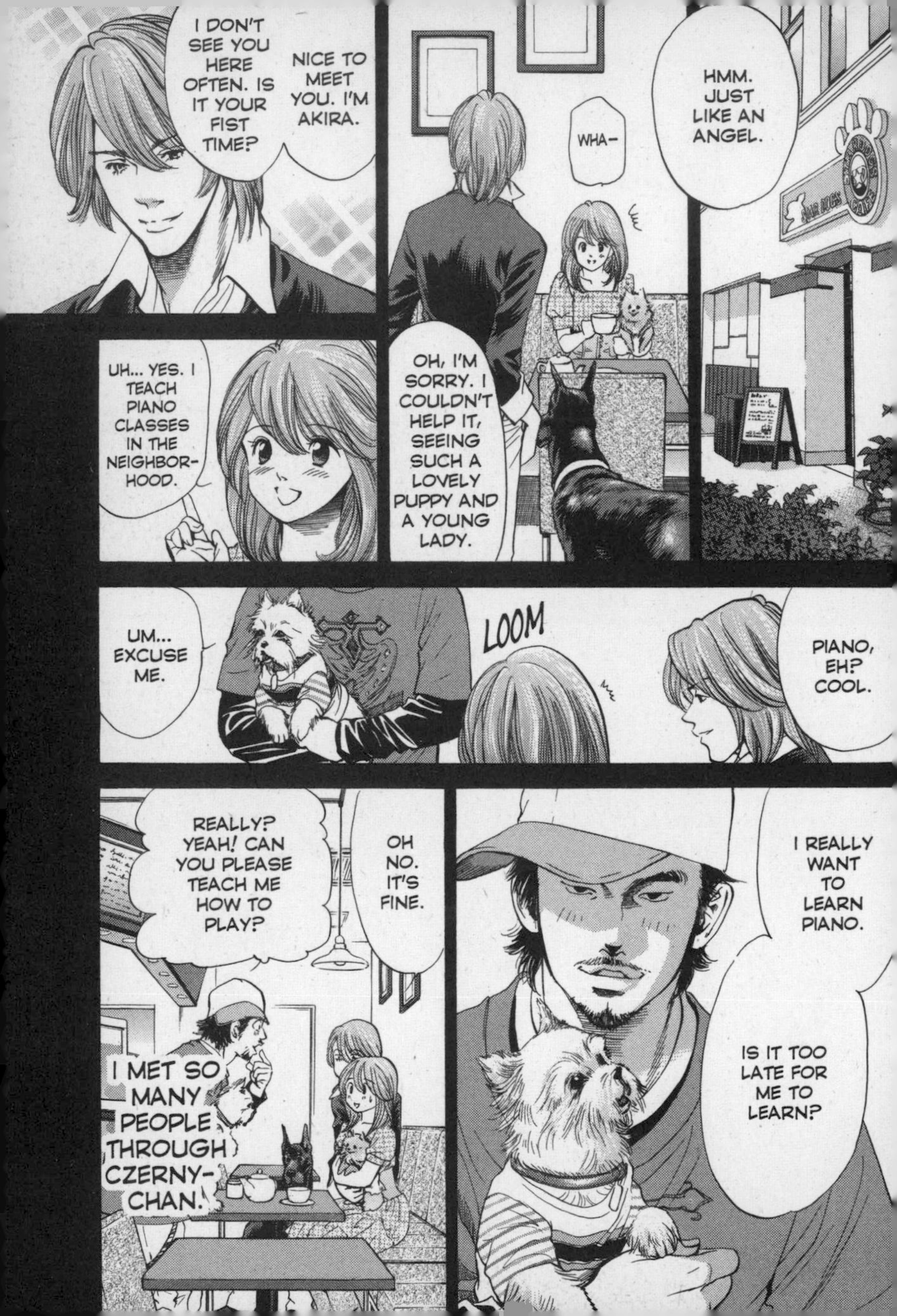
HMM. JUST LIKE AN ANGEL.
WHA-
OH, I'M SORRY. I COULDN'T HELP IT, SEEING SUCH A LOVELY PUPPY AND A YOUNG LADY.
NICE TO MEET YOU. I'M AKIRA.
I DON'T SEE YOU HERE OFTEN. IS IT YOUR FIST TIME?
UH... YES. I TEACH PIANO CLASSES IN THE NEIGHBOR-HOOD.
PIANO, EH? COOL.
LOOM
UM... EXCUSE ME.
I REALLY WANT TO LEARN PIANO.
IS IT TOO LATE FOR ME TO LEARN?
OH NO. IT'S FINE.
REALLY? YEAH! CAN YOU PLEASE TEACH ME HOW TO PLAY?
I MET SO MANY PEOPLE THROUGH CZERNY-CHAN.

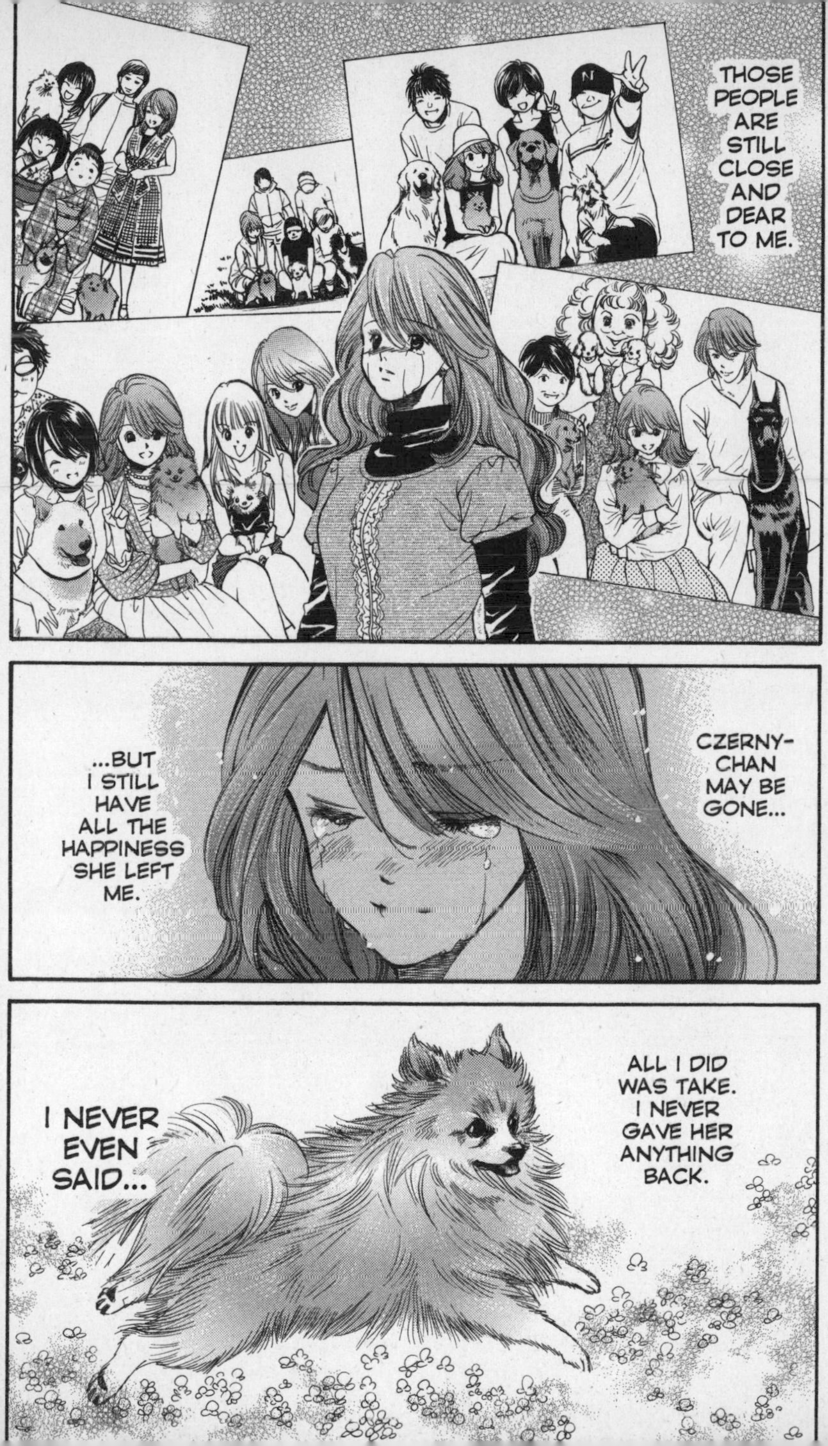
THOSE PEOPLE ARE STILL CLOSE AND DEAR TO ME.
CZERNY-CHAN MAY BE GONE...
...BUT I STILL HAVE ALL THE HAPPINESS SHE LEFT ME.
ALL I DID WAS TAKE. I NEVER GAVE HER ANYTHING BACK.
I NEVER EVEN SAID...

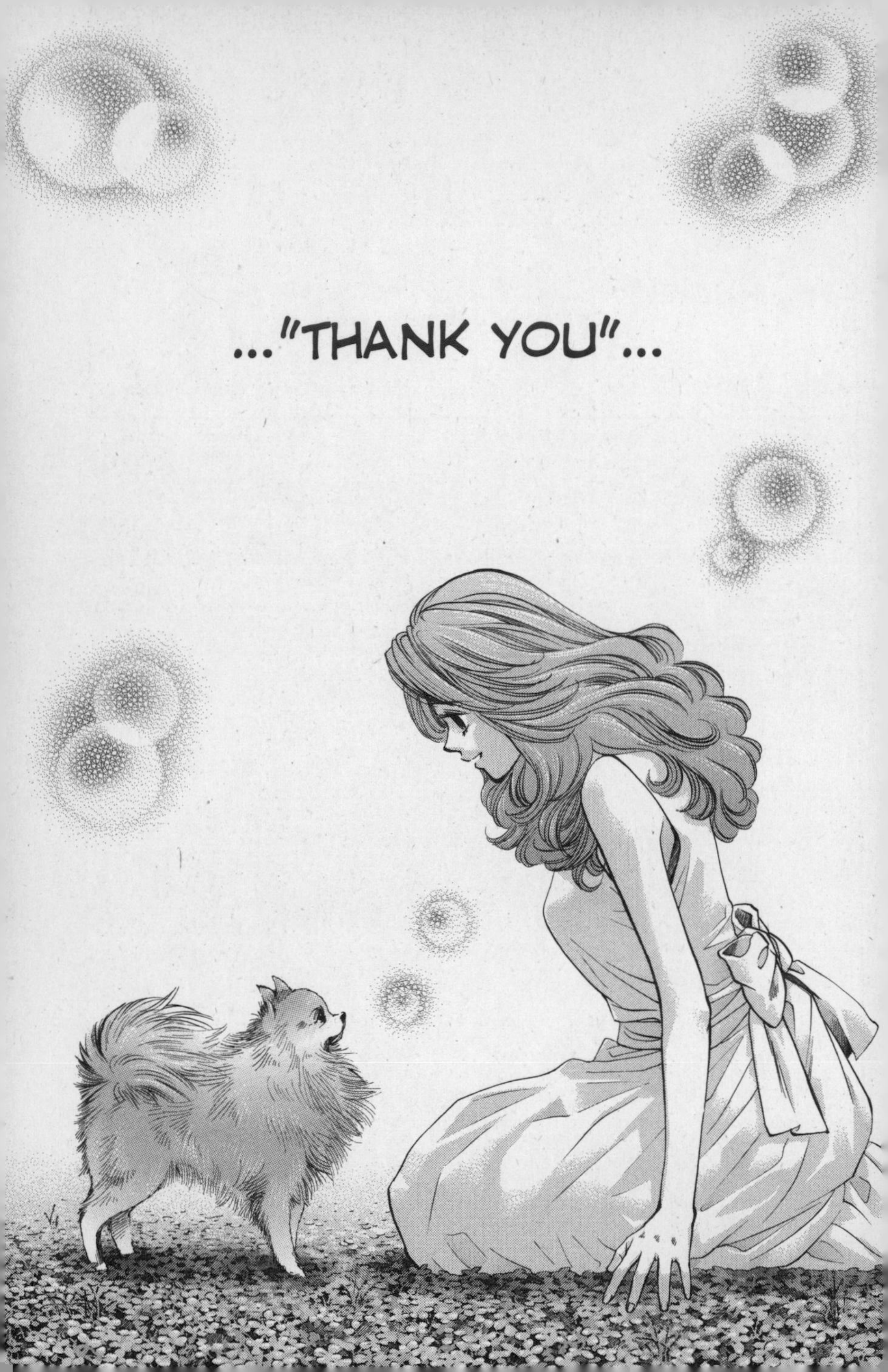
..."THANK YOU"...

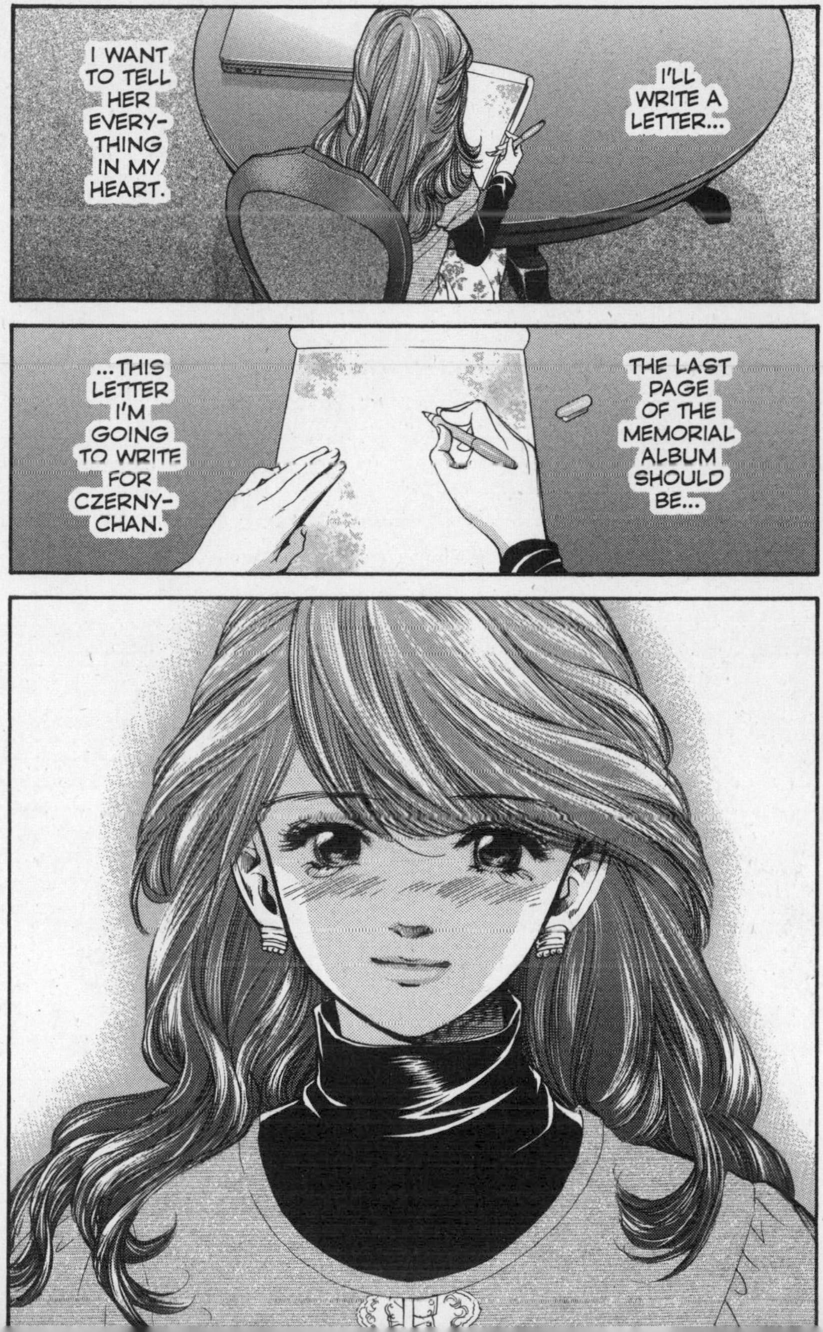
I'LL WRITE A LETTER...
I WANT TO TELL HER EVERY-THING IN MY HEART.
THE LAST PAGE OF THE MEMORIAL ALBUM SHOULD BE...
...THIS LETTER I'M GOING TO WRITE FOR CZERNY-CHAN.

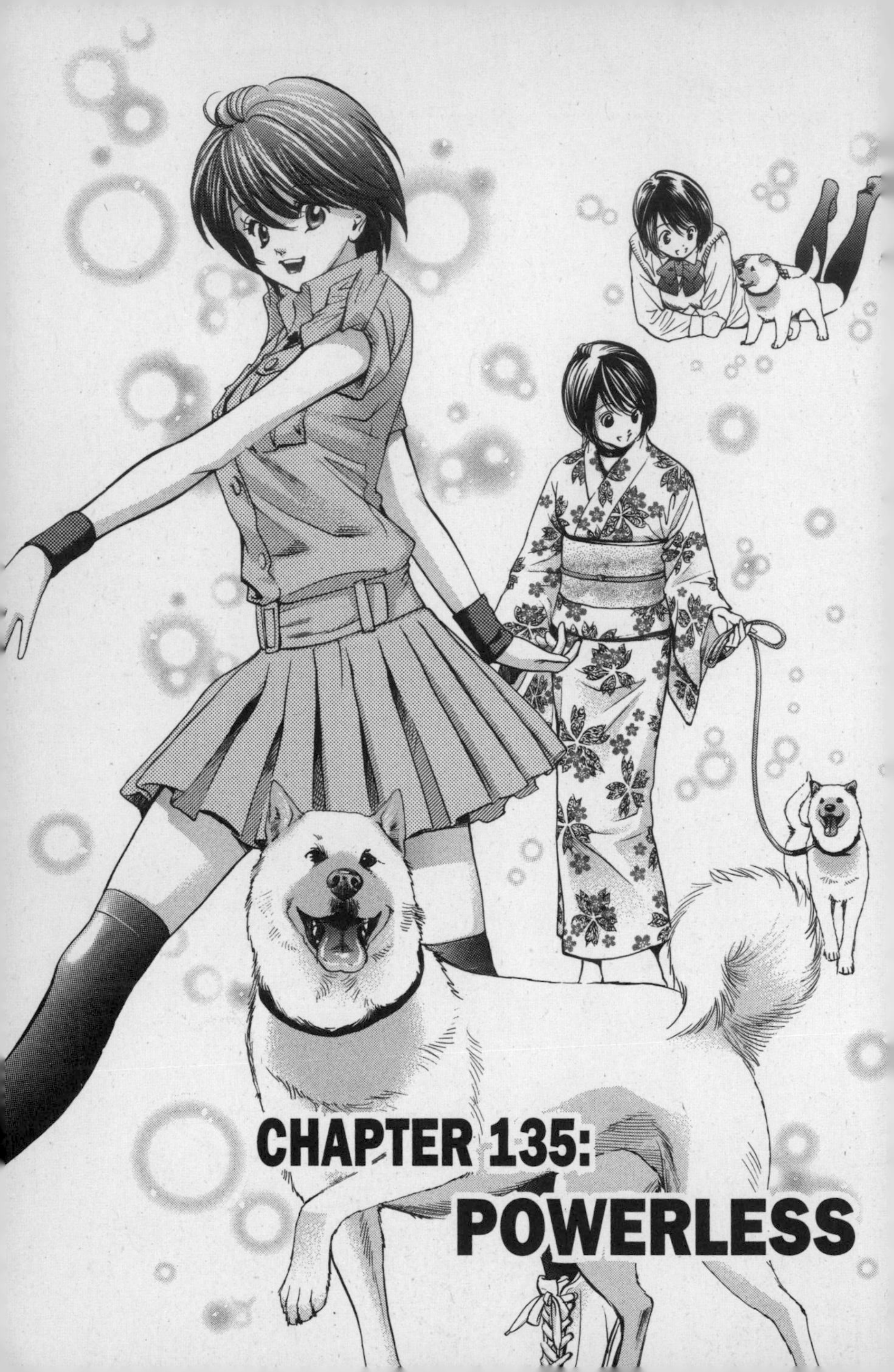
CHAPTER 135:
POWERLESS

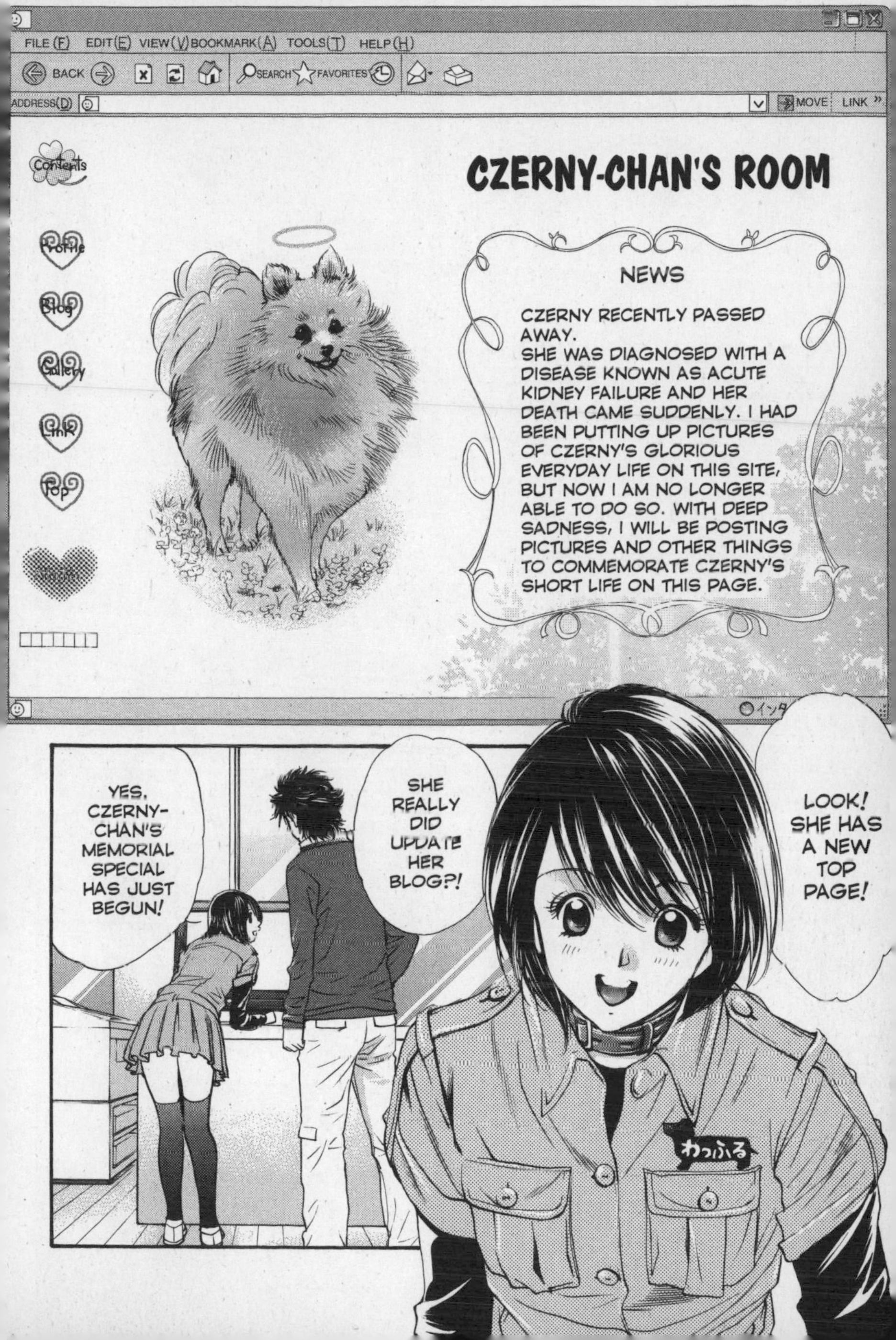
FILE (F) EDIT (E) VIEW (V) BOOKMARK (A) TOOLS (T) HELP (H)
BACK
SEARCH FAVORITES
ADDRESS (D)
MOVE LINK
Contents
Profile
Blog
Gallery
Link
Top
CZERNY-CHAN'S ROOM
NEWS
CZERNY RECENTLY PASSED AWAY.
SHE WAS DIAGNOSED WITH A DISEASE KNOWN AS ACUTE KIDNEY FAILURE AND HER DEATH CAME SUDDENLY. I HAD BEEN PUTTING UP PICTURES OF CZERNY'S GLORIOUS EVERYDAY LIFE ON THIS SITE, BUT NOW I AM NO LONGER ABLE TO DO SO. WITH DEEP SADNESS, I WILL BE POSTING PICTURES AND OTHER THINGS TO COMMEMORATE CZERNY'S SHORT LIFE ON THIS PAGE.
LOOK! SHE HAS A NEW TOP PAGE!
わっふる
SHE REALLY DID UPDATE HER BLOG?!
YES, CZERNY-CHAN'S MEMORIAL SPECIAL HAS JUST BEGUN!

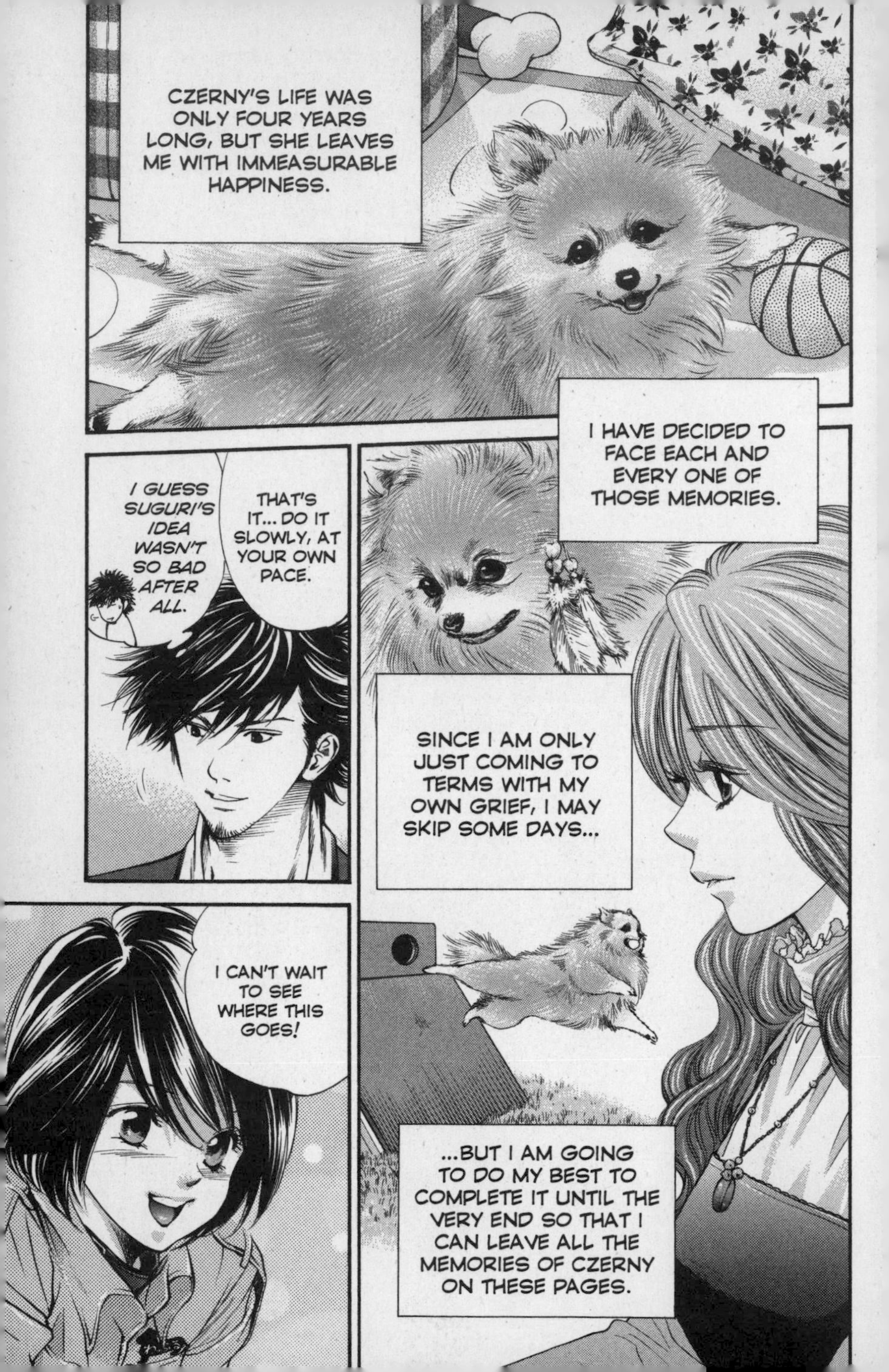
CZERNY'S LIFE WAS ONLY FOUR YEARS LONG, BUT SHE LEAVES ME WITH IMMEASURABLE HAPPINESS.
I HAVE DECIDED TO FACE EACH AND EVERY ONE OF THOSE MEMORIES.
SINCE I AM ONLY JUST COMING TO TERMS WITH MY OWN GRIEF, I MAY SKIP SOME DAYS...
...BUT I AM GOING TO DO MY BEST TO COMPLETE IT UNTIL THE VERY END SO THAT I CAN LEAVE ALL THE MEMORIES OF CZERNY ON THESE PAGES.
THAT'S IT... DO IT SLOWLY, AT YOUR OWN PACE.
I GUESS SUGURI'S IDEA WASN'T SO BAD AFTER ALL.
I CAN'T WAIT TO SEE WHERE THIS GOES!

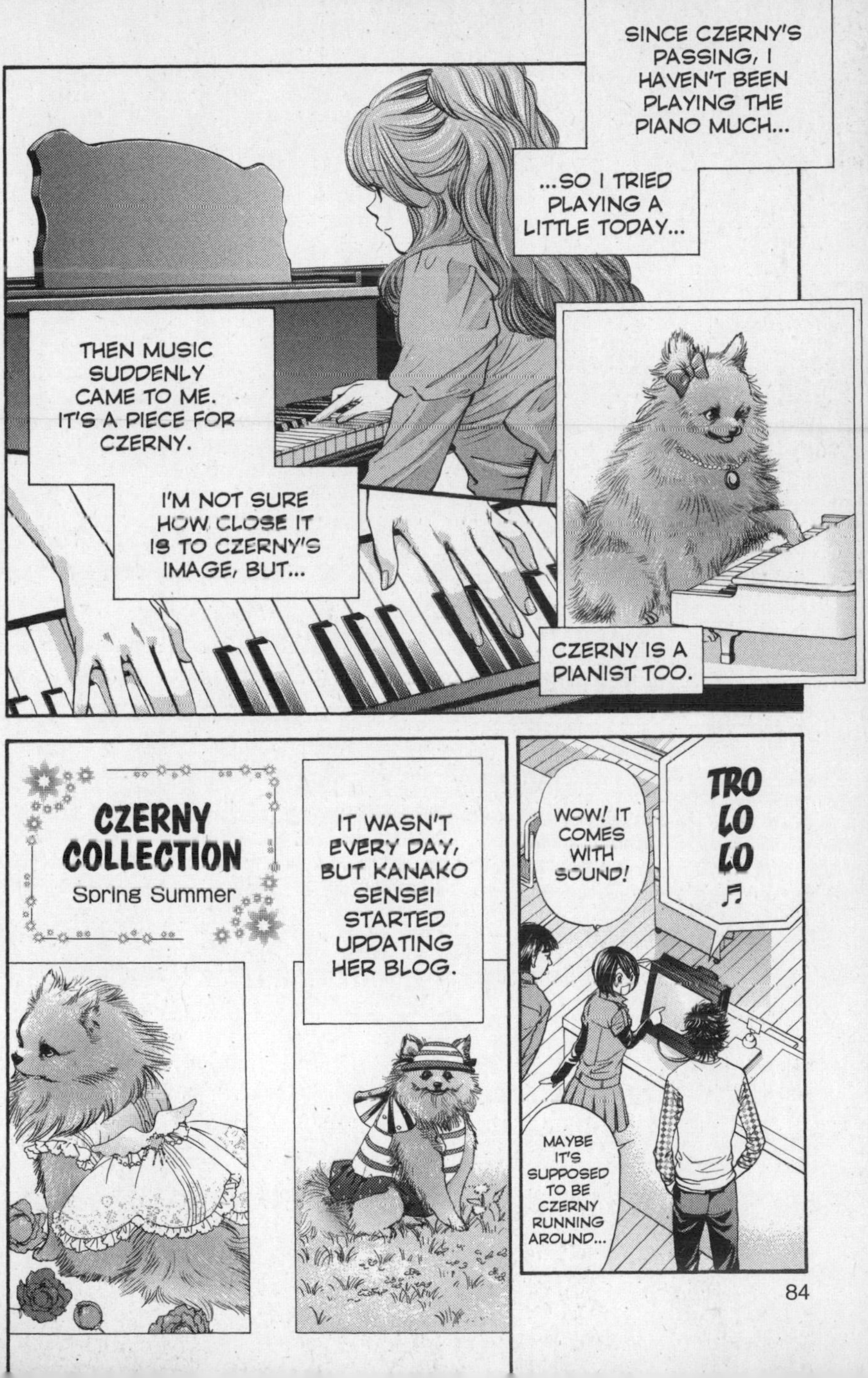
SINCE CZERNY'S PASSING, I HAVEN'T BEEN PLAYING THE PIANO MUCH...
...SO I TRIED PLAYING A LITTLE TODAY...
THEN MUSIC SUDDENLY CAME TO ME. IT'S A PIECE FOR CZERNY.
I'M NOT SURE HOW CLOSE IT IS TO CZERNY'S IMAGE, BUT...
CZERNY IS A PIANIST TOO.
TRO LO LO ♬
WOW! IT COMES WITH SOUND!
MAYBE IT'S SUPPOSED TO BE CZERNY RUNNING AROUND...
IT WASN'T EVERY DAY, BUT KANAKO SENSEI STARTED UPDATING HER BLOG.
CZERNY COLLECTION
Spring Summer

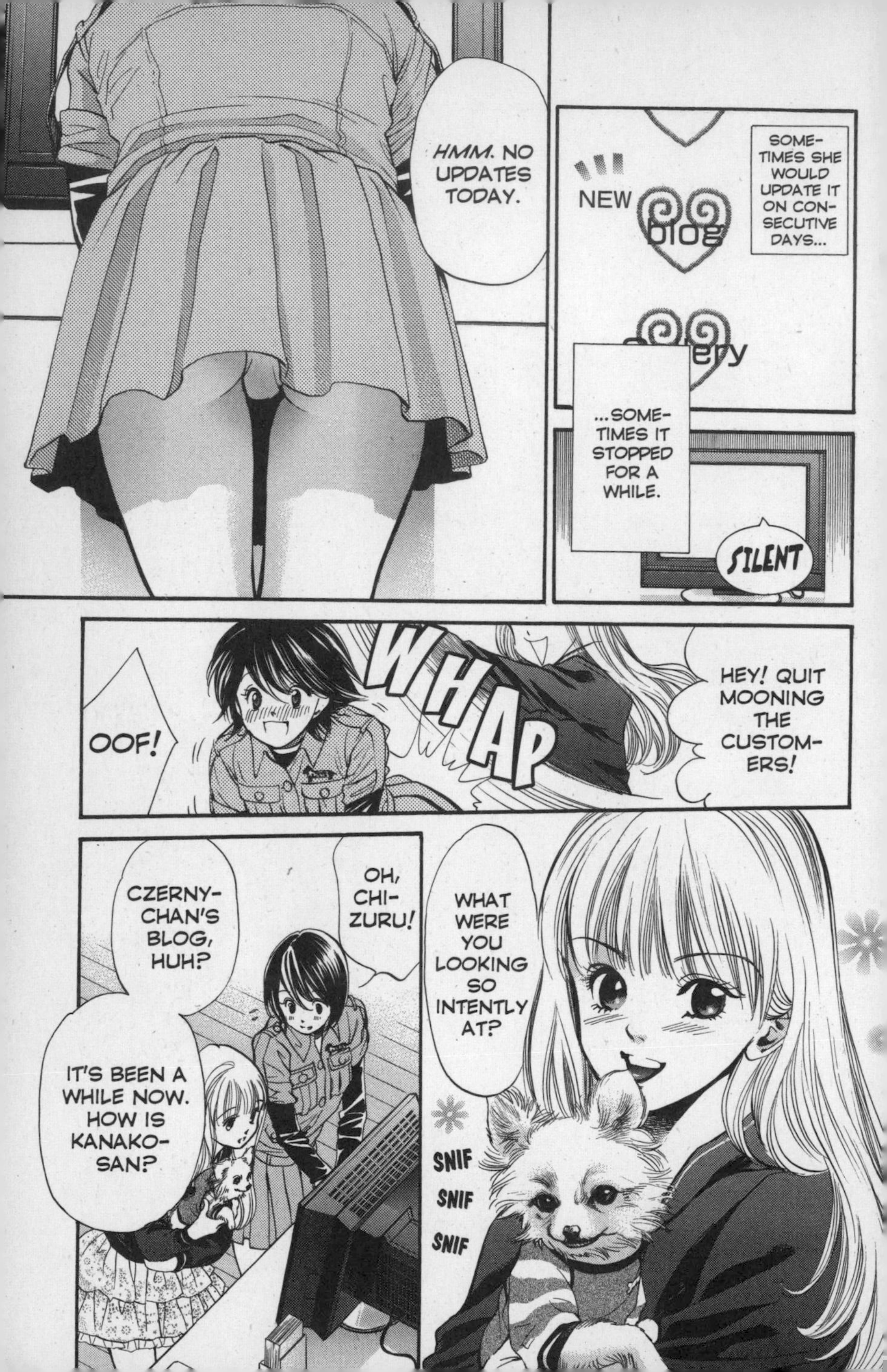
NEW
blog
SOMETIMES SHE WOULD UPDATE IT ON CONSECUTIVE DAYS...
...SOMETIMES IT STOPPED FOR A WHILE.
SILENT
HMM. NO UPDATES TODAY.
HEY! QUIT MOONING THE CUSTOMERS!
WHAP
OOF!
WHAT WERE YOU LOOKING SO INTENTLY AT?
SNIF
SNIF
SNIF
OH, CHIZURU!
CZERNY-CHAN'S BLOG, HUH?
IT'S BEEN A WHILE NOW. HOW IS KANAKO-SAN?

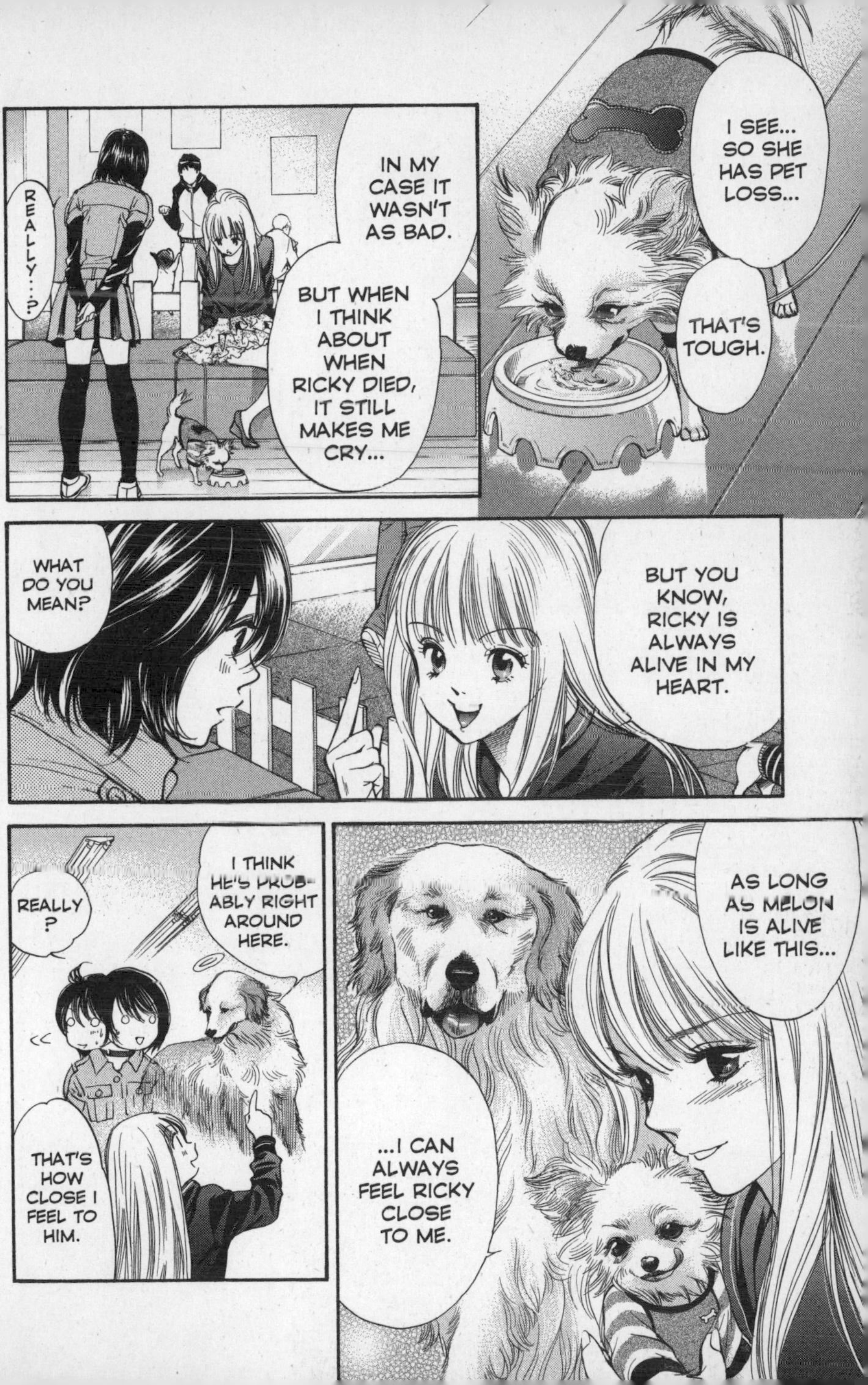
I SEE... SO SHE HAS PET LOSS...
THAT'S TOUGH.
IN MY CASE IT WASN'T AS BAD.
BUT WHEN I THINK ABOUT WHEN RICKY DIED, IT STILL MAKES ME CRY...
REALLY...?
BUT YOU KNOW, RICKY IS ALWAYS ALIVE IN MY HEART.
WHAT DO YOU MEAN?
AS LONG AS MELON IS ALIVE LIKE THIS...
...I CAN ALWAYS FEEL RICKY CLOSE TO ME.
I THINK HE'S PROB-ABLY RIGHT AROUND HERE.
REALLY?
THAT'S HOW CLOSE I FEEL TO HIM.

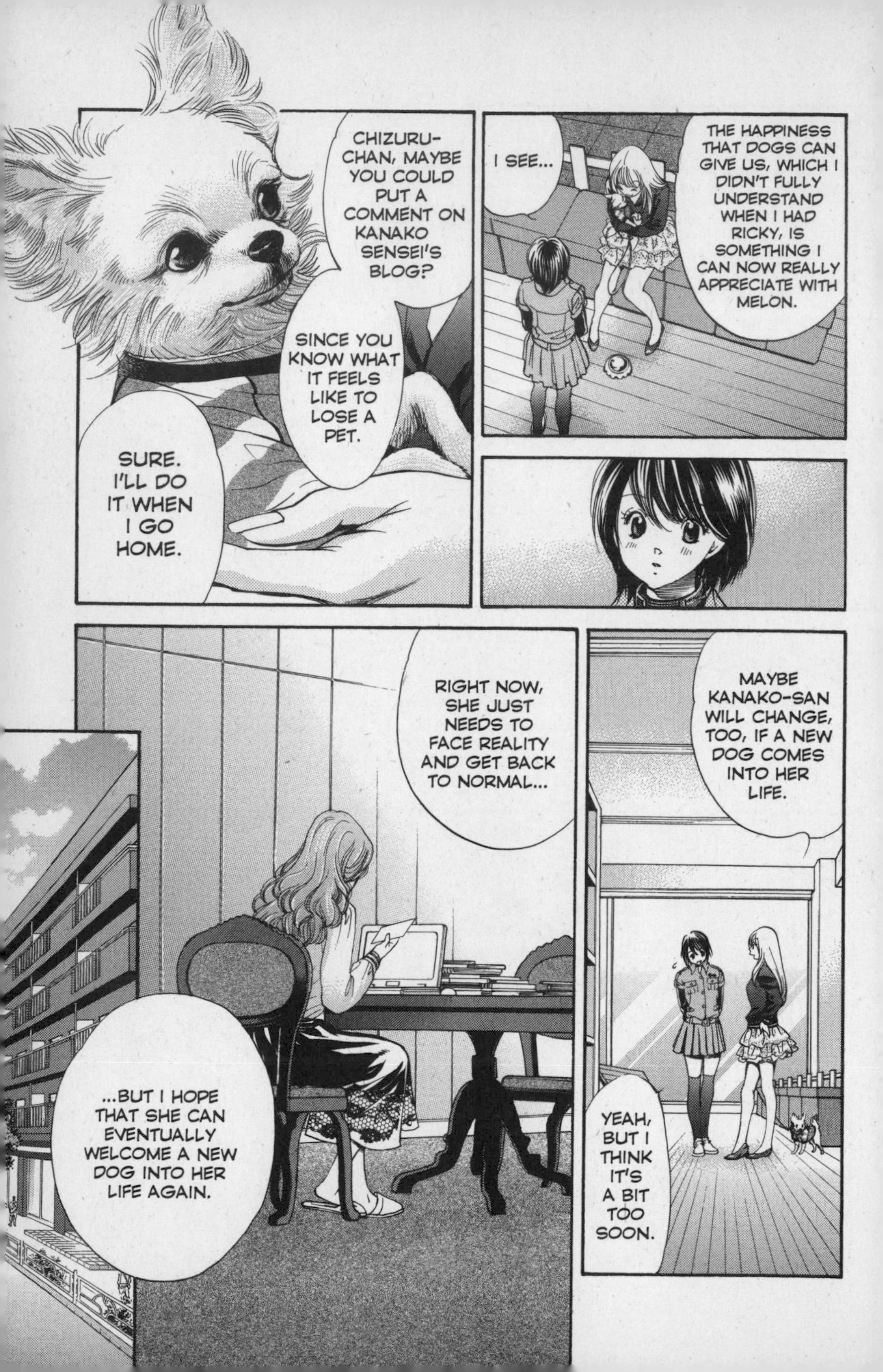
THE HAPPINESS THAT DOGS CAN GIVE US, WHICH I DIDN'T FULLY UNDERSTAND WHEN I HAD RICKY, IS SOMETHING I CAN NOW REALLY APPRECIATE WITH MELON.
I SEE...
CHIZURU-CHAN, MAYBE YOU COULD PUT A COMMENT ON KANAKO SENSEI'S BLOG?
SINCE YOU KNOW WHAT IT FEELS LIKE TO LOSE A PET.
SURE. I'LL DO IT WHEN I GO HOME.
MAYBE KANAKO-SAN WILL CHANGE, TOO, IF A NEW DOG COMES INTO HER LIFE.
YEAH, BUT I THINK IT'S A BIT TOO SOON.
RIGHT NOW, SHE JUST NEEDS TO FACE REALITY AND GET BACK TO NORMAL...
...BUT I HOPE THAT SHE CAN EVENTUALLY WELCOME A NEW DOG INTO HER LIFE AGAIN.

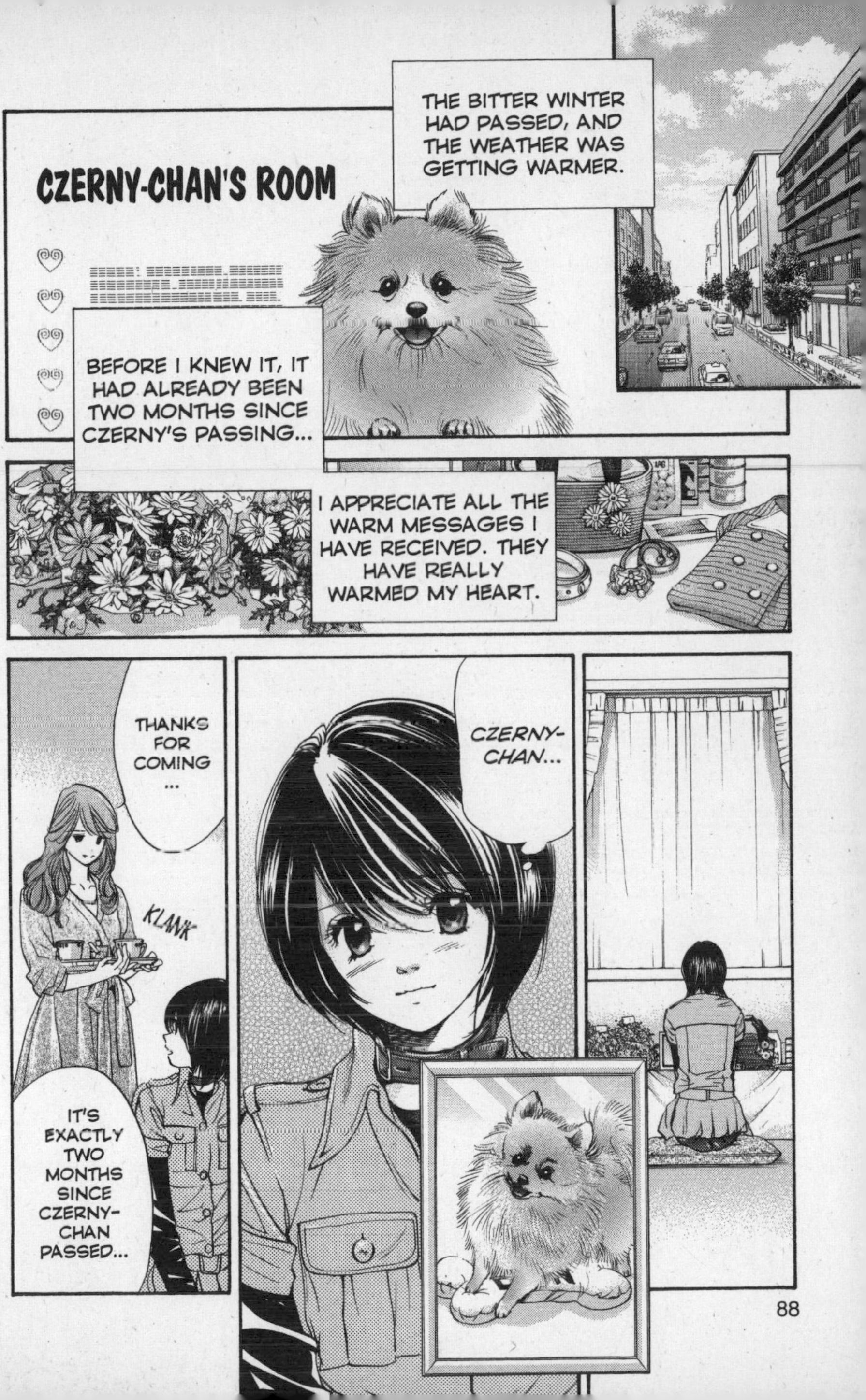
THE BITTER WINTER HAD PASSED, AND THE WEATHER WAS GETTING WARMER.
CZERNY-CHAN'S ROOM
BEFORE I KNEW IT, IT HAD ALREADY BEEN TWO MONTHS SINCE CZERNY'S PASSING...
I APPRECIATE ALL THE WARM MESSAGES I HAVE RECEIVED. THEY HAVE REALLY WARMED MY HEART.
CZERNY-CHAN...
THANKS FOR COMING ...
KLANK
IT'S EXACTLY TWO MONTHS SINCE CZERNY-CHAN PASSED...

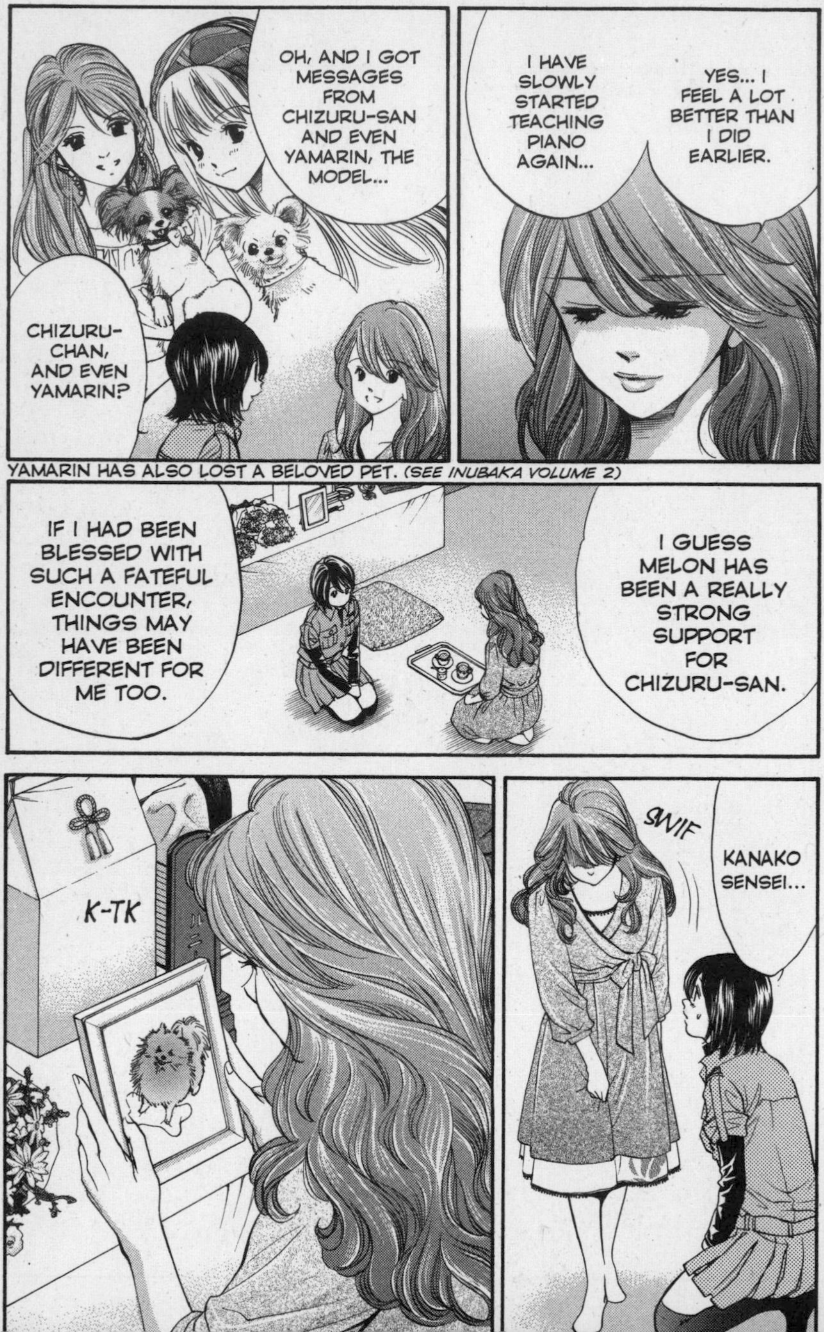
YES... I FEEL A LOT BETTER THAN I DID EARLIER.
I HAVE SLOWLY STARTED TEACHING PIANO AGAIN...
OH, AND I GOT MESSAGES FROM CHIZURU-SAN AND EVEN YAMARIN, THE MODEL...
CHIZURU-CHAN, AND EVEN YAMARIN?
YAMARIN HAS ALSO LOST A BELOVED PET. (SEE INUBAKA VOLUME 2)
I GUESS MELON HAS BEEN A REALLY STRONG SUPPORT FOR CHIZURU-SAN.
IF I HAD BEEN BLESSED WITH SUCH A FATEFUL ENCOUNTER, THINGS MAY HAVE BEEN DIFFERENT FOR ME TOO.
SWIF
KANAKO SENSEI...
K-TK

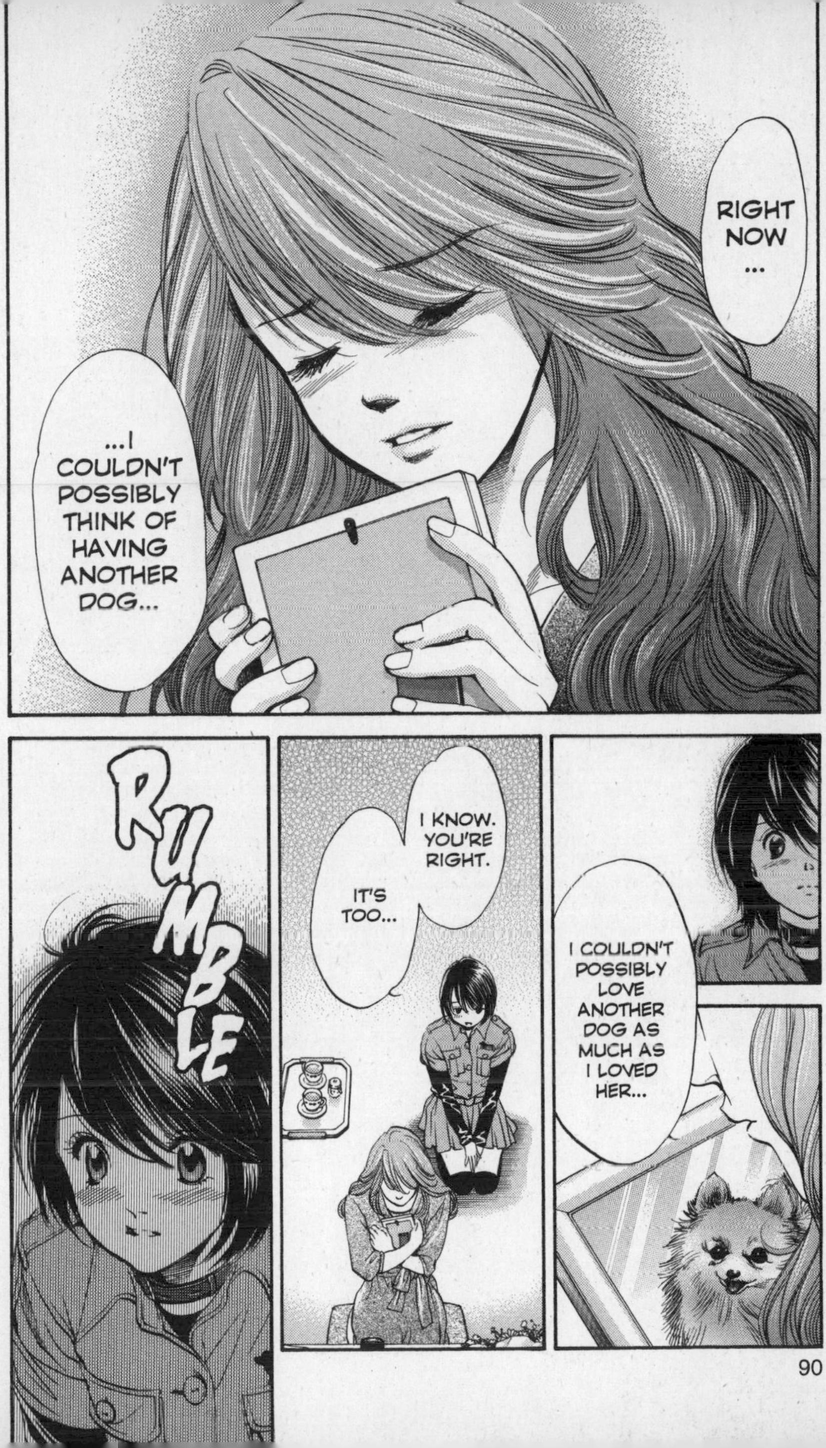
RIGHT NOW ...
...I COULDN'T POSSIBLY THINK OF HAVING ANOTHER DOG...
I COULDN'T POSSIBLY LOVE ANOTHER DOG AS MUCH AS I LOVED HER...
I KNOW. YOU'RE RIGHT.
IT'S TOO...
RUMBLE

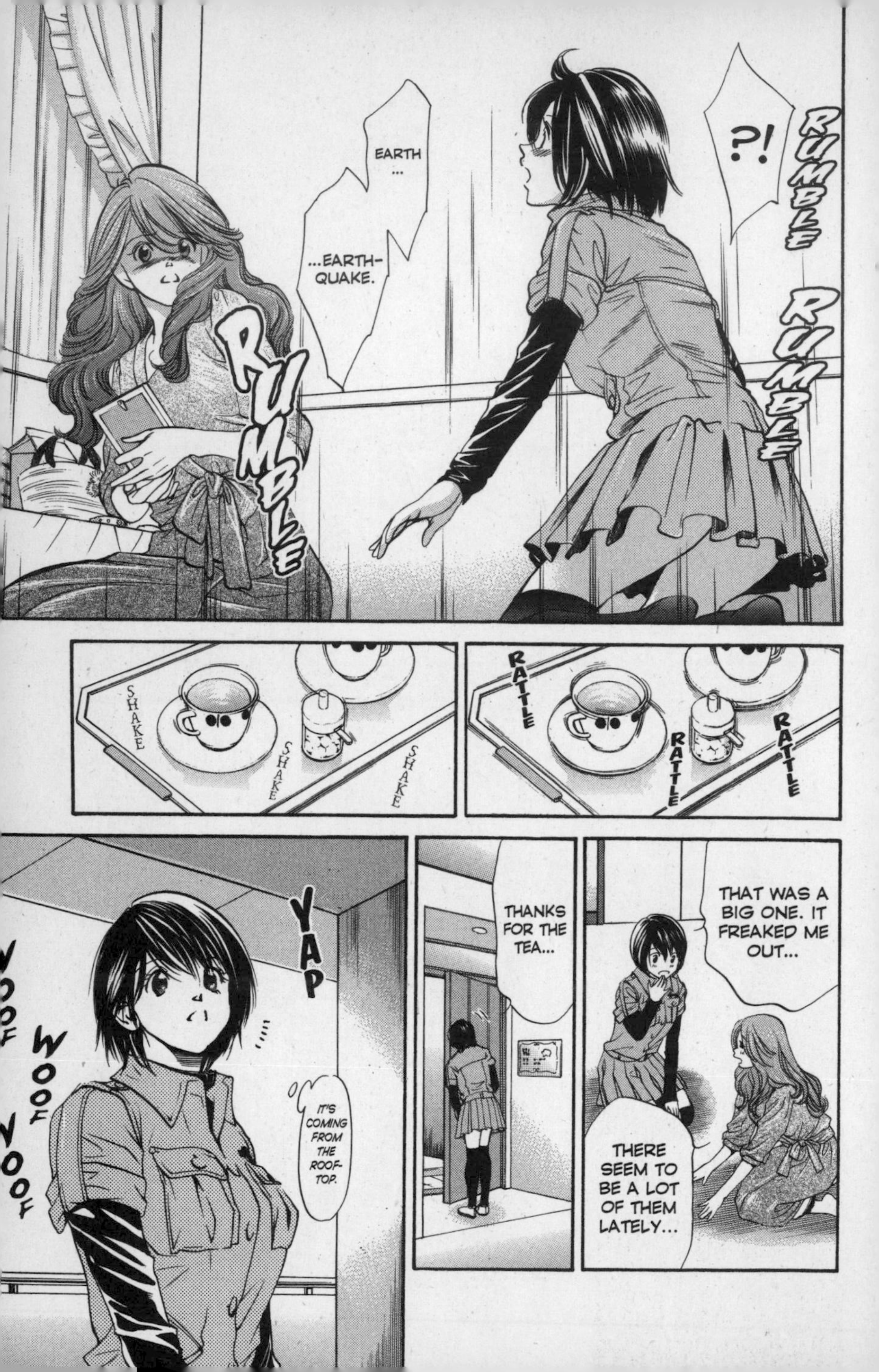
RUMBLE
?!
RUMBLE RUMBLE
EARTH ...
...EARTH-QUAKE.
RUMBLE
RATTLE
RATTLE RATTLE
SHAKE
SHAKE
SHAKE
THAT WAS A BIG ONE. IT FREAKED ME OUT...
THERE SEEM TO BE A LOT OF THEM LATELY...
THANKS FOR THE TEA...
YAP
WOOF WOOF WOOF
.....
IT'S COMING FROM THE ROOF-TOP.

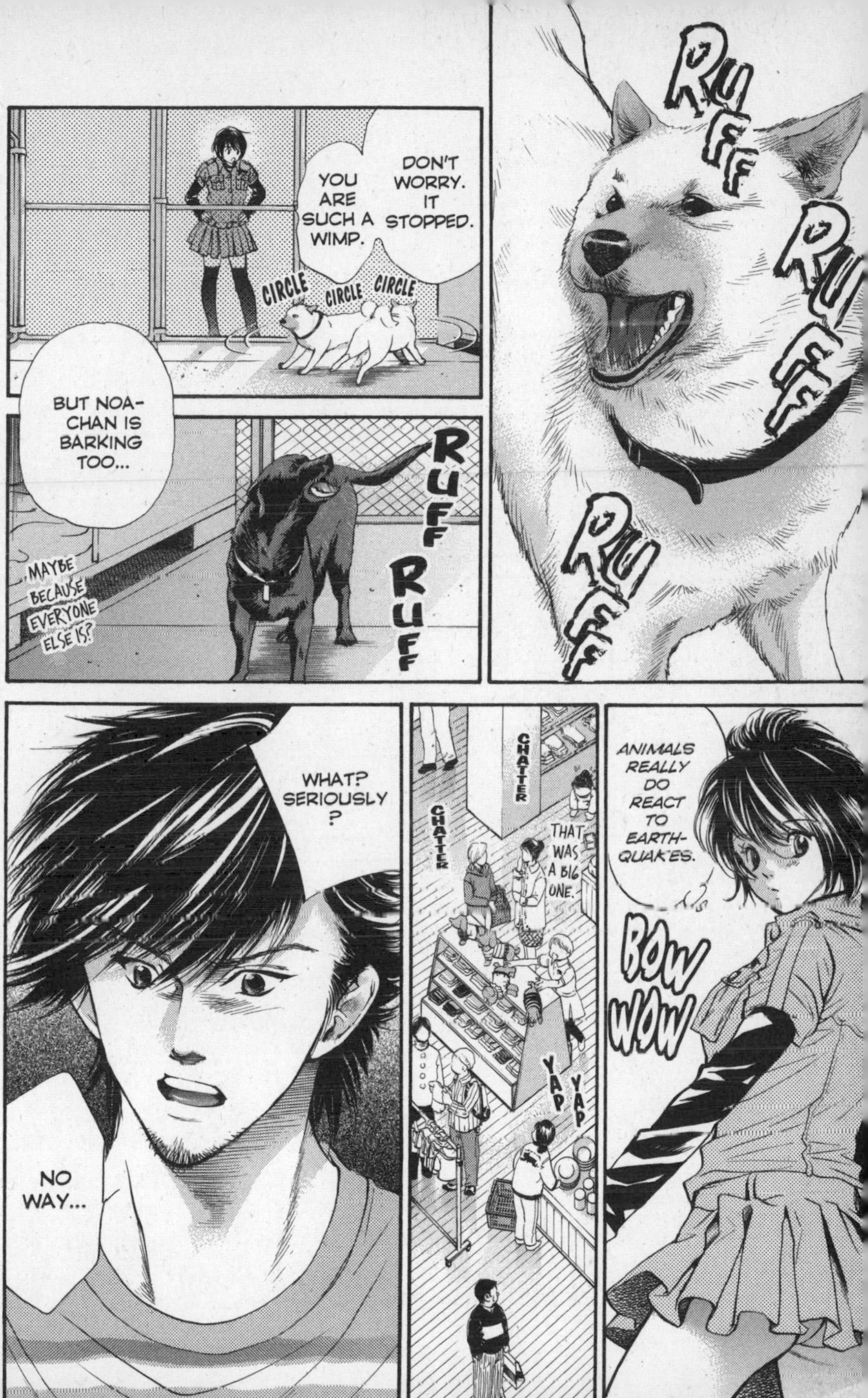
RUFF
RUFF
RUFF
DON'T WORRY. IT STOPPED.
YOU ARE SUCH A WIMP.
CIRCLE CIRCLE CIRCLE
BUT NOA-CHAN IS BARKING TOO...
RUFF RUFF
MAYBE BECAUSE EVERYONE ELSE IS?
ANIMALS REALLY DO REACT TO EARTHQUAKES.
BOW WOW
CHATTER
CHATTER
THAT WAS A BIG ONE.
YAP YAP
WHAT? SERIOUSLY?
NO WAY...

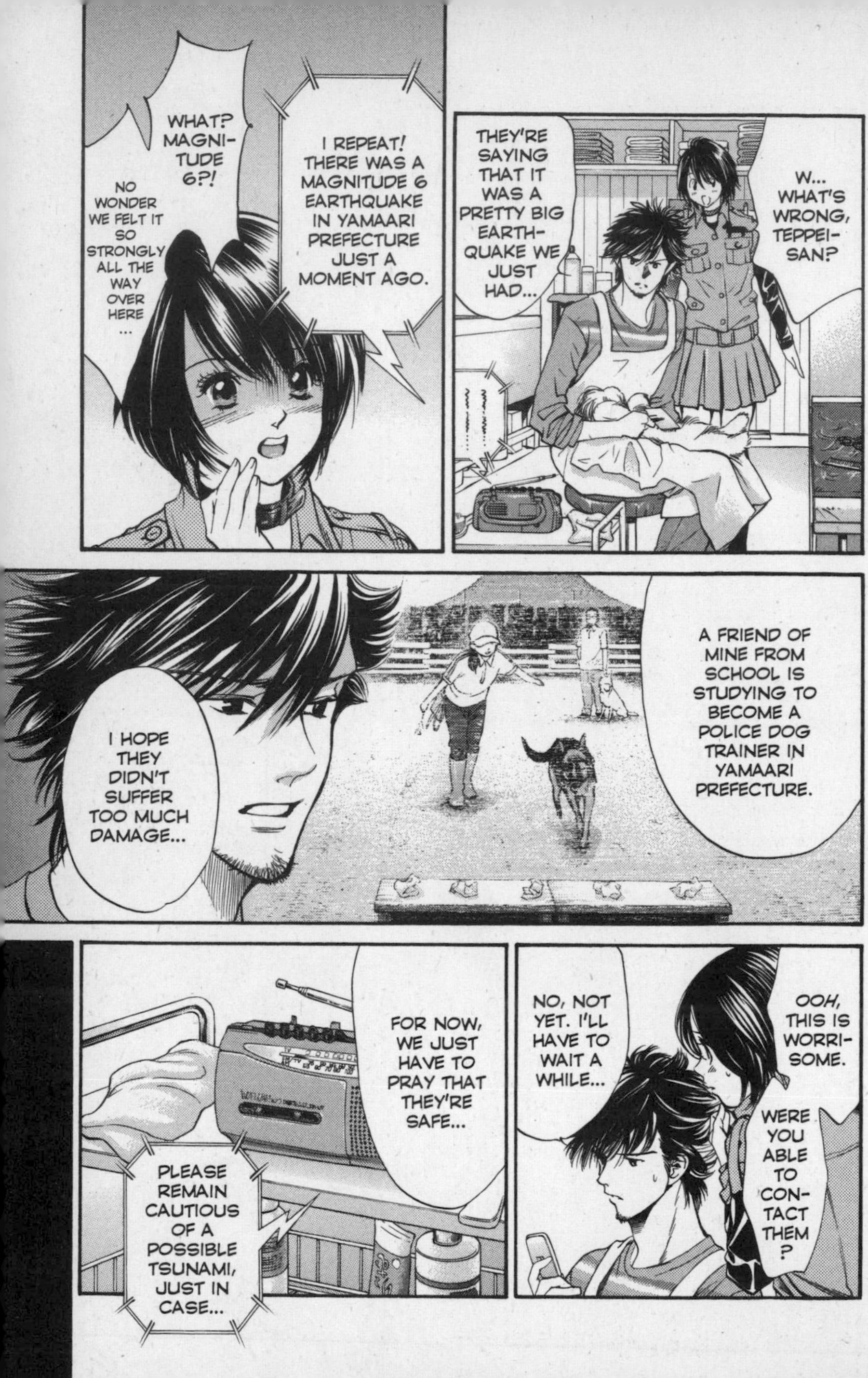
W... WHAT'S WRONG, TEPPEI-SAN?
THEY'RE SAYING THAT IT WAS A PRETTY BIG EARTHQUAKE WE JUST HAD...
I REPEAT! THERE WAS A MAGNITUDE 6 EARTHQUAKE IN YAMAARI PREFECTURE JUST A MOMENT AGO.
WHAT? MAGNITUDE 6?!
NO WONDER WE FELT IT SO STRONGLY ALL THE WAY OVER HERE...
A FRIEND OF MINE FROM SCHOOL IS STUDYING TO BECOME A POLICE DOG TRAINER IN YAMAARI PREFECTURE.
I HOPE THEY DIDN'T SUFFER TOO MUCH DAMAGE...
OOH, THIS IS WORRISOME.
WERE YOU ABLE TO CONTACT THEM?
NO, NOT YET. I'LL HAVE TO WAIT A WHILE...
FOR NOW, WE JUST HAVE TO PRAY THAT THEY'RE SAFE...
PLEASE REMAIN CAUTIOUS OF A POSSIBLE TSUNAMI, JUST IN CASE...

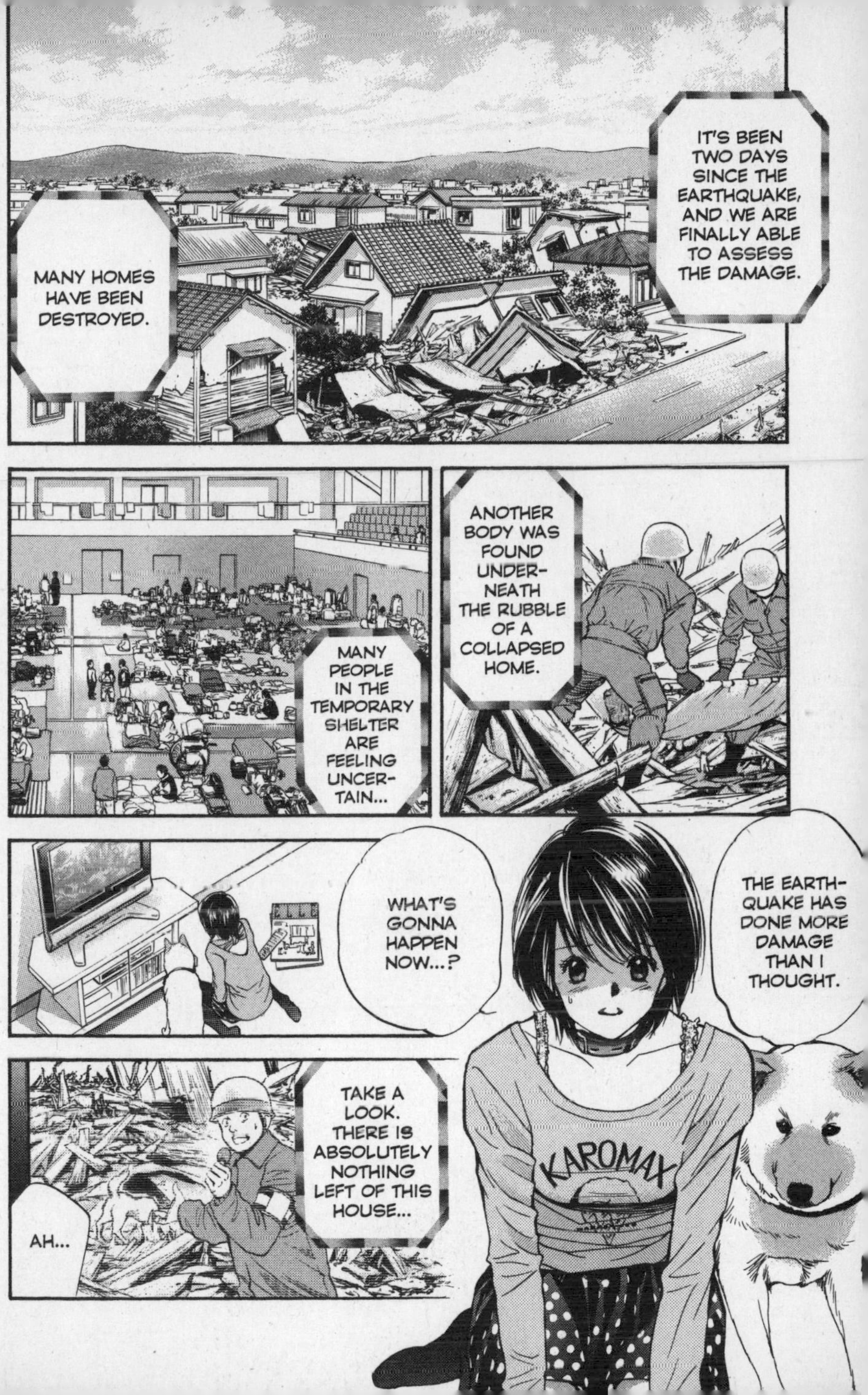
IT'S BEEN TWO DAYS SINCE THE EARTHQUAKE, AND WE ARE FINALLY ABLE TO ASSESS THE DAMAGE.
MANY HOMES HAVE BEEN DESTROYED.
ANOTHER BODY WAS FOUND UNDER-NEATH THE RUBBLE OF A COLLAPSED HOME.
MANY PEOPLE IN THE TEMPORARY SHELTER ARE FEELING UNCER-TAIN...
THE EARTH-QUAKE HAS DONE MORE DAMAGE THAN I THOUGHT.
WHAT'S GONNA HAPPEN NOW...?
KAROMAX
TAKE A LOOK. THERE IS ABSOLUTELY NOTHING LEFT OF THIS HOUSE...
AH...

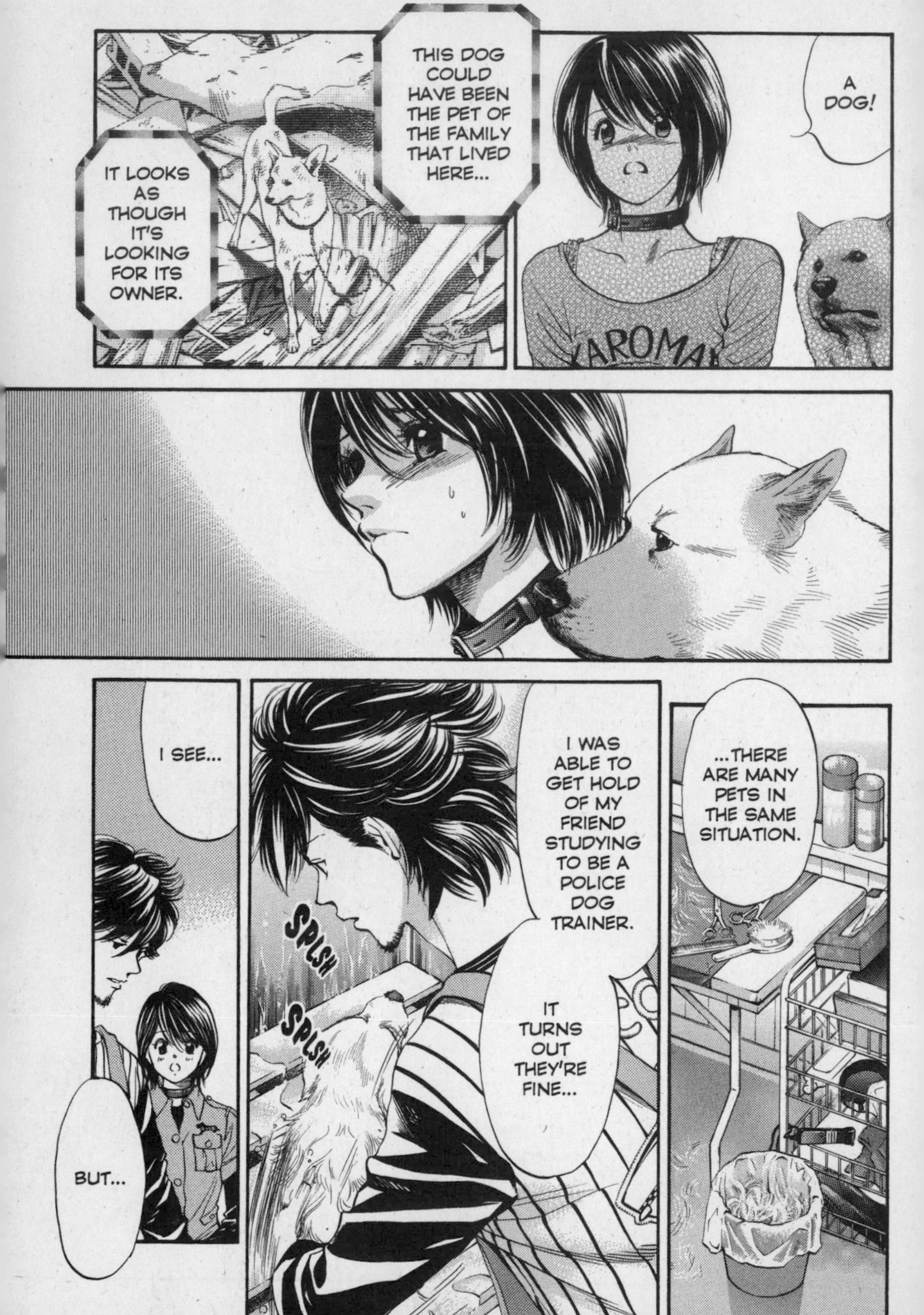
A DOG!
THIS DOG COULD HAVE BEEN THE PET OF THE FAMILY THAT LIVED HERE...
IT LOOKS AS THOUGH IT'S LOOKING FOR ITS OWNER.
...THERE ARE MANY PETS IN THE SAME SITUATION.
I WAS ABLE TO GET HOLD OF MY FRIEND STUDYING TO BE A POLICE DOG TRAINER.
IT TURNS OUT THEY'RE FINE...
SPLSH
SPLSH
I SEE...
BUT...

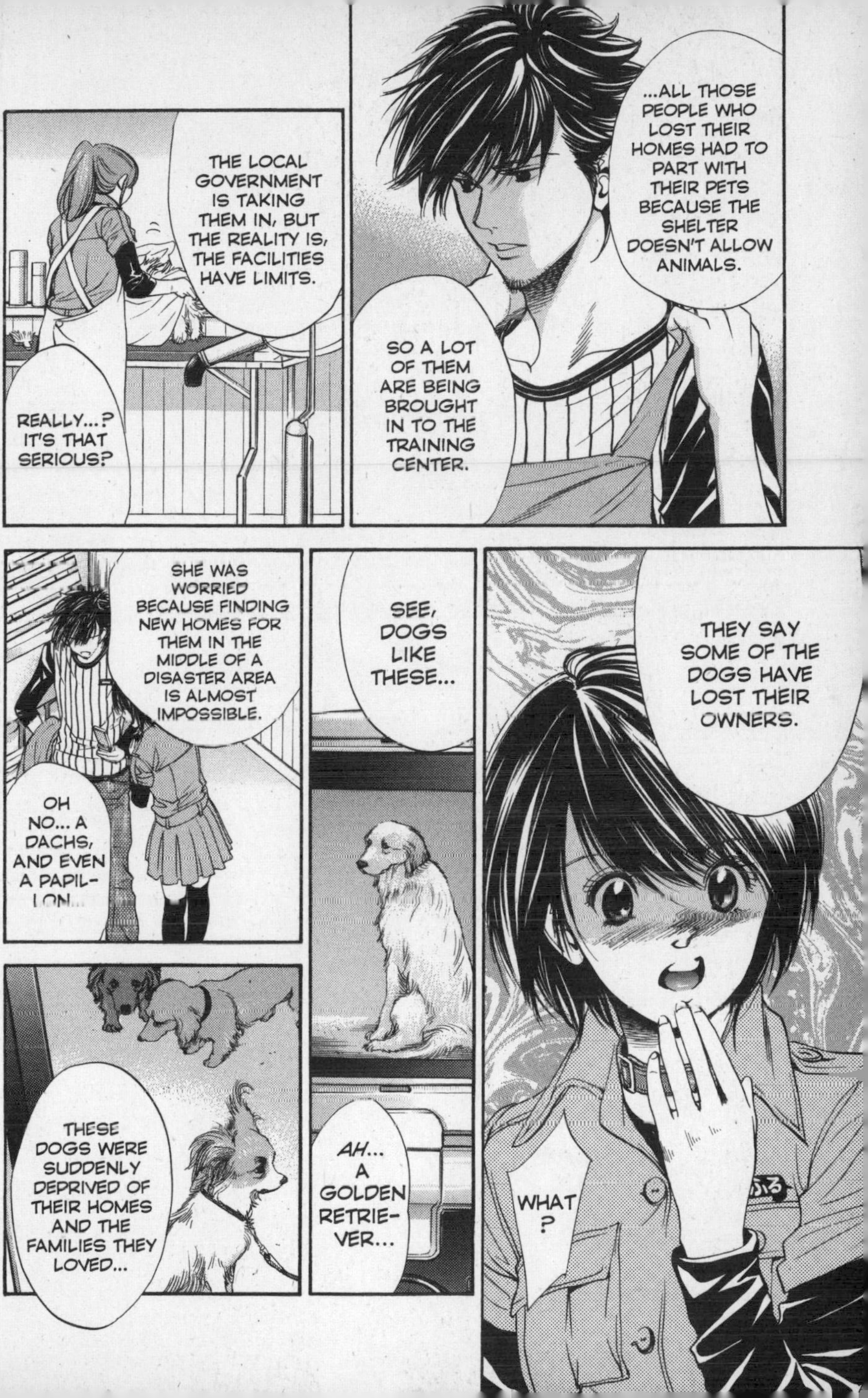
...ALL THOSE PEOPLE WHO LOST THEIR HOMES HAD TO PART WITH THEIR PETS BECAUSE THE SHELTER DOESN'T ALLOW ANIMALS.
SO A LOT OF THEM ARE BEING BROUGHT IN TO THE TRAINING CENTER.
THE LOCAL GOVERNMENT IS TAKING THEM IN, BUT THE REALITY IS, THE FACILITIES HAVE LIMITS.
REALLY...? IT'S THAT SERIOUS?
THEY SAY SOME OF THE DOGS HAVE LOST THEIR OWNERS.
WHAT?
SEE, DOGS LIKE THESE...
AH... A GOLDEN RETRIEVER...
SHE WAS WORRIED BECAUSE FINDING NEW HOMES FOR THEM IN THE MIDDLE OF A DISASTER AREA IS ALMOST IMPOSSIBLE.
OH NO... A DACHS, AND EVEN A PAPILLON...
THESE DOGS WERE SUDDENLY DEPRIVED OF THEIR HOMES AND THE FAMILIES THEY LOVED...

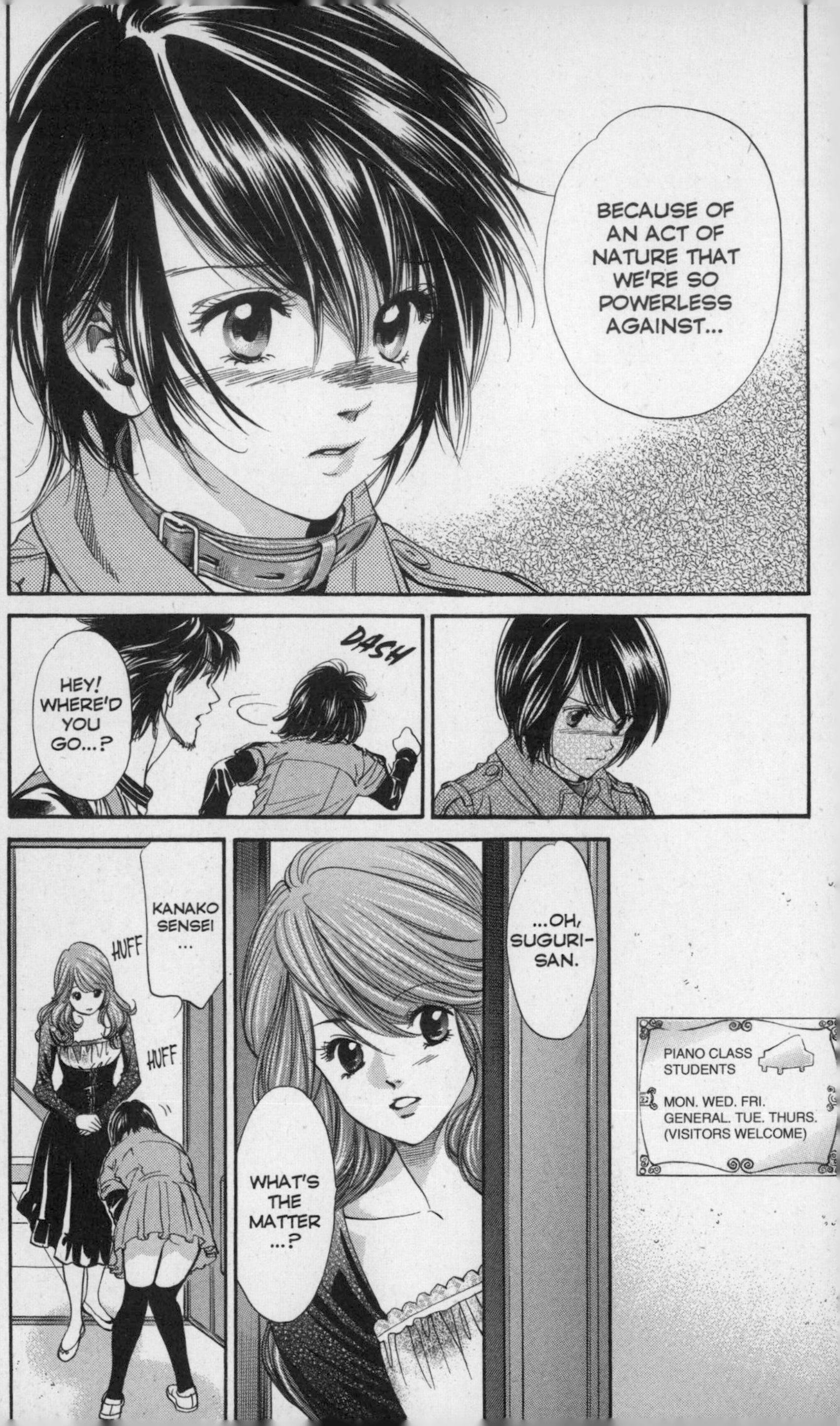
BECAUSE OF AN ACT OF NATURE THAT WE'RE SO POWERLESS AGAINST...
DASH
HEY! WHERE'D YOU GO...?
PIANO CLASS STUDENTS
MON. WED. FRI.
GENERAL. TUE. THURS.
(VISITORS WELCOME)
...OH, SUGURI-SAN.
WHAT'S THE MATTER...?
KANAKO SENSEI...
HUFF
HUFF

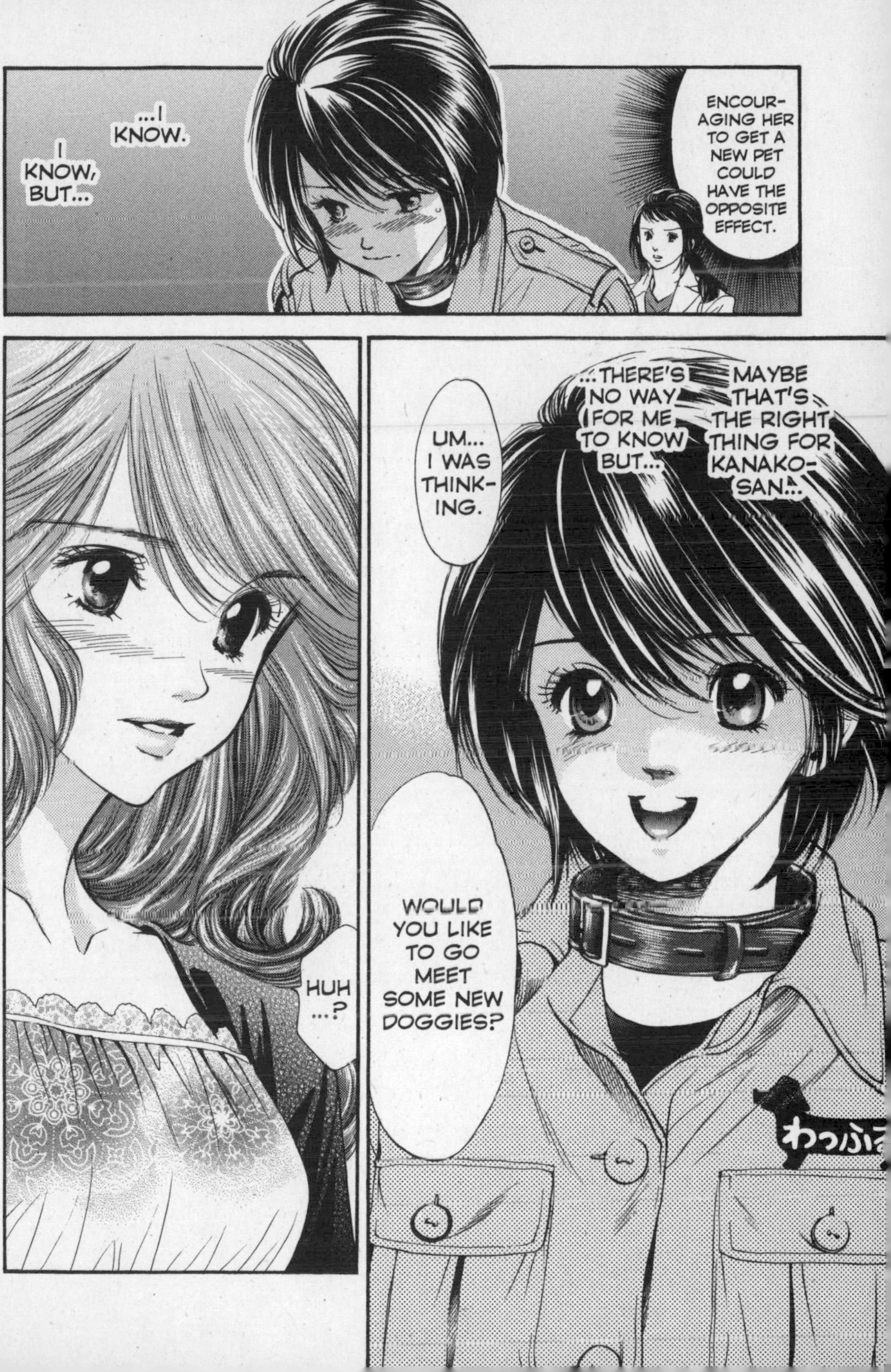
ENCOURAGING HER TO GET A NEW PET COULD HAVE THE OPPOSITE EFFECT.
...I KNOW.
I KNOW, BUT...
MAYBE THAT'S THE RIGHT THING FOR KANAKO-SAN...
...THERE'S NO WAY FOR ME TO KNOW BUT...
UM... I WAS THINKING.
WOULD YOU LIKE TO GO MEET SOME NEW DOGGIES?
HUH ...?

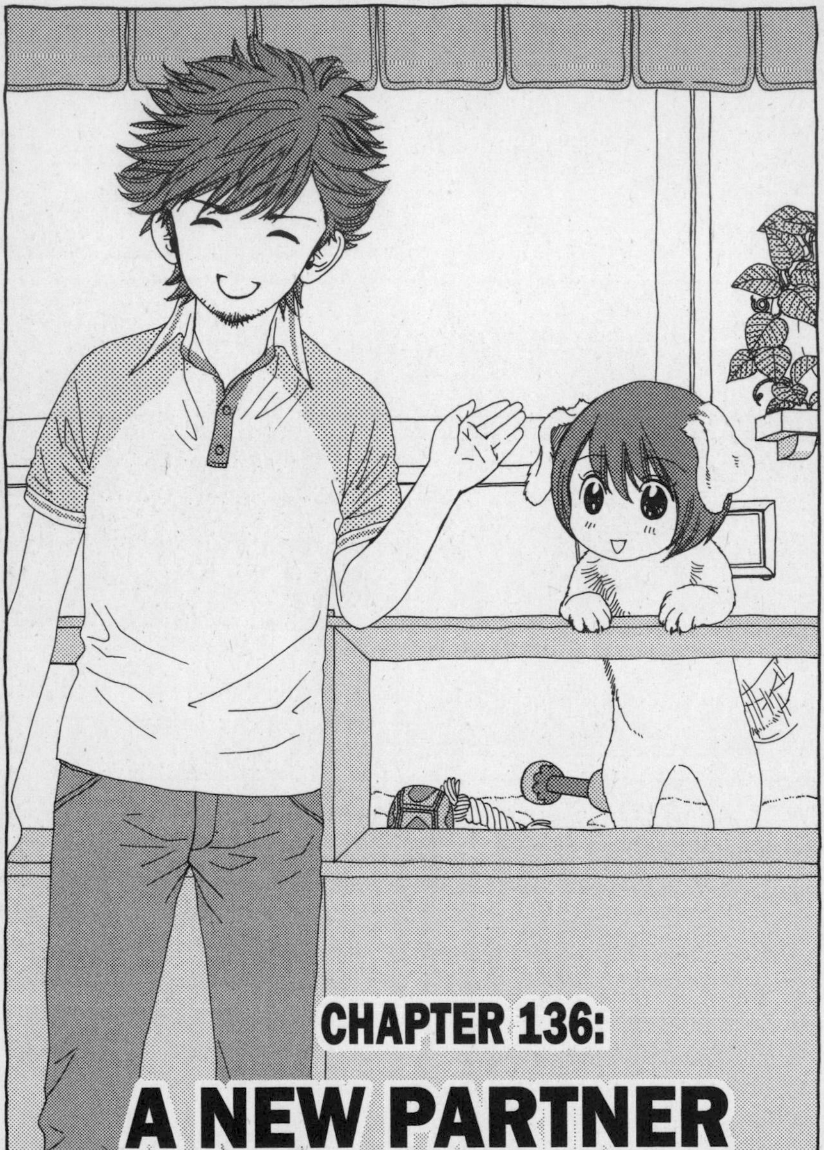
CHAPTER 136:
A NEW PARTNER

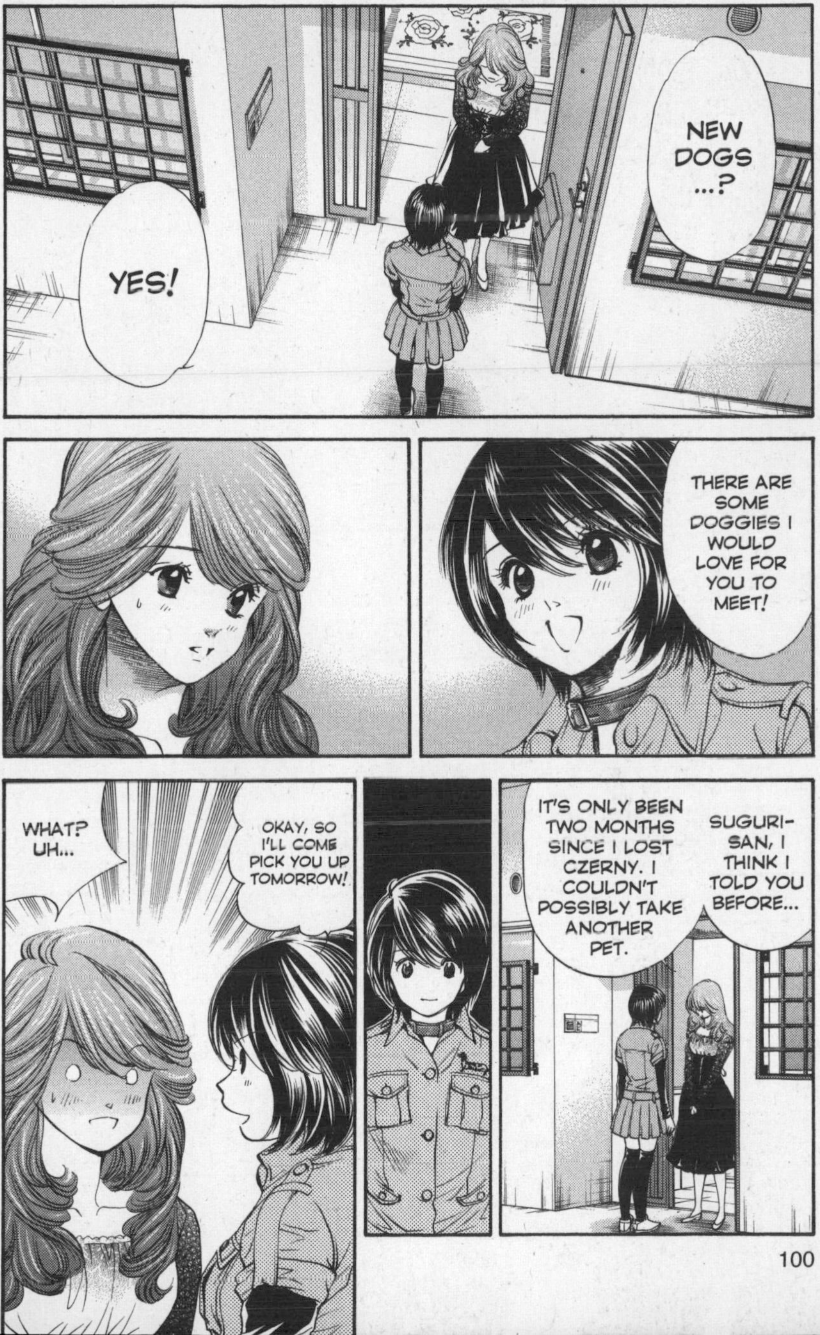
NEW DOGS ...?
YES!
THERE ARE SOME DOGGIES I WOULD LOVE FOR YOU TO MEET!
SUGURI-SAN, I THINK I TOLD YOU BEFORE...
IT'S ONLY BEEN TWO MONTHS SINCE I LOST CZERNY. I COULDN'T POSSIBLY TAKE ANOTHER PET.
OKAY, SO I'LL COME PICK YOU UP TOMORROW!
WHAT? UH...

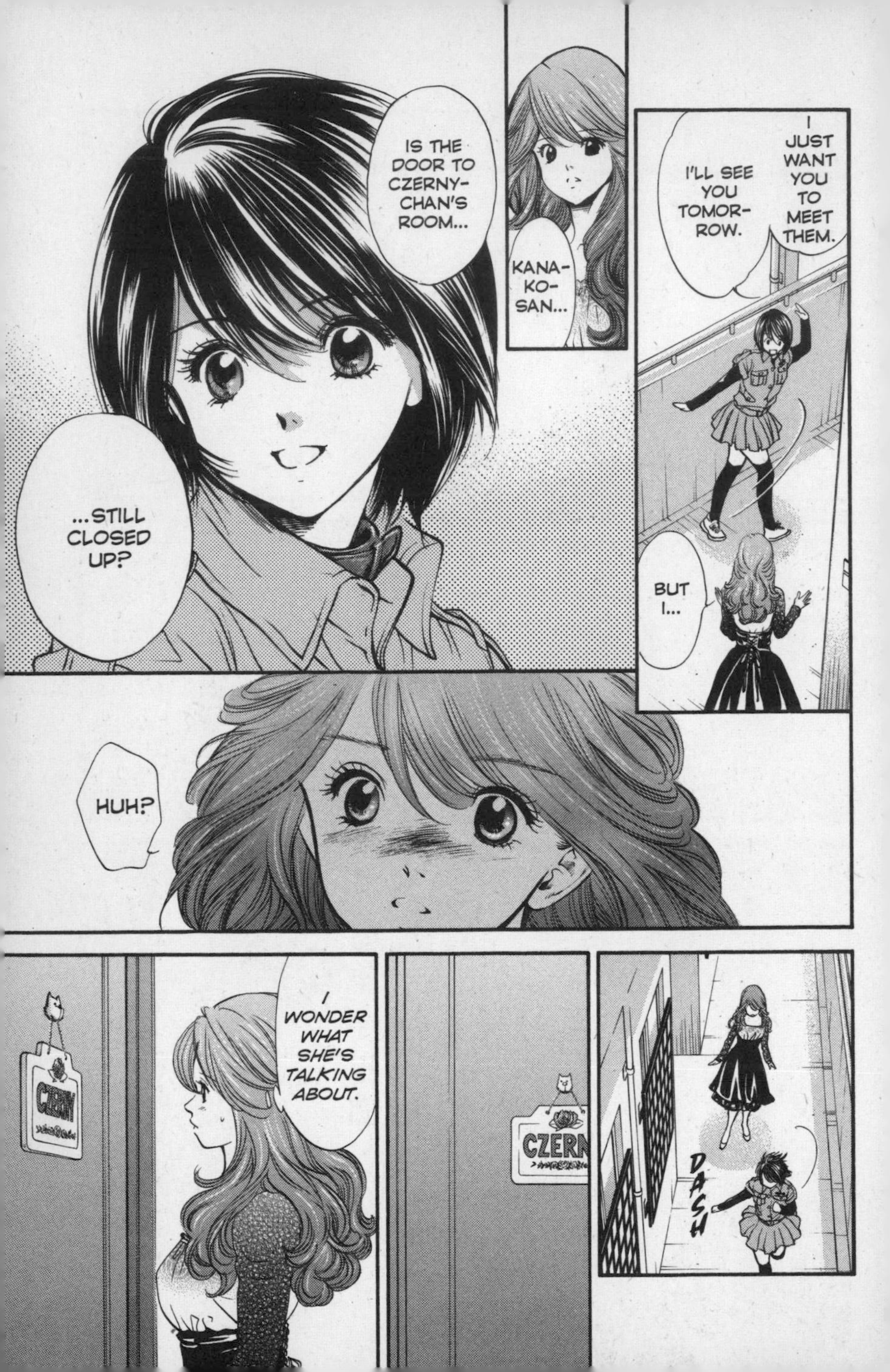
I JUST WANT YOU TO MEET THEM.
I'LL SEE YOU TOMORROW.
BUT I...
KANA-KO-SAN...
IS THE DOOR TO CZERNY-CHAN'S ROOM...
...STILL CLOSED UP?
HUH?
DASH
CZERNY
CZERNY
I WONDER WHAT SHE'S TALKING ABOUT.

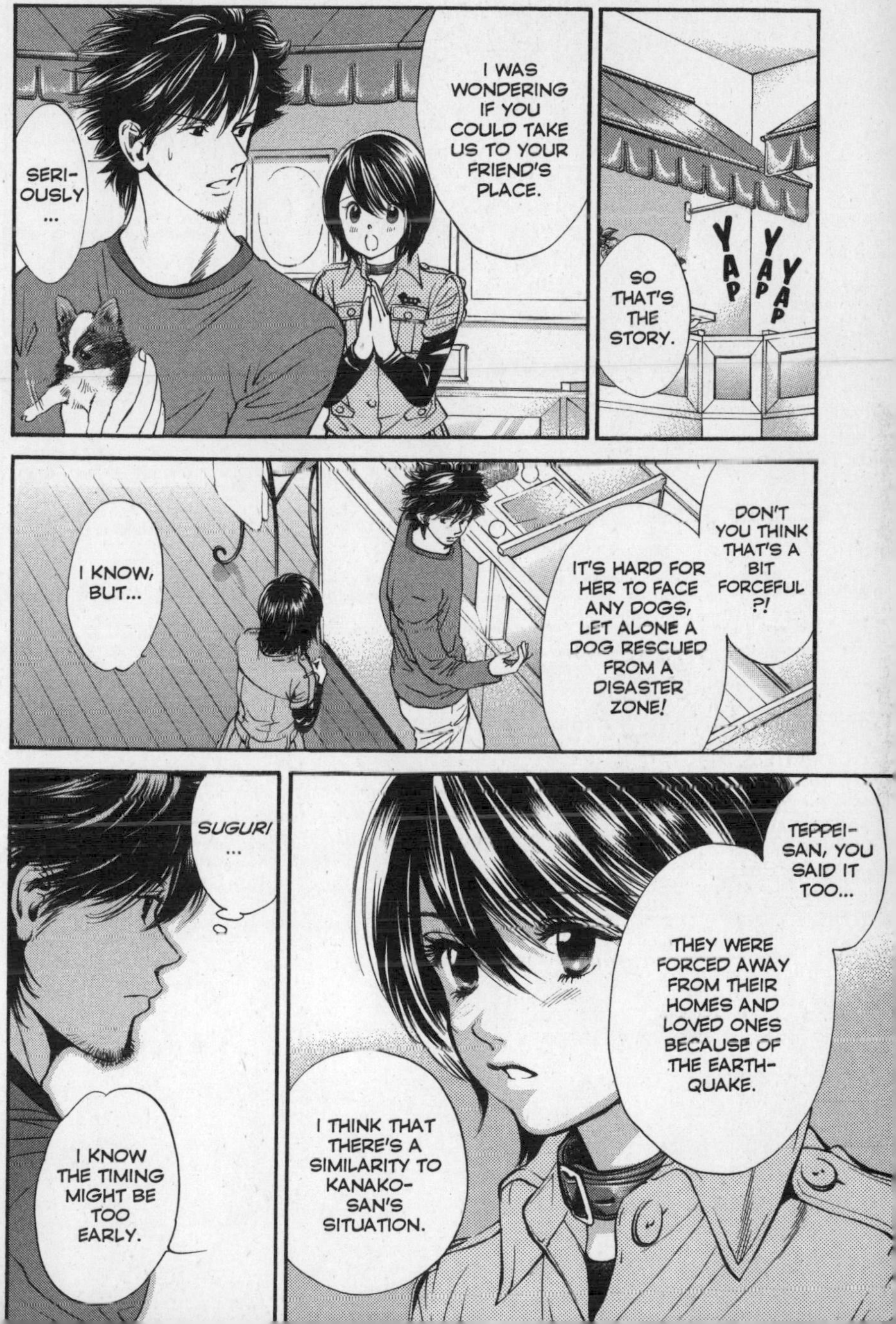
YAP YAP YAP
SO THAT'S THE STORY.
I WAS WONDERING IF YOU COULD TAKE US TO YOUR FRIEND'S PLACE.
SERI-OUSLY ...
DON'T YOU THINK THAT'S A BIT FORCEFUL ?!
IT'S HARD FOR HER TO FACE ANY DOGS, LET ALONE A DOG RESCUED FROM A DISASTER ZONE!
I KNOW, BUT...
TEPPEI-SAN, YOU SAID IT TOO...
THEY WERE FORCED AWAY FROM THEIR HOMES AND LOVED ONES BECAUSE OF THE EARTH-QUAKE.
I THINK THAT THERE'S A SIMILARITY TO KANAKO-SAN'S SITUATION.
SUGURI ...
I KNOW THE TIMING MIGHT BE TOO EARLY.

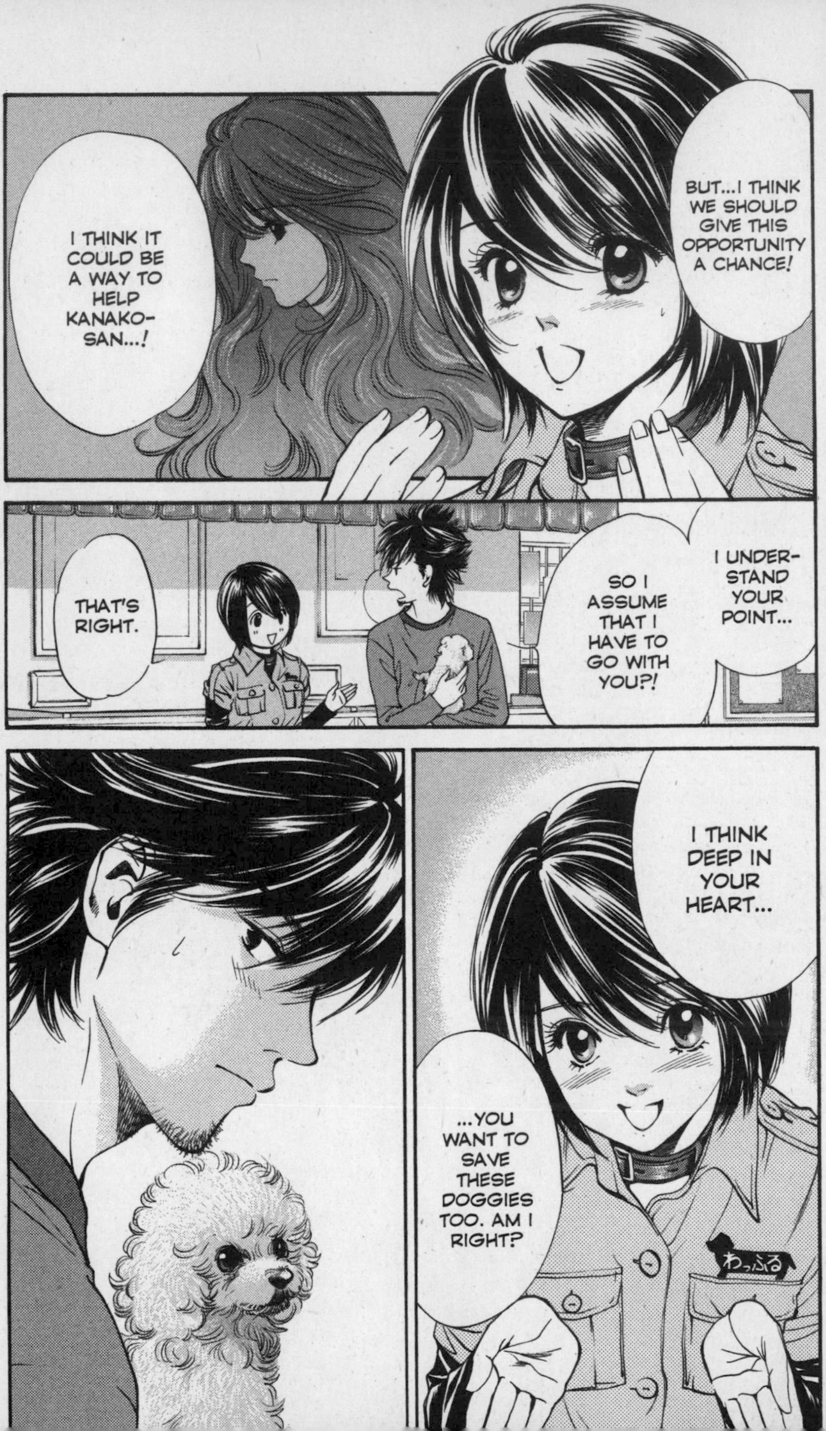
BUT...I THINK WE SHOULD GIVE THIS OPPORTUNITY A CHANCE!
I THINK IT COULD BE A WAY TO HELP KANAKO-SAN...!
I UNDER-STAND YOUR POINT...
SO I ASSUME THAT I HAVE TO GO WITH YOU?!
THAT'S RIGHT.
I THINK DEEP IN YOUR HEART...
...YOU WANT TO SAVE THESE DOGGIES TOO. AM I RIGHT?
わっふる

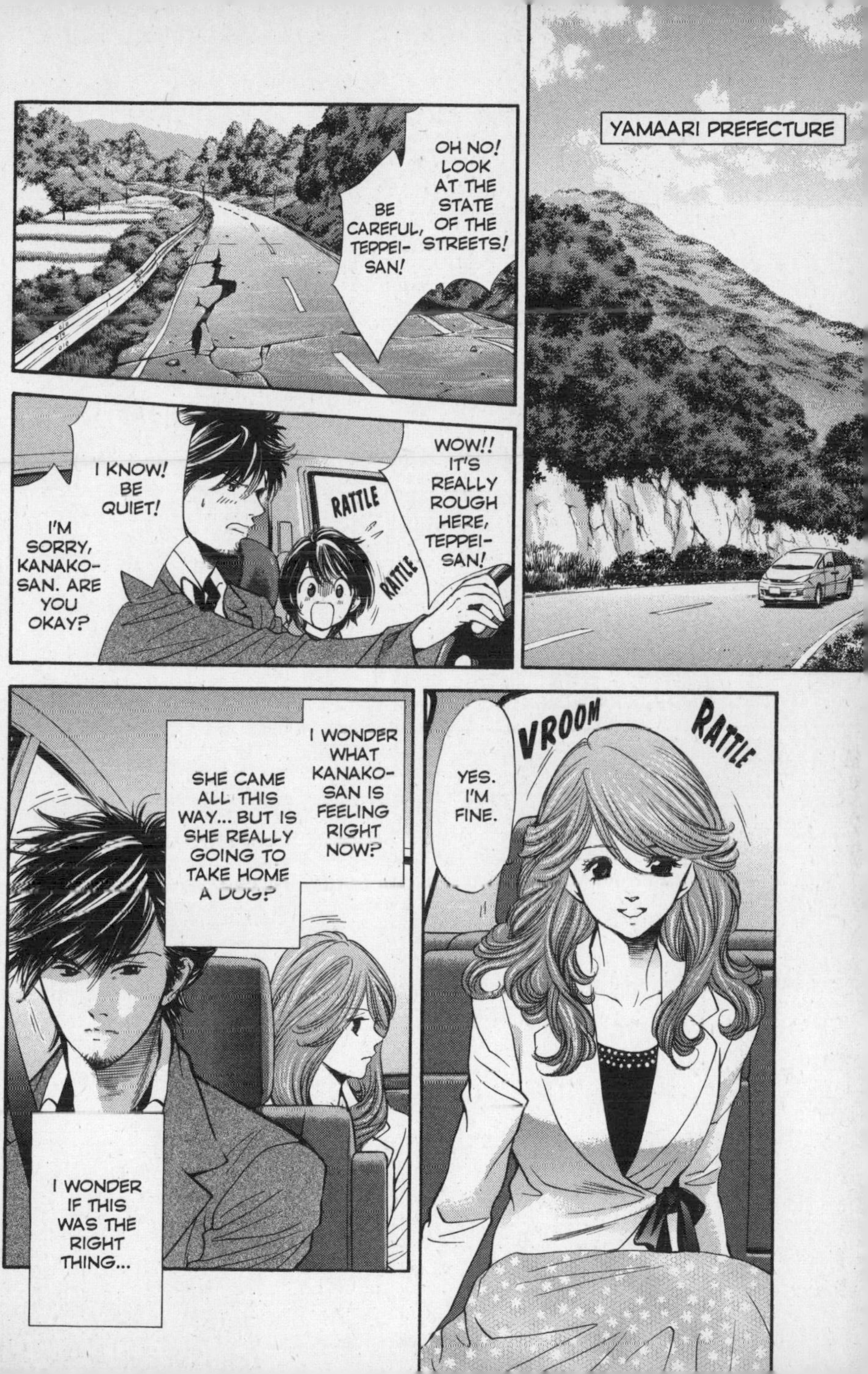
YAMAARI PREFECTURE
OH NO! LOOK AT THE STATE OF THE STREETS!
BE CAREFUL, TEPPEI-SAN!
WOW!! IT'S REALLY ROUGH HERE, TEPPEI-SAN!
RATTLE
RATTLE
I KNOW! BE QUIET!
I'M SORRY, KANAKO-SAN. ARE YOU OKAY?
RATTLE
VROOM
YES. I'M FINE.
I WONDER WHAT KANAKO-SAN IS FEELING RIGHT NOW?
SHE CAME ALL THIS WAY... BUT IS SHE REALLY GOING TO TAKE HOME A DOG?
I WONDER IF THIS WAS THE RIGHT THING...

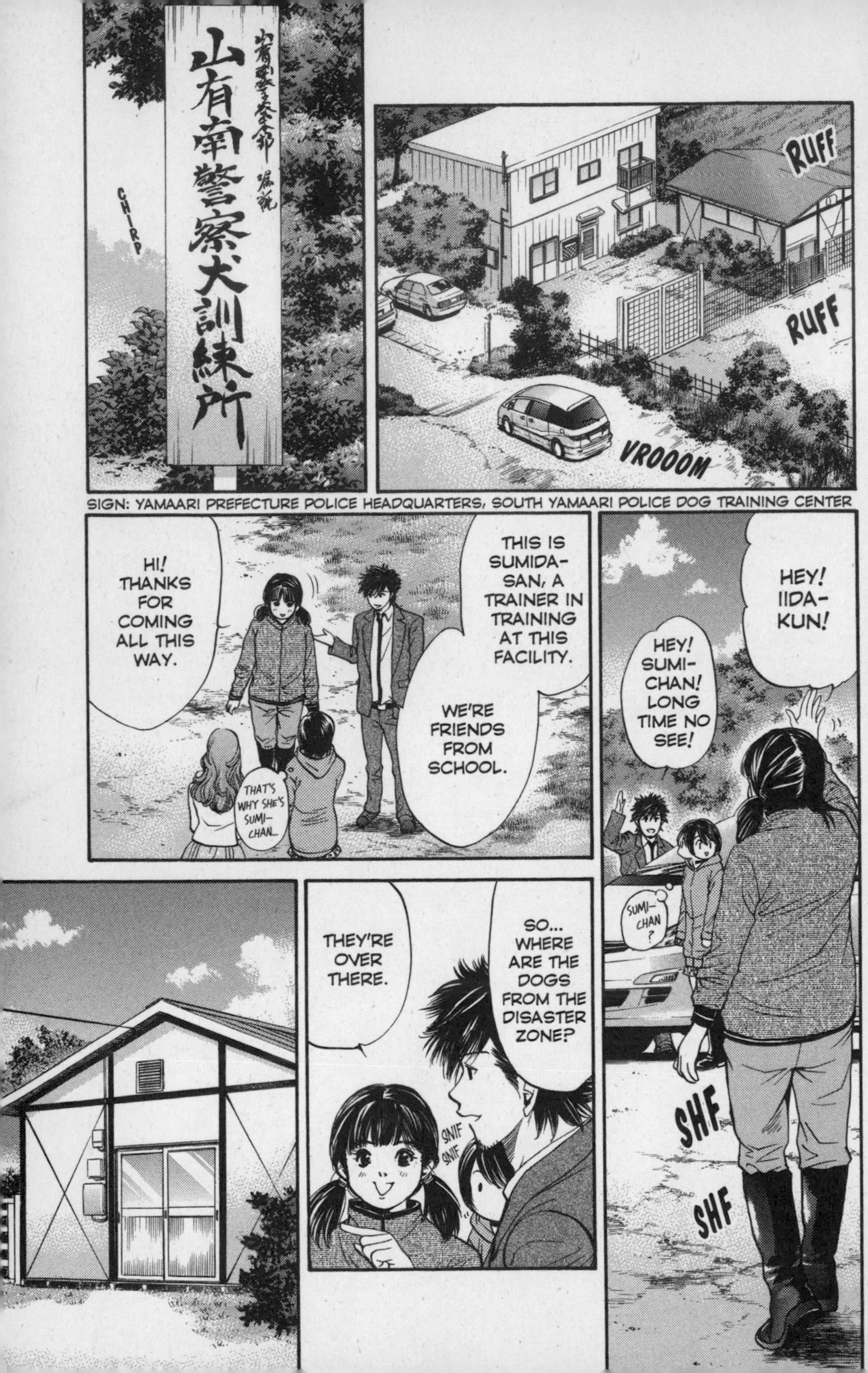
RUFF
RUFF
VROOOM
山有南警察犬訓練所
CHIRP
SIGN: YAMAARI PREFECTURE POLICE HEADQUARTERS, SOUTH YAMAARI POLICE DOG TRAINING CENTER
HEY! IIDA-KUN!
HEY! SUMI-CHAN! LONG TIME NO SEE!
SUMI-CHAN?
SHF
SHF
THIS IS SUMIDA-SAN, A TRAINER IN TRAINING AT THIS FACILITY.
WE'RE FRIENDS FROM SCHOOL.
HI! THANKS FOR COMING ALL THIS WAY.
THAT'S WHY SHE'S SUMI-CHAN...
SO... WHERE ARE THE DOGS FROM THE DISASTER ZONE?
THEY'RE OVER THERE.
SNIF SNIF

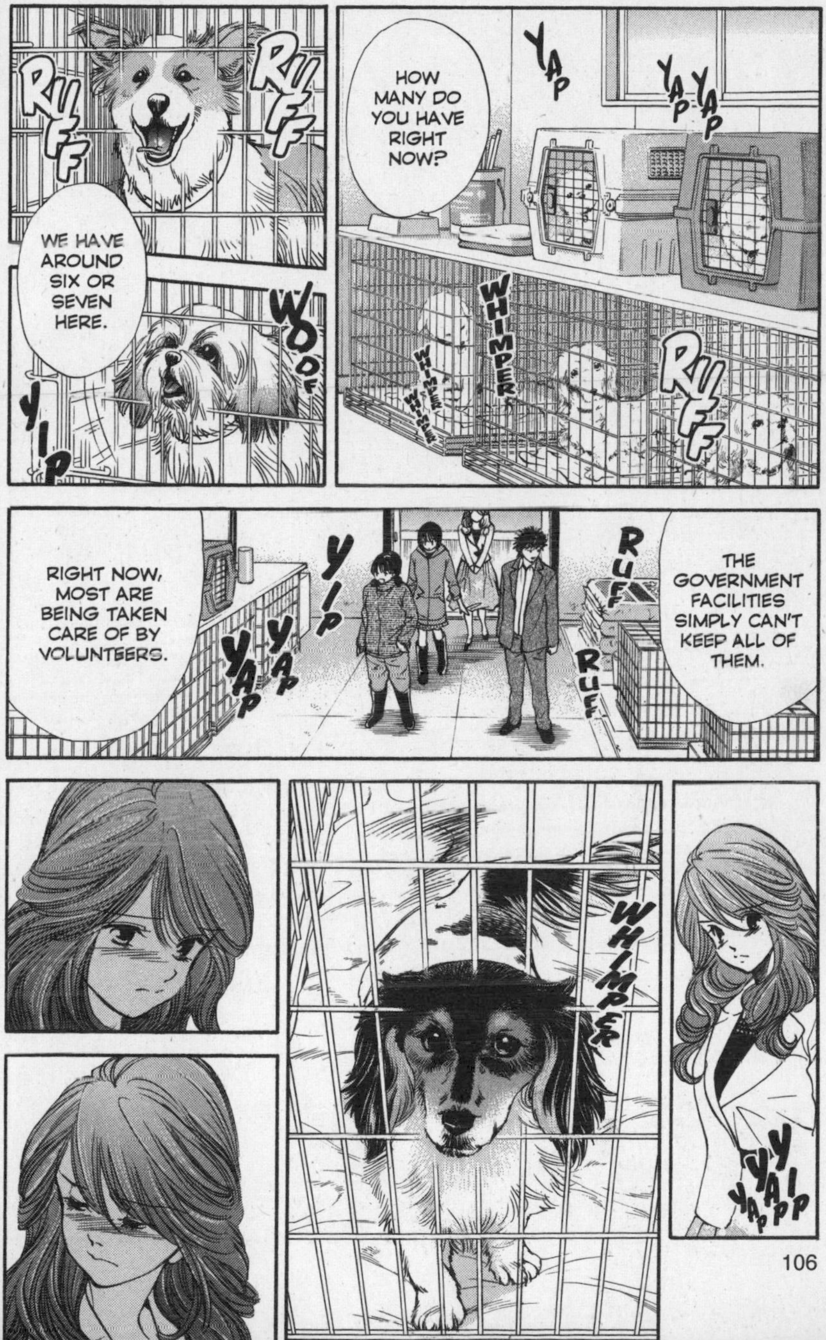
YAP
YAP YAP
HOW MANY DO YOU HAVE RIGHT NOW?
WHIMPER
WHIMPER WHIMPER
RUFF
RUFF
RUFF
WE HAVE AROUND SIX OR SEVEN HERE.
WOOF
YIP
THE GOVERNMENT FACILITIES SIMPLY CAN'T KEEP ALL OF THEM.
RUFF
RUFF
YIP
YAP
YAP
RIGHT NOW, MOST ARE BEING TAKEN CARE OF BY VOLUNTEERS.
YIP
YAP
YAP
WHIMPER

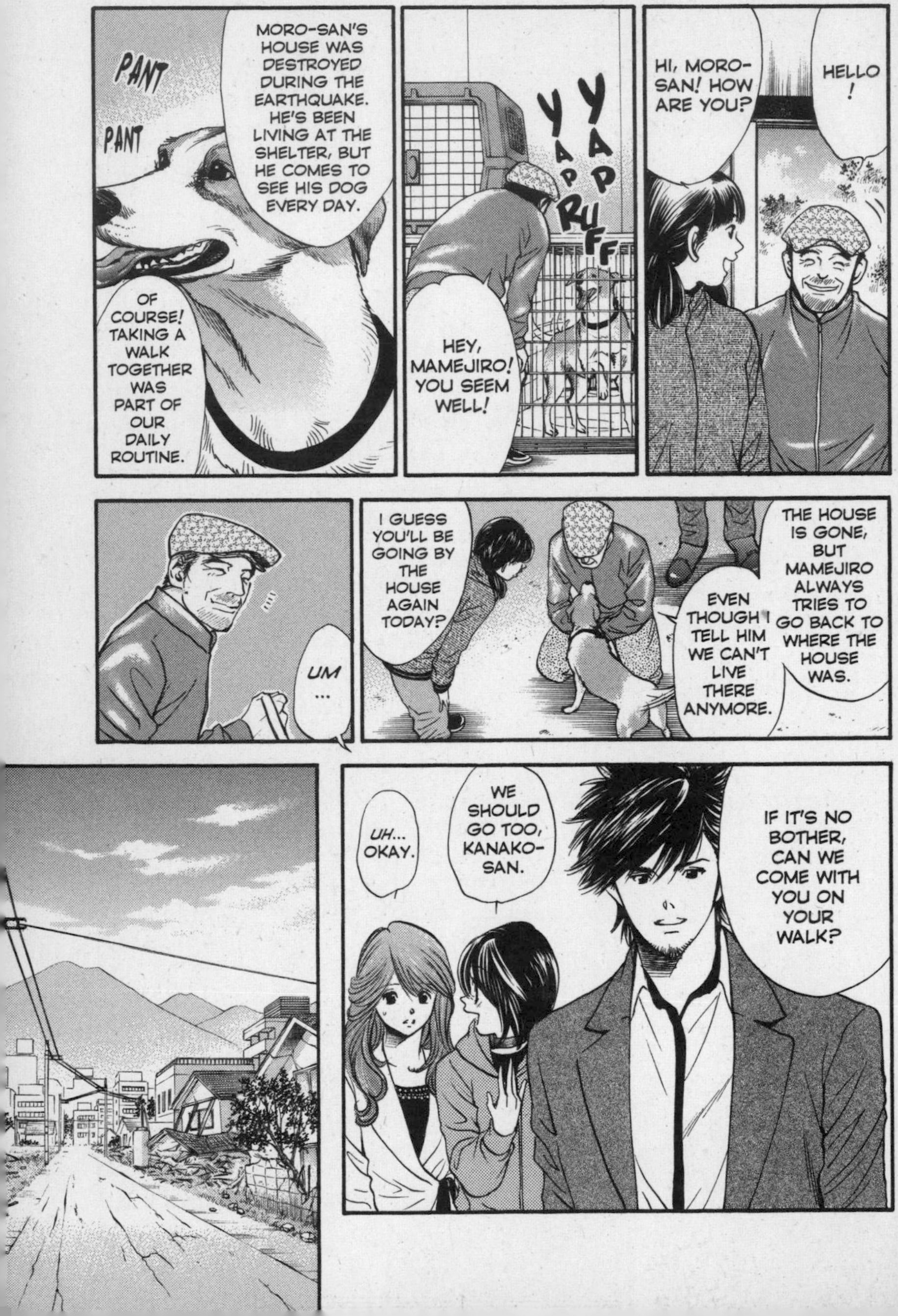
HELLO!
HI, MORO-SAN! HOW ARE YOU?
YAP YAP
RUFF
HEY, MAMEJIRO! YOU SEEM WELL!
MORO-SAN'S HOUSE WAS DESTROYED DURING THE EARTHQUAKE. HE'S BEEN LIVING AT THE SHELTER, BUT HE COMES TO SEE HIS DOG EVERY DAY.
PANT
PANT
OF COURSE! TAKING A WALK TOGETHER WAS PART OF OUR DAILY ROUTINE.
THE HOUSE IS GONE, BUT MAMEJIRO ALWAYS TRIES TO GO BACK TO WHERE THE HOUSE WAS.
EVEN THOUGH I TELL HIM WE CAN'T LIVE THERE ANYMORE.
I GUESS YOU'LL BE GOING BY THE HOUSE AGAIN TODAY?
...
UM ...
IF IT'S NO BOTHER, CAN WE COME WITH YOU ON YOUR WALK?
WE SHOULD GO TOO, KANAKO-SAN.
UH... OKAY.

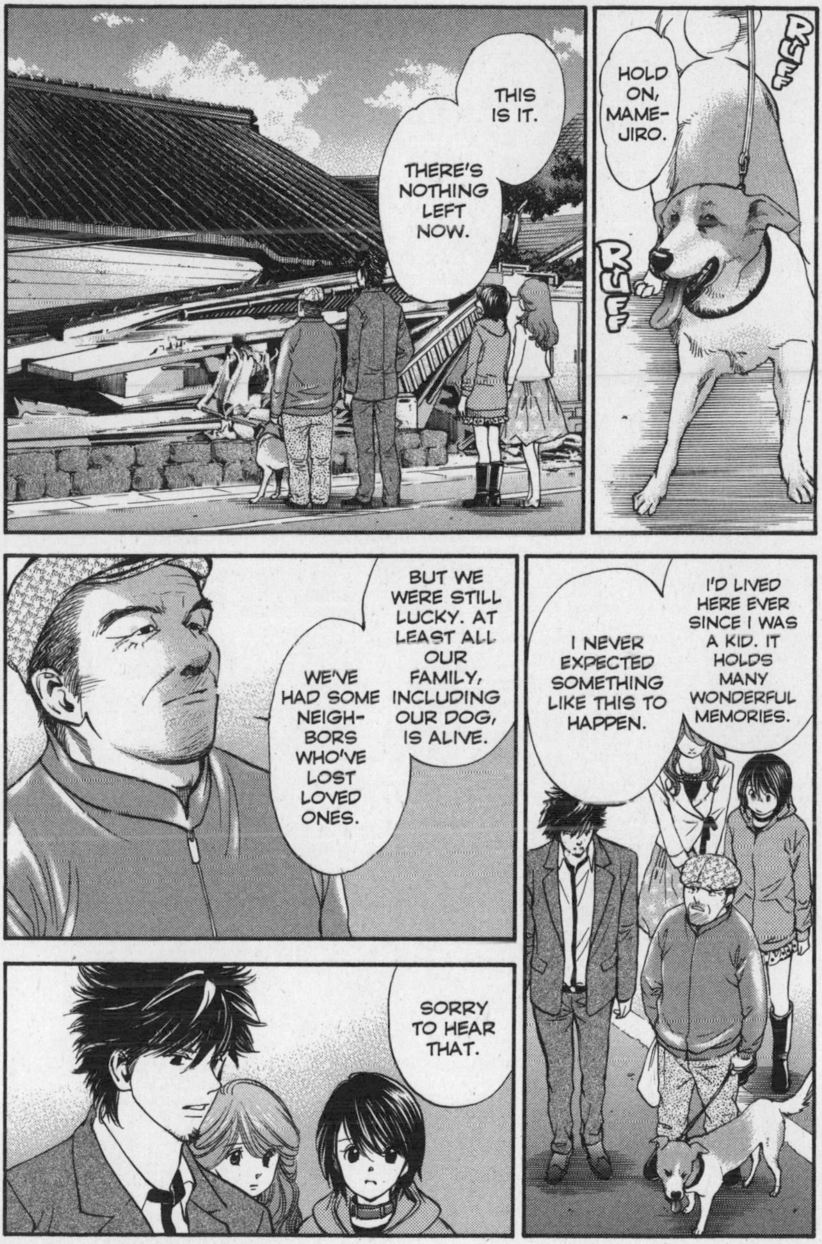
RUFF
HOLD ON, MAMEJIRO.
RUFF
THIS IS IT.
THERE'S NOTHING LEFT NOW.
I'D LIVED HERE EVER SINCE I WAS A KID. IT HOLDS MANY WONDERFUL MEMORIES.
I NEVER EXPECTED SOMETHING LIKE THIS TO HAPPEN.
BUT WE WERE STILL LUCKY. AT LEAST ALL OUR FAMILY, INCLUDING OUR DOG, IS ALIVE.
WE'VE HAD SOME NEIGHBORS WHO'VE LOST LOVED ONES.
SORRY TO HEAR THAT.

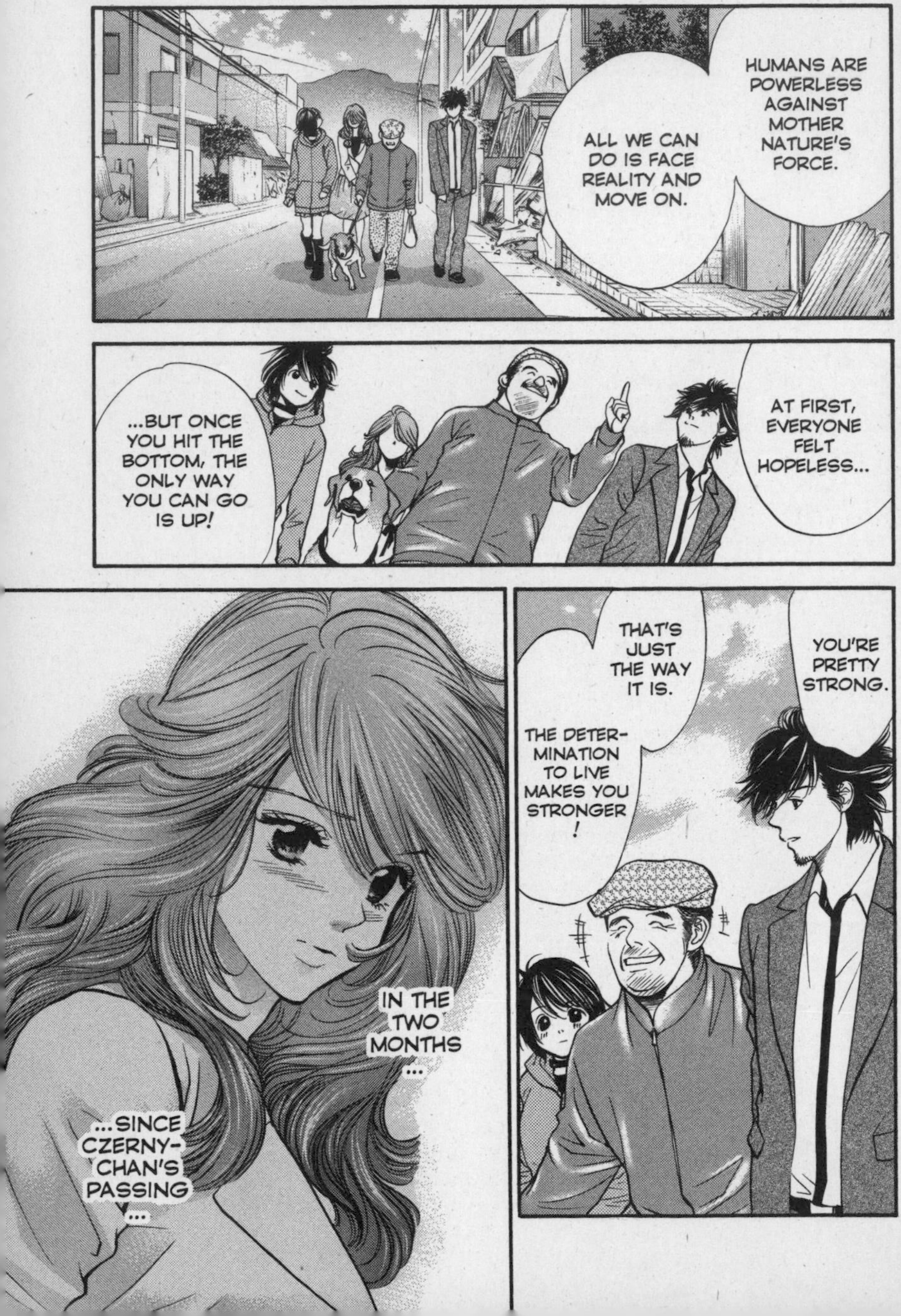
HUMANS ARE POWERLESS AGAINST MOTHER NATURE'S FORCE.
ALL WE CAN DO IS FACE REALITY AND MOVE ON.
AT FIRST, EVERYONE FELT HOPELESS...
...BUT ONCE YOU HIT THE BOTTOM, THE ONLY WAY YOU CAN GO IS UP!
YOU'RE PRETTY STRONG.
THAT'S JUST THE WAY IT IS.
THE DETER-MINATION TO LIVE MAKES YOU STRONGER!
IN THE TWO MONTHS...
...SINCE CZERNY-CHAN'S PASSING...

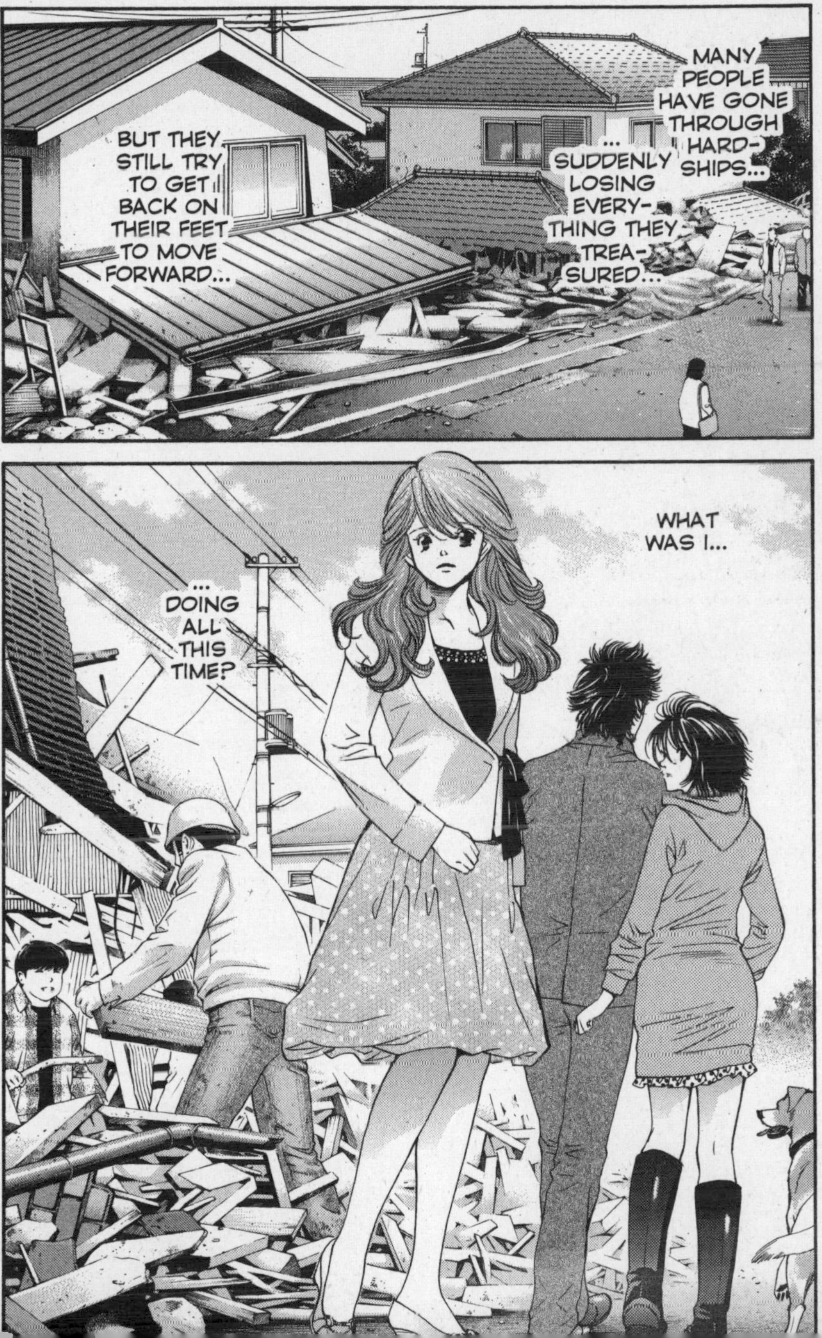
MANY PEOPLE HAVE GONE THROUGH HARDSHIPS...
... SUDDENLY LOSING EVERYTHING THEY TREASURED...
BUT THEY STILL TRY TO GET BACK ON THEIR FEET TO MOVE FORWARD...
WHAT WAS I...
... DOING ALL THIS TIME?

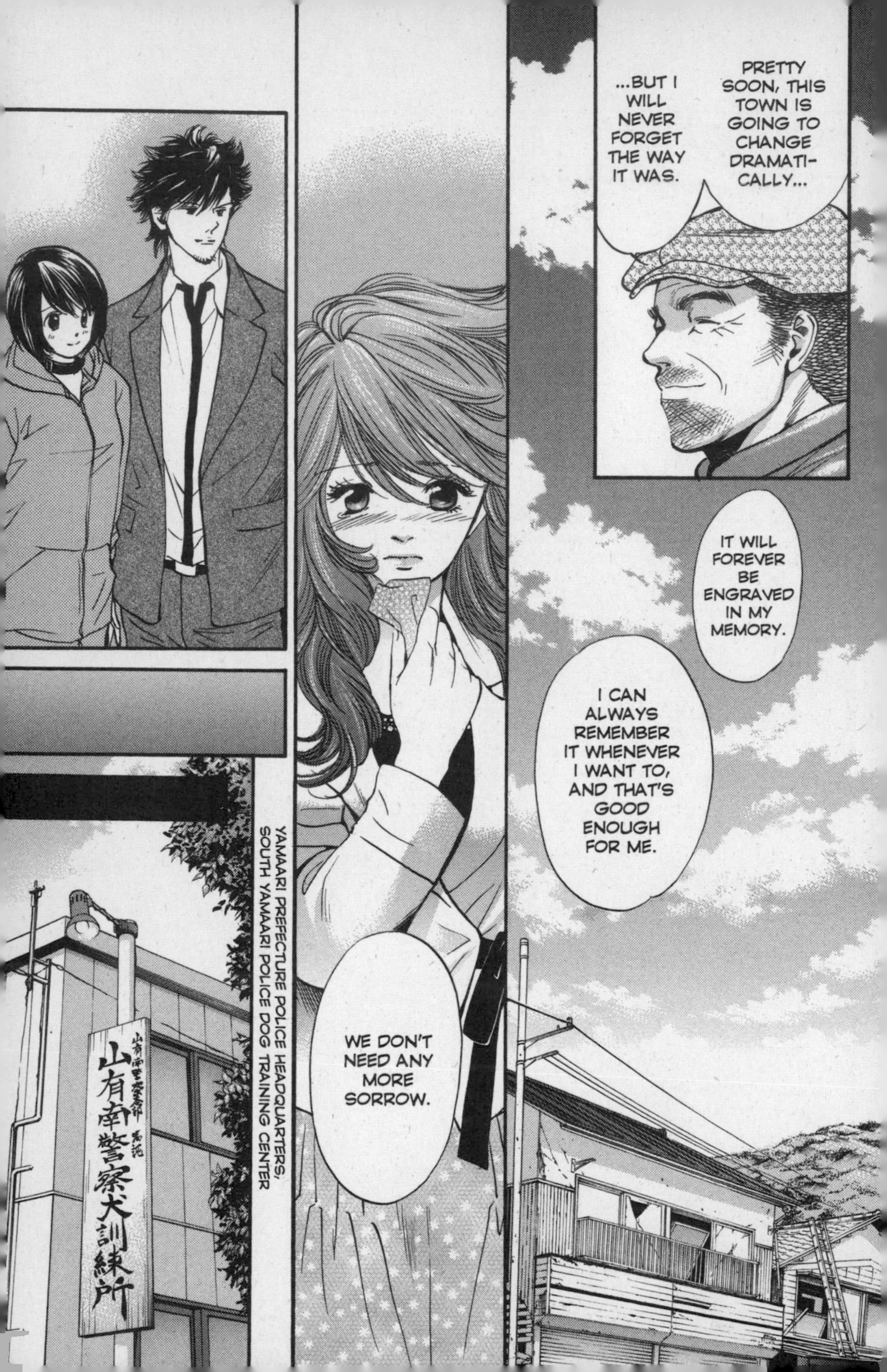
PRETTY SOON, THIS TOWN IS GOING TO CHANGE DRAMATI-CALLY...
...BUT I WILL NEVER FORGET THE WAY IT WAS.
IT WILL FOREVER BE ENGRAVED IN MY MEMORY.
I CAN ALWAYS REMEMBER IT WHENEVER I WANT TO, AND THAT'S GOOD ENOUGH FOR ME.
WE DON'T NEED ANY MORE SORROW.
YAMAARI PREFECTURE POLICE HEADQUARTERS, SOUTH YAMAARI POLICE DOG TRAINING CENTER
山有南警察犬訓練所

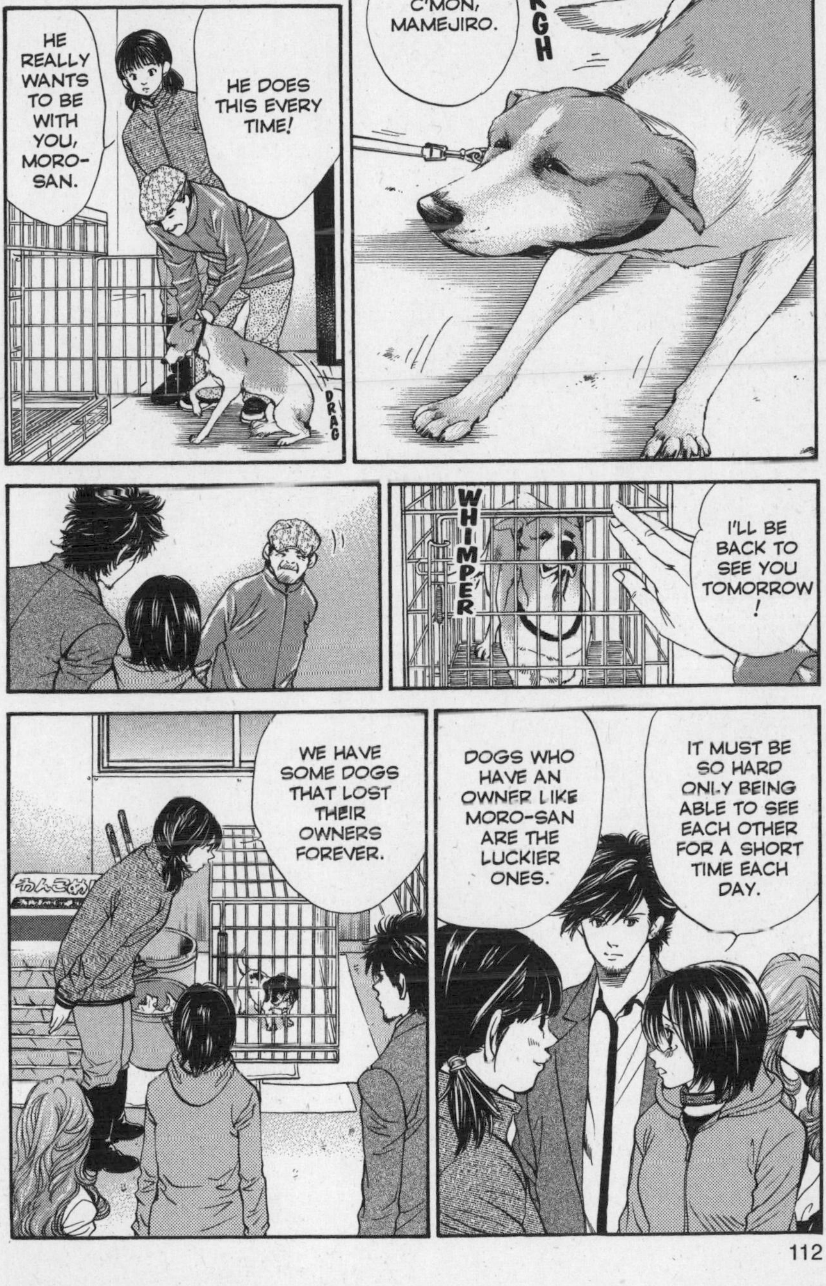
C'MON, MAMEJIRO.
URGH
HE DOES THIS EVERY TIME!
HE REALLY WANTS TO BE WITH YOU, MORO-SAN.
DRAG
I'LL BE BACK TO SEE YOU TOMORROW!
WHIMPER
IT MUST BE SO HARD ONLY BEING ABLE TO SEE EACH OTHER FOR A SHORT TIME EACH DAY.
DOGS WHO HAVE AN OWNER LIKE MORO-SAN ARE THE LUCKIER ONES.
WE HAVE SOME DOGS THAT LOST THEIR OWNERS FOREVER.

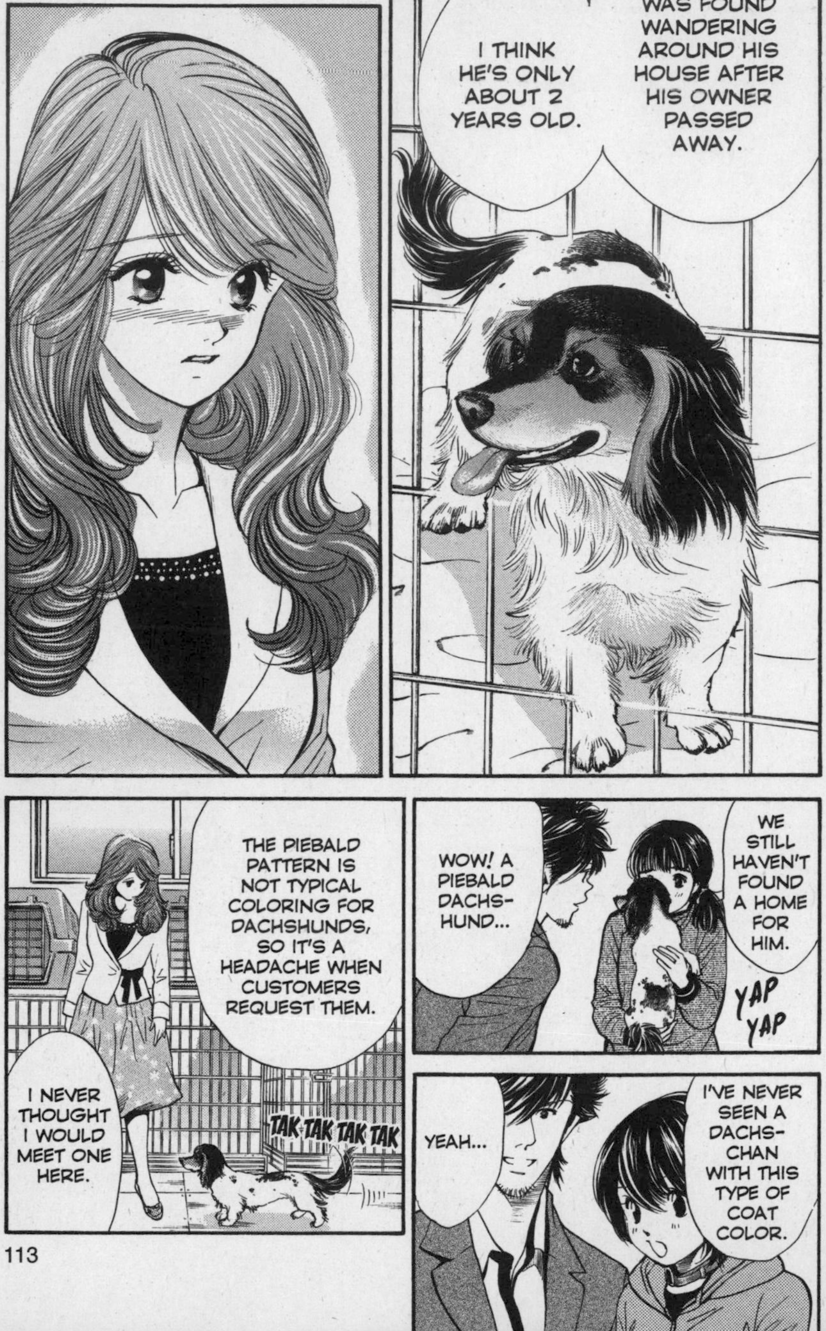
THIS DOG WAS FOUND WANDERING AROUND HIS HOUSE AFTER HIS OWNER PASSED AWAY.
I THINK HE'S ONLY ABOUT 2 YEARS OLD.
WE STILL HAVEN'T FOUND A HOME FOR HIM.
WOW! A PIEBALD DACHS-HUND...
YAP YAP
I'VE NEVER SEEN A DACHS-CHAN WITH THIS TYPE OF COAT COLOR.
YEAH...
THE PIEBALD PATTERN IS NOT TYPICAL COLORING FOR DACHSHUNDS, SO IT'S A HEADACHE WHEN CUSTOMERS REQUEST THEM.
I NEVER THOUGHT I WOULD MEET ONE HERE.
TAK TAK TAK TAK

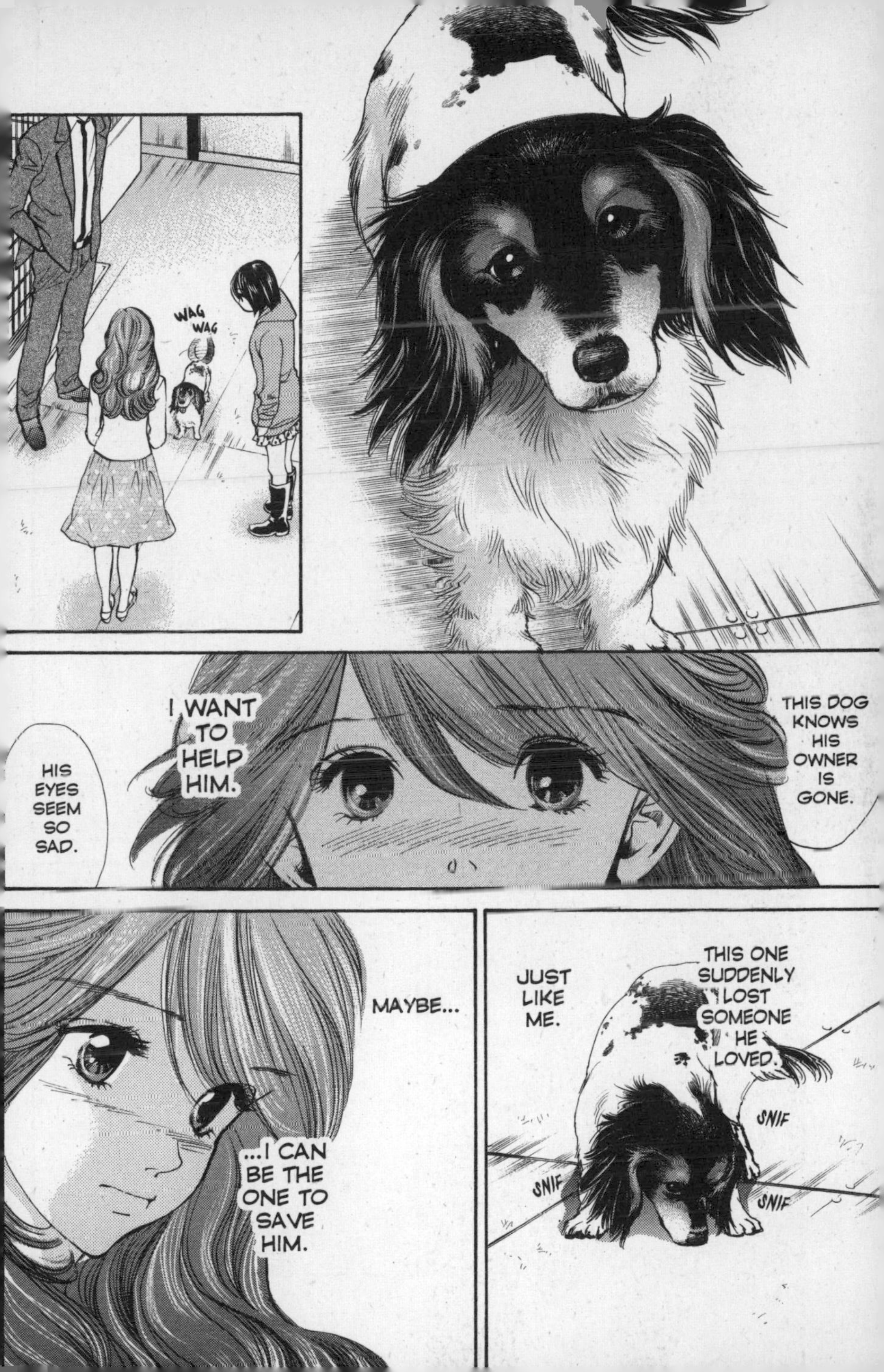
WAG WAG
THIS DOG KNOWS HIS OWNER IS GONE.
I WANT TO HELP HIM.
HIS EYES SEEM SO SAD.
THIS ONE SUDDENLY LOST SOMEONE HE LOVED.
JUST LIKE ME.
SNIF
SNIF
SNIF
MAYBE...
...I CAN BE THE ONE TO SAVE HIM.

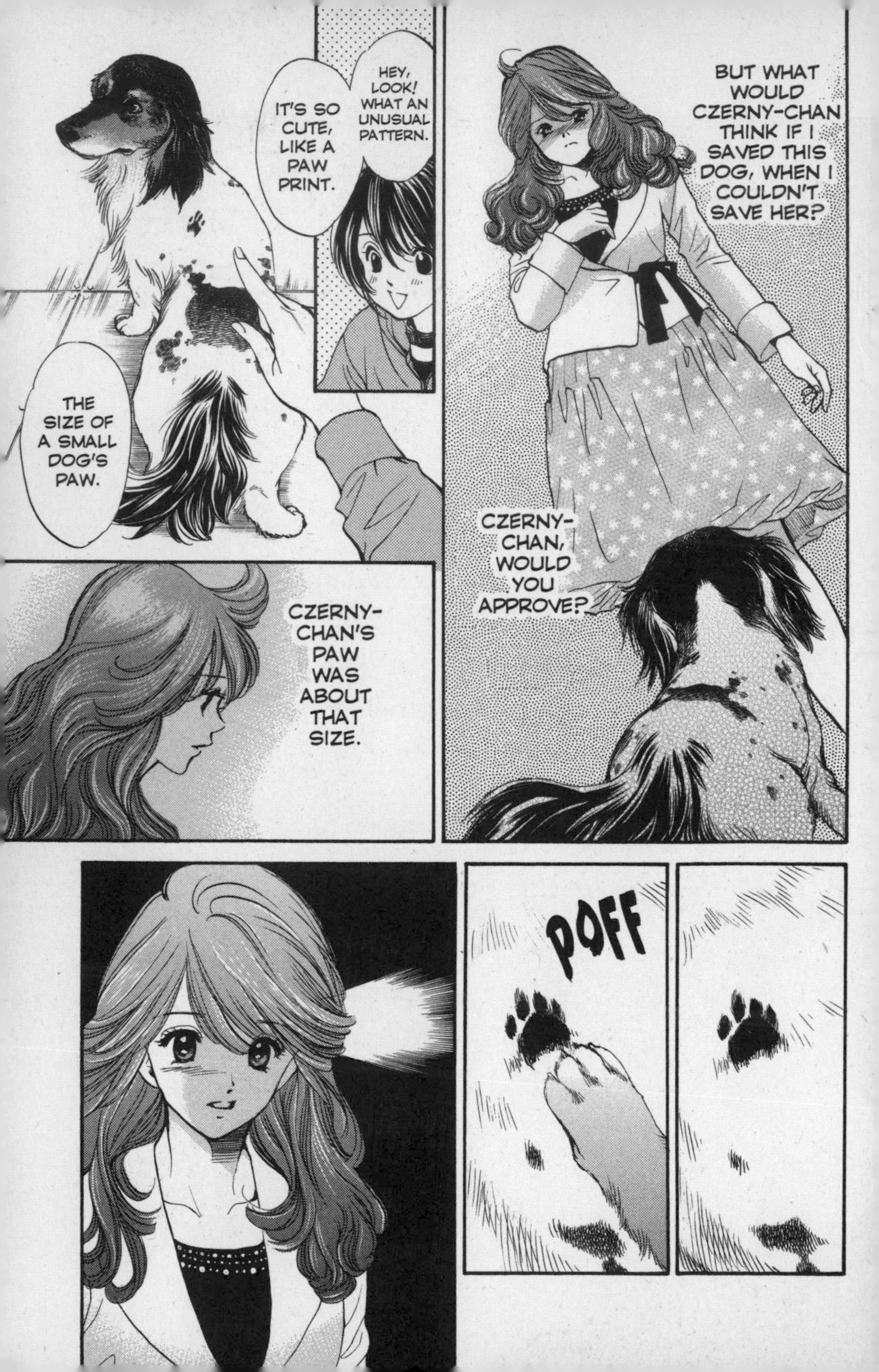
BUT WHAT WOULD CZERNY-CHAN THINK IF I SAVED THIS DOG, WHEN I COULDN'T SAVE HER?
CZERNY-CHAN, WOULD YOU APPROVE?
HEY, LOOK! WHAT AN UNUSUAL PATTERN.
IT'S SO CUTE, LIKE A PAW PRINT.
THE SIZE OF A SMALL DOG'S PAW.
CZERNY-CHAN'S PAW WAS ABOUT THAT SIZE.
POFF

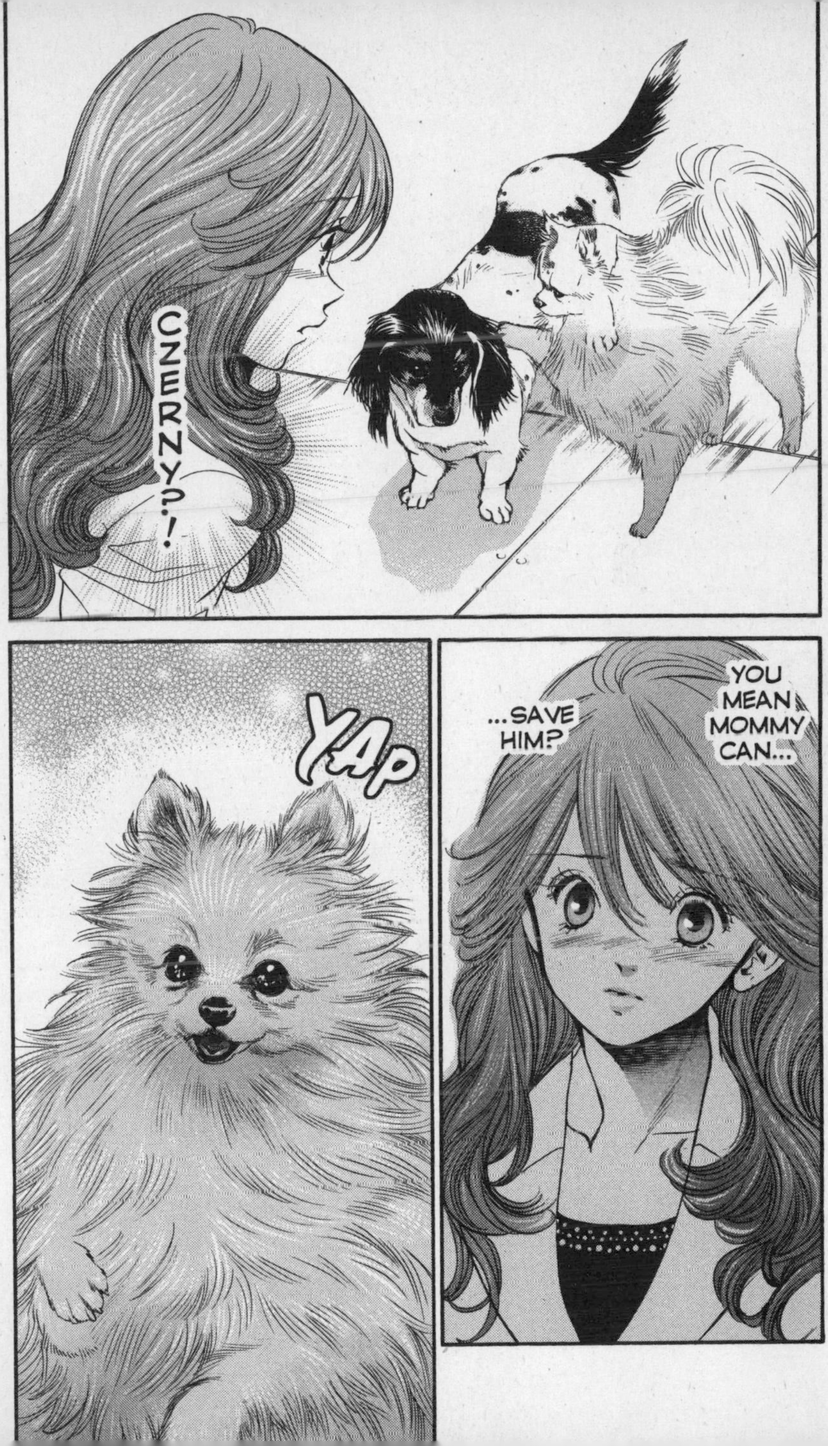
CZERNY?!
YOU MEAN MOMMY CAN...
...SAVE HIM?
YAP

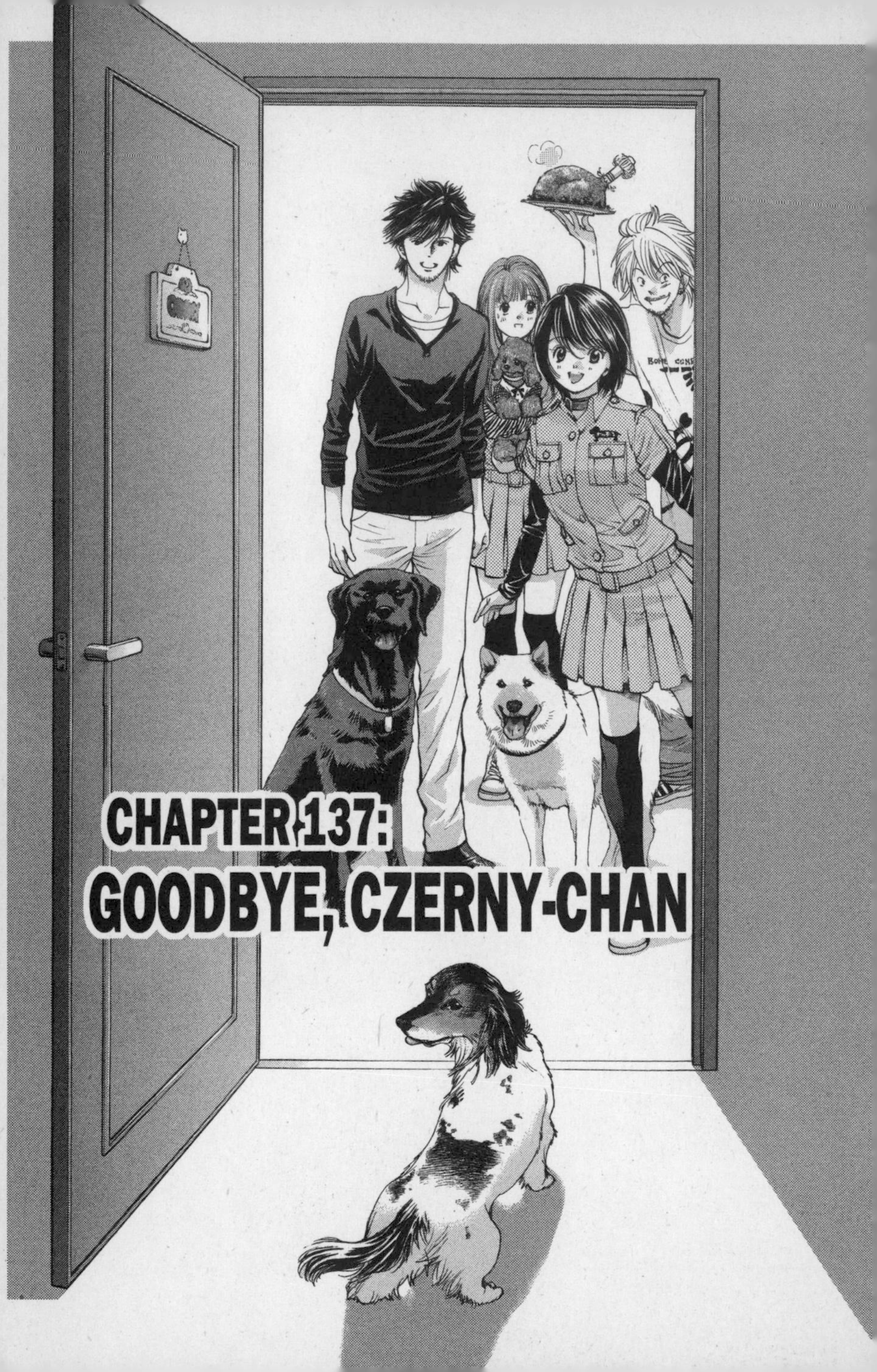

CHAPTER 137: GOODBYE, CZERNY-CHAN

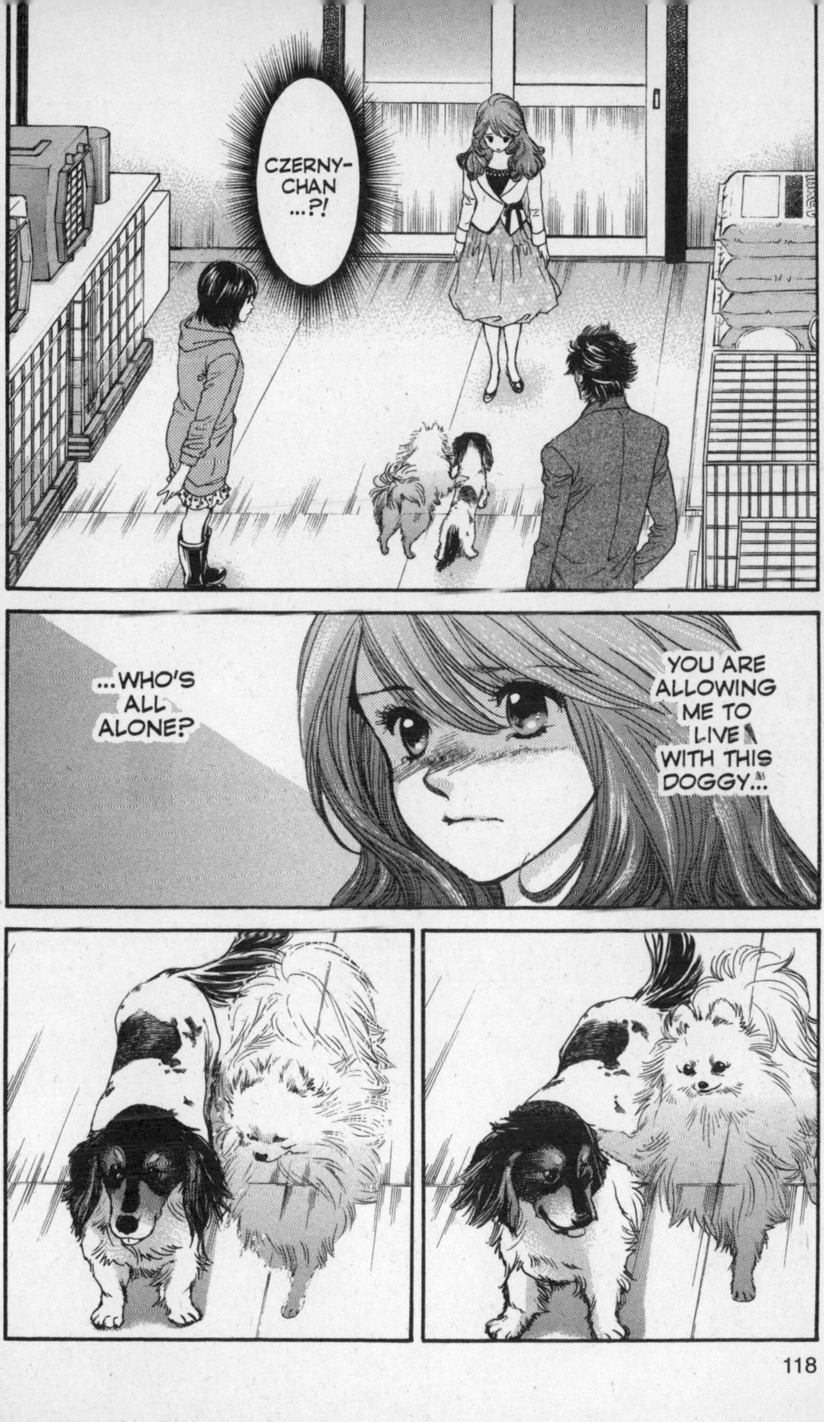
CZERNY-CHAN ...?!
YOU ARE ALLOWING ME TO LIVE WITH THIS DOGGY...
...WHO'S ALL ALONE?

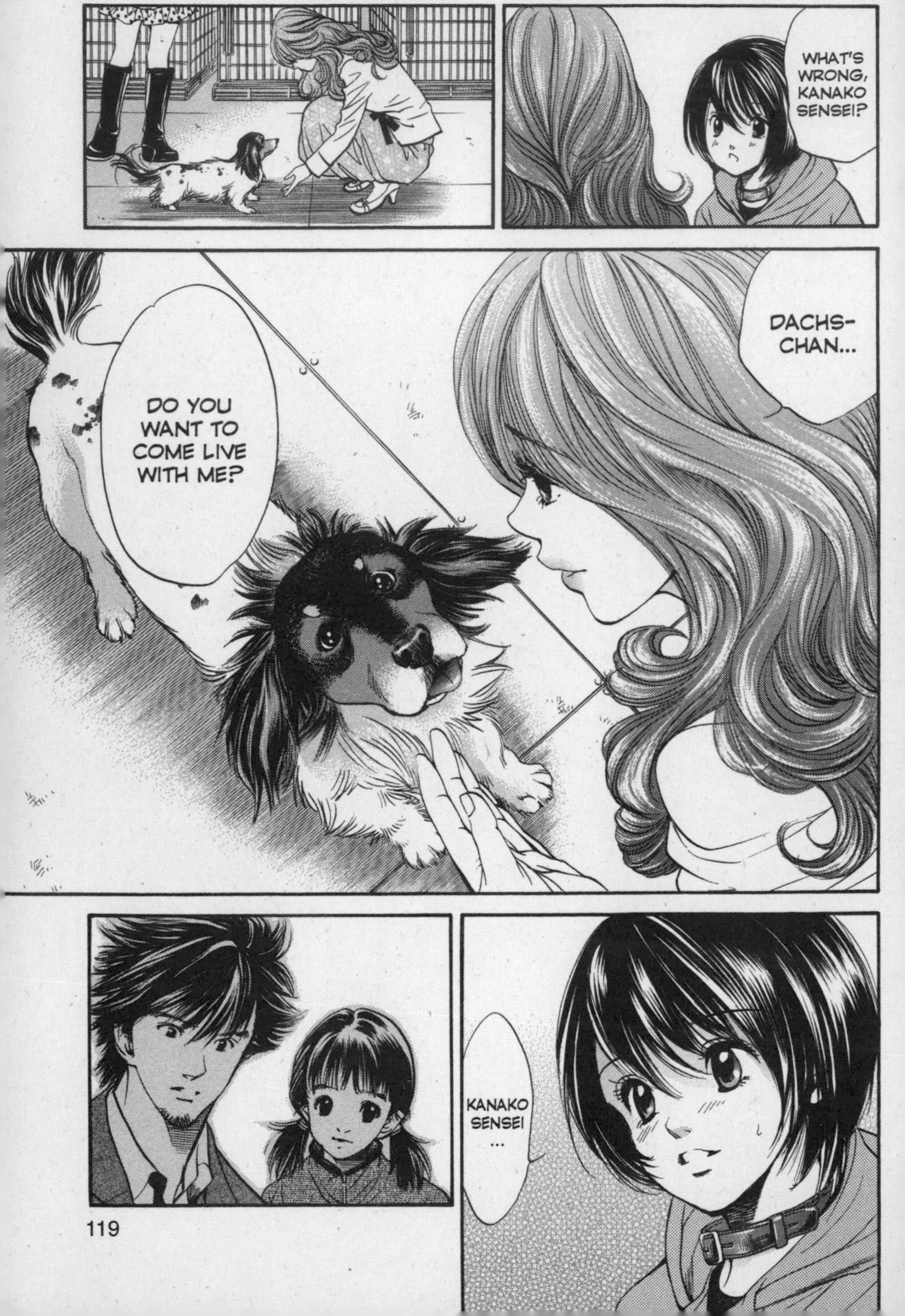
WHAT'S WRONG, KANAKO SENSEI?
DACHS-CHAN...
DO YOU WANT TO COME LIVE WITH ME?
KANAKO SENSEI ...

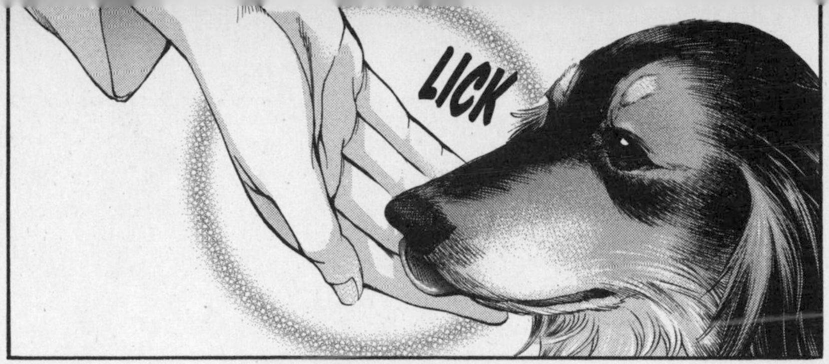
LICK
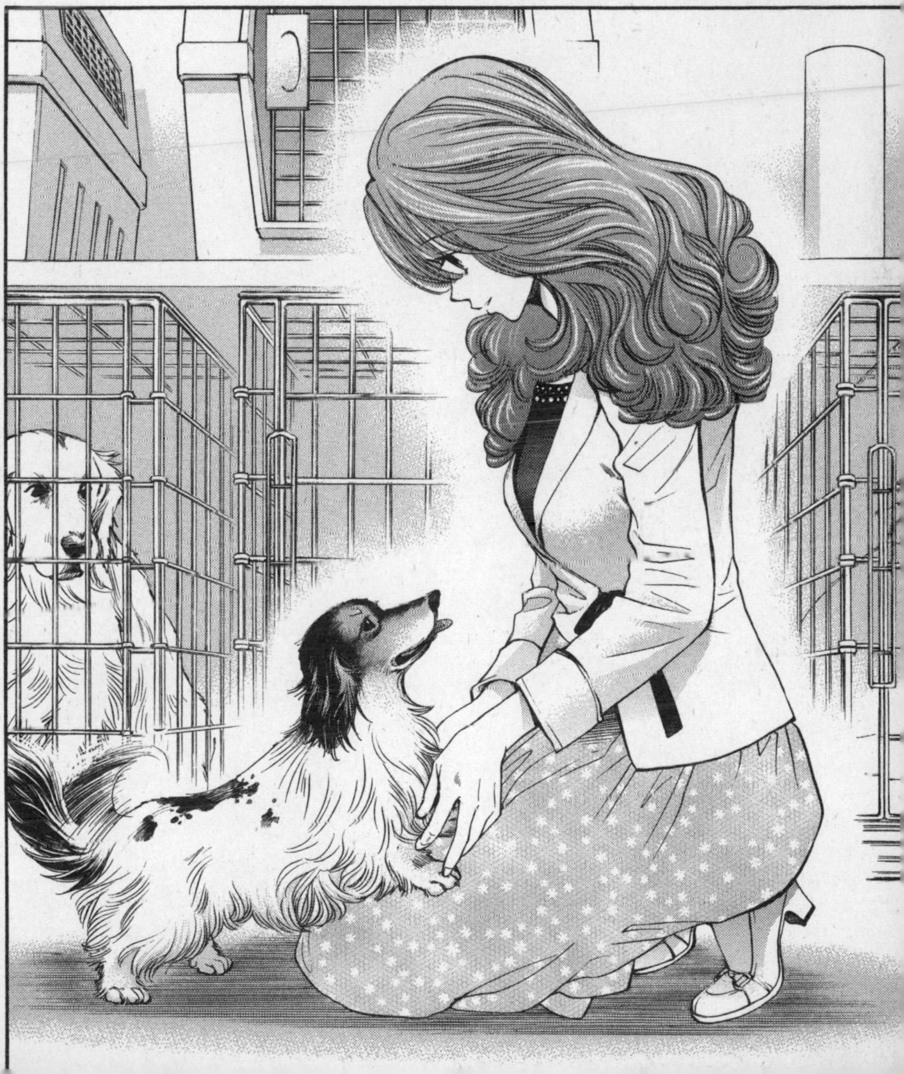

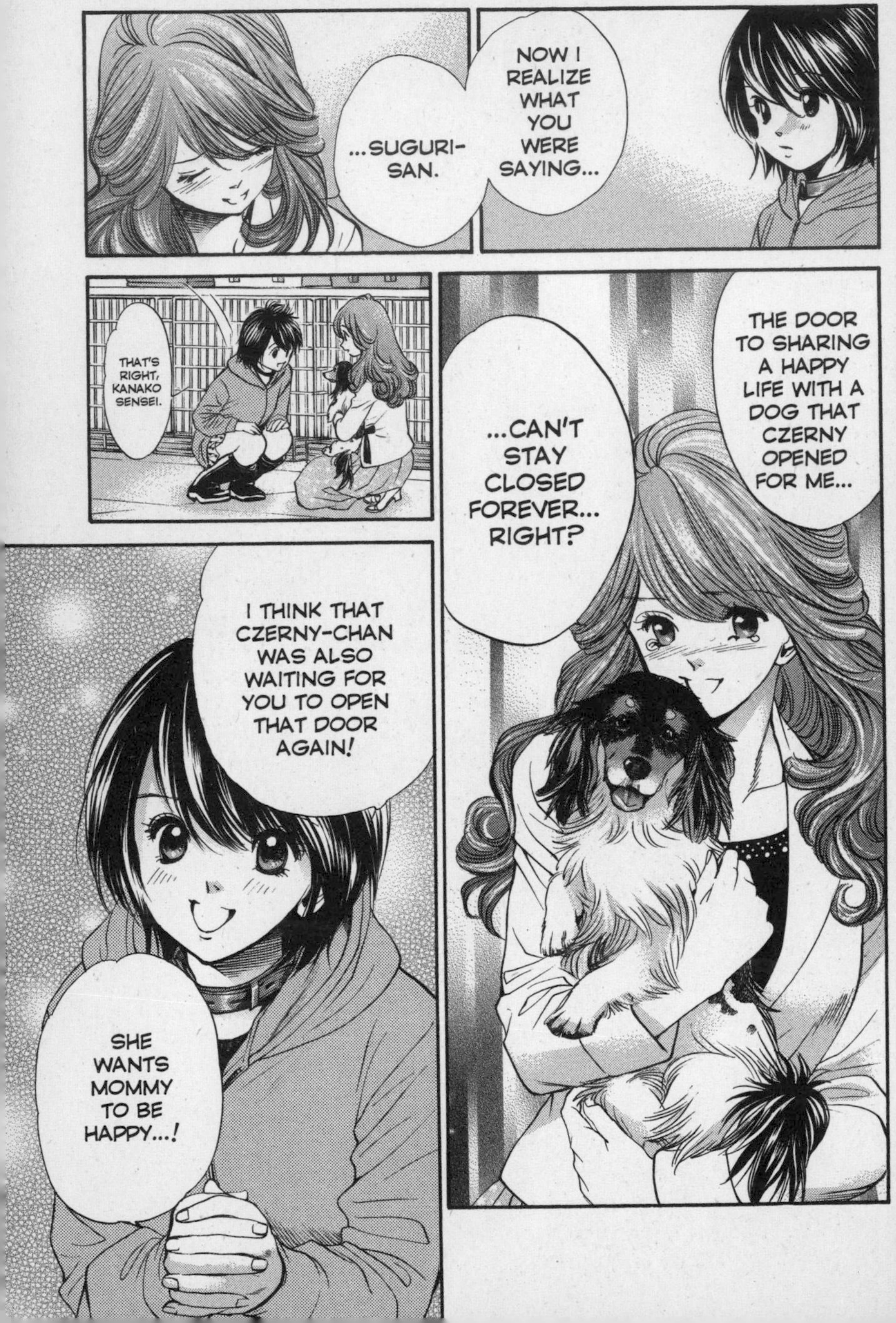
NOW I REALIZE WHAT YOU WERE SAYING...
...SUGURI-SAN.
THE DOOR TO SHARING A HAPPY LIFE WITH A DOG THAT CZERNY OPENED FOR ME...
...CAN'T STAY CLOSED FOREVER... RIGHT?
THAT'S RIGHT, KANAKO SENSEI.
I THINK THAT CZERNY-CHAN WAS ALSO WAITING FOR YOU TO OPEN THAT DOOR AGAIN!
SHE WANTS MOMMY TO BE HAPPY...!

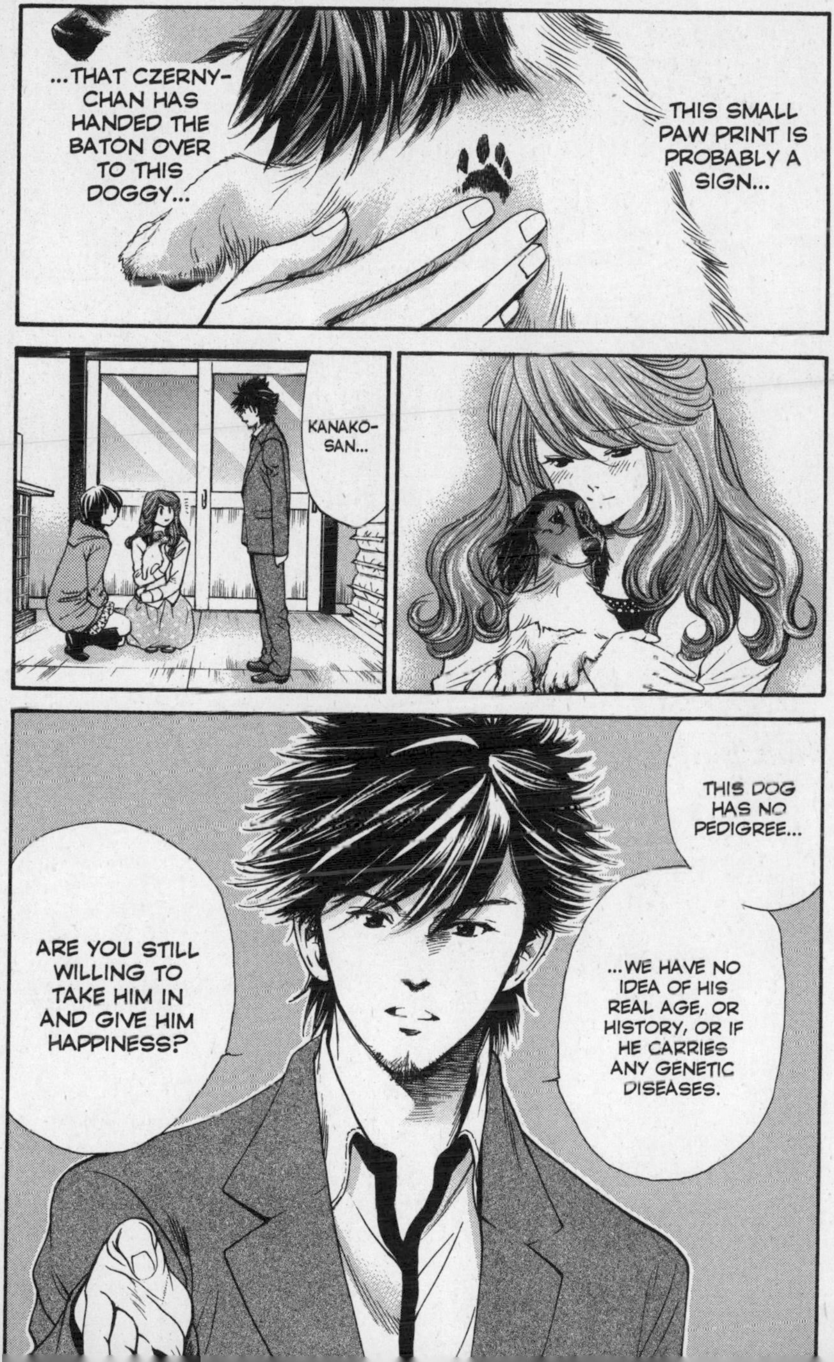
THIS SMALL PAW PRINT IS PROBABLY A SIGN...
...THAT CZERNY-CHAN HAS HANDED THE BATON OVER TO THIS DOGGY...
KANAKO-SAN...
THIS DOG HAS NO PEDIGREE...
...WE HAVE NO IDEA OF HIS REAL AGE, OR HISTORY, OR IF HE CARRIES ANY GENETIC DISEASES.
ARE YOU STILL WILLING TO TAKE HIM IN AND GIVE HIM HAPPINESS?

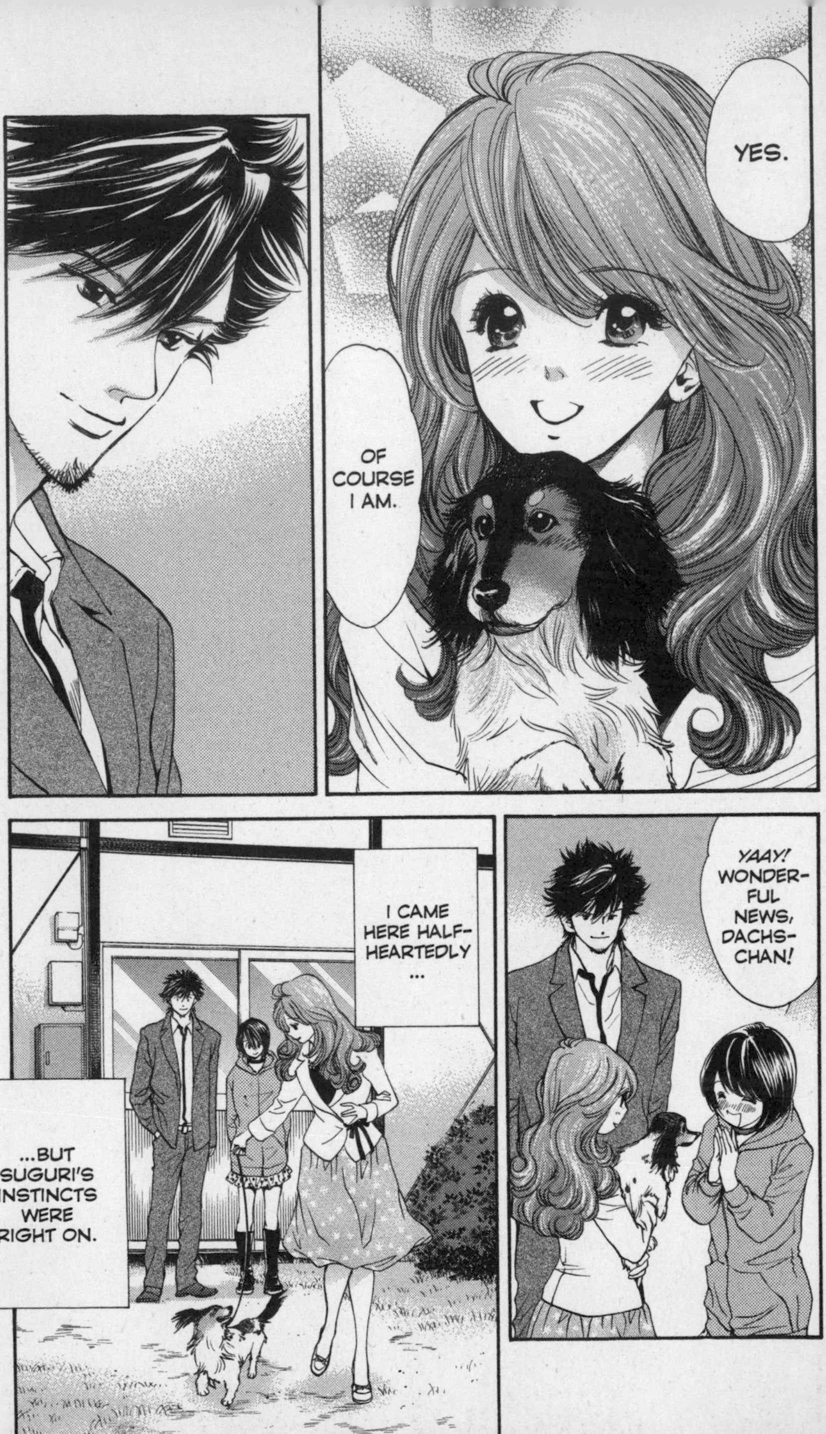
YES.
OF COURSE I AM.
YAAY! WONDERFUL NEWS, DACHS-CHAN!
I CAME HERE HALF-HEARTEDLY...
...BUT SUGURI'S INSTINCTS WERE RIGHT ON.

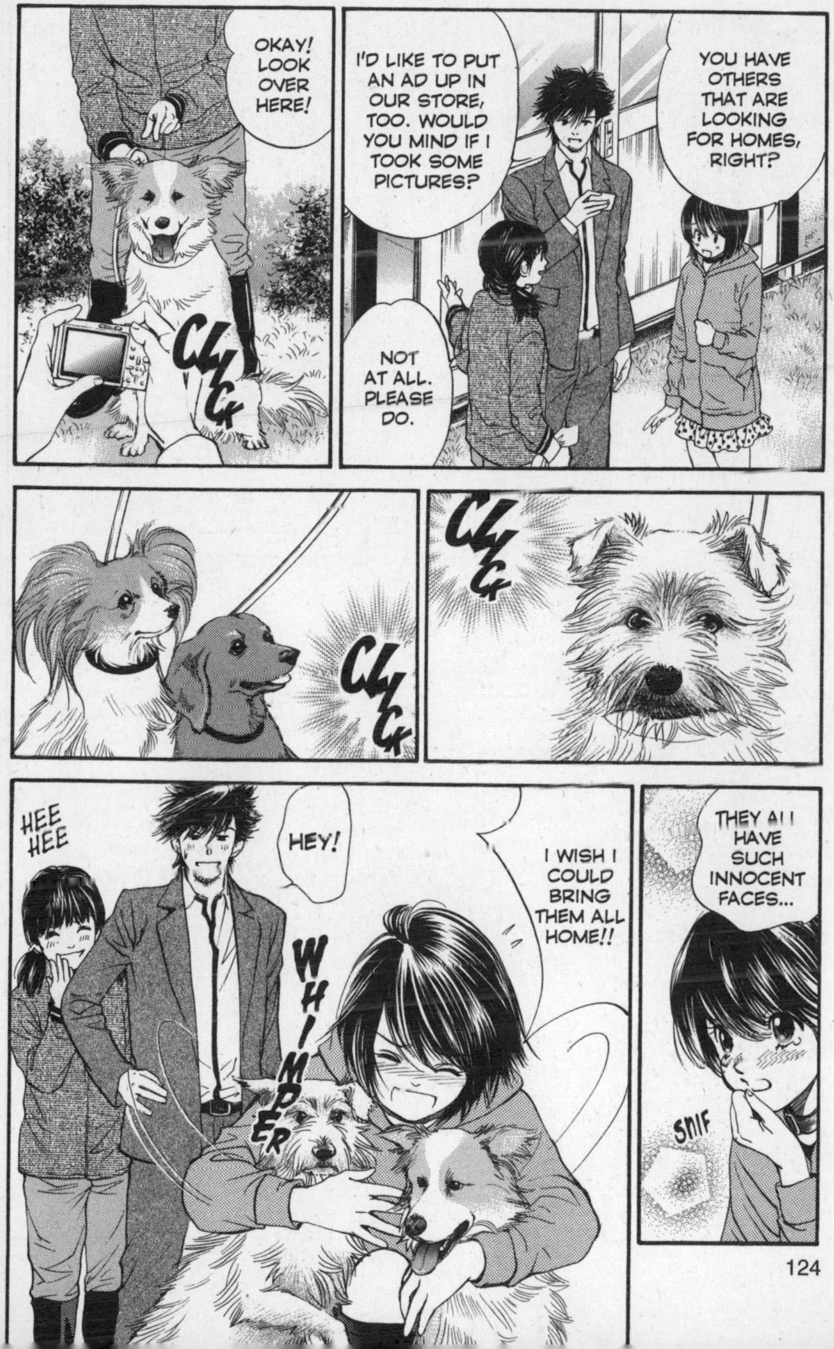
YOU HAVE OTHERS THAT ARE LOOKING FOR HOMES, RIGHT?
I'D LIKE TO PUT AN AD UP IN OUR STORE, TOO. WOULD YOU MIND IF I TOOK SOME PICTURES?
NOT AT ALL. PLEASE DO.
OKAY! LOOK OVER HERE!
CLICK
CLICK
CLICK
THEY ALL HAVE SUCH INNOCENT FACES...
SNIF
I WISH I COULD BRING THEM ALL HOME!!
HEY!
HEE HEE
WHIMPER

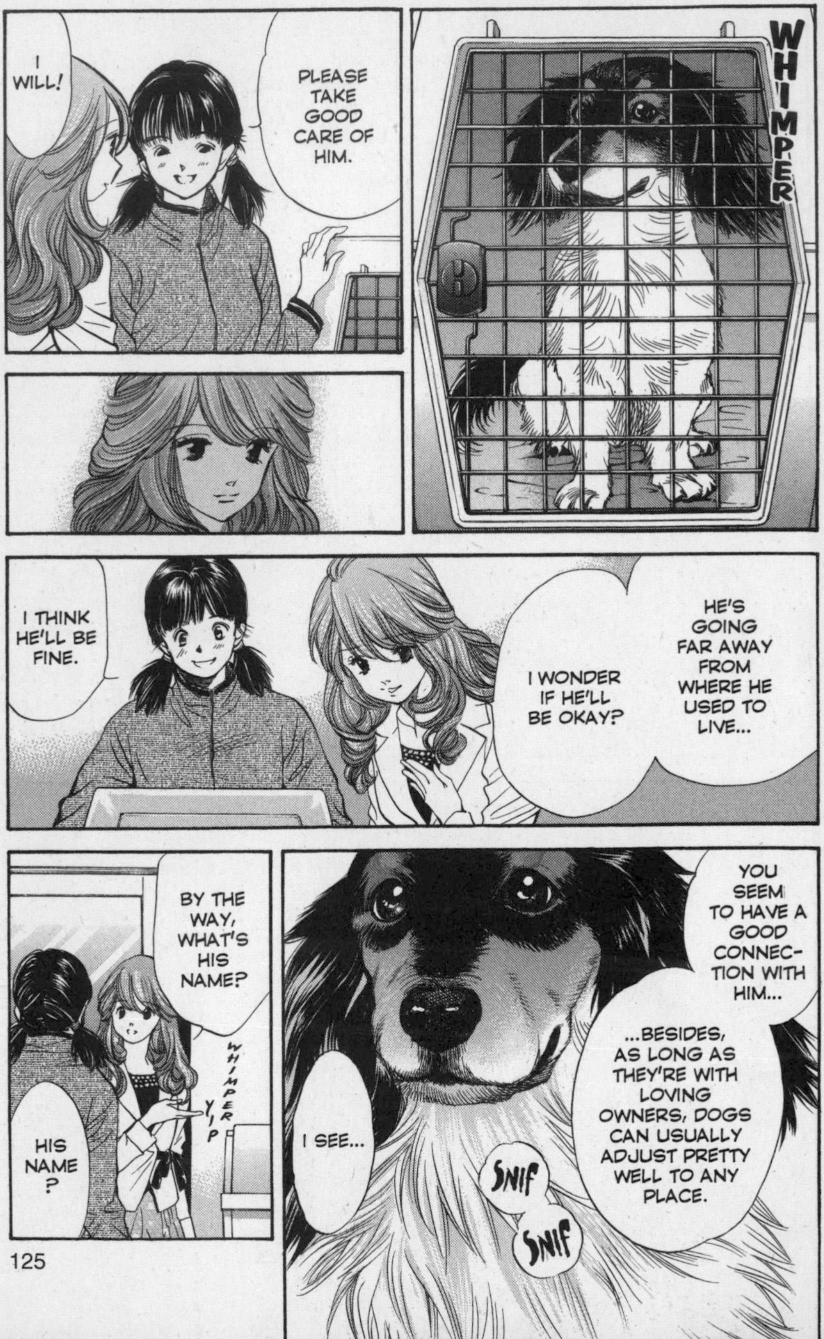
WHIMPER
PLEASE TAKE GOOD CARE OF HIM.
I WILL!
HE'S GOING FAR AWAY FROM WHERE HE USED TO LIVE...
I WONDER IF HE'LL BE OKAY?
I THINK HE'LL BE FINE.
YOU SEEM TO HAVE A GOOD CONNECTION WITH HIM...
...BESIDES, AS LONG AS THEY'RE WITH LOVING OWNERS, DOGS CAN USUALLY ADJUST PRETTY WELL TO ANY PLACE.
I SEE...
SNIF
SNIF
BY THE WAY, WHAT'S HIS NAME?
WHIMPER
YIP
HIS NAME?

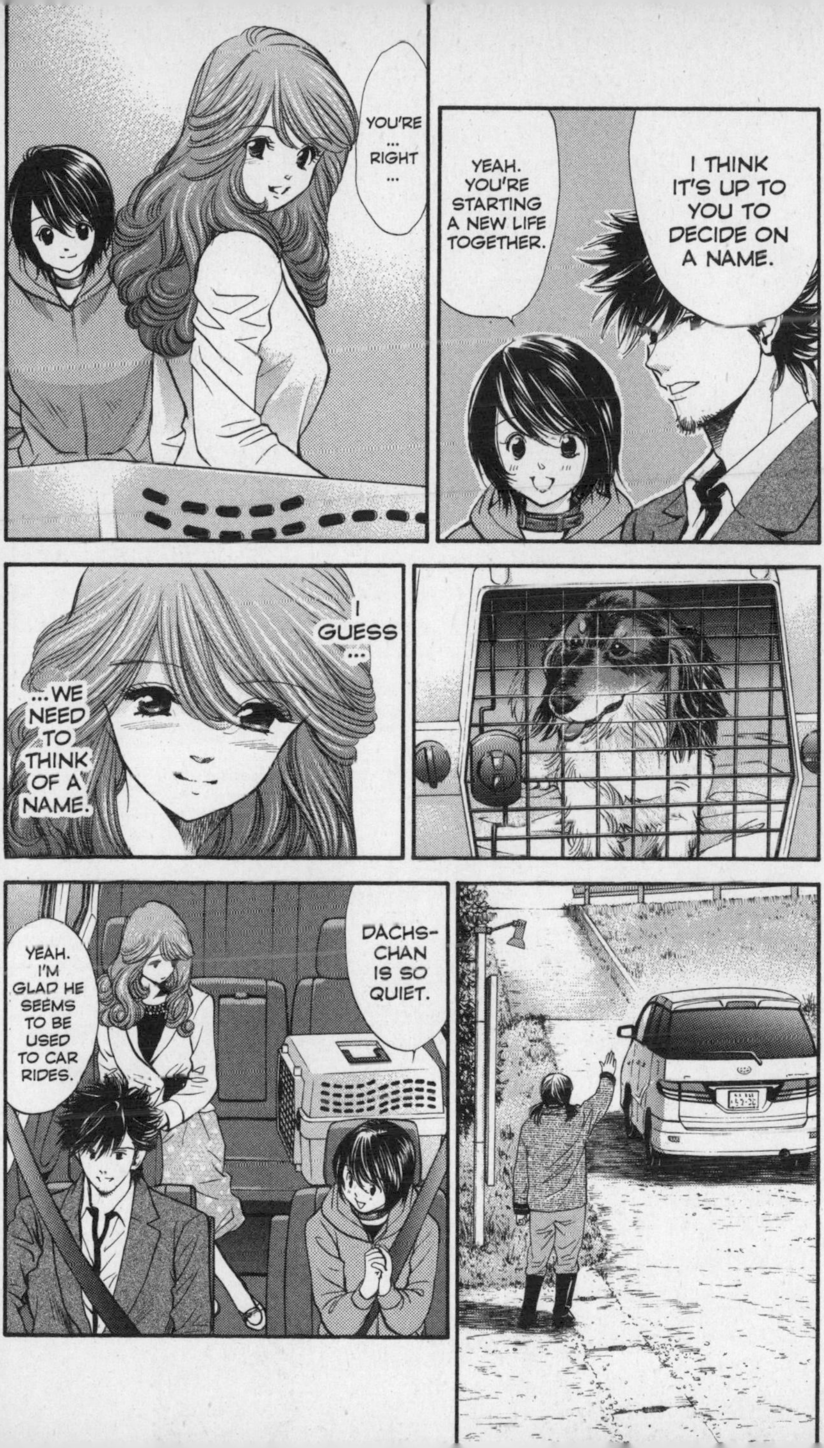
I THINK IT'S UP TO YOU TO DECIDE ON A NAME.
YEAH. YOU'RE STARTING A NEW LIFE TOGETHER.
YOU'RE ... RIGHT ...
I GUESS ...
...WE NEED TO THINK OF A NAME.
DACHS-CHAN IS SO QUIET.
YEAH. I'M GLAD HE SEEMS TO BE USED TO CAR RIDES.

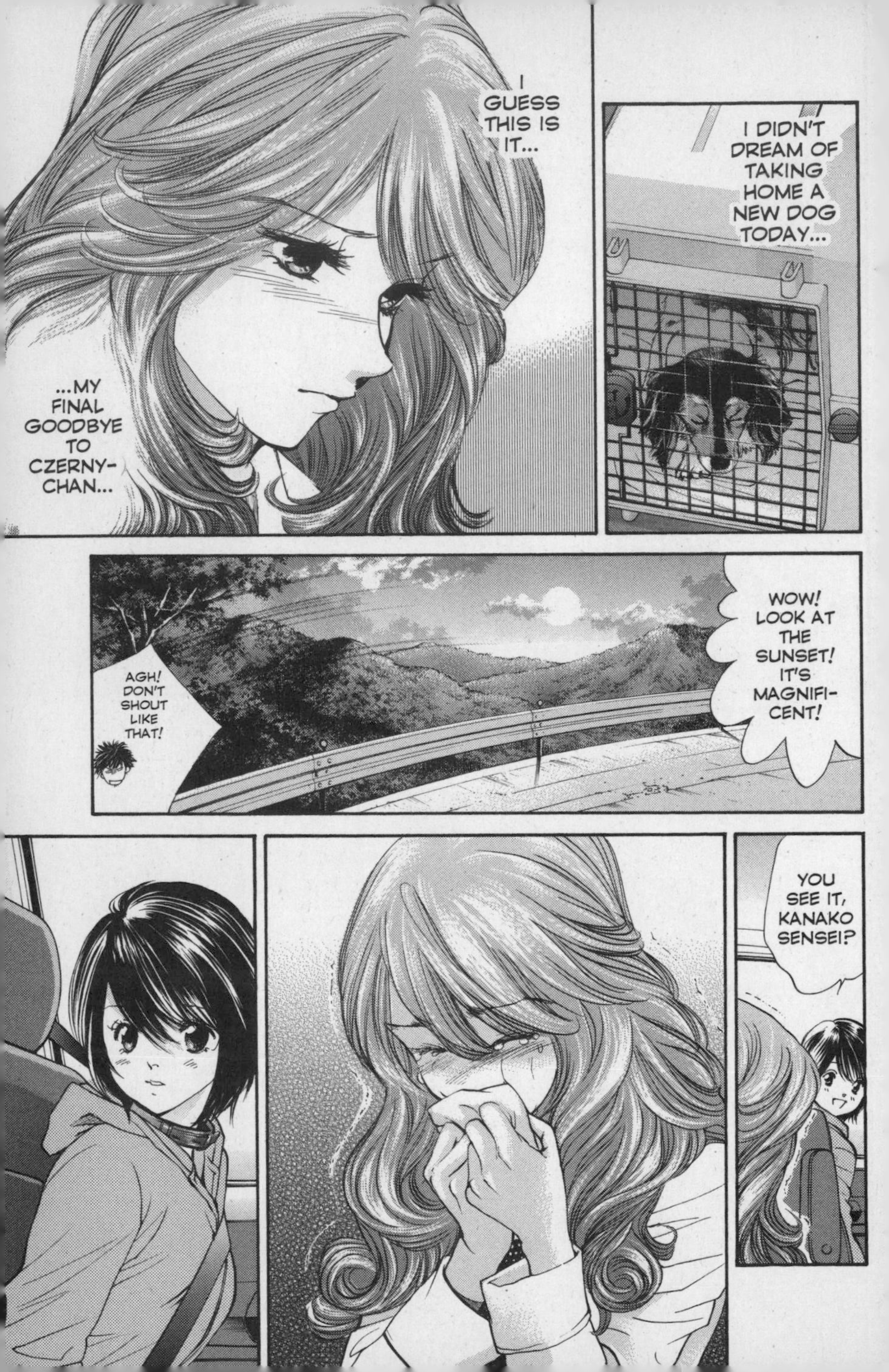
I DIDN'T DREAM OF TAKING HOME A NEW DOG TODAY...
I GUESS THIS IS IT...
...MY FINAL GOODBYE TO CZERNY-CHAN...
WOW! LOOK AT THE SUNSET! IT'S MAGNIFI-CENT!
AGH! DON'T SHOUT LIKE THAT!
YOU SEE IT, KANAKO SENSEI?

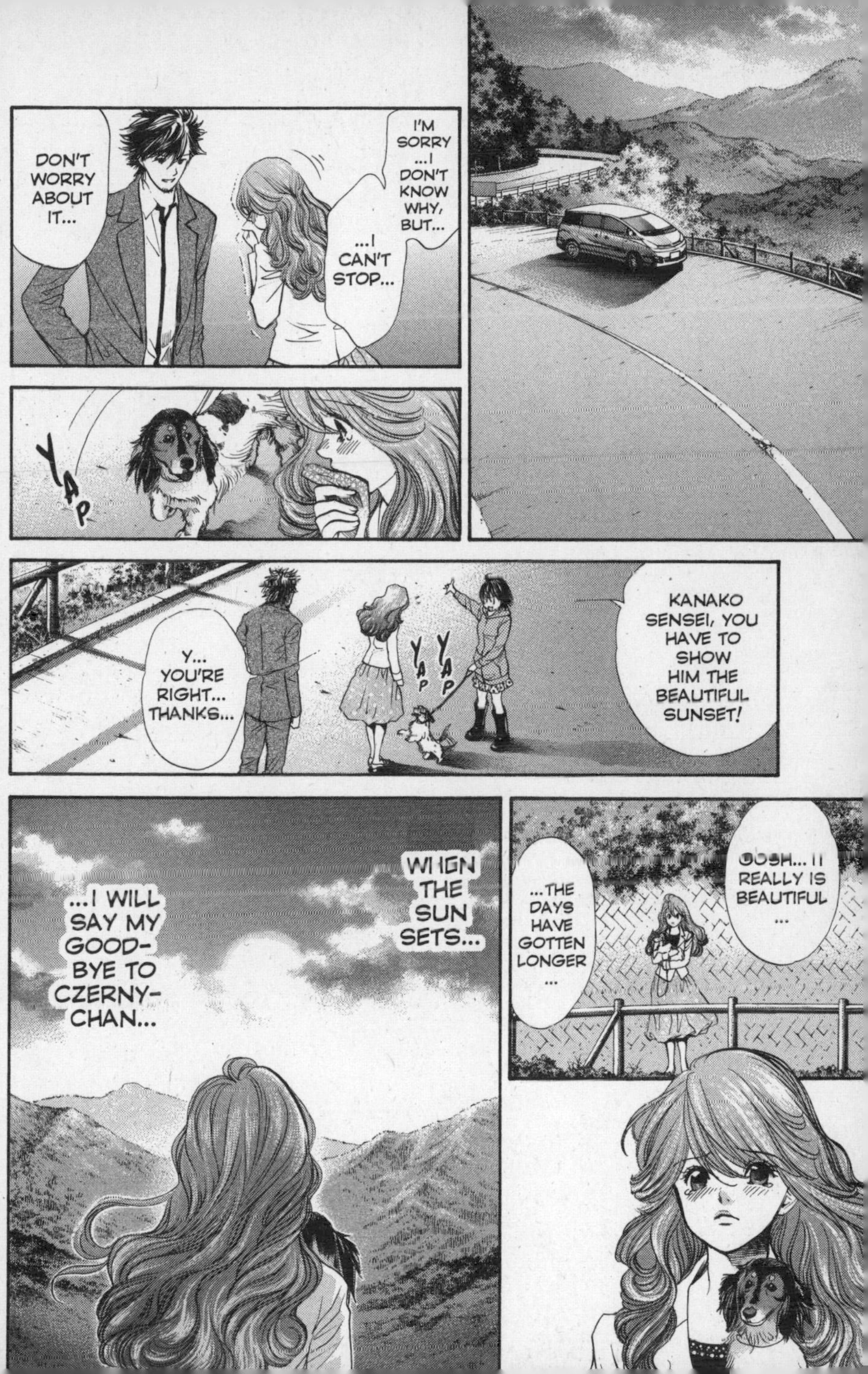
I'M SORRY ...I DON'T KNOW WHY, BUT...
...I CAN'T STOP...
DON'T WORRY ABOUT IT...
YAP
KANAKO SENSEI, YOU HAVE TO SHOW HIM THE BEAUTIFUL SUNSET!
YAP YAP
Y... YOU'RE RIGHT... THANKS...
GOSH... IT REALLY IS BEAUTIFUL...
...THE DAYS HAVE GOTTEN LONGER...
WHEN THE SUN SETS...
...I WILL SAY MY GOOD-BYE TO CZERNY-CHAN...

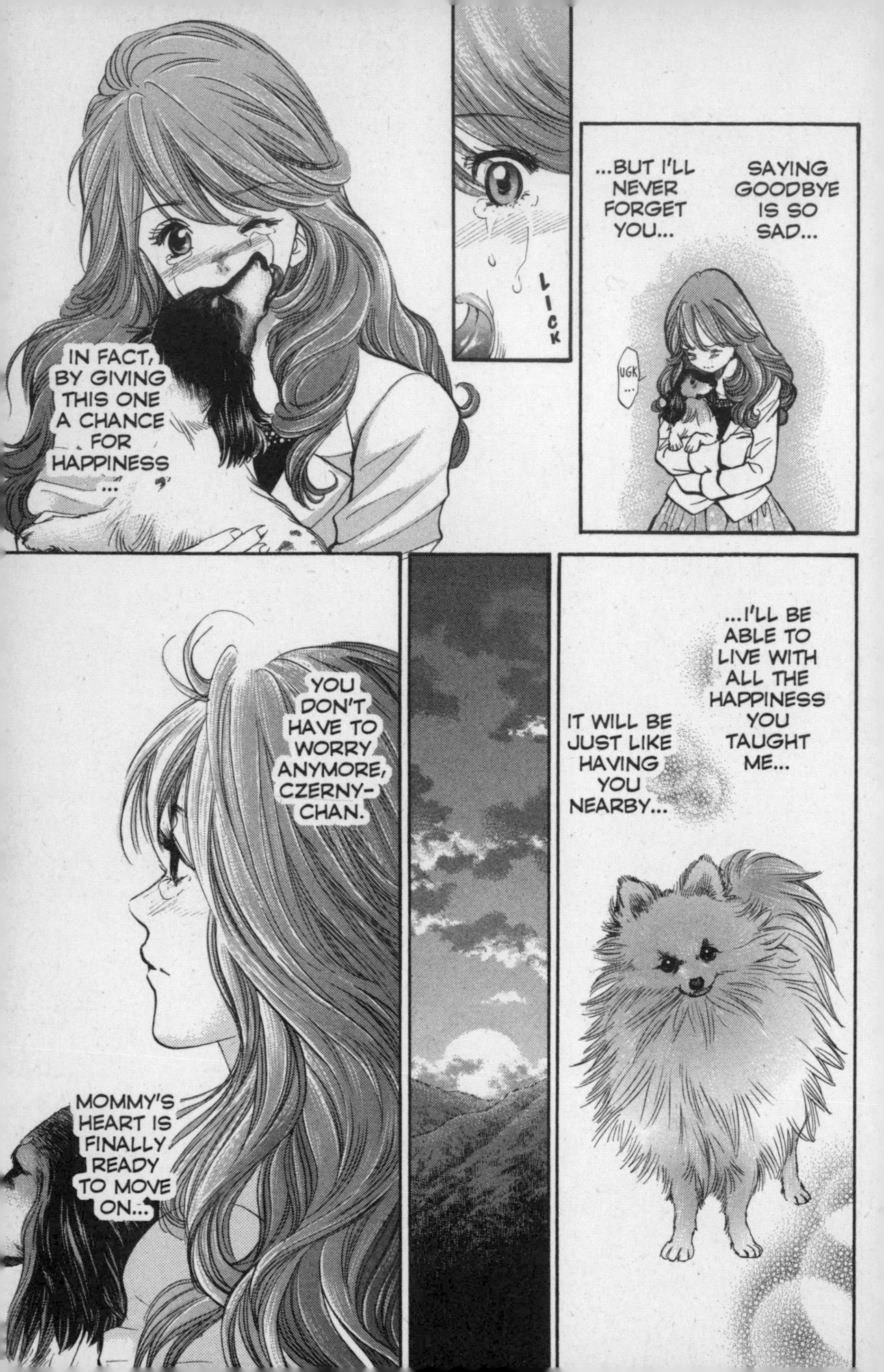
SAYING GOODBYE IS SO SAD...
...BUT I'LL NEVER FORGET YOU...
UGK...
LICK
IN FACT, BY GIVING THIS ONE A CHANCE FOR HAPPINESS...
...I'LL BE ABLE TO LIVE WITH ALL THE HAPPINESS YOU TAUGHT ME...
IT WILL BE JUST LIKE HAVING YOU NEARBY...
YOU DON'T HAVE TO WORRY ANYMORE, CZERNY-CHAN.
MOMMY'S HEART IS FINALLY READY TO MOVE ON...

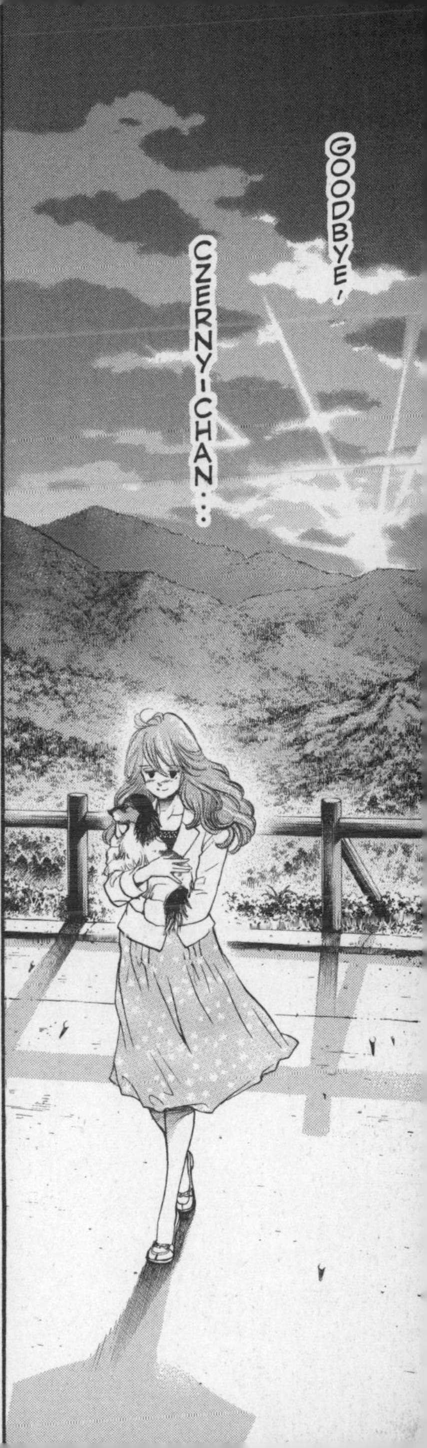
GOODBYE,
CZERNYI-CHAN...

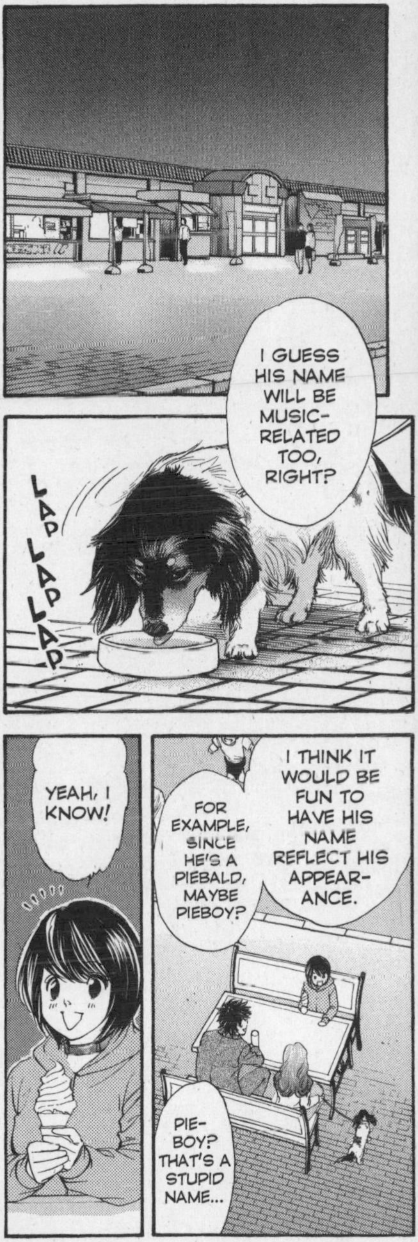
I GUESS HIS NAME WILL BE MUSIC-RELATED TOO, RIGHT?
LAP LAP LAP LAP
I THINK IT WOULD BE FUN TO HAVE HIS NAME REFLECT HIS APPEARANCE.
FOR EXAMPLE, SINCE HE'S A PIEBALD, MAYBE PIEBOY?
PIE-BOY? THAT'S A STUPID NAME...
YEAH, I KNOW!

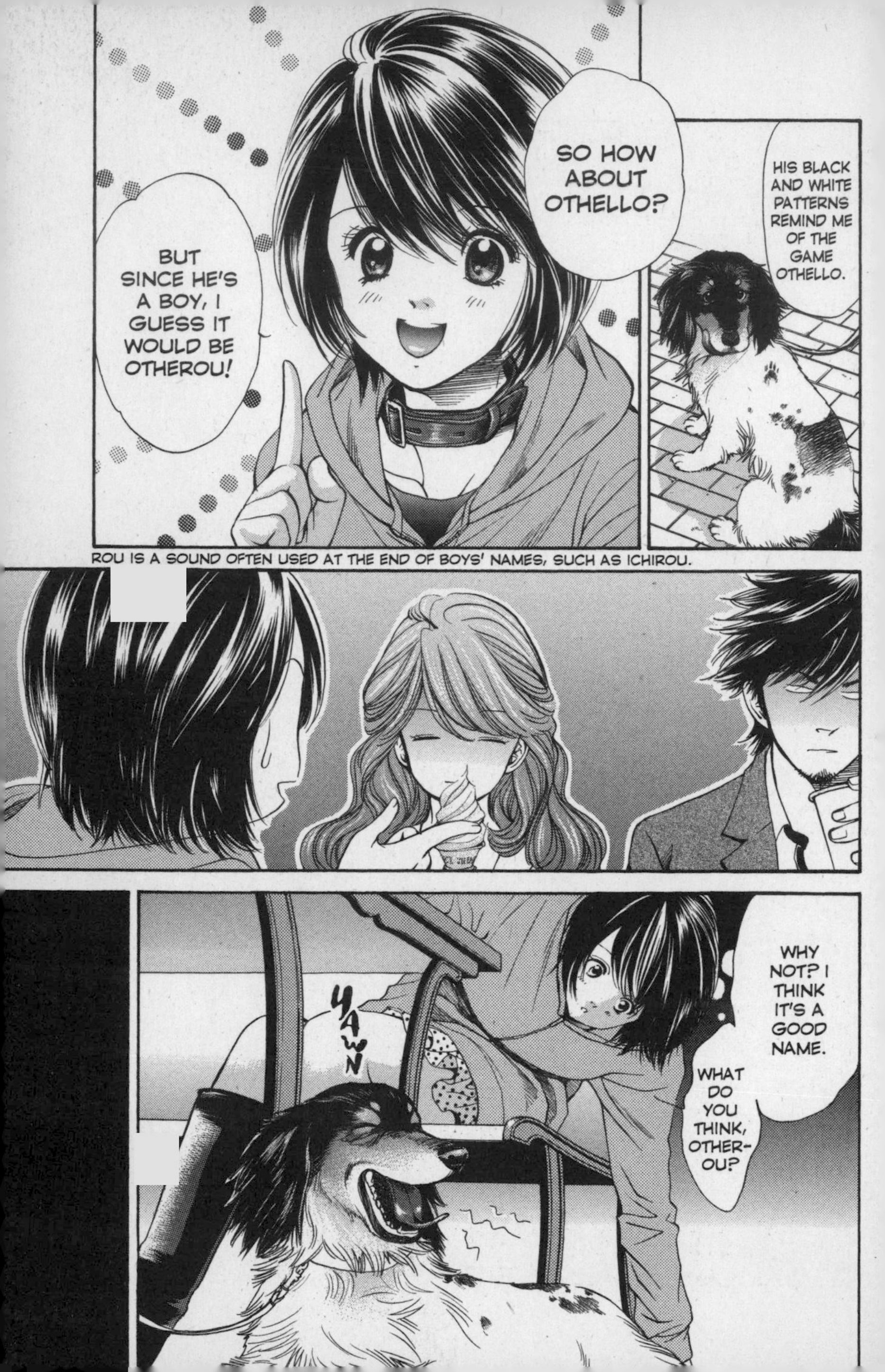
HIS BLACK AND WHITE PATTERNS REMIND ME OF THE GAME OTHELLO.
SO HOW ABOUT OTHELLO?
BUT SINCE HE'S A BOY, I GUESS IT WOULD BE OTHEROU!
ROU IS A SOUND OFTEN USED AT THE END OF BOYS' NAMES, SUCH AS ICHIROU.
WHY NOT? I THINK IT'S A GOOD NAME.
WHAT DO YOU THINK, OTHER-OU?
YAWN

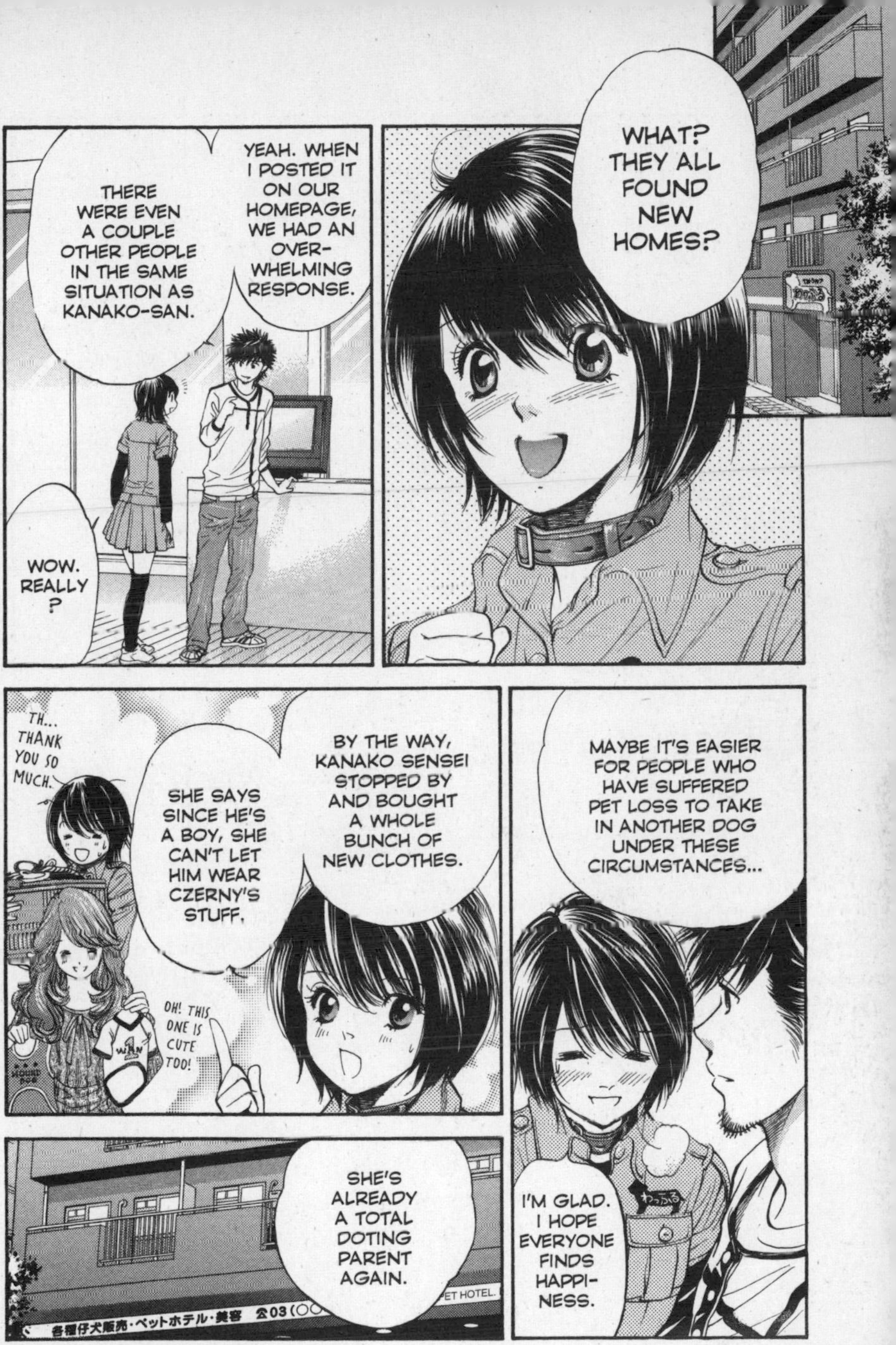
WHAT? THEY ALL FOUND NEW HOMES?
YEAH. WHEN I POSTED IT ON OUR HOMEPAGE, WE HAD AN OVER-WHELMING RESPONSE.
THERE WERE EVEN A COUPLE OTHER PEOPLE IN THE SAME SITUATION AS KANAKO-SAN.
WOW. REALLY?
MAYBE IT'S EASIER FOR PEOPLE WHO HAVE SUFFERED PET LOSS TO TAKE IN ANOTHER DOG UNDER THESE CIRCUMSTANCES...
I'M GLAD. I HOPE EVERYONE FINDS HAPPI-NESS.
BY THE WAY, KANAKO SENSEI STOPPED BY AND BOUGHT A WHOLE BUNCH OF NEW CLOTHES.
SHE SAYS SINCE HE'S A BOY, SHE CAN'T LET HIM WEAR CZERNY'S STUFF.
TH... THANK YOU SO MUCH.
OH! THIS ONE IS CUTE TOO!
SHE'S ALREADY A TOTAL DOTING PARENT AGAIN.
PET HOTEL.
各種仔犬販売・ペットホテル・美容 ☎03(○○

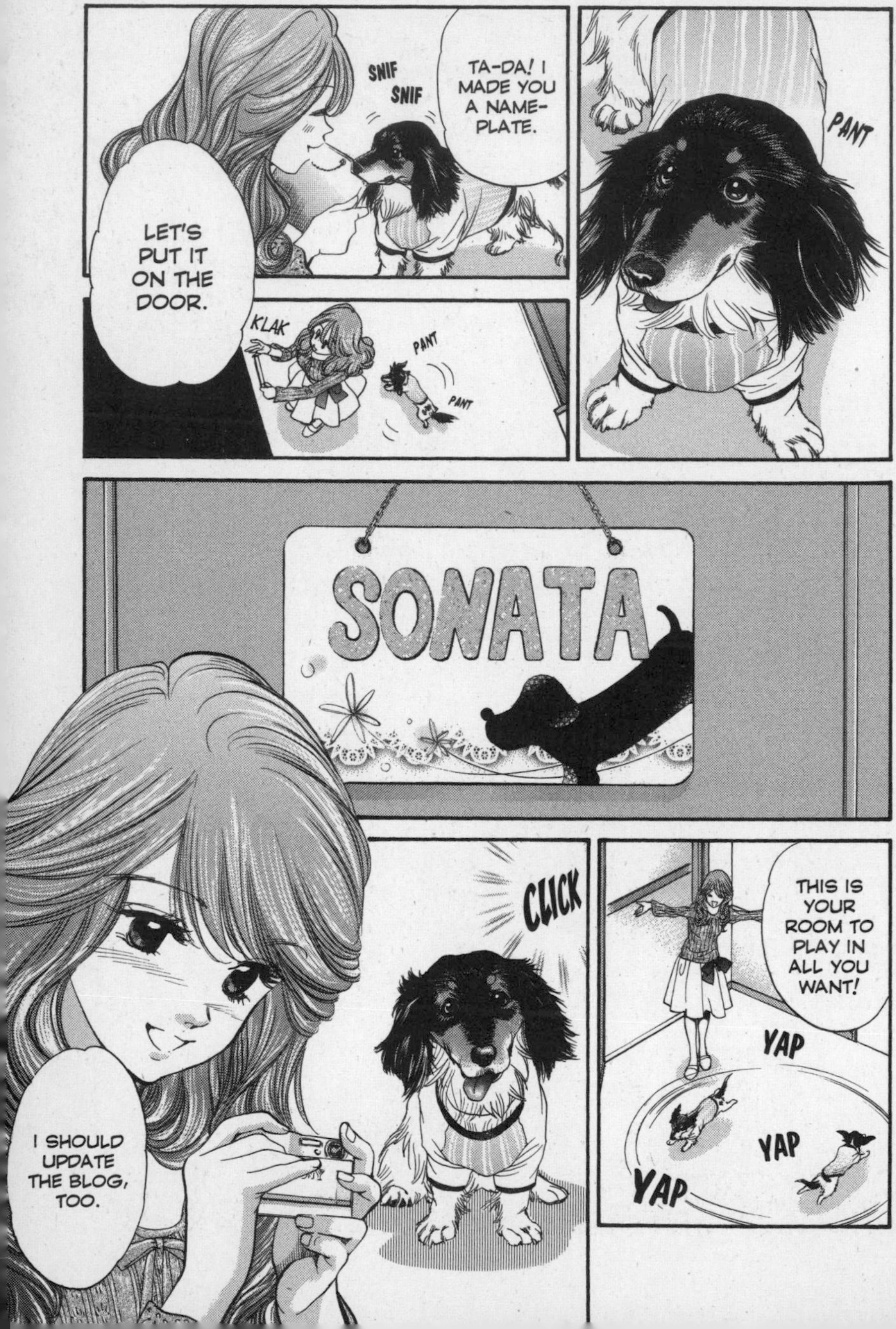
PANT
TA-DA! I MADE YOU A NAME-PLATE.
SNIF SNIF
LET'S PUT IT ON THE DOOR.
PANT
PANT
KLAK
SONATA
THIS IS YOUR ROOM TO PLAY IN ALL YOU WANT!
YAP
YAP
YAP
CLICK
I SHOULD UPDATE THE BLOG, TOO.

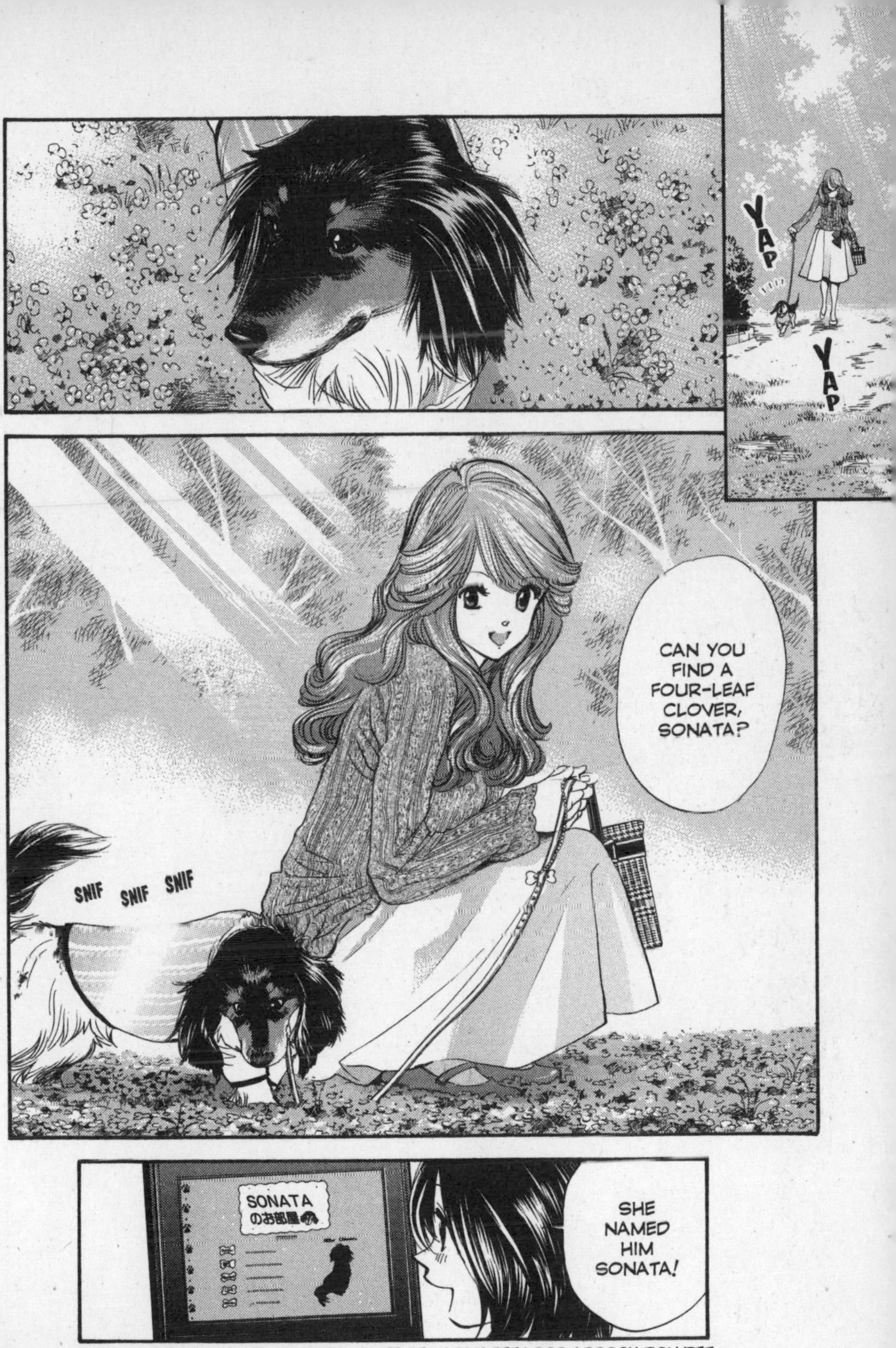
YAP
YAP
YAP
YAP
CAN YOU FIND A FOUR-LEAF CLOVER, SONATA?
SNIF SNIF SNIF
SHE NAMED HIM SONATA!
SONATA のお部屋

SPECIAL THANKS TO MR. YOSHIDA, CHIEF OF JAPAN PET LOSS ASSOCIATION/PET LOSS COUNSELOR (CH. 129 [VOL. 12] THROUGH CH. 137 [VOL. 13])

CHAPTER 138: LET'S MAKE A PHOTO BOOK

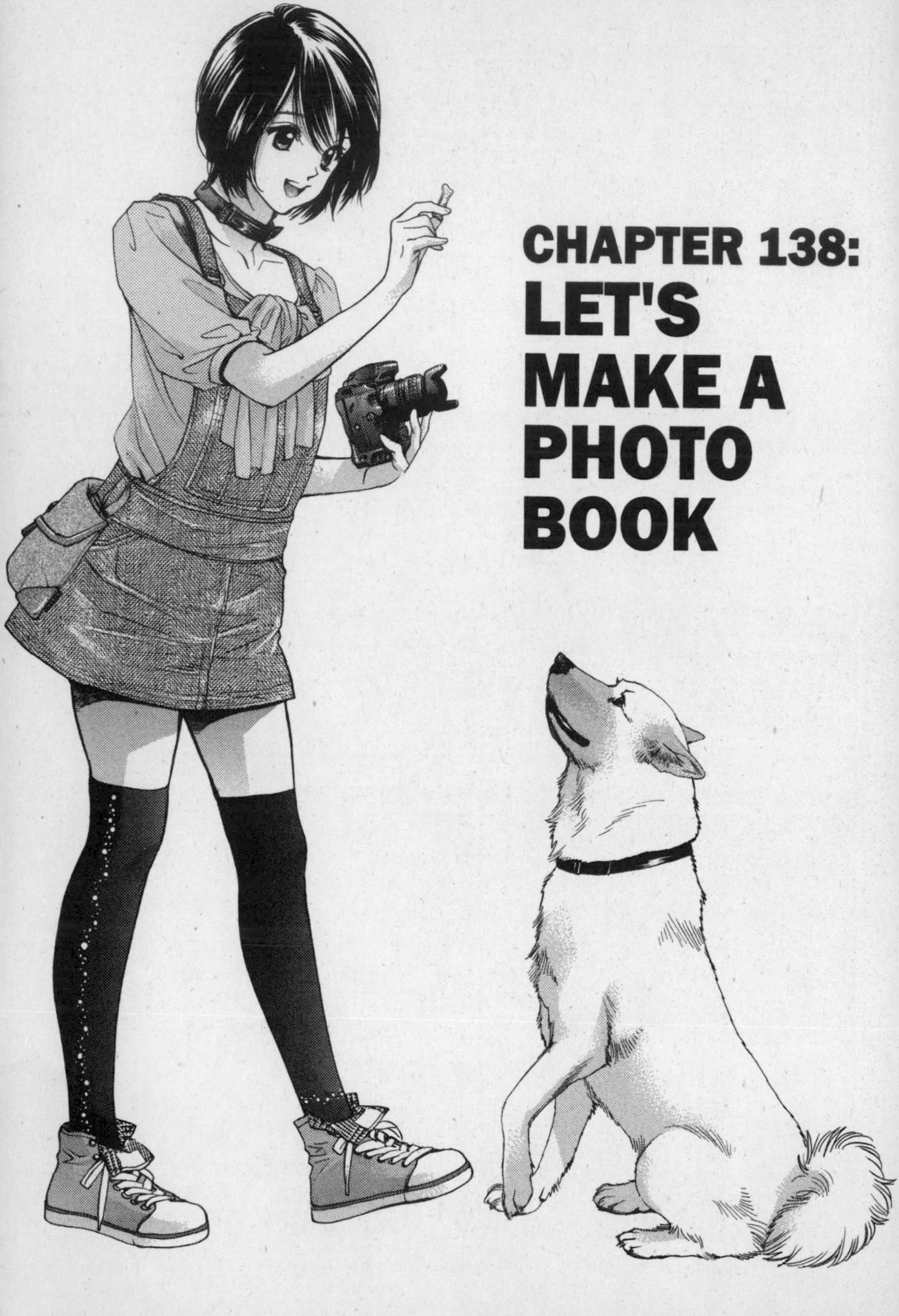

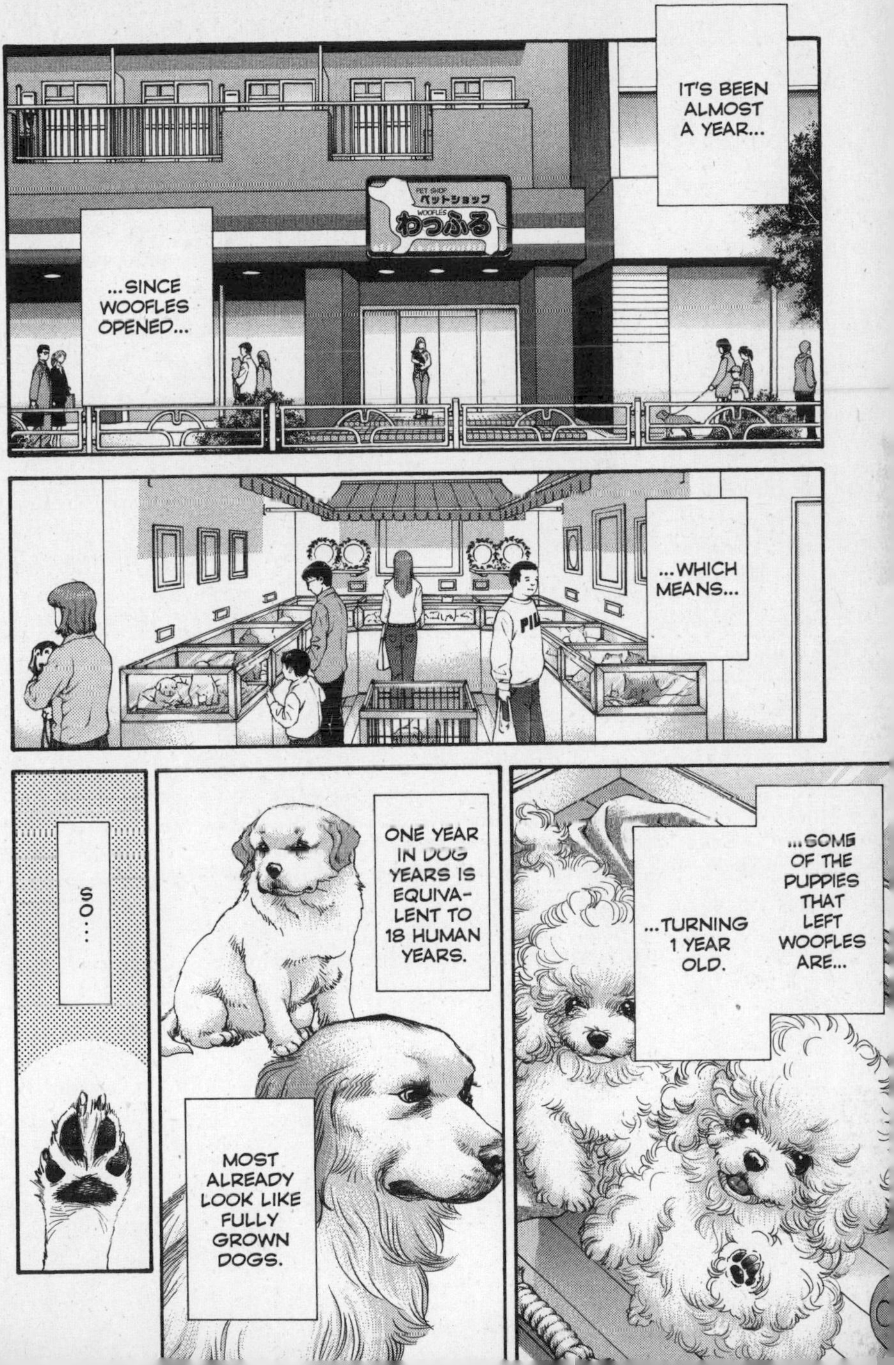
IT'S BEEN ALMOST A YEAR...
PET SHOP
ペットショップ
WOOFLES
わっふる
...SINCE WOOFLES OPENED...
...WHICH MEANS...
...SOME OF THE PUPPIES THAT LEFT WOOFLES ARE...
...TURNING 1 YEAR OLD.
ONE YEAR IN DOG YEARS IS EQUIVA-LENT TO 18 HUMAN YEARS.
MOST ALREADY LOOK LIKE FULLY GROWN DOGS.
SO...

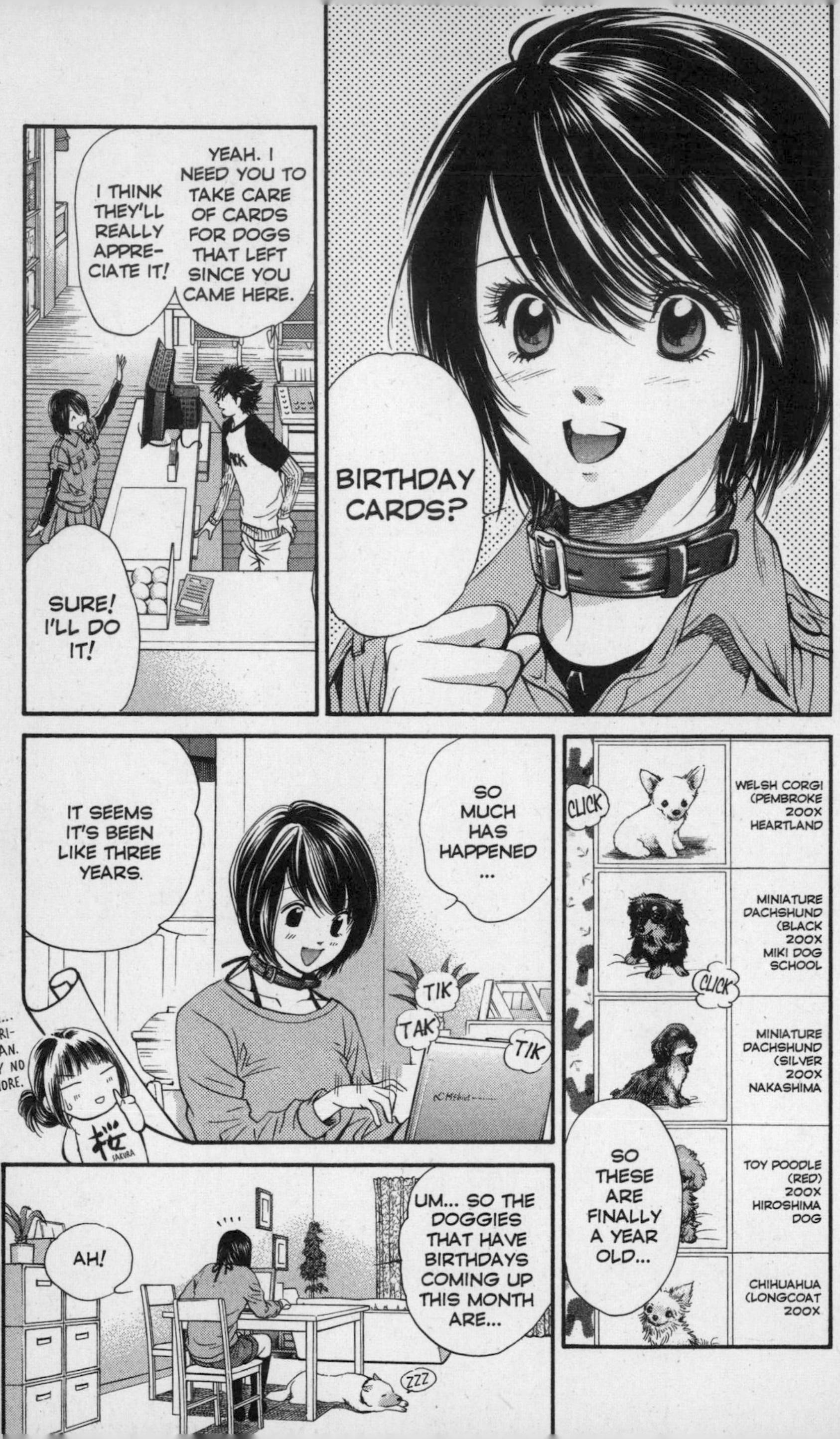
BIRTHDAY CARDS?
YEAH. I NEED YOU TO TAKE CARE OF CARDS FOR DOGS THAT LEFT SINCE YOU CAME HERE.
I THINK THEY'LL REALLY APPRECIATE IT!
SURE! I'LL DO IT!
CLICK
WELSH CORGI (PEMBROKE 200X HEARTLAND
MINIATURE DACHSHUND (BLACK 200X MIKI DOG SCHOOL
CLICK
MINIATURE DACHSHUND (SILVER 200X NAKASHIMA
TOY POODLE (RED) 200X HIROSHIMA DOG
CHIHUAHUA (LONGCOAT 200X
SO THESE ARE FINALLY A YEAR OLD...
SO MUCH HAS HAPPENED...
IT SEEMS IT'S BEEN LIKE THREE YEARS.
TIK
TAK
TIK
SHHH... SUGURI-CHAN. SAY NO MORE.
SAKURA
UM... SO THE DOGGIES THAT HAVE BIRTHDAYS COMING UP THIS MONTH ARE...
AH!
ZZZ

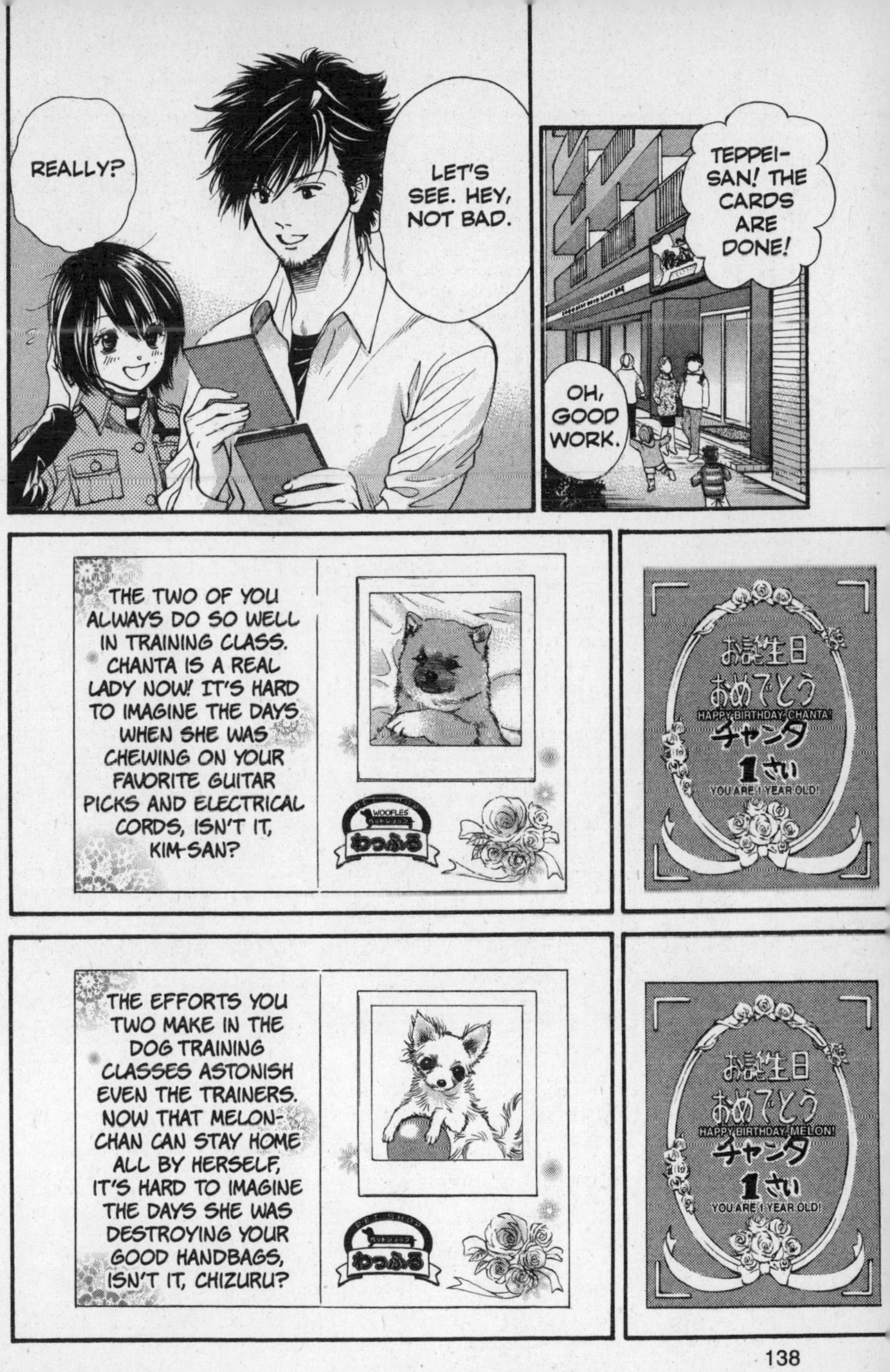
TEPPEI-SAN! THE CARDS ARE DONE!
OH, GOOD WORK.
LET'S SEE. HEY, NOT BAD.
REALLY?
お誕生日
おめでとう
HAPPY BIRTHDAY, CHANTA!
チャンタ
1さい
YOU ARE 1 YEAR OLD!
THE TWO OF YOU ALWAYS DO SO WELL IN TRAINING CLASS. CHANTA IS A REAL LADY NOW! IT'S HARD TO IMAGINE THE DAYS WHEN SHE WAS CHEWING ON YOUR FAVORITE GUITAR PICKS AND ELECTRICAL CORDS, ISN'T IT, KIM-SAN?
WOOFLES
わっふる
お誕生日
おめでとう
HAPPY BIRTHDAY, MELON!
チャンタ
1さい
YOU ARE 1 YEAR OLD!
THE EFFORTS YOU TWO MAKE IN THE DOG TRAINING CLASSES ASTONISH EVEN THE TRAINERS. NOW THAT MELON-CHAN CAN STAY HOME ALL BY HERSELF, IT'S HARD TO IMAGINE THE DAYS SHE WAS DESTROYING YOUR GOOD HANDBAGS, ISN'T IT, CHIZURU?
わっふる

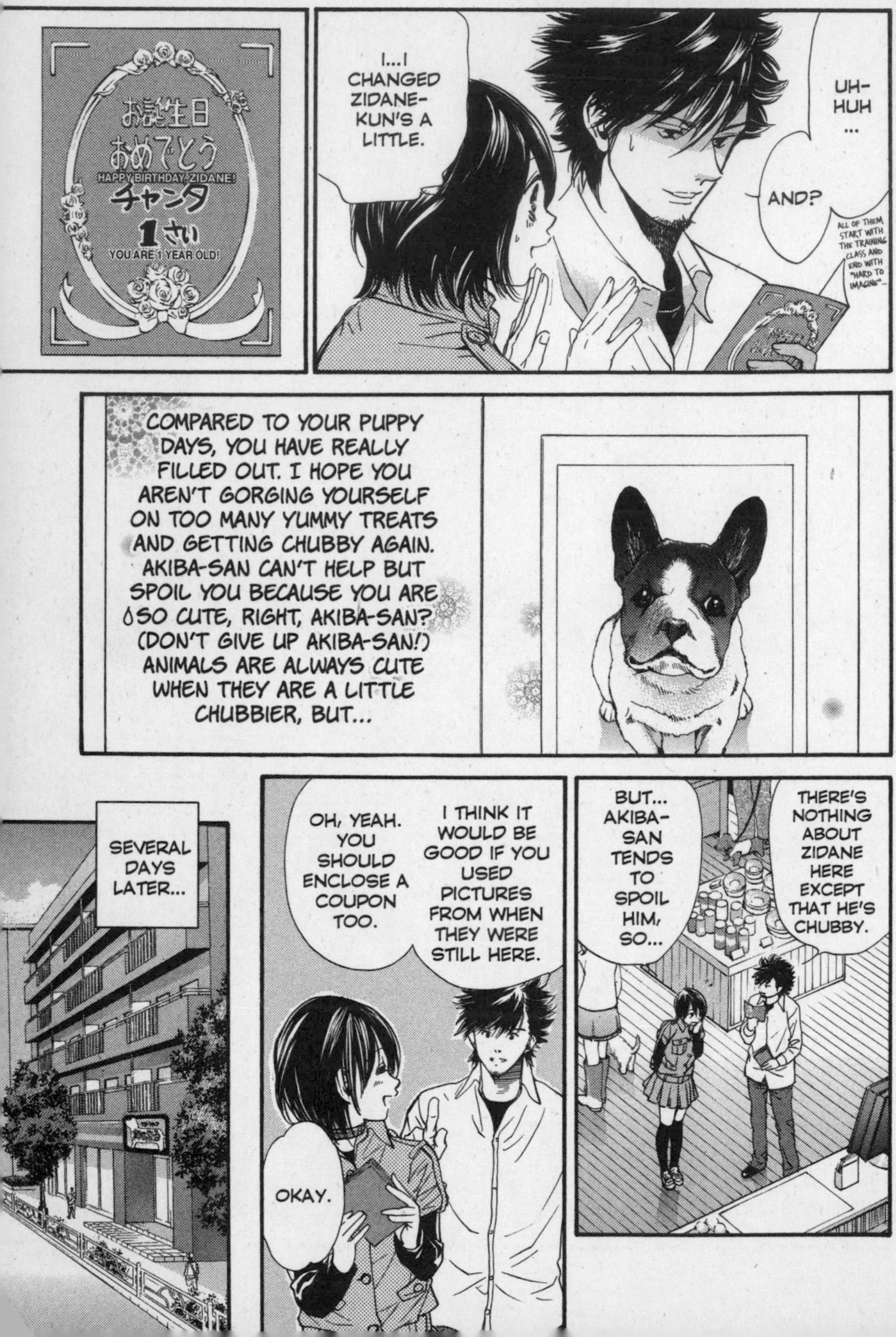
UH-HUH ...
AND?
ALL OF THEM START WITH THE TRAINING CLASS AND END WITH "HARD TO IMAGINE"...
I...I CHANGED ZIDANE-KUN'S A LITTLE.
お誕生日
おめでとう
HAPPY BIRTHDAY, ZIDANE!
チャンタ
1さい
YOU ARE 1 YEAR OLD!
COMPARED TO YOUR PUPPY DAYS, YOU HAVE REALLY FILLED OUT. I HOPE YOU AREN'T GORGING YOURSELF ON TOO MANY YUMMY TREATS AND GETTING CHUBBY AGAIN. AKIBA-SAN CAN'T HELP BUT SPOIL YOU BECAUSE YOU ARE SO CUTE, RIGHT, AKIBA-SAN? (DON'T GIVE UP AKIBA-SAN!) ANIMALS ARE ALWAYS CUTE WHEN THEY ARE A LITTLE CHUBBIER, BUT...
THERE'S NOTHING ABOUT ZIDANE HERE EXCEPT THAT HE'S CHUBBY.
BUT... AKIBA-SAN TENDS TO SPOIL HIM, SO...
I THINK IT WOULD BE GOOD IF YOU USED PICTURES FROM WHEN THEY WERE STILL HERE.
OH, YEAH. YOU SHOULD ENCLOSE A COUPON TOO.
OKAY.
SEVERAL DAYS LATER...

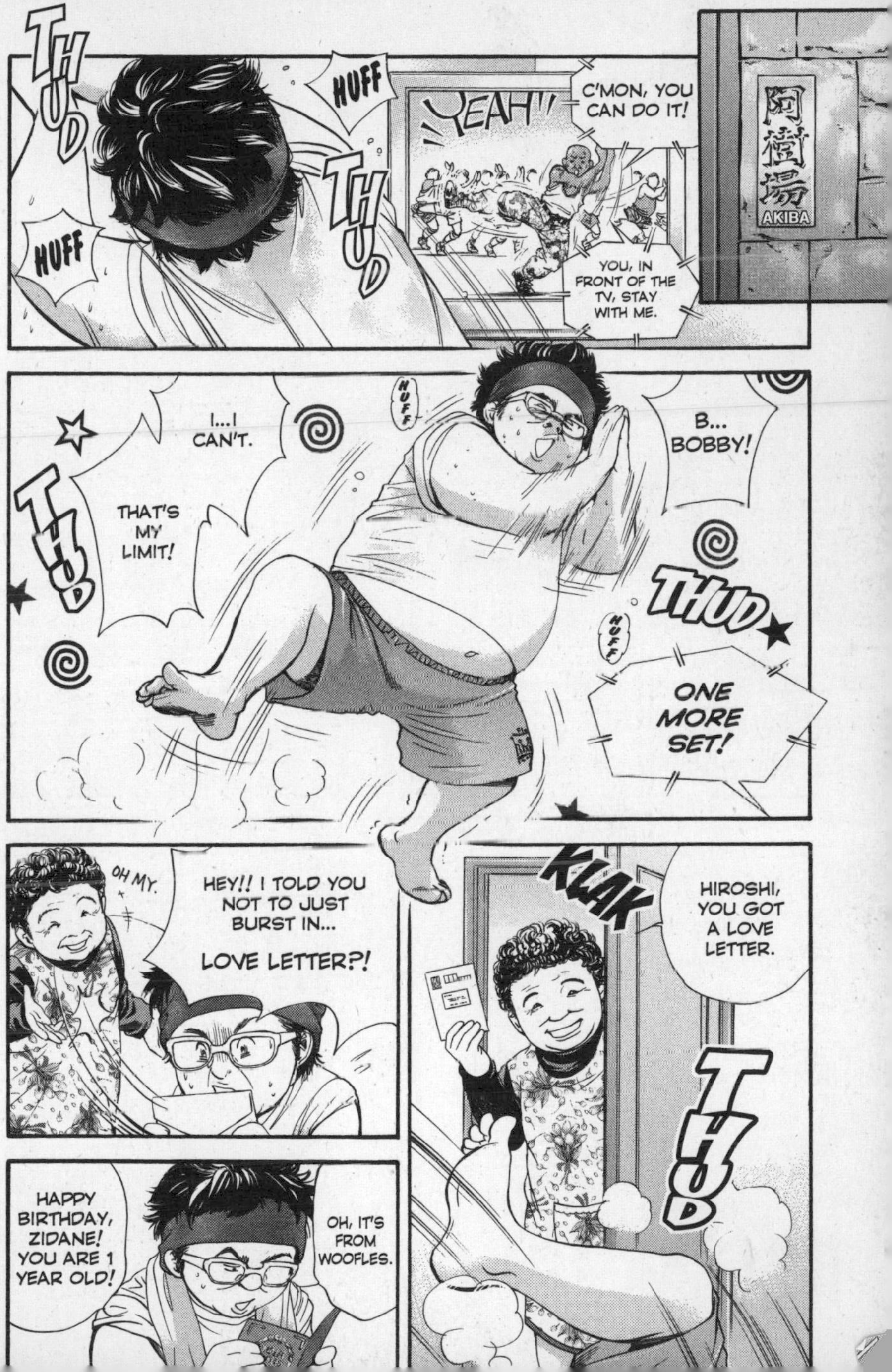
AKIBA
C'MON, YOU CAN DO IT!
YEAH!!
YOU, IN FRONT OF THE TV, STAY WITH ME.
HUFF
THUD
THUD
HUFF
B... BOBBY!
HUFF
THUD
HUFF
ONE MORE SET!
I...I CAN'T.
THAT'S MY LIMIT!
THUD
KLAK
HIROSHI, YOU GOT A LOVE LETTER.
THUD
OH MY.
HEY!! I TOLD YOU NOT TO JUST BURST IN...
LOVE LETTER?!
OH, IT'S FROM WOOFLES.
HAPPY BIRTHDAY, ZIDANE! YOU ARE 1 YEAR OLD!

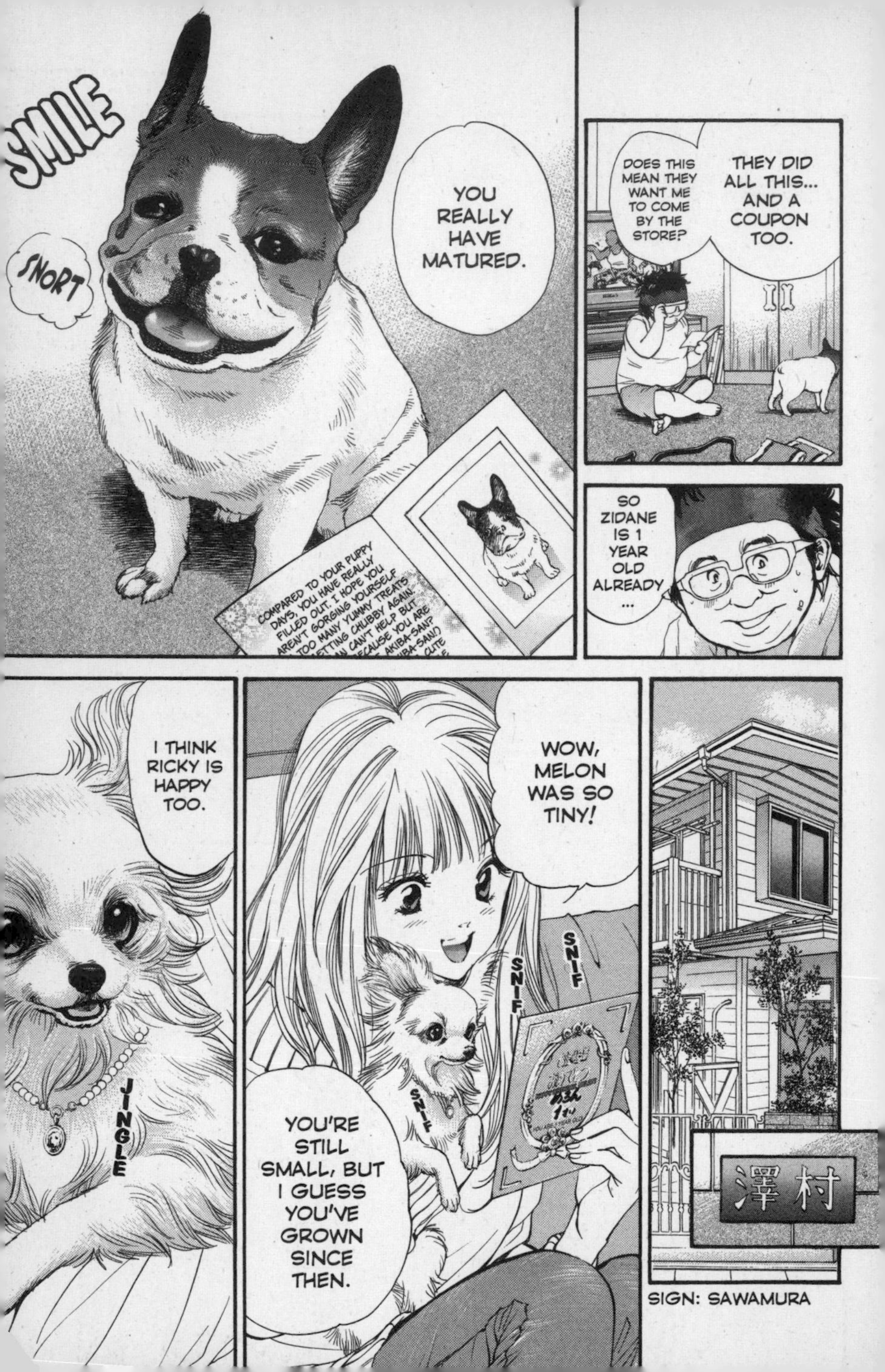
THEY DID ALL THIS... AND A COUPON TOO.
DOES THIS MEAN THEY WANT ME TO COME BY THE STORE?
SO ZIDANE IS 1 YEAR OLD ALREADY...
YOU REALLY HAVE MATURED.
SMILE
SNORT
COMPARED TO YOUR PUPPY DAYS, YOU HAVE REALLY FILLED OUT. I HOPE YOU AREN'T GORGING YOURSELF ON TOO MANY YUMMY TREATS. GETTING CHUBBY AGAIN.
澤村
SIGN: SAWAMURA
WOW, MELON WAS SO TINY!
SNIF
SNIF
YOU'RE STILL SMALL, BUT I GUESS YOU'VE GROWN SINCE THEN.
I THINK RICKY IS HAPPY TOO.
JINGLE

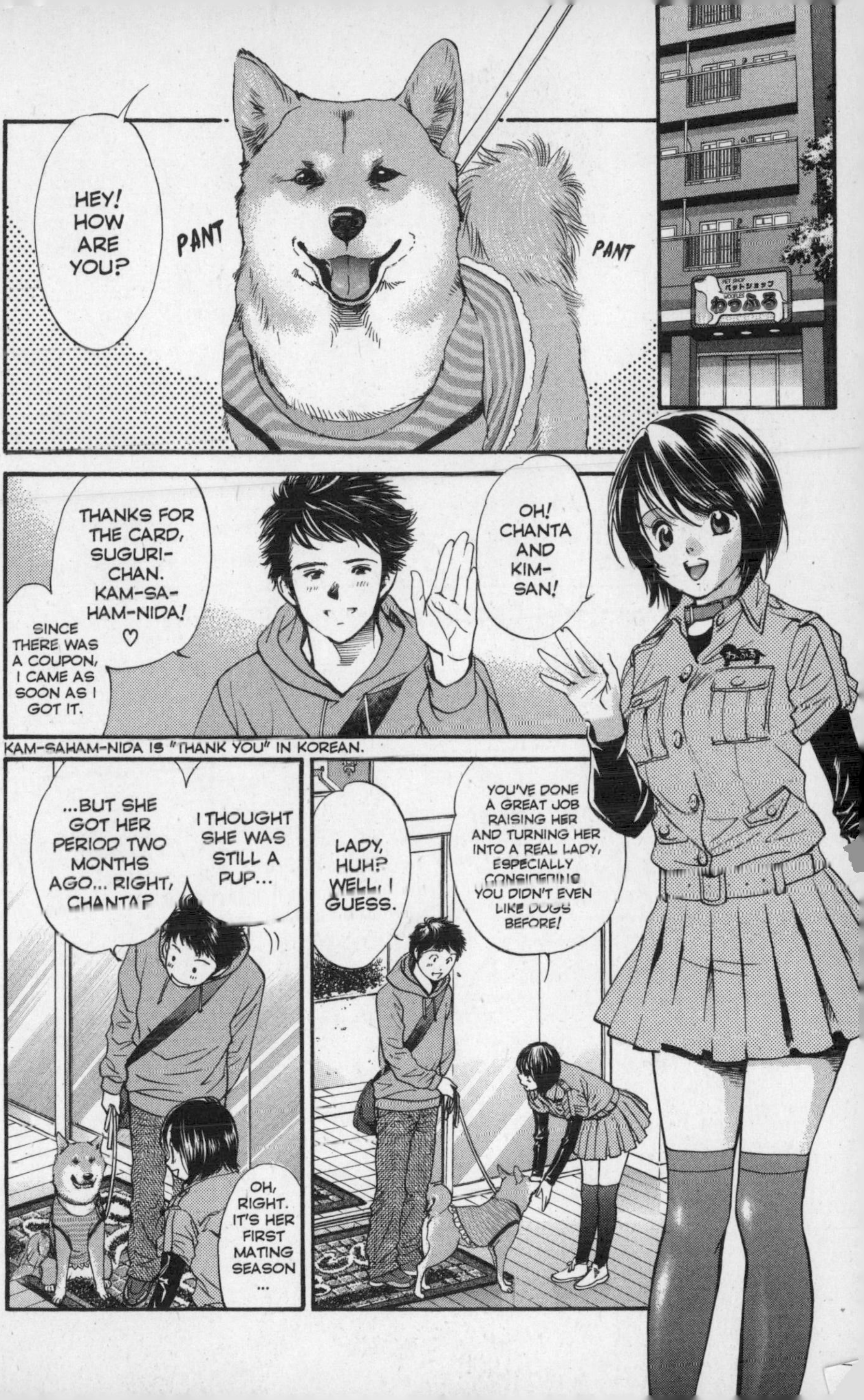
PANT
PANT
HEY! HOW ARE YOU?
OH! CHANTA AND KIM-SAN!
THANKS FOR THE CARD, SUGURI-CHAN. KAM-SA-HAM-NIDA! ♡
SINCE THERE WAS A COUPON, I CAME AS SOON AS I GOT IT.
YOU'VE DONE A GREAT JOB RAISING HER AND TURNING HER INTO A REAL LADY, ESPECIALLY CONSIDERING YOU DIDN'T EVEN LIKE DOGS BEFORE!
LADY, HUH? WELL, I GUESS.
I THOUGHT SHE WAS STILL A PUP...
...BUT SHE GOT HER PERIOD TWO MONTHS AGO... RIGHT, CHANTA?
OH, RIGHT. IT'S HER FIRST MATING SEASON ...

KAM-SAHAM-NIDA IS "THANK YOU" IN KOREAN.

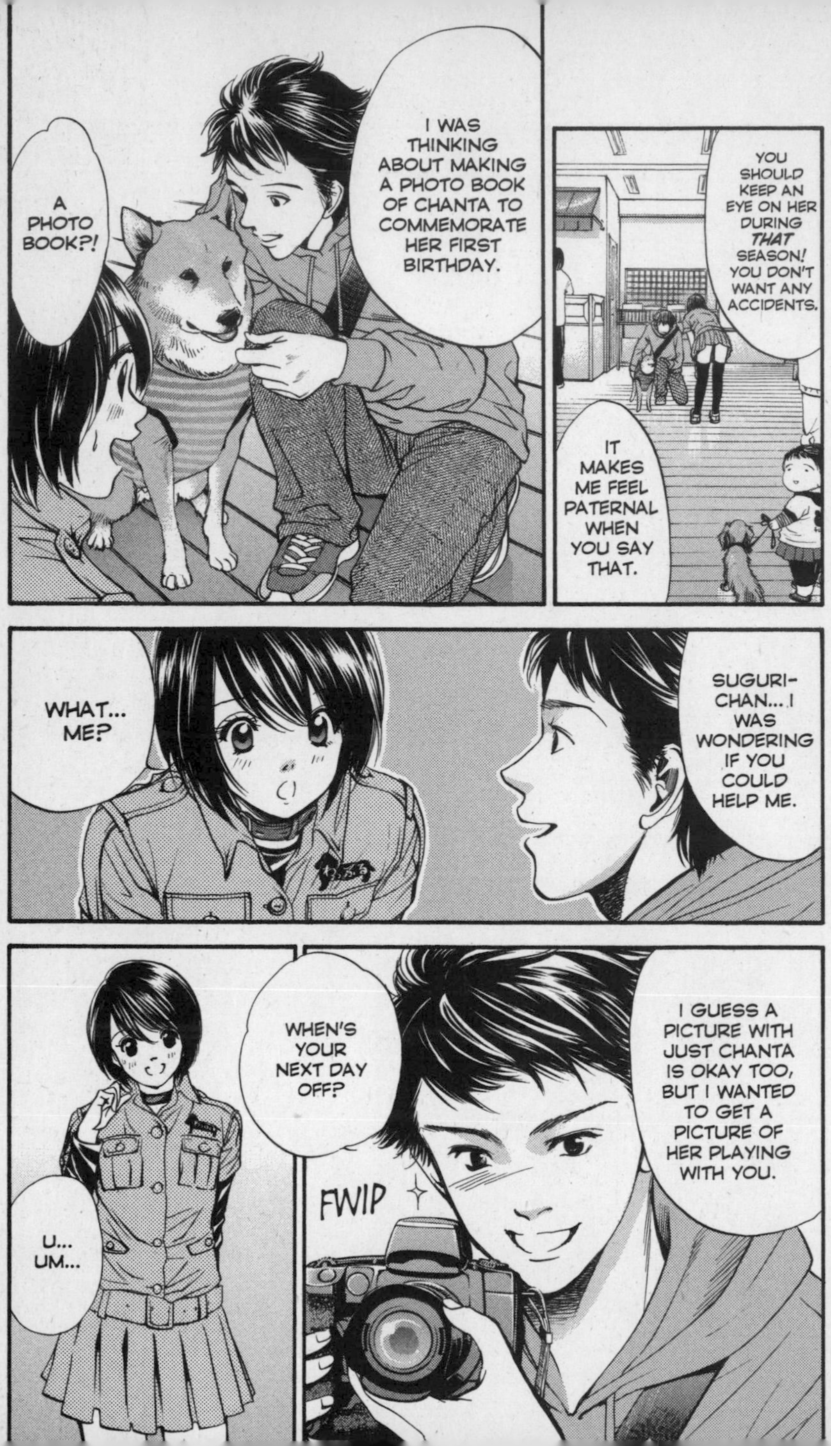
YOU SHOULD KEEP AN EYE ON HER DURING *THAT* SEASON! YOU DON'T WANT ANY ACCIDENTS.
IT MAKES ME FEEL PATERNAL WHEN YOU SAY THAT.
I WAS THINKING ABOUT MAKING A PHOTO BOOK OF CHANTA TO COMMEMORATE HER FIRST BIRTHDAY.
A PHOTO BOOK?!
SUGURI-CHAN... I WAS WONDERING IF YOU COULD HELP ME.
WHAT... ME?
I GUESS A PICTURE WITH JUST CHANTA IS OKAY TOO, BUT I WANTED TO GET A PICTURE OF HER PLAYING WITH YOU.
FWIP
WHEN'S YOUR NEXT DAY OFF?
U... UM...

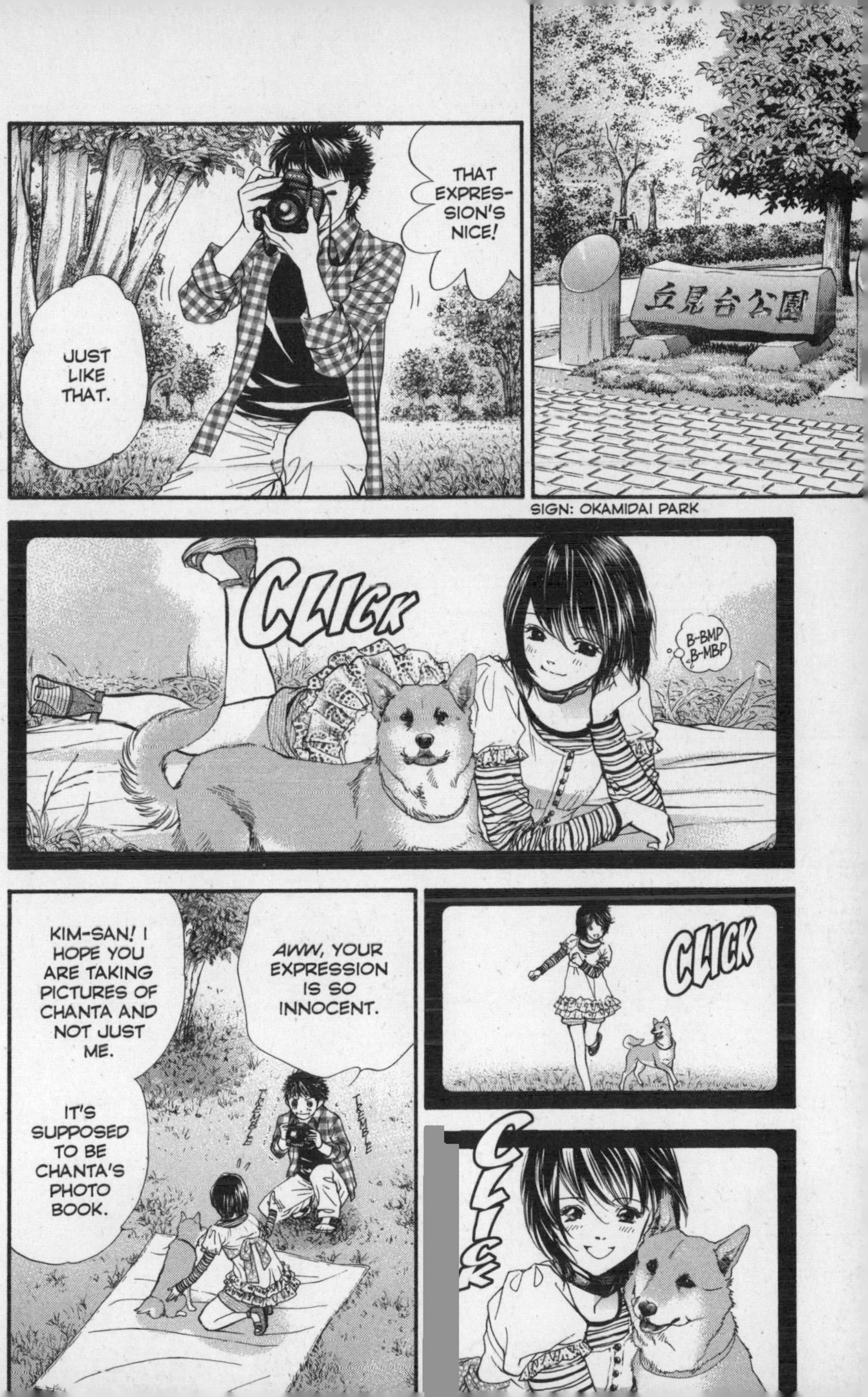
丘見台公園
SIGN: OKAMIDAI PARK
THAT EXPRESSION'S NICE!
JUST LIKE THAT.
B-BMP B-MBP
CLICK
CLICK
CLICK
AWW, YOUR EXPRESSION IS SO INNOCENT.
KIM-SAN! I HOPE YOU ARE TAKING PICTURES OF CHANTA AND NOT JUST ME.
IT'S SUPPOSED TO BE CHANTA'S PHOTO BOOK.
TREMBLE
TREMBLE

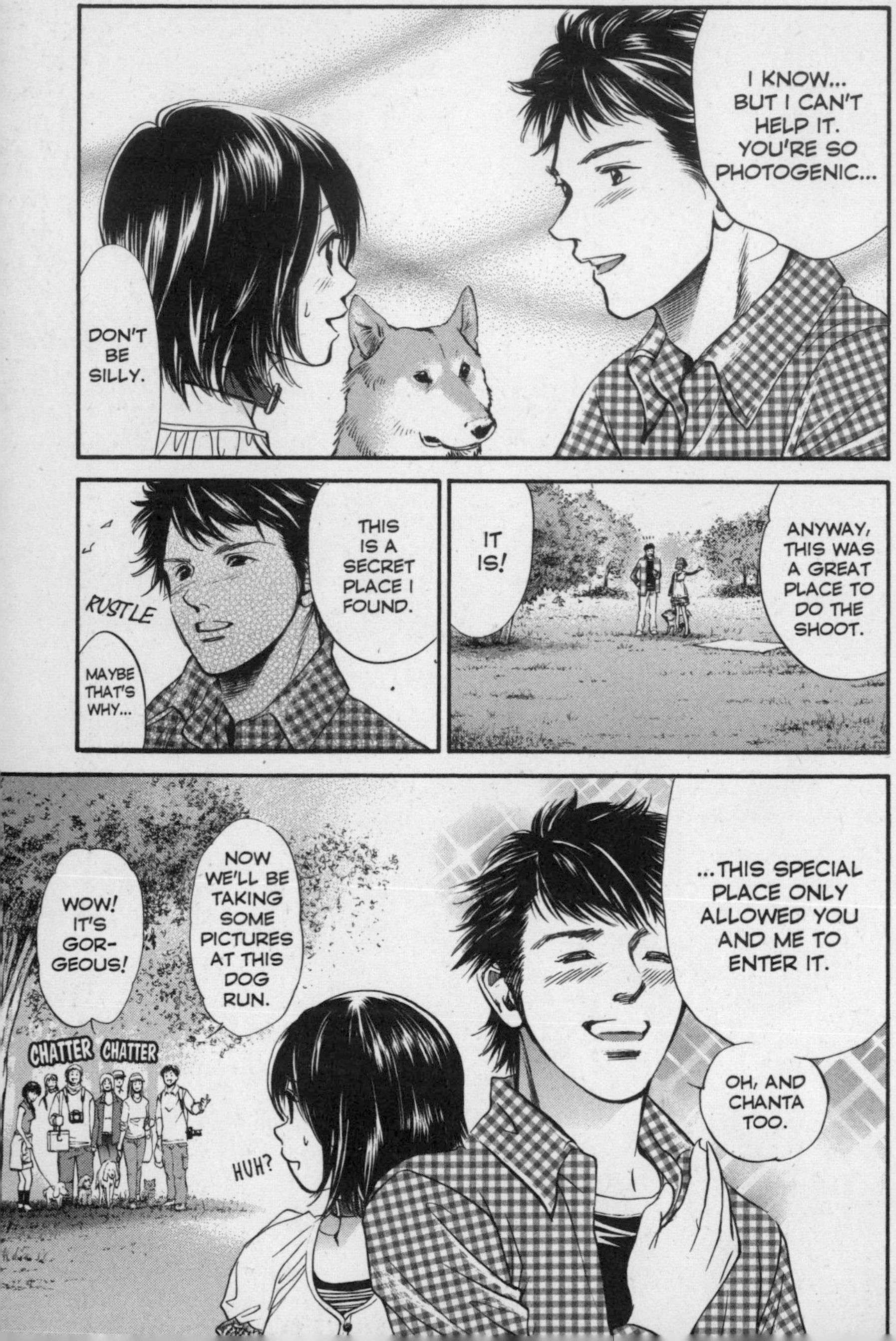
I KNOW... BUT I CAN'T HELP IT. YOU'RE SO PHOTOGENIC...
DON'T BE SILLY.
ANYWAY, THIS WAS A GREAT PLACE TO DO THE SHOOT.
IT IS!
THIS IS A SECRET PLACE I FOUND.
RUSTLE
MAYBE THAT'S WHY...
...THIS SPECIAL PLACE ONLY ALLOWED YOU AND ME TO ENTER IT.
OH, AND CHANTA TOO.
HUH?
NOW WE'LL BE TAKING SOME PICTURES AT THIS DOG RUN.
WOW! IT'S GOR-GEOUS!
CHATTER CHATTER

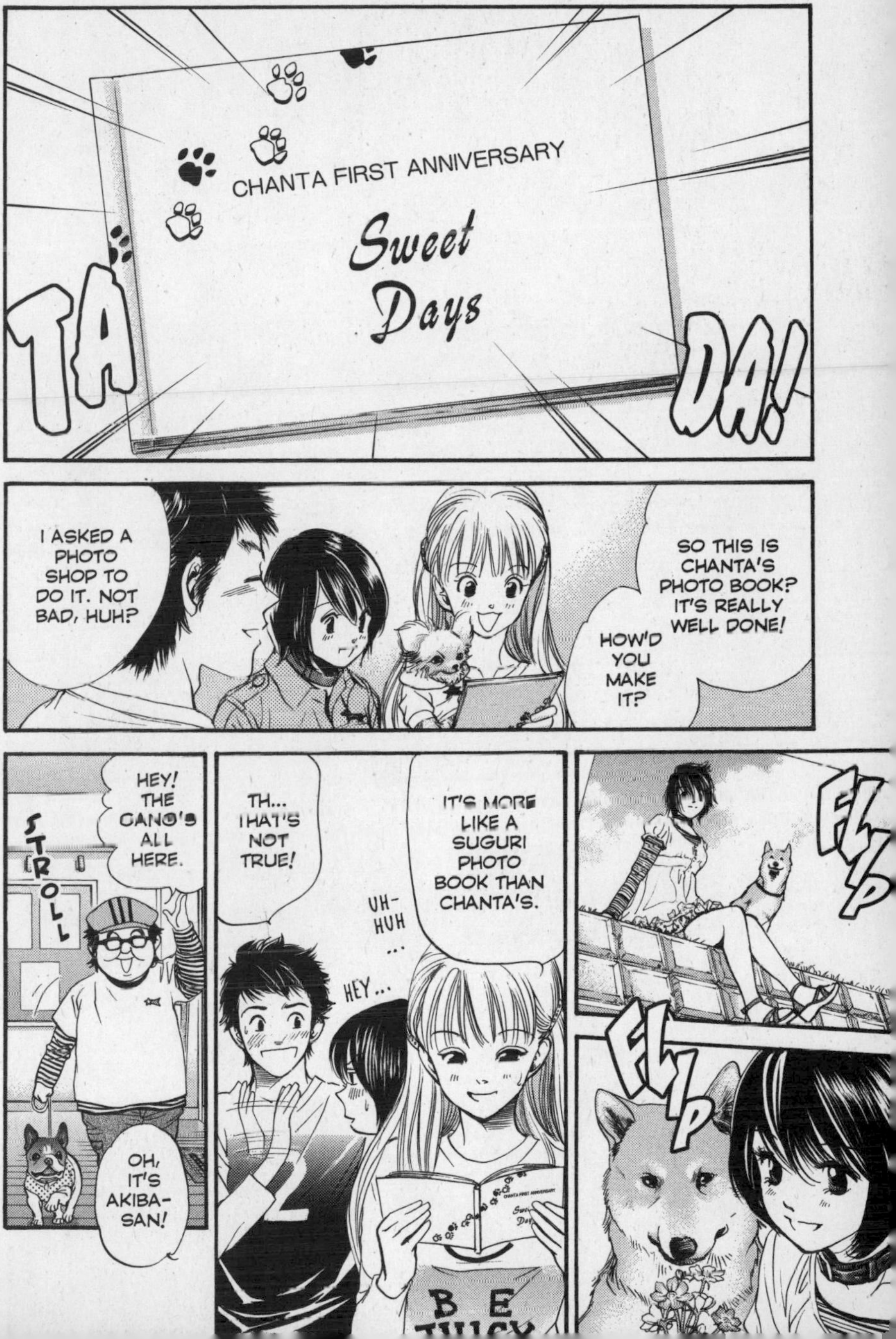
CHANTA FIRST ANNIVERSARY
Sweet Days
TA
DA!
SO THIS IS CHANTA'S PHOTO BOOK? IT'S REALLY WELL DONE!
HOW'D YOU MAKE IT?
I ASKED A PHOTO SHOP TO DO IT. NOT BAD, HUH?
FLIP
FLIP
IT'S MORE LIKE A SUGURI PHOTO BOOK THAN CHANTA'S.
UH-HUH ...
TH... THAT'S NOT TRUE!
HEY...
HEY! THE GANG'S ALL HERE.
STROLL
OH, IT'S AKIBA-SAN!

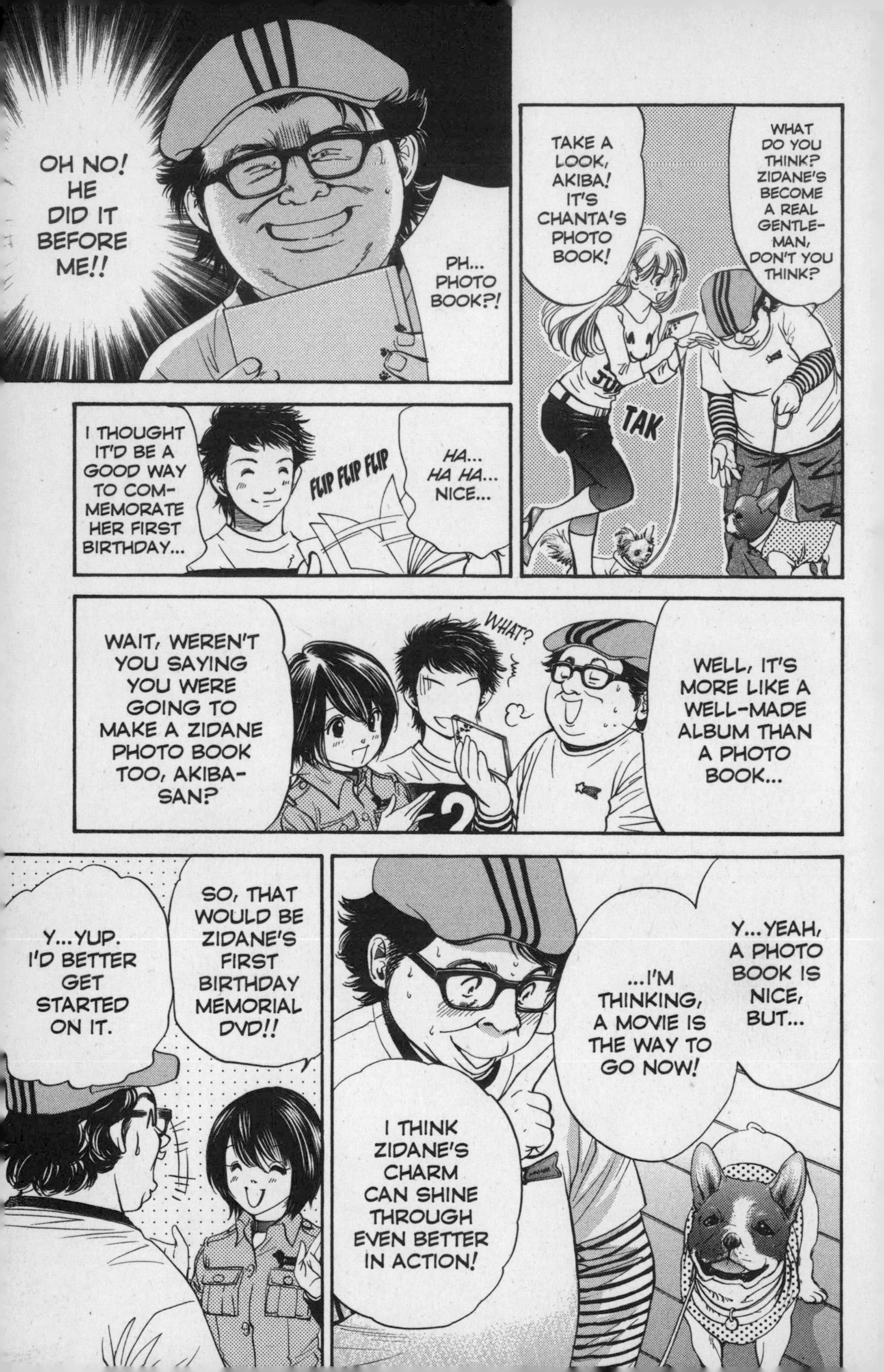
WHAT DO YOU THINK? ZIDANE'S BECOME A REAL GENTLE-MAN, DON'T YOU THINK?
TAKE A LOOK, AKIBA! IT'S CHANTA'S PHOTO BOOK!
TAK
PH... PHOTO BOOK?!
OH NO! HE DID IT BEFORE ME!!
HA... HA HA... NICE...
FLIP FLIP FLIP
I THOUGHT IT'D BE A GOOD WAY TO COM-MEMORATE HER FIRST BIRTHDAY...
WELL, IT'S MORE LIKE A WELL-MADE ALBUM THAN A PHOTO BOOK...
WHAT?
WAIT, WEREN'T YOU SAYING YOU WERE GOING TO MAKE A ZIDANE PHOTO BOOK TOO, AKIBA-SAN?
Y...YEAH, A PHOTO BOOK IS NICE, BUT...
...I'M THINKING, A MOVIE IS THE WAY TO GO NOW!
I THINK ZIDANE'S CHARM CAN SHINE THROUGH EVEN BETTER IN ACTION!
SO, THAT WOULD BE ZIDANE'S FIRST BIRTHDAY MEMORIAL DVD!!
Y...YUP. I'D BETTER GET STARTED ON IT.

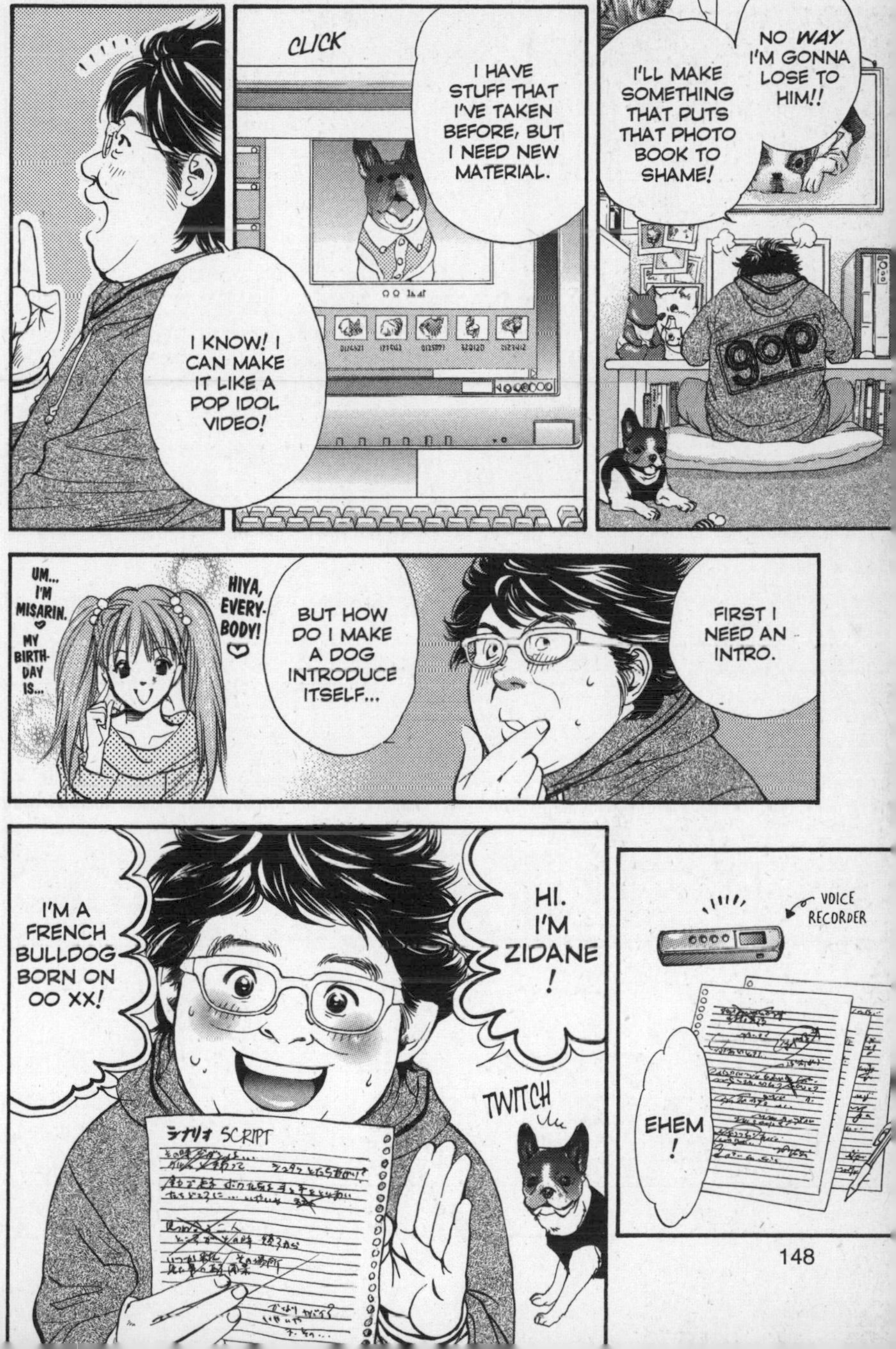
NO WAY I'M GONNA LOSE TO HIM!!
I'LL MAKE SOMETHING THAT PUTS THAT PHOTO BOOK TO SHAME!
CLICK
I HAVE STUFF THAT I'VE TAKEN BEFORE, BUT I NEED NEW MATERIAL.
I KNOW! I CAN MAKE IT LIKE A POP IDOL VIDEO!
FIRST I NEED AN INTRO.
BUT HOW DO I MAKE A DOG INTRODUCE ITSELF...
HIYA, EVERYBODY!
UM... I'M MISARIN. MY BIRTHDAY IS...
VOICE RECORDER
EHEM!
HI. I'M ZIDANE!
I'M A FRENCH BULLDOG BORN ON OO XX!
TWITCH
SCRIPT

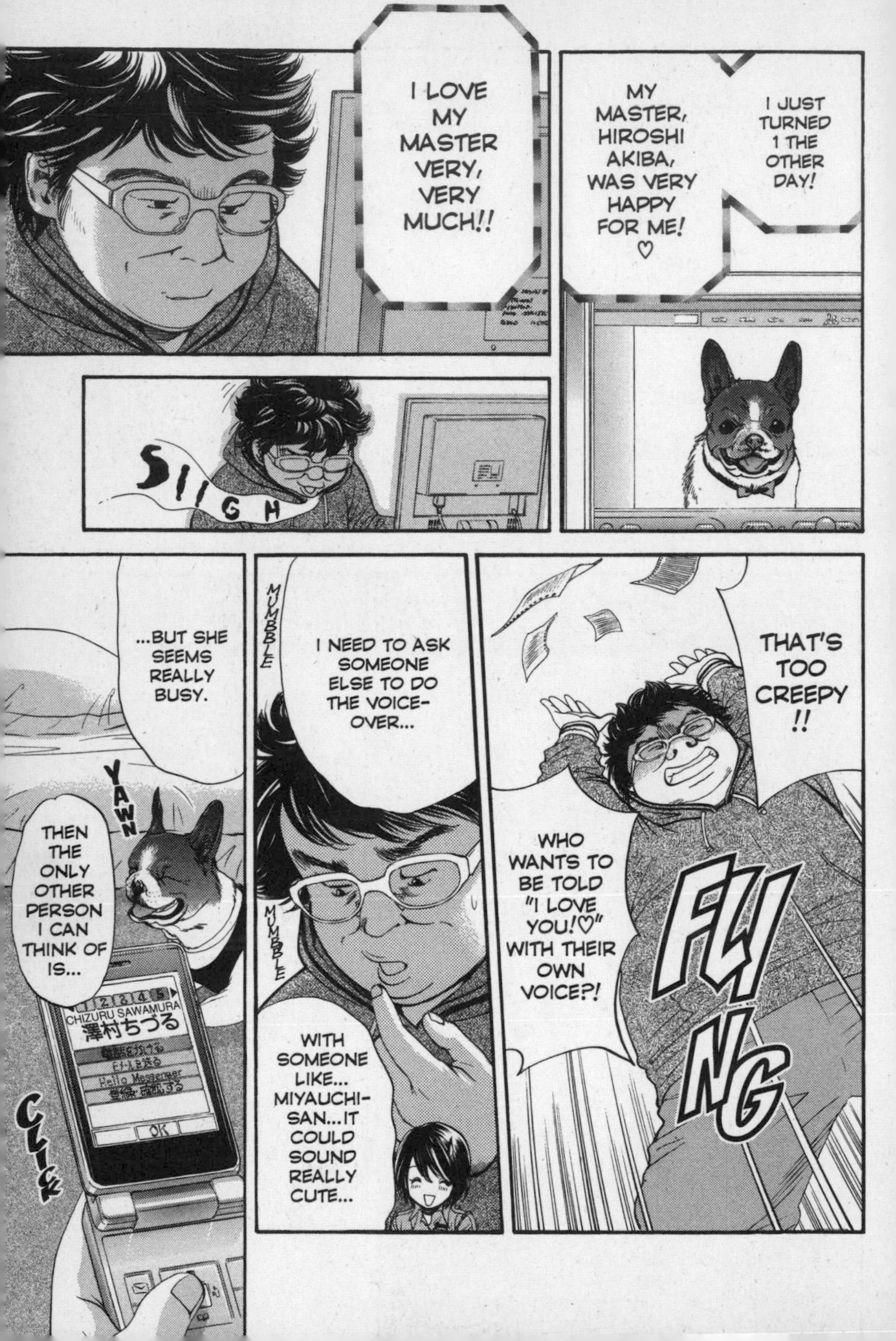
I JUST TURNED 1 THE OTHER DAY!
MY MASTER, HIROSHI AKIBA, WAS VERY HAPPY FOR ME! ♡
I LOVE MY MASTER VERY, VERY MUCH!!
SIIGH
THAT'S TOO CREEPY!!
WHO WANTS TO BE TOLD "I LOVE YOU!♡" WITH THEIR OWN VOICE?!
FLING
MUMBLE
I NEED TO ASK SOMEONE ELSE TO DO THE VOICE-OVER...
MUMBLE
WITH SOMEONE LIKE... MIYAUCHI-SAN...IT COULD SOUND REALLY CUTE...
...BUT SHE SEEMS REALLY BUSY.
YAWN
THEN THE ONLY OTHER PERSON I CAN THINK OF IS...
1 2 3 4 5
CHIZURU SAWAMURA
澤村ちづる
Hello Messenger
OK
CLICK

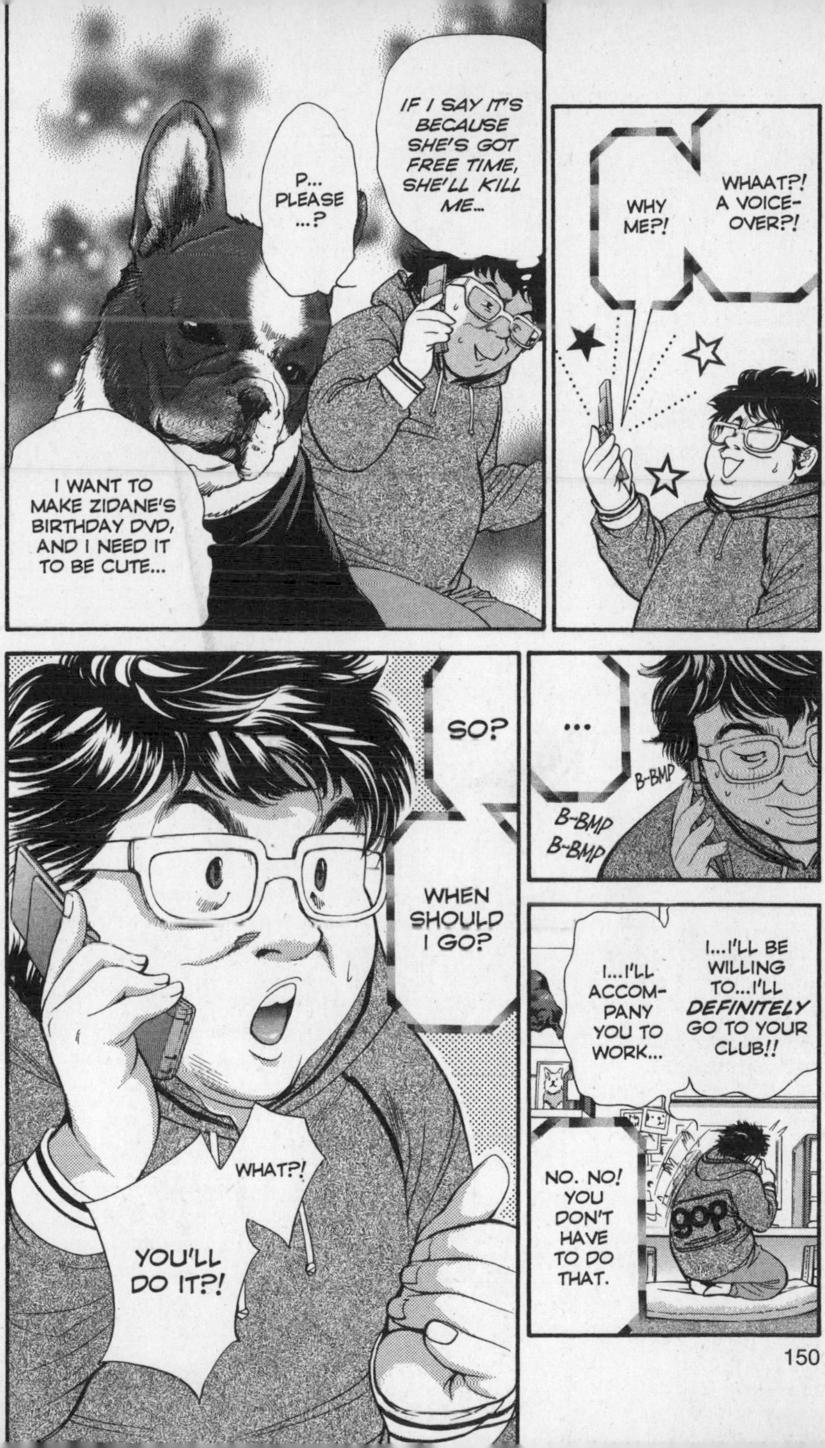
WHAAT?! A VOICE-OVER?!
WHY ME?!
IF I SAY IT'S BECAUSE SHE'S GOT FREE TIME, SHE'LL KILL ME...
P... PLEASE ...?
I WANT TO MAKE ZIDANE'S BIRTHDAY DVD, AND I NEED IT TO BE CUTE...
...
B-BMP
B-BMP
B-BMP
I...I'LL BE WILLING TO...I'LL *DEFINITELY* GO TO YOUR CLUB!!
I...I'LL ACCOMPANY YOU TO WORK...
NO. NO! YOU DON'T HAVE TO DO THAT.
SO?
WHEN SHOULD I GO?
WHAT?!
YOU'LL DO IT?!

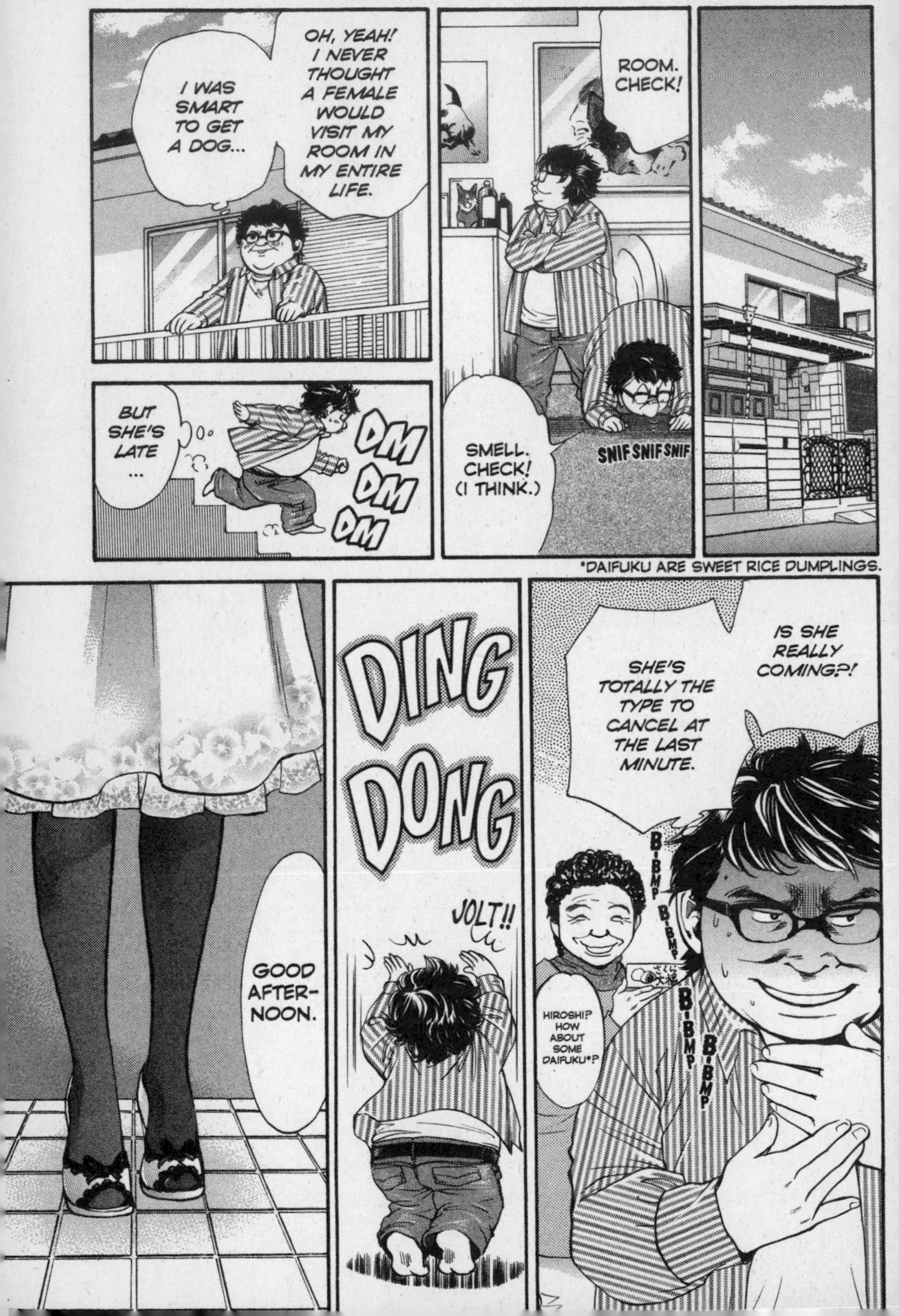
ROOM. CHECK!
SNIF SNIF SNIF
SMELL. CHECK! (I THINK.)
OH, YEAH! I NEVER THOUGHT A FEMALE WOULD VISIT MY ROOM IN MY ENTIRE LIFE.
I WAS SMART TO GET A DOG...
BUT SHE'S LATE ...
DM DM DM
IS SHE REALLY COMING?!
SHE'S TOTALLY THE TYPE TO CANCEL AT THE LAST MINUTE.
B-BMP B-BMP B-BMP B-BMP
HIROSHI? HOW ABOUT SOME DAIFUKU*?
DING DONG
JOLT!!
GOOD AFTER-NOON.

*DAIFUKU ARE SWEET RICE DUMPLINGS.

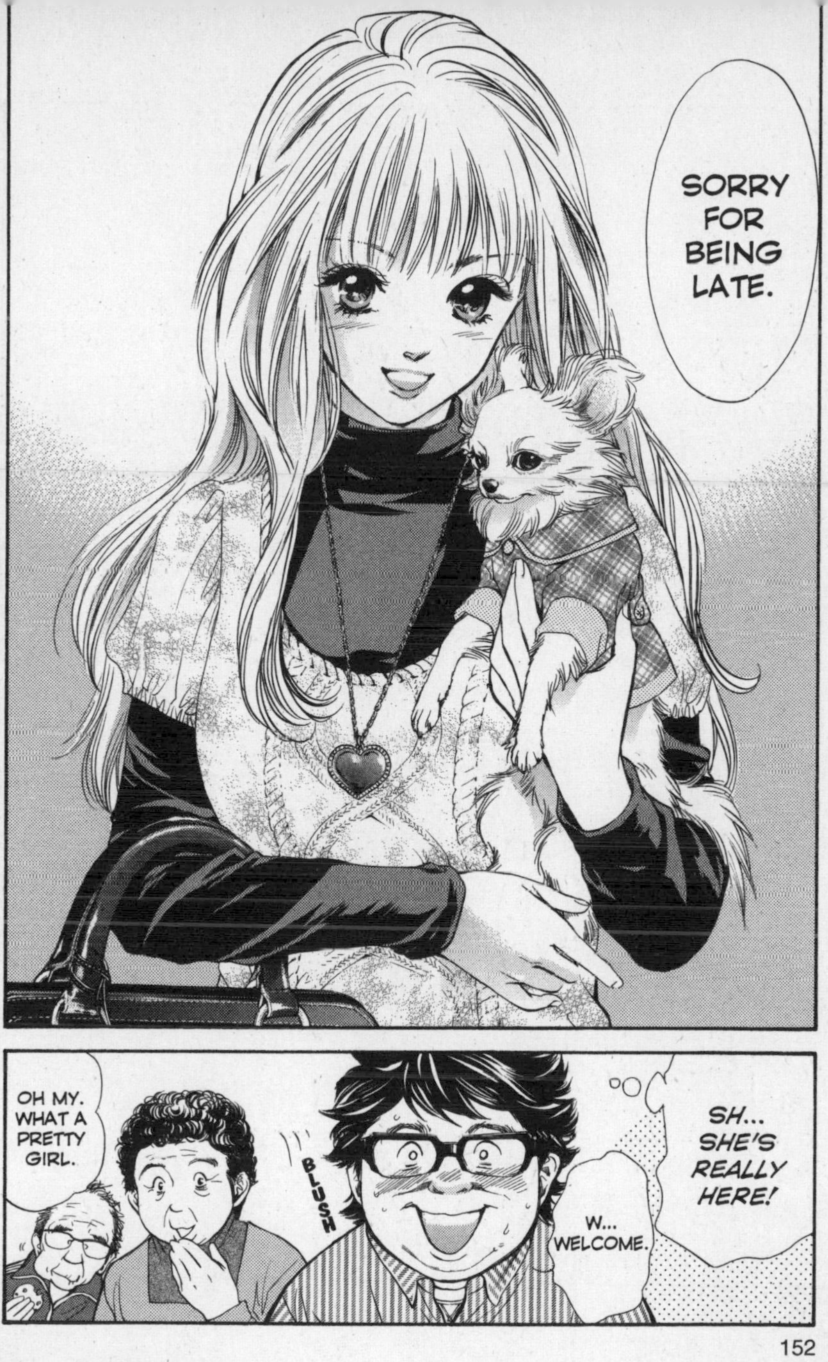
SORRY FOR BEING LATE.
SH... SHE'S REALLY HERE!
W... WELCOME.
BLUSH
OH MY. WHAT A PRETTY GIRL.

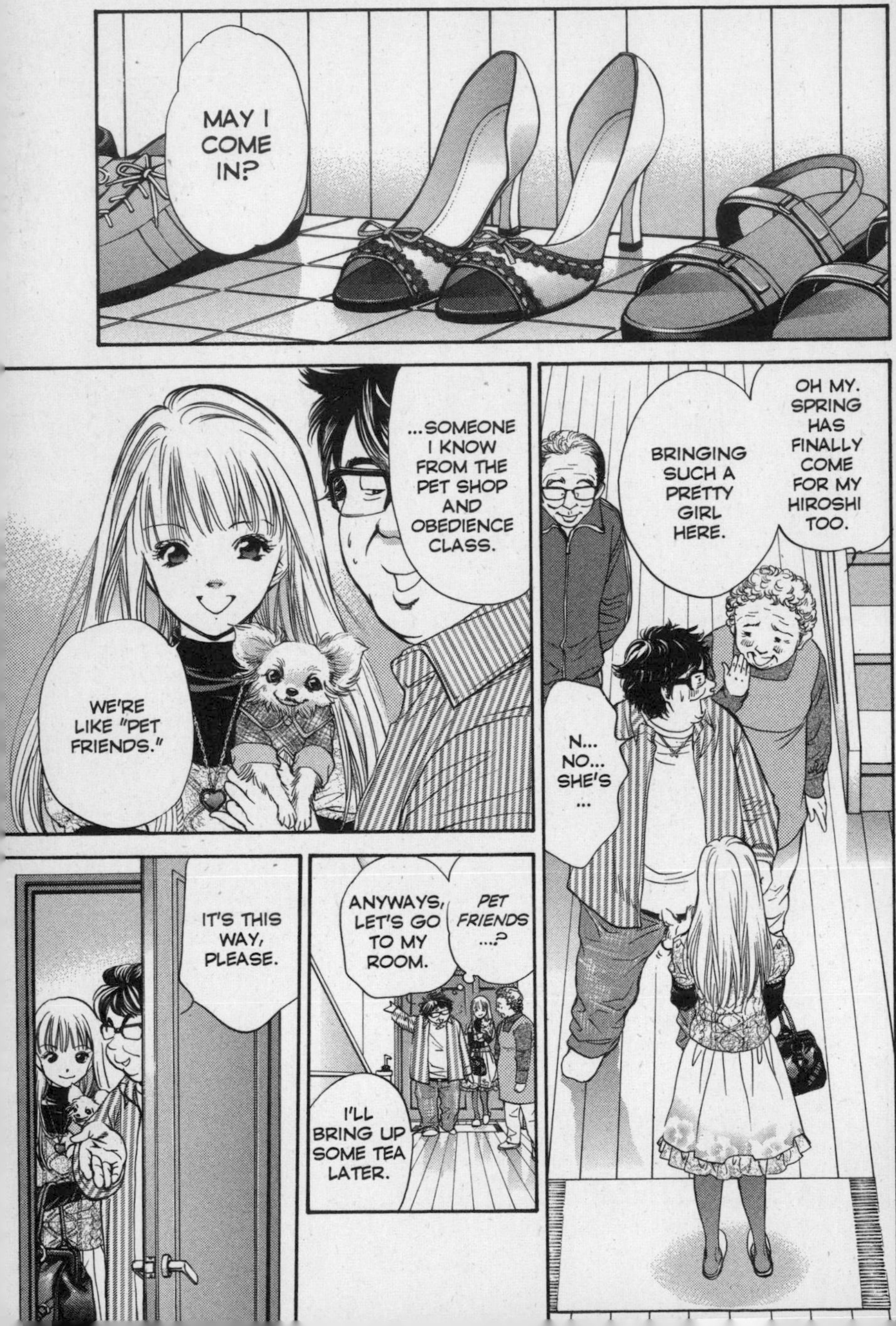
MAY I COME IN?
OH MY. SPRING HAS FINALLY COME FOR MY HIROSHI TOO.
BRINGING SUCH A PRETTY GIRL HERE.
N... NO... SHE'S ...
...SOMEONE I KNOW FROM THE PET SHOP AND OBEDIENCE CLASS.
WE'RE LIKE "PET FRIENDS."
PET FRIENDS ...?
ANYWAYS, LET'S GO TO MY ROOM.
I'LL BRING UP SOME TEA LATER.
IT'S THIS WAY, PLEASE.

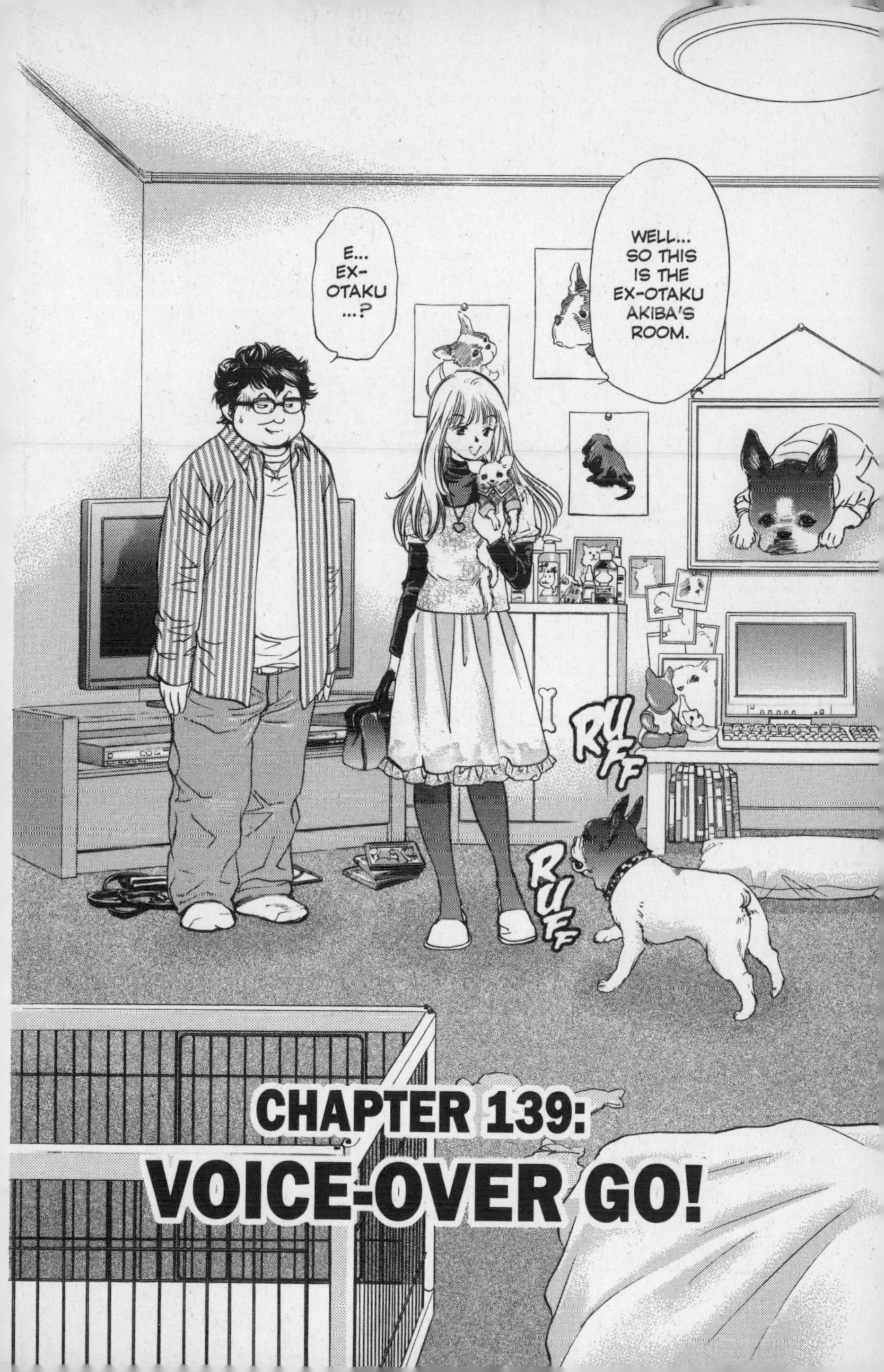
WELL... SO THIS IS THE EX-OTAKU AKIBA'S ROOM.
E... EX-OTAKU ...?
RUFF
RUFF
CHAPTER 139:
VOICE-OVER GO!

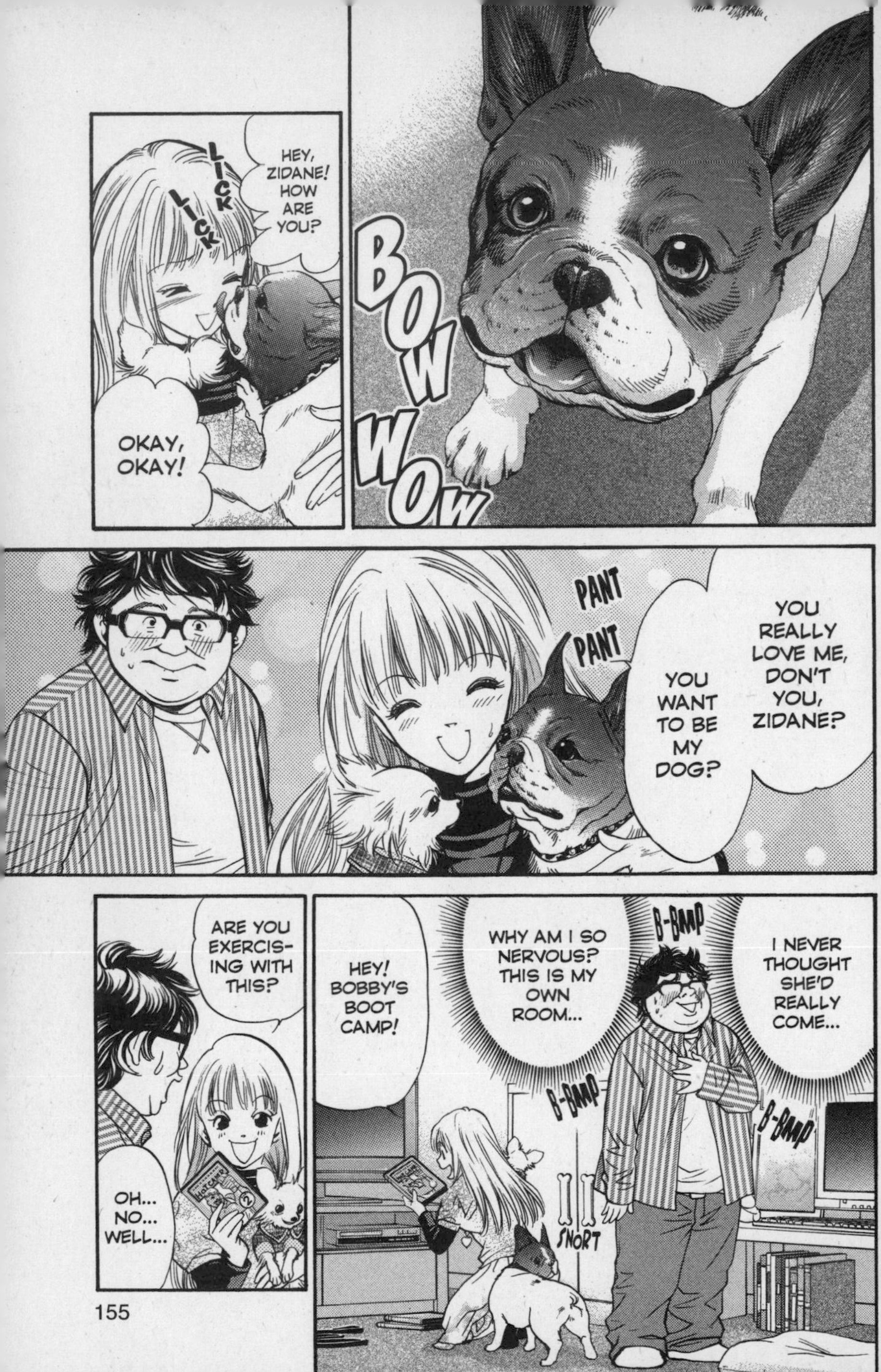
BOW WOW WOW
LICK LICK
HEY, ZIDANE! HOW ARE YOU?
OKAY, OKAY!
PANT PANT
YOU REALLY LOVE ME, DON'T YOU, ZIDANE?
YOU WANT TO BE MY DOG?
I NEVER THOUGHT SHE'D REALLY COME...
B-BMP
WHY AM I SO NERVOUS? THIS IS MY OWN ROOM...
B-BMP B-BMP
HEY! BOBBY'S BOOT CAMP!
SNORT
ARE YOU EXERCIS-ING WITH THIS?
OH... NO... WELL...

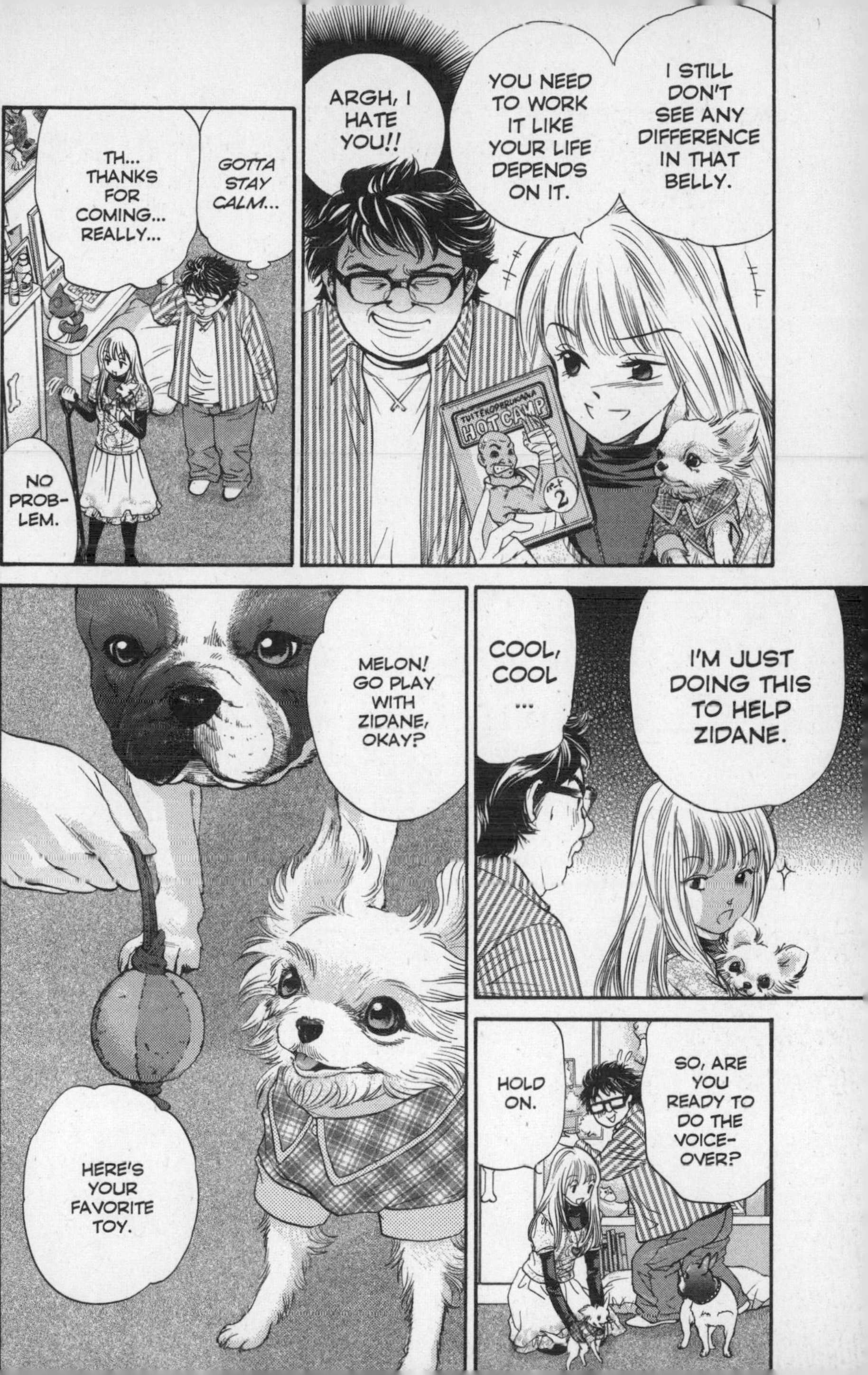
I STILL DON'T SEE ANY DIFFERENCE IN THAT BELLY.
YOU NEED TO WORK IT LIKE YOUR LIFE DEPENDS ON IT.
ARGH, I HATE YOU!!
HOT CAMP
GOTTA STAY CALM...
TH... THANKS FOR COMING... REALLY...
NO PROB-LEM.
I'M JUST DOING THIS TO HELP ZIDANE.
COOL, COOL ...
SO, ARE YOU READY TO DO THE VOICE-OVER?
HOLD ON.
MELON! GO PLAY WITH ZIDANE, OKAY?
HERE'S YOUR FAVORITE TOY.

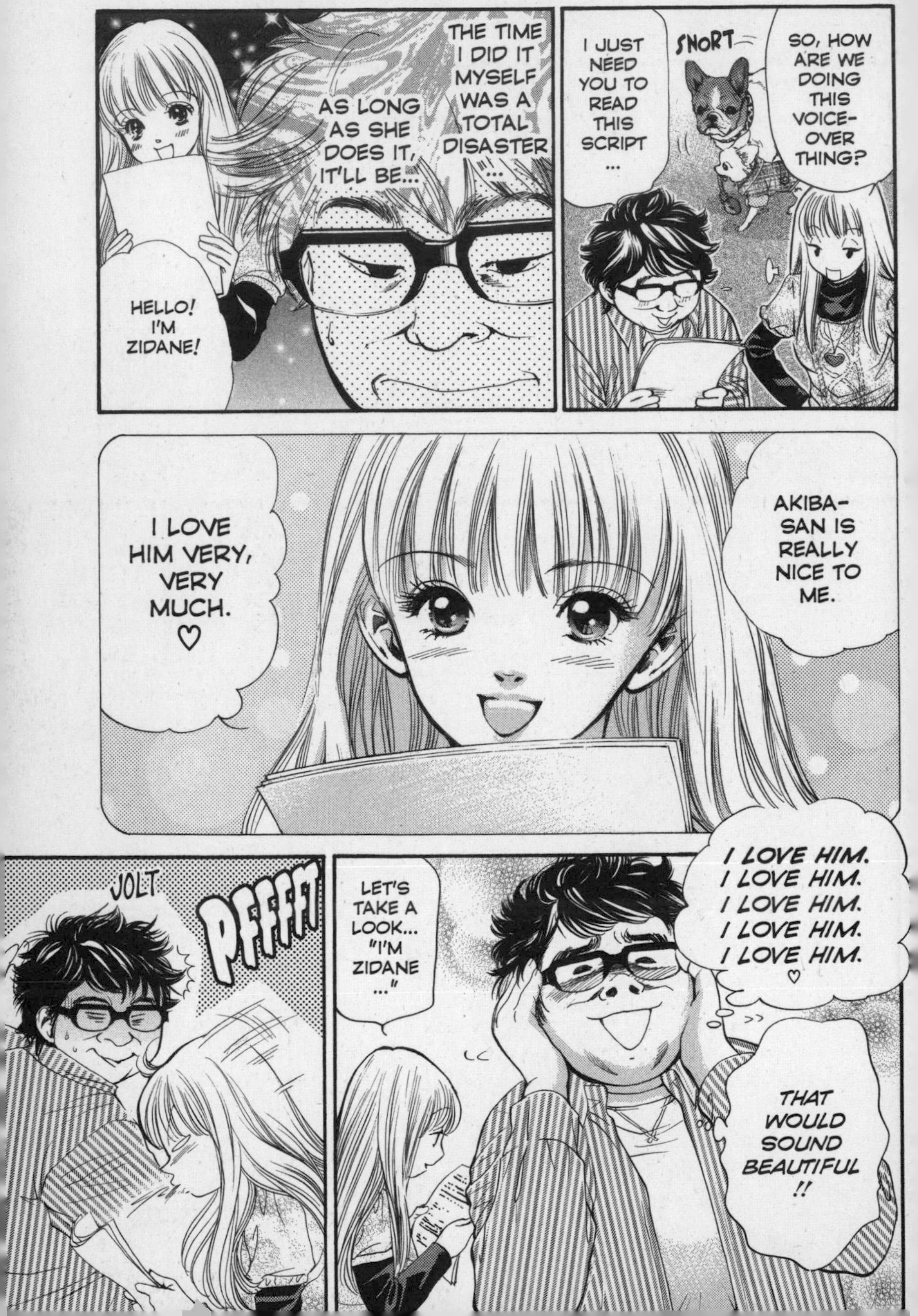
SO, HOW ARE WE DOING THIS VOICE-OVER THING?
SNORT
I JUST NEED YOU TO READ THIS SCRIPT ...
THE TIME I DID IT MYSELF WAS A TOTAL DISASTER ...
AS LONG AS SHE DOES IT, IT'LL BE...
HELLO! I'M ZIDANE!
AKIBA-SAN IS REALLY NICE TO ME.
I LOVE HIM VERY, VERY MUCH. ♡
I LOVE HIM. I LOVE HIM. I LOVE HIM. I LOVE HIM. I LOVE HIM. ♡
LET'S TAKE A LOOK... "I'M ZIDANE ..."
THAT WOULD SOUND BEAUTIFUL !!
PFFFFT
JOLT

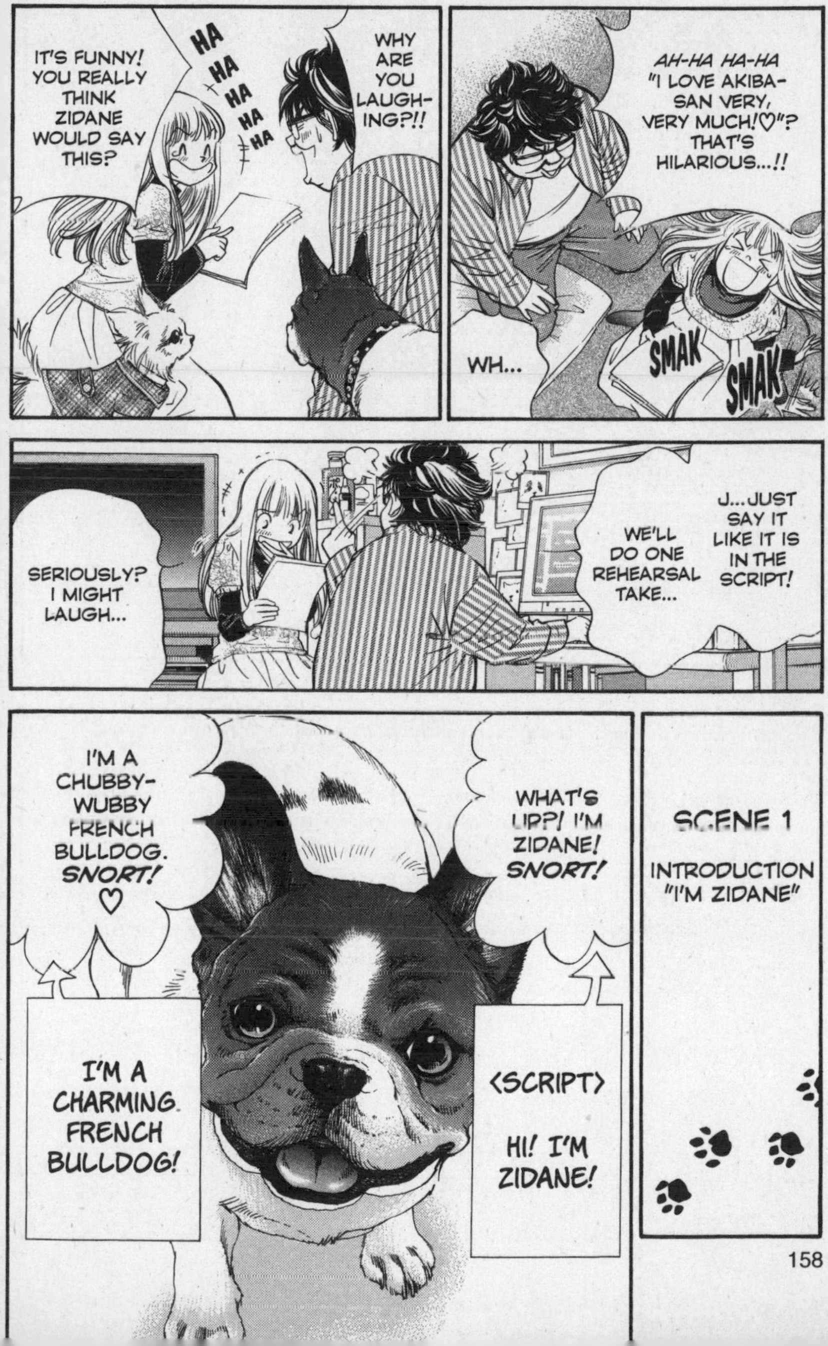
AH-HA HA-HA "I LOVE AKIBA-SAN VERY, VERY MUCH!♡"? THAT'S HILARIOUS...!!
WH...
SMAK
SMAK
WHY ARE YOU LAUGHING?!!
HA HA HA HA HA
IT'S FUNNY! YOU REALLY THINK ZIDANE WOULD SAY THIS?
J...JUST SAY IT LIKE IT IS IN THE SCRIPT!
WE'LL DO ONE REHEARSAL TAKE...
SERIOUSLY? I MIGHT LAUGH...
SCENE 1
INTRODUCTION "I'M ZIDANE"
<SCRIPT>
HI! I'M ZIDANE!
WHAT'S UP?! I'M ZIDANE! SNORT!
I'M A CHARMING FRENCH BULLDOG!
I'M A CHUBBY-WUBBY FRENCH BULLDOG. SNORT! ♡

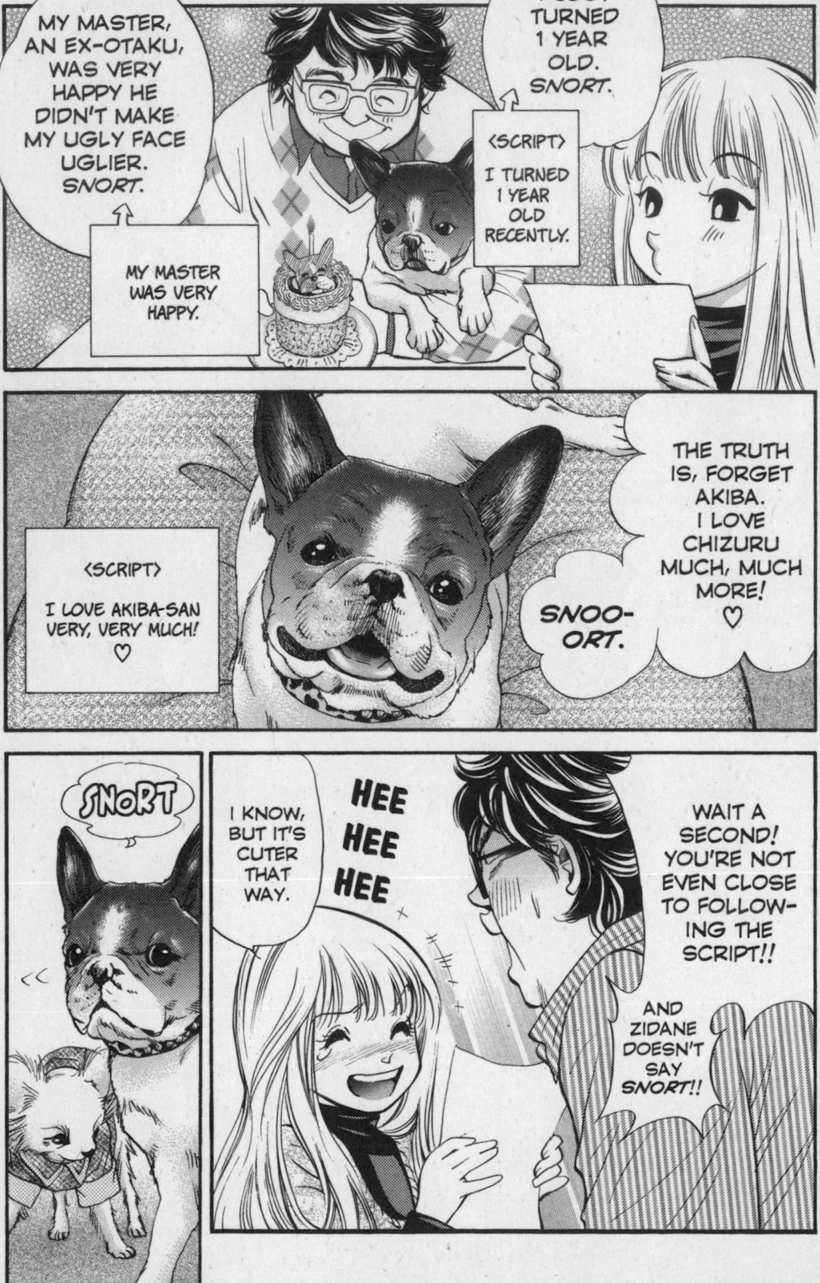
I JUST TURNED 1 YEAR OLD. SNORT.
<SCRIPT> I TURNED 1 YEAR OLD RECENTLY.
MY MASTER, AN EX-OTAKU, WAS VERY HAPPY HE DIDN'T MAKE MY UGLY FACE UGLIER. SNORT.
MY MASTER WAS VERY HAPPY.
THE TRUTH IS, FORGET AKIBA. I LOVE CHIZURU MUCH, MUCH MORE! ♡
SNOO-ORT.
<SCRIPT> I LOVE AKIBA-SAN VERY, VERY MUCH! ♡
WAIT A SECOND! YOU'RE NOT EVEN CLOSE TO FOLLOW-ING THE SCRIPT!!
AND ZIDANE DOESN'T SAY SNORT!!
HEE HEE HEE
I KNOW, BUT IT'S CUTER THAT WAY.
SNORT

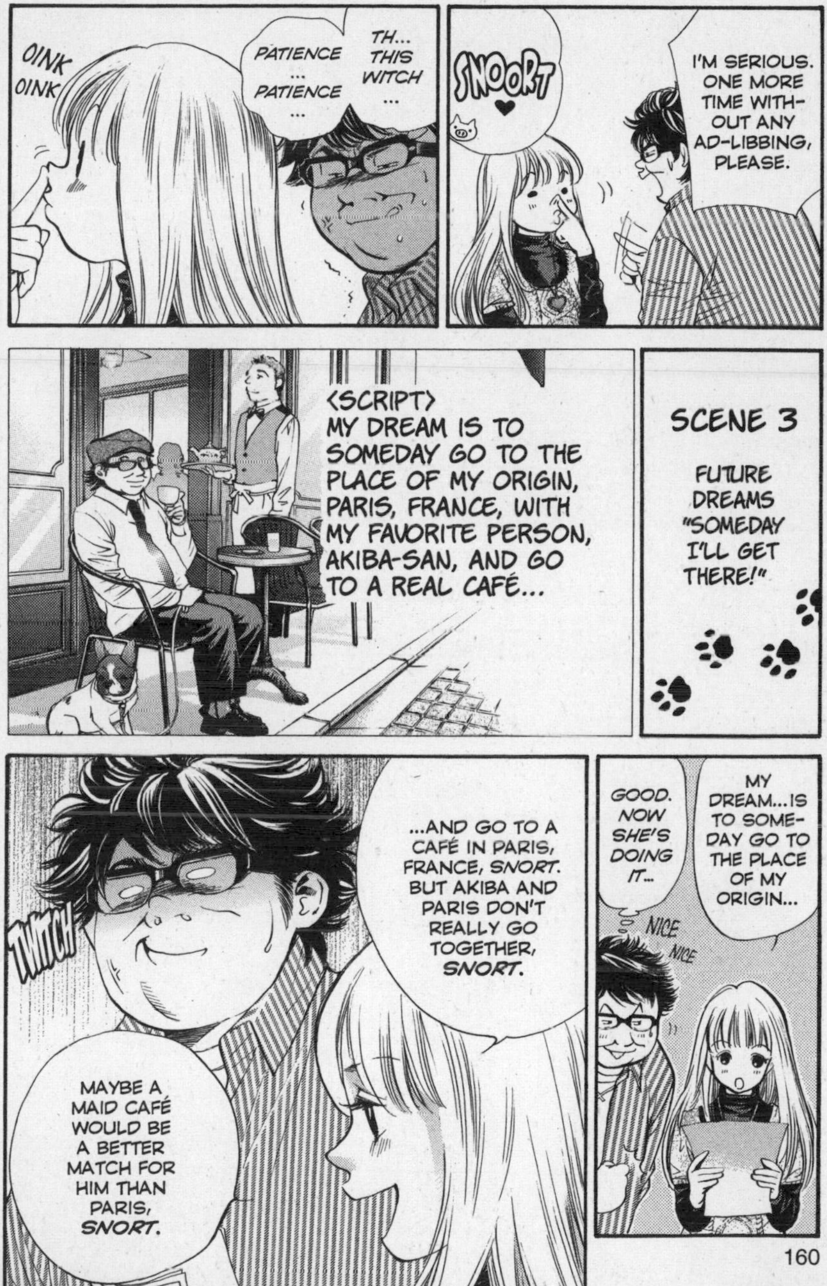
I'M SERIOUS. ONE MORE TIME WITHOUT ANY AD-LIBBING, PLEASE.
SNOORT ♥
TH... THIS WITCH ...
PATIENCE ... PATIENCE ...
OINK OINK
SCENE 3
FUTURE DREAMS "SOMEDAY I'LL GET THERE!"
<SCRIPT> MY DREAM IS TO SOMEDAY GO TO THE PLACE OF MY ORIGIN, PARIS, FRANCE, WITH MY FAVORITE PERSON, AKIBA-SAN, AND GO TO A REAL CAFÉ...
MY DREAM...IS TO SOMEDAY GO TO THE PLACE OF MY ORIGIN...
GOOD. NOW SHE'S DOING IT...
NICE NICE
...AND GO TO A CAFÉ IN PARIS, FRANCE, *SNORT*. BUT AKIBA AND PARIS DON'T REALLY GO TOGETHER, *SNORT*.
TWITCH
MAYBE A MAID CAFÉ WOULD BE A BETTER MATCH FOR HIM THAN PARIS, *SNORT*.

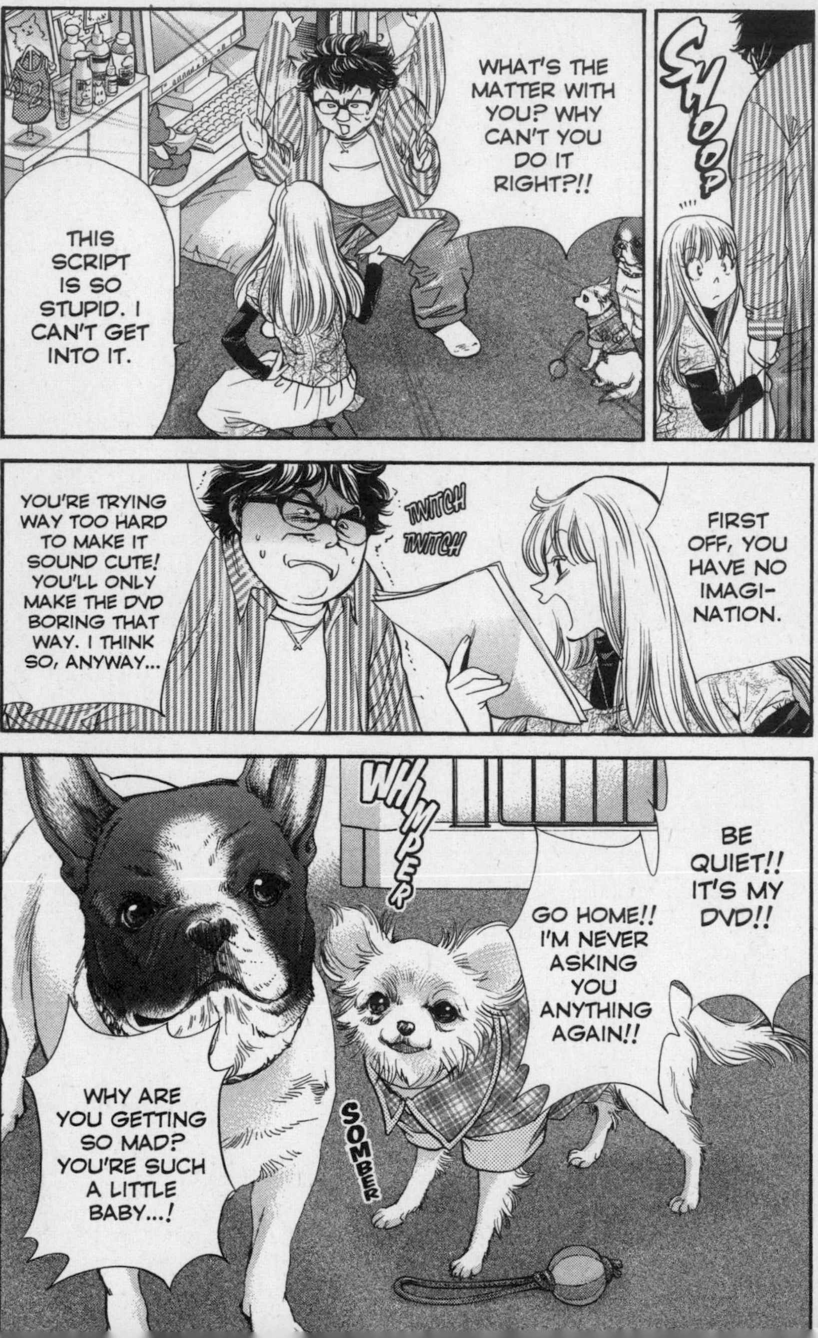
SHOOP
WHAT'S THE MATTER WITH YOU? WHY CAN'T YOU DO IT RIGHT?!!
THIS SCRIPT IS SO STUPID. I CAN'T GET INTO IT.
FIRST OFF, YOU HAVE NO IMAGI-NATION.
TWITCH TWITCH
YOU'RE TRYING WAY TOO HARD TO MAKE IT SOUND CUTE! YOU'LL ONLY MAKE THE DVD BORING THAT WAY. I THINK SO, ANYWAY...
BE QUIET!! IT'S MY DVD!!
WHIMPER
GO HOME!! I'M NEVER ASKING YOU ANYTHING AGAIN!!
SOMBER
WHY ARE YOU GETTING SO MAD? YOU'RE SUCH A LITTLE BABY...!

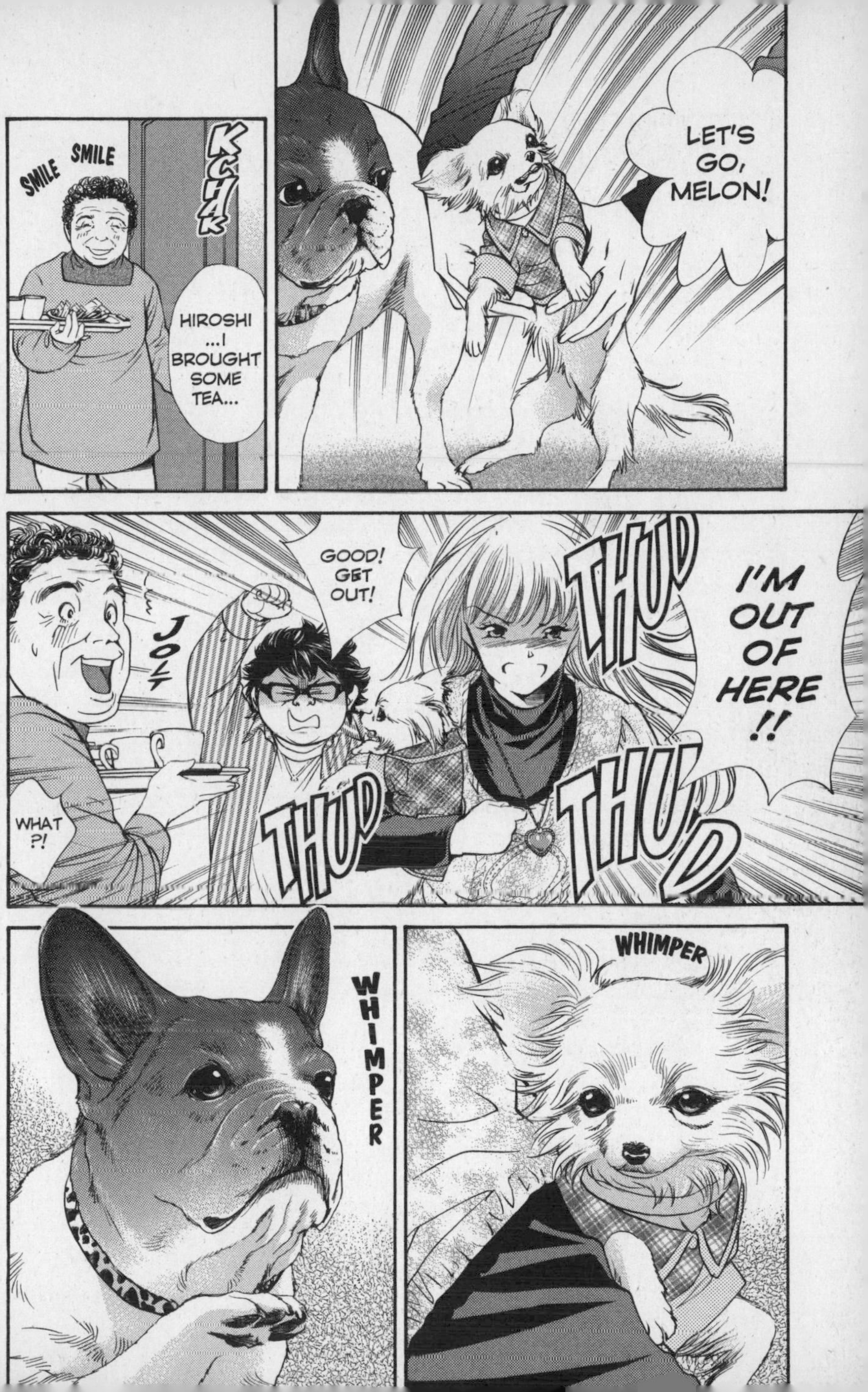
LET'S GO, MELON!
SMILE SMILE
KCHAK
HIROSHI ...I BROUGHT SOME TEA...
I'M OUT OF HERE!!
THUD
THUD
GOOD! GET OUT!
JOLT
THUD
WHAT ?!
WHIMPER
WHIMPER

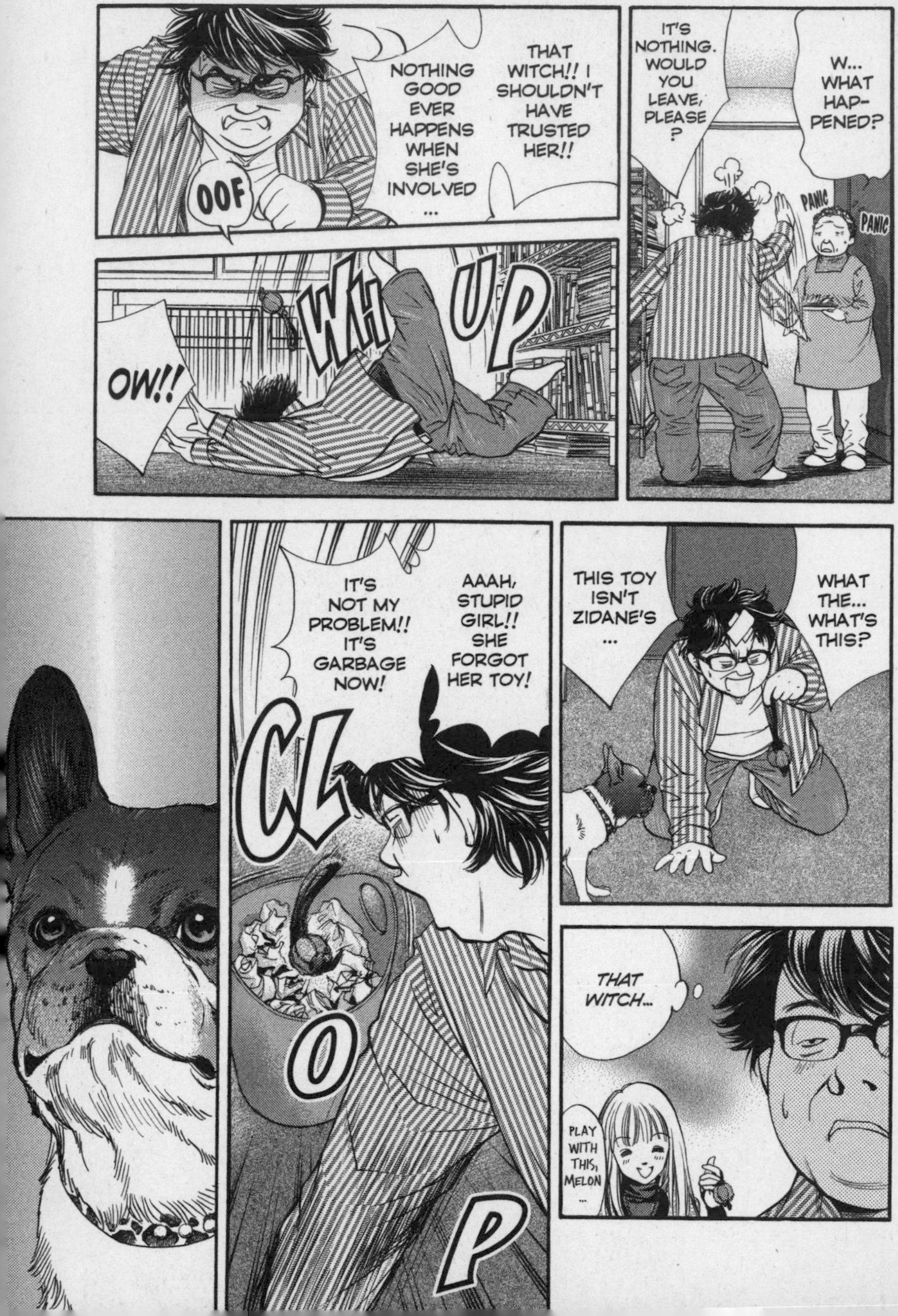
W... WHAT HAP-PENED?
IT'S NOTHING. WOULD YOU LEAVE, PLEASE?
PANIC
PANIC
THAT WITCH!! I SHOULDN'T HAVE TRUSTED HER!!
NOTHING GOOD EVER HAPPENS WHEN SHE'S INVOLVED...
OOF
WHUP
OW!!
WHAT THE... WHAT'S THIS?
THIS TOY ISN'T ZIDANE'S...
THAT WITCH...
PLAY WITH THIS, MELON...
AAAH, STUPID GIRL!! SHE FORGOT HER TOY!
IT'S NOT MY PROBLEM!! IT'S GARBAGE NOW!
CLOP

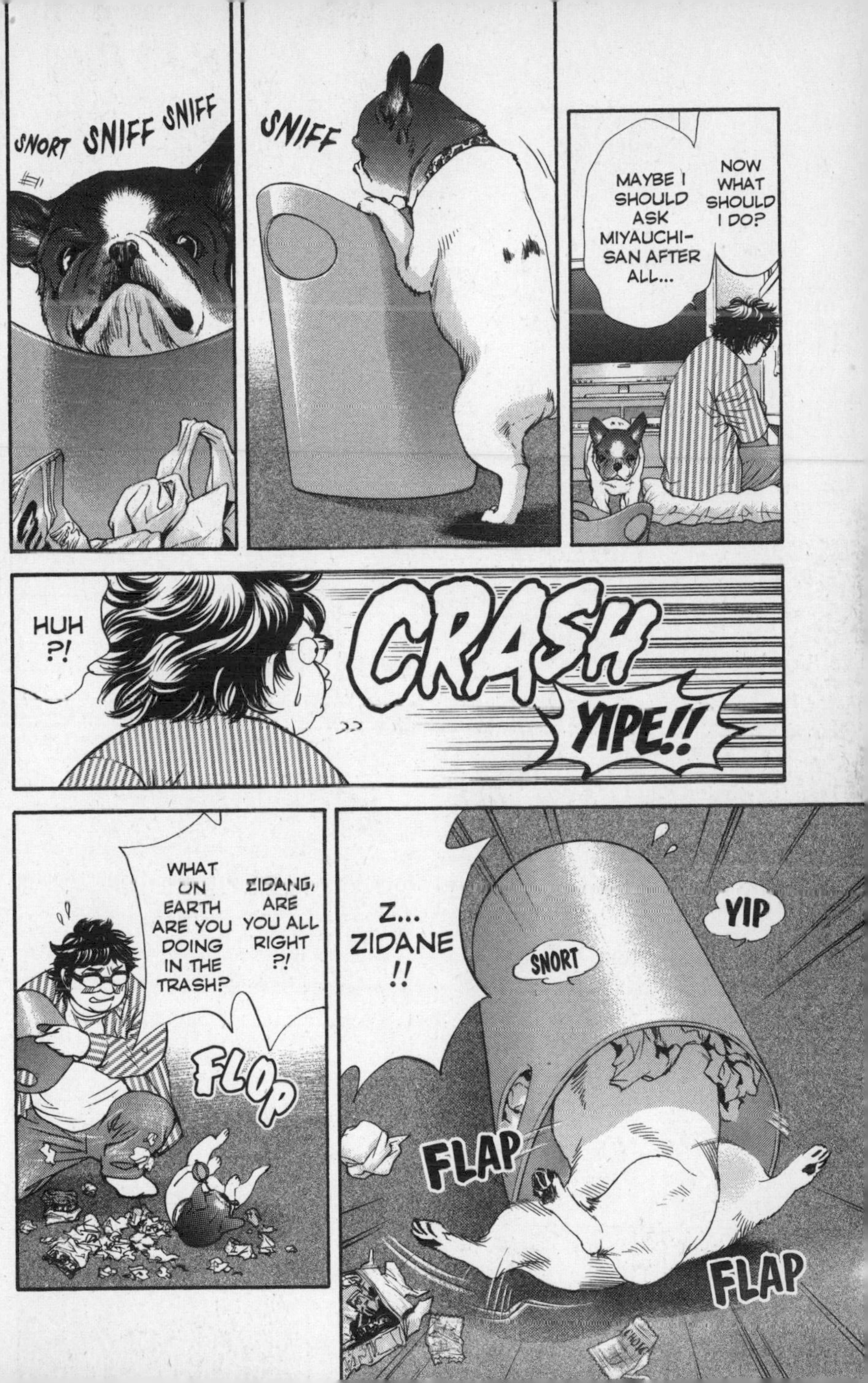
NOW WHAT SHOULD I DO?
MAYBE I SHOULD ASK MIYAUCHI-SAN AFTER ALL...
SNIFF
SNIFF SNIFF
SNORT
CRASH
YIPE!!
HUH?!
YIP
SNORT
Z... ZIDANE!!
FLAP
FLAP
ZIDANE, ARE YOU ALL RIGHT?!
WHAT ON EARTH ARE YOU DOING IN THE TRASH?
FLOP

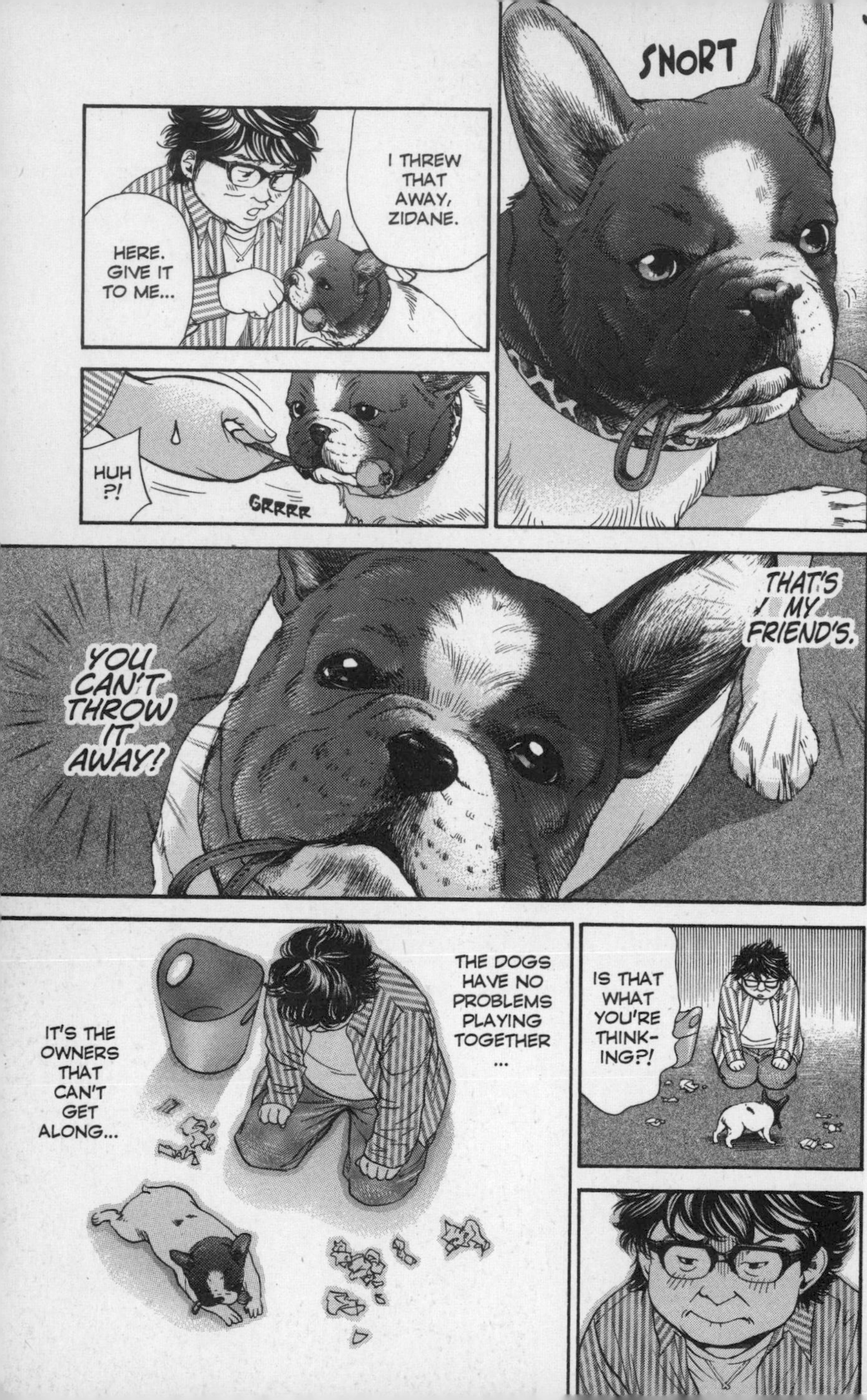
SNORT
I THREW THAT AWAY, ZIDANE.
HERE. GIVE IT TO ME...
HUH?!
GRRRR
THAT'S MY FRIEND'S.
YOU CAN'T THROW IT AWAY!
IS THAT WHAT YOU'RE THINKING?!
THE DOGS HAVE NO PROBLEMS PLAYING TOGETHER ...
IT'S THE OWNERS THAT CAN'T GET ALONG...

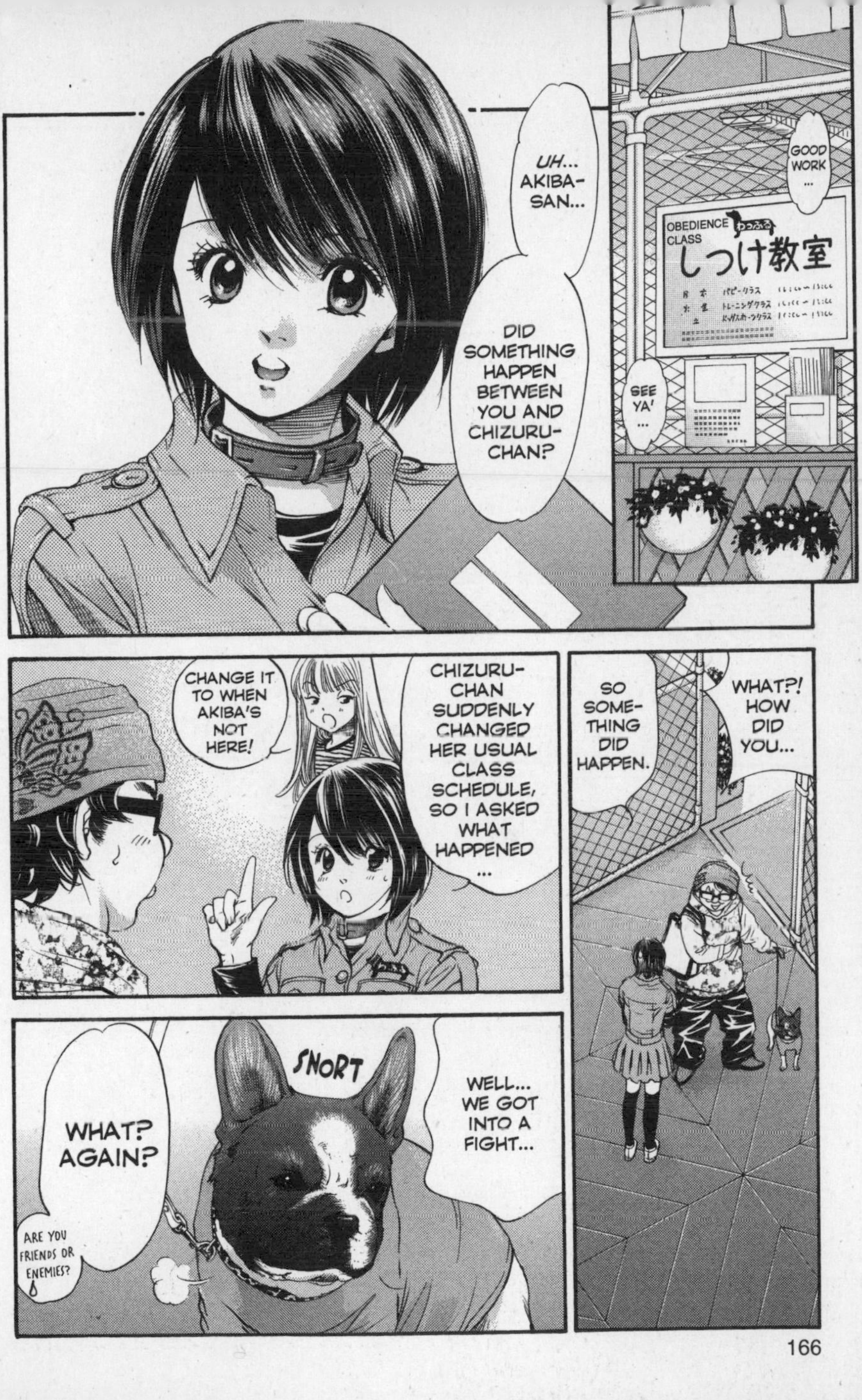
GOOD WORK ...
OBEDIENCE CLASS
しつけ教室
SEE YA' ...
UH... AKIBA-SAN...
DID SOMETHING HAPPEN BETWEEN YOU AND CHIZURU-CHAN?
WHAT?! HOW DID YOU...
SO SOMETHING DID HAPPEN.
CHIZURU-CHAN SUDDENLY CHANGED HER USUAL CLASS SCHEDULE, SO I ASKED WHAT HAPPENED ...
CHANGE IT TO WHEN AKIBA'S NOT HERE!
WELL... WE GOT INTO A FIGHT...
SNORT
WHAT? AGAIN?
ARE YOU FRIENDS OR ENEMIES?

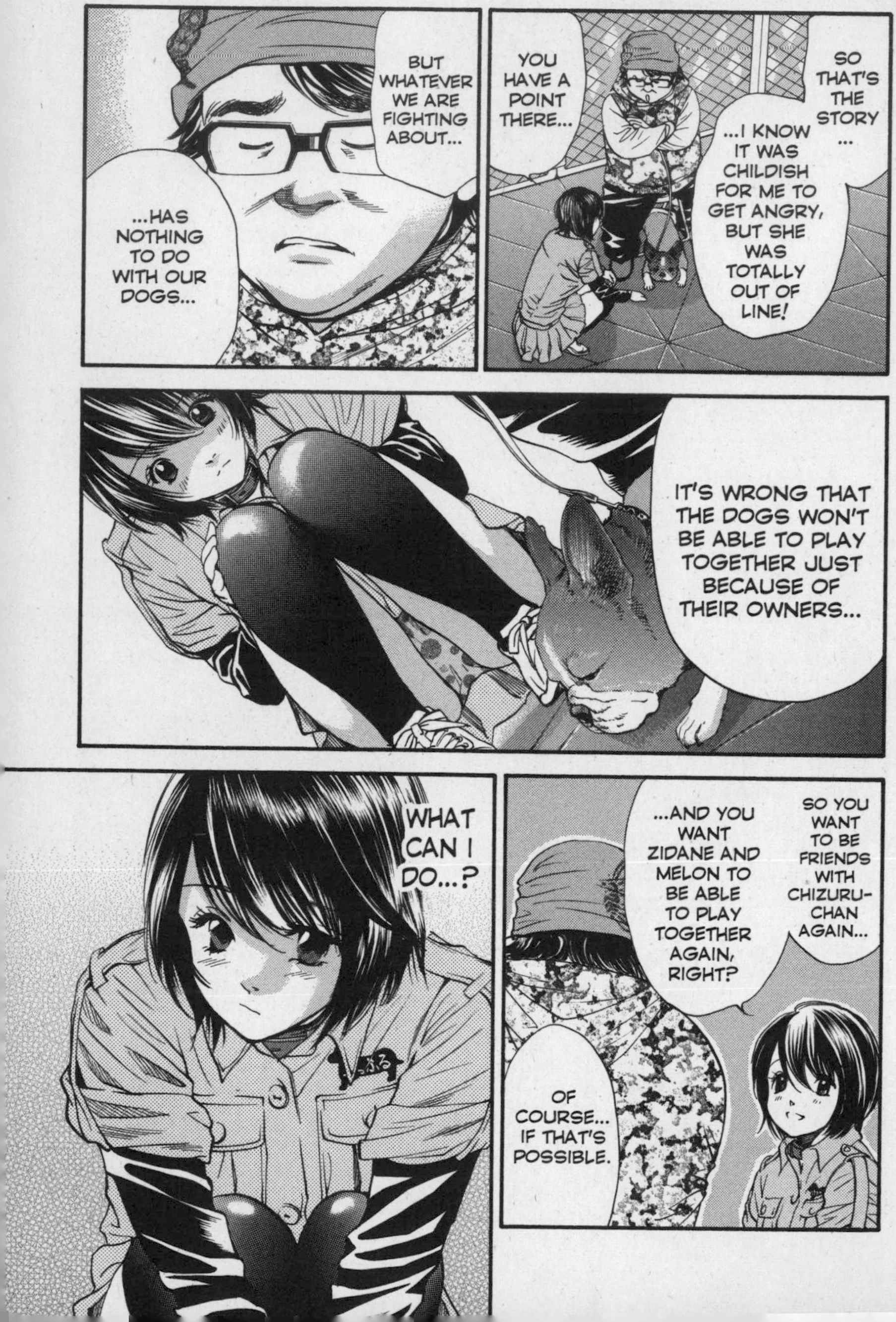
SO THAT'S THE STORY...
...I KNOW IT WAS CHILDISH FOR ME TO GET ANGRY, BUT SHE WAS TOTALLY OUT OF LINE!
YOU HAVE A POINT THERE...
BUT WHATEVER WE ARE FIGHTING ABOUT...
...HAS NOTHING TO DO WITH OUR DOGS...
IT'S WRONG THAT THE DOGS WON'T BE ABLE TO PLAY TOGETHER JUST BECAUSE OF THEIR OWNERS...
SO YOU WANT TO BE FRIENDS WITH CHIZURU-CHAN AGAIN...
...AND YOU WANT ZIDANE AND MELON TO BE ABLE TO PLAY TOGETHER AGAIN, RIGHT?
OF COURSE... IF THAT'S POSSIBLE.
WHAT CAN I DO...?

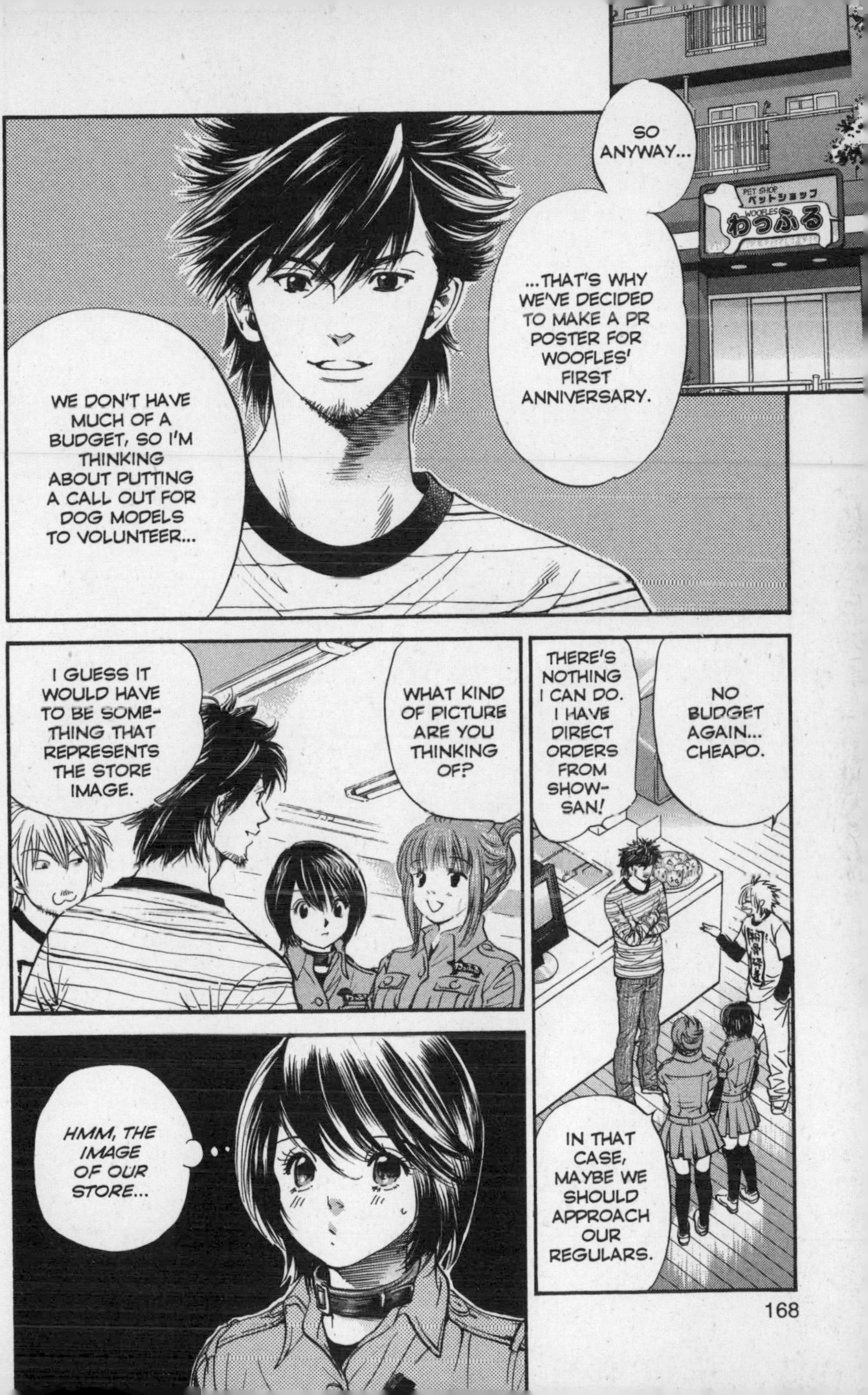

SO ANYWAY...
PET SHOP
ペットショップ
WOOFLES
わっふる
...THAT'S WHY WE'VE DECIDED TO MAKE A PR POSTER FOR WOOFLES' FIRST ANNIVERSARY.
WE DON'T HAVE MUCH OF A BUDGET, SO I'M THINKING ABOUT PUTTING A CALL OUT FOR DOG MODELS TO VOLUNTEER...
NO BUDGET AGAIN... CHEAPO.
THERE'S NOTHING I CAN DO. I HAVE DIRECT ORDERS FROM SHOW-SAN!
IN THAT CASE, MAYBE WE SHOULD APPROACH OUR REGULARS.
WHAT KIND OF PICTURE ARE YOU THINKING OF?
I GUESS IT WOULD HAVE TO BE SOME-THING THAT REPRESENTS THE STORE IMAGE.
HMM, THE IMAGE OF OUR STORE...

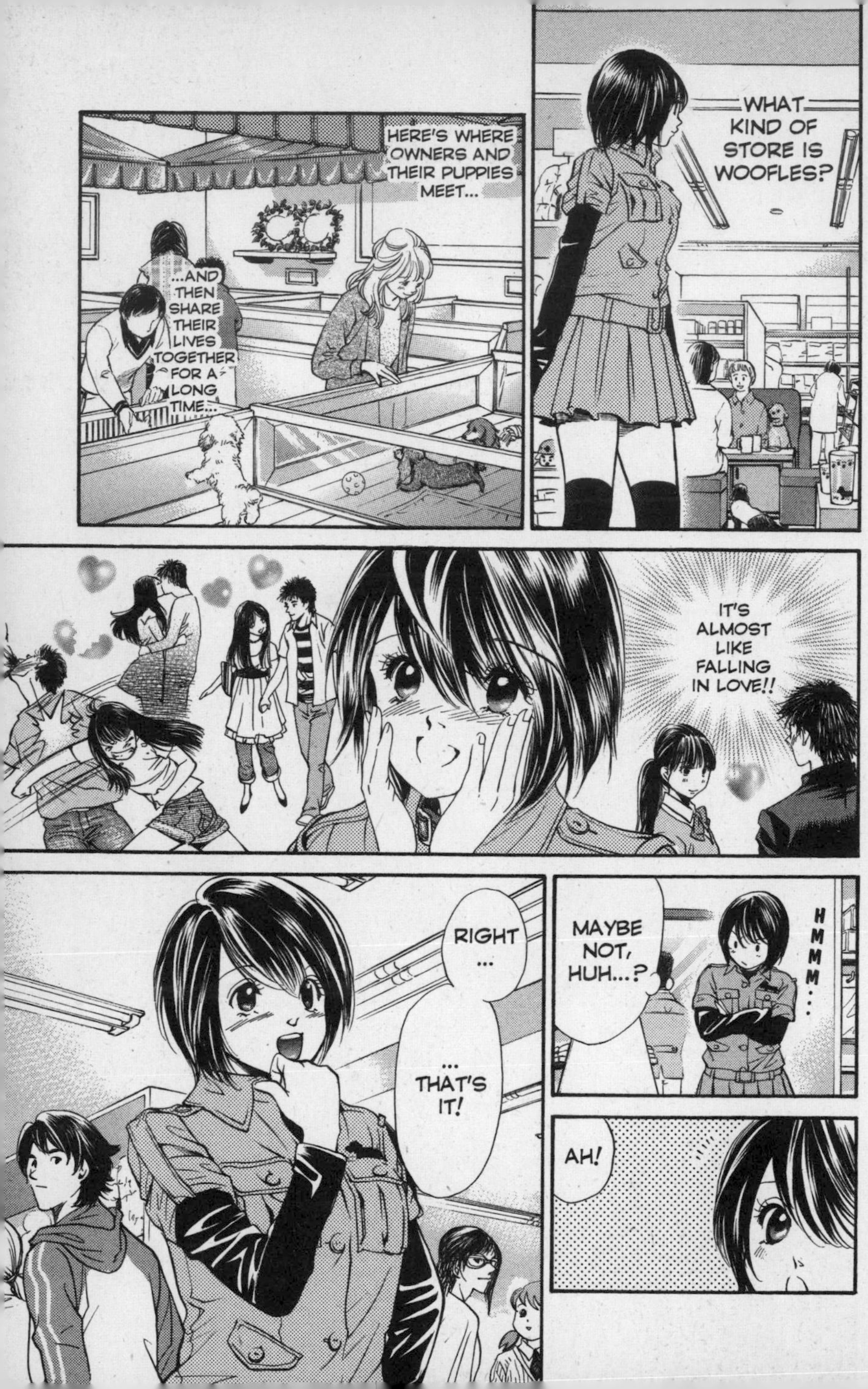
WHAT KIND OF STORE IS WOOFLES?
HERE'S WHERE OWNERS AND THEIR PUPPIES MEET...
...AND THEN SHARE THEIR LIVES TOGETHER FOR A LONG TIME...
IT'S ALMOST LIKE FALLING IN LOVE!!
HMMM...
MAYBE NOT, HUH...?
AH!
RIGHT...
...THAT'S IT!

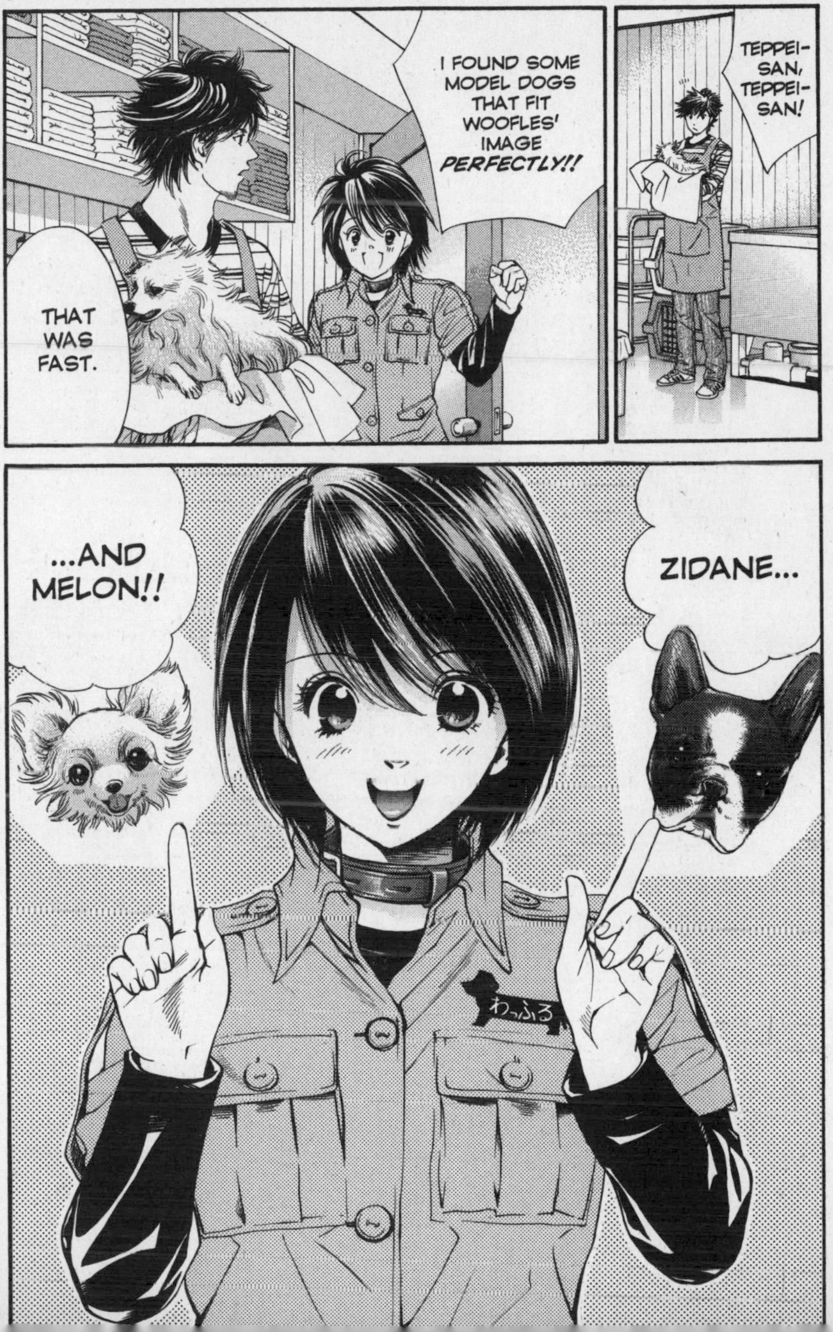
TEPPEI-SAN, TEPPEI-SAN!
I FOUND SOME MODEL DOGS THAT FIT WOOFLES' IMAGE PERFECTLY!!
THAT WAS FAST.
ZIDANE...
...AND MELON!!
わっふる

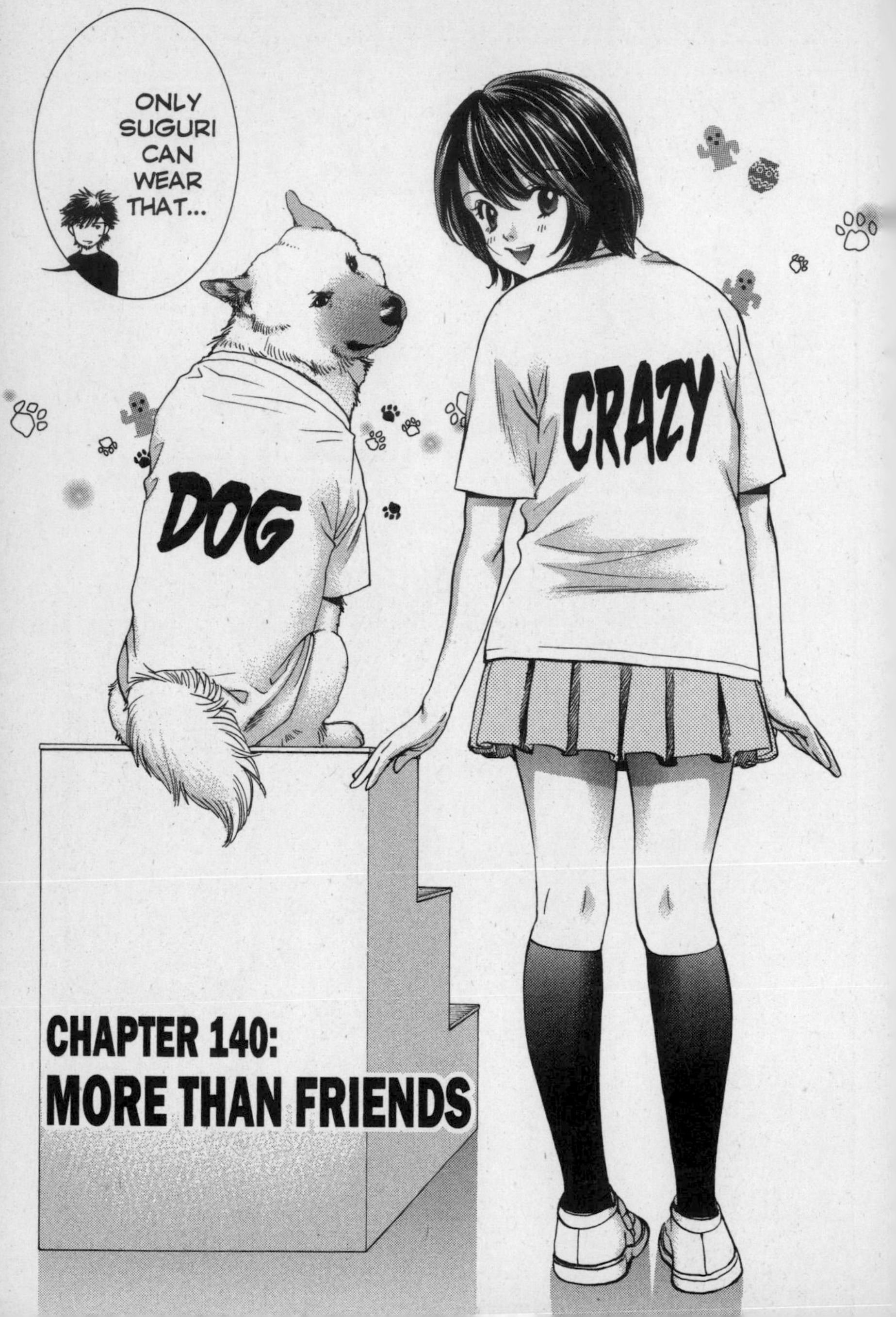
ONLY SUGURI CAN WEAR THAT...
DOG
CRAZY

CHAPTER 140: MORE THAN FRIENDS

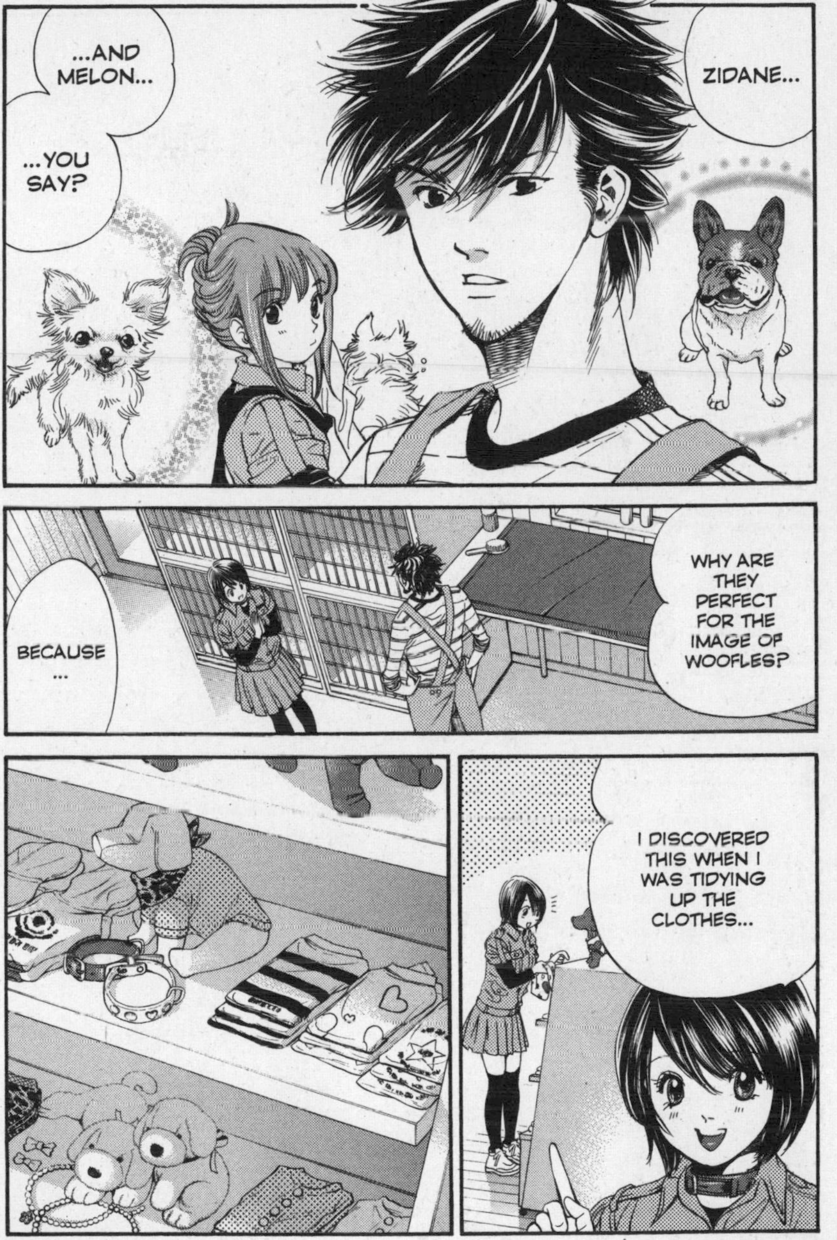
ZIDANE...
...AND MELON...
...YOU SAY?
WHY ARE THEY PERFECT FOR THE IMAGE OF WOOFLES?
BECAUSE ...
I DISCOVERED THIS WHEN I WAS TIDYING UP THE CLOTHES...

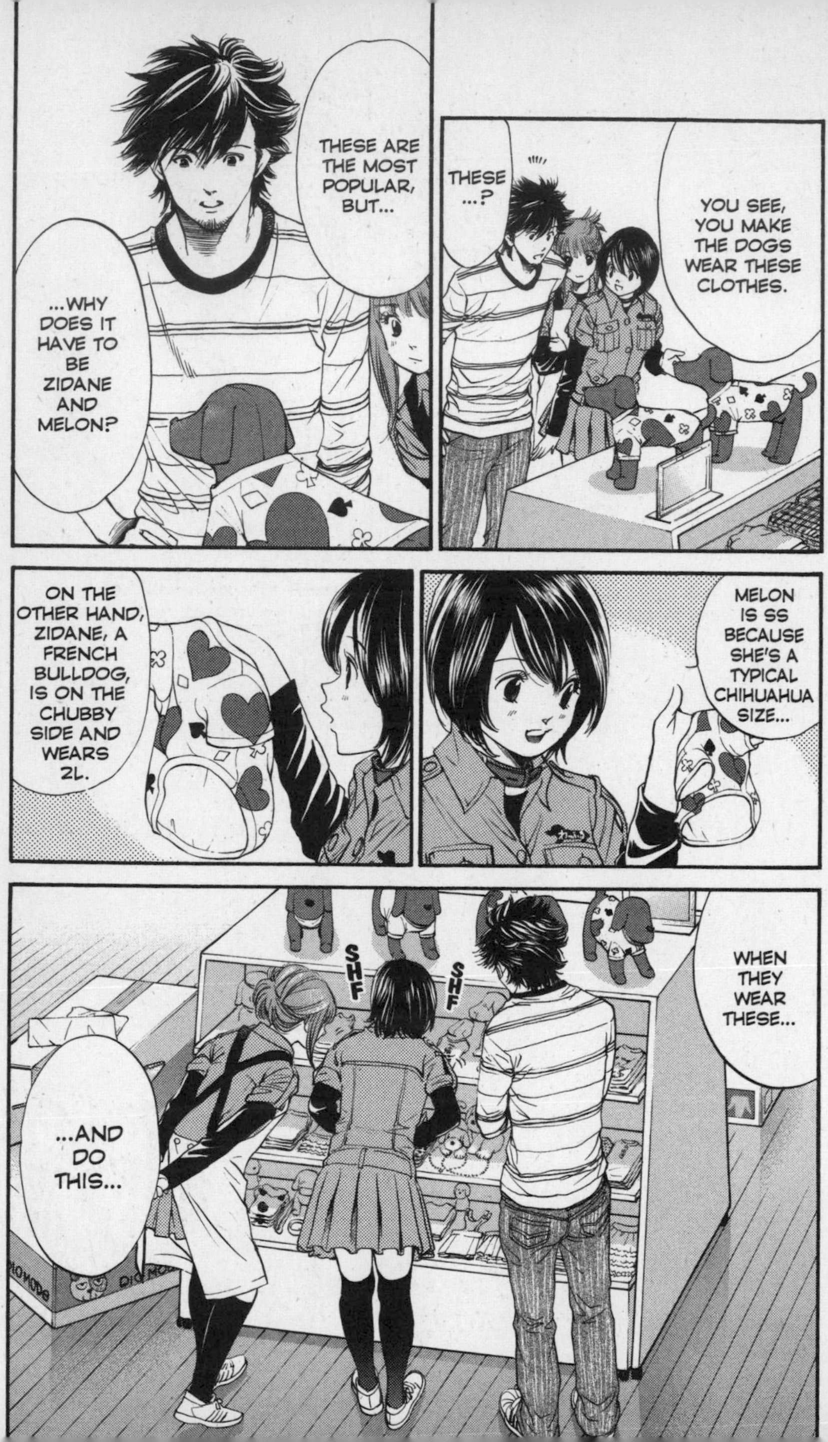
YOU SEE, YOU MAKE THE DOGS WEAR THESE CLOTHES.
THESE ...?
THESE ARE THE MOST POPULAR, BUT...
...WHY DOES IT HAVE TO BE ZIDANE AND MELON?
MELON IS SS BECAUSE SHE'S A TYPICAL CHIHUAHUA SIZE...
ON THE OTHER HAND, ZIDANE, A FRENCH BULLDOG, IS ON THE CHUBBY SIDE AND WEARS 2L.
WHEN THEY WEAR THESE...
SHF
SHF
...AND DO THIS...

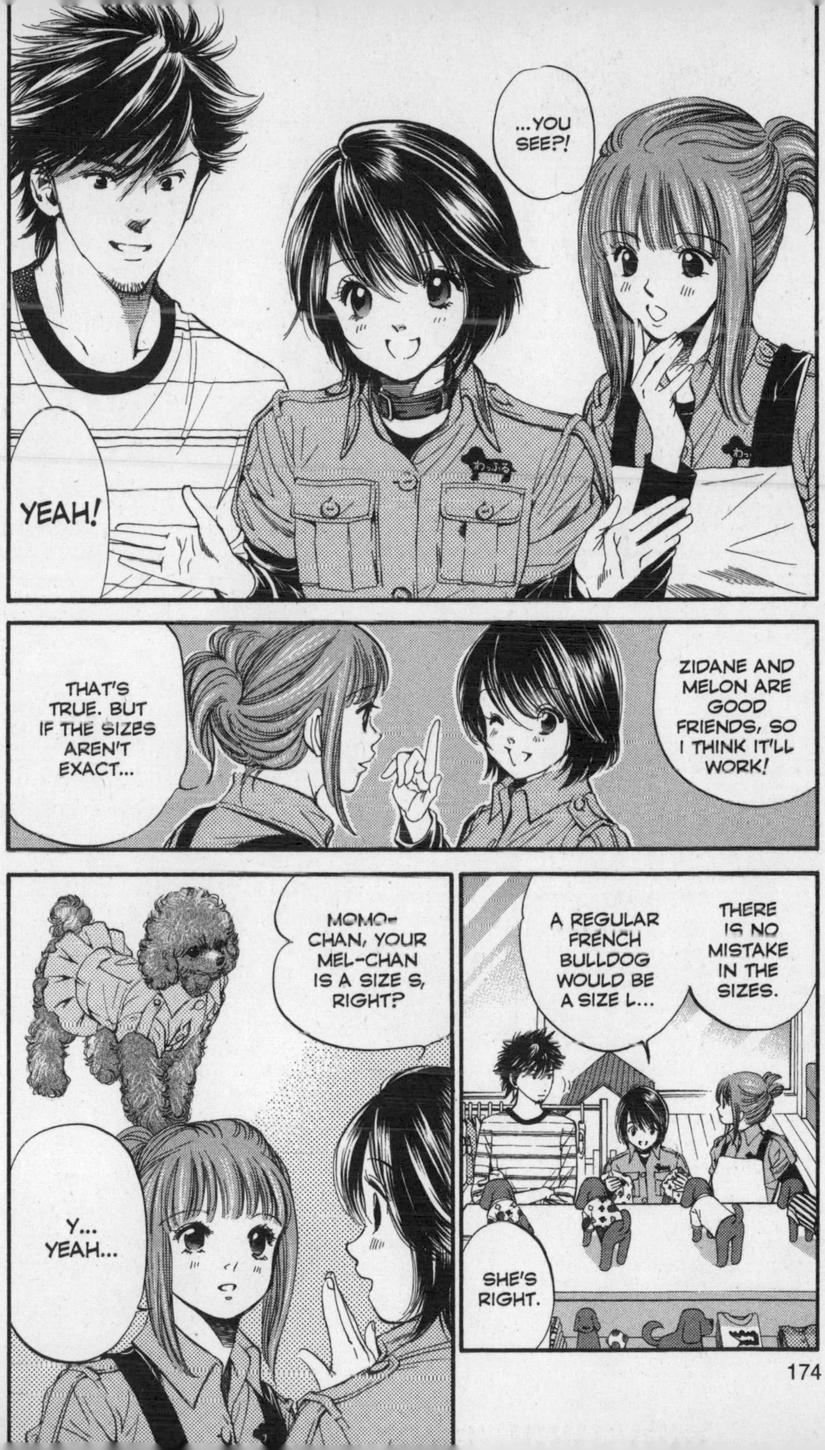
...YOU SEE?!
YEAH!
ZIDANE AND MELON ARE GOOD FRIENDS, SO I THINK IT'LL WORK!
THAT'S TRUE. BUT IF THE SIZES AREN'T EXACT...
THERE IS NO MISTAKE IN THE SIZES.
A REGULAR FRENCH BULLDOG WOULD BE A SIZE L...
SHE'S RIGHT.
MOMO-CHAN, YOUR MEL-CHAN IS A SIZE S, RIGHT?
Y... YEAH...

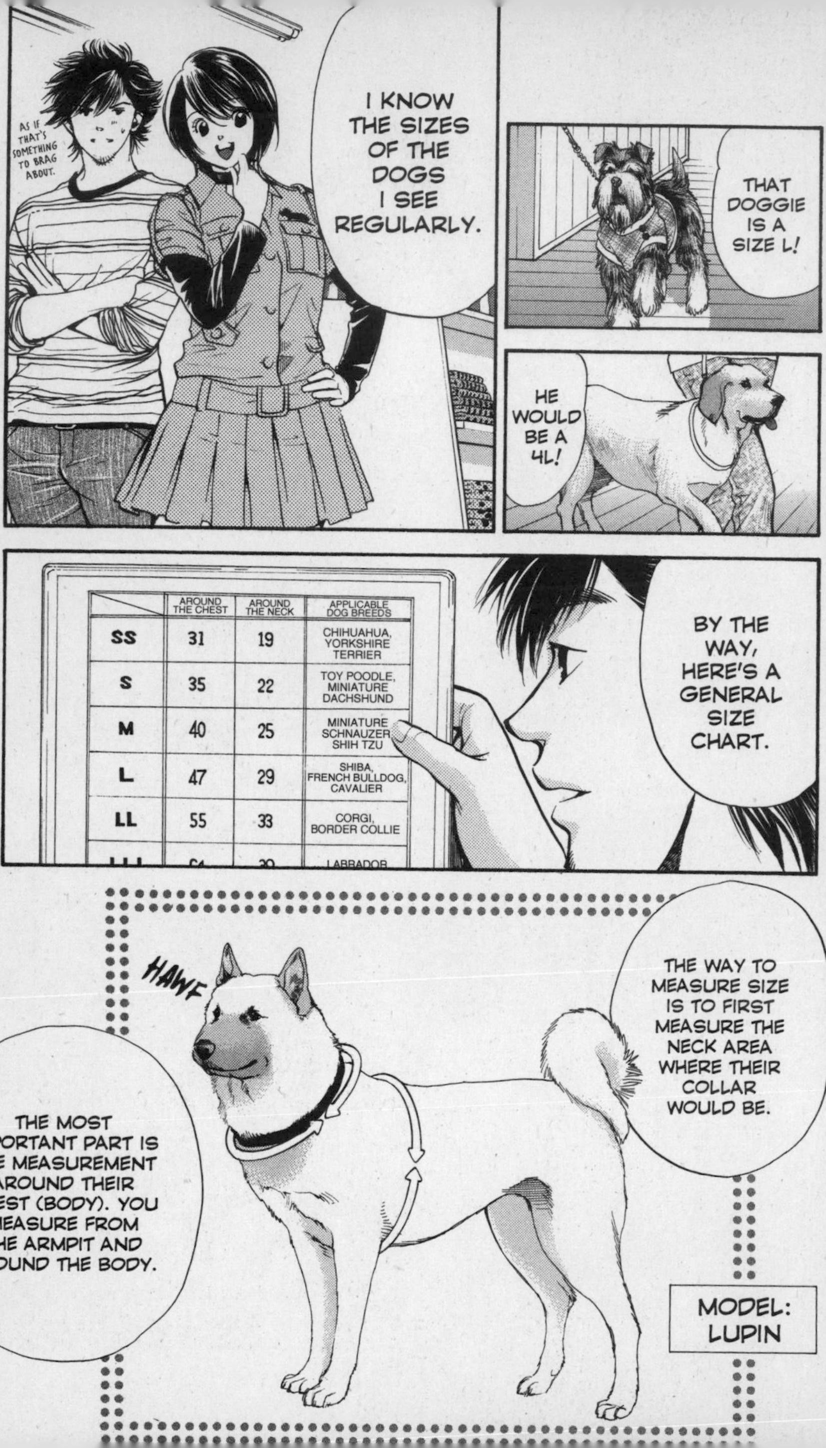
THAT DOGGIE IS A SIZE L!
HE WOULD BE A 4L!
I KNOW THE SIZES OF THE DOGS I SEE REGULARLY.
AS IF THAT'S SOMETHING TO BRAG ABOUT.
BY THE WAY, HERE'S A GENERAL SIZE CHART.
AROUND THE CHEST
AROUND THE NECK
APPLICABLE DOG BREEDS
SS 31 19 CHIHUAHUA, YORKSHIRE TERRIER
S 35 22 TOY POODLE, MINIATURE DACHSHUND
M 40 25 MINIATURE SCHNAUZER SHIH TZU
L 47 29 SHIBA, FRENCH BULLDOG, CAVALIER
LL 55 33 CORGI, BORDER COLLIE
THE WAY TO MEASURE SIZE IS TO FIRST MEASURE THE NECK AREA WHERE THEIR COLLAR WOULD BE.
HAWF
THE MOST IMPORTANT PART IS THE MEASUREMENT AROUND THEIR CHEST (BODY). YOU MEASURE FROM THE ARMPIT AND AROUND THE BODY.
MODEL: LUPIN

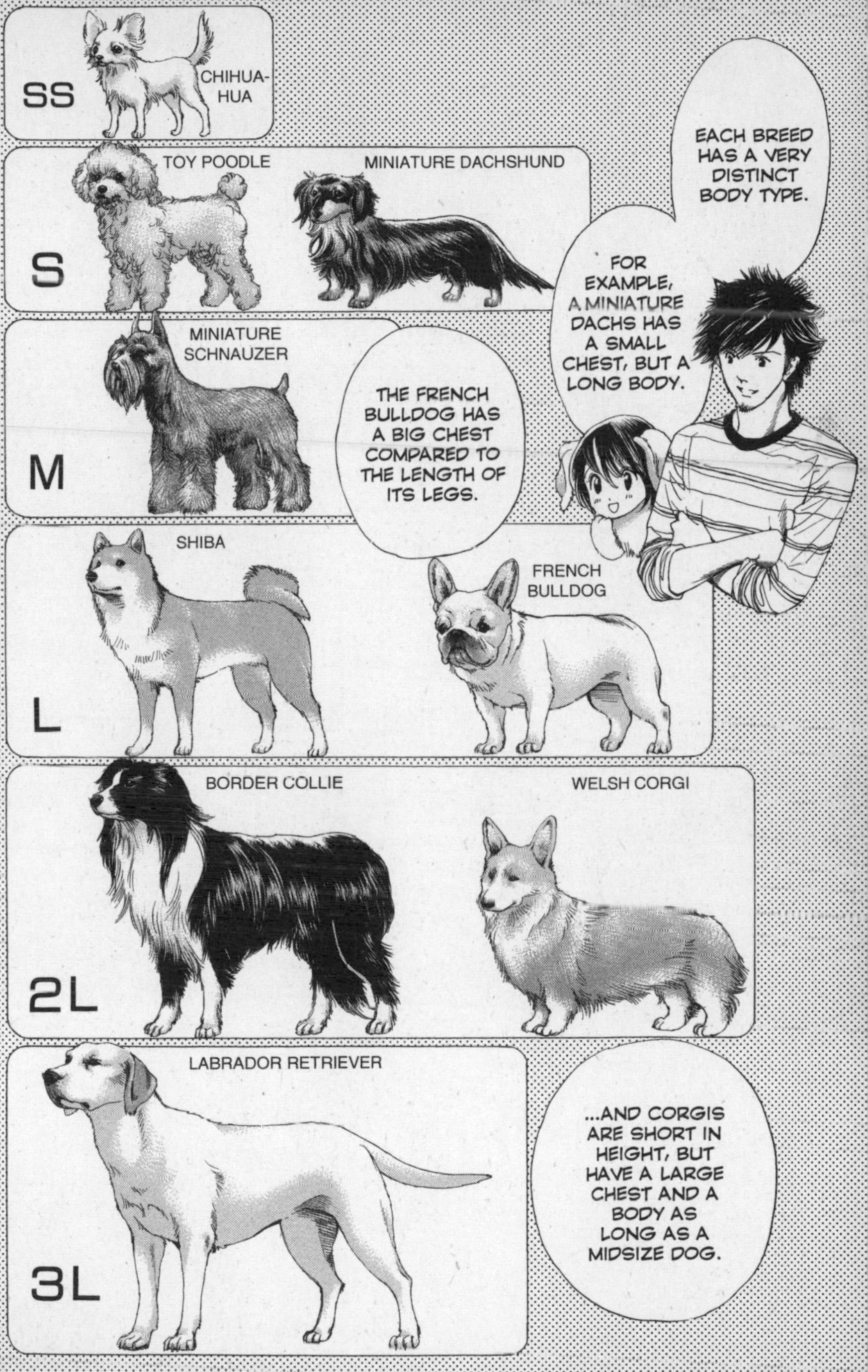

SS
CHIHUA-HUA
EACH BREED HAS A VERY DISTINCT BODY TYPE.
MINIATURE DACHSHUND
TOY POODLE
S
FOR EXAMPLE, A MINIATURE DACHS HAS A SMALL CHEST, BUT A LONG BODY.
THE FRENCH BULLDOG HAS A BIG CHEST COMPARED TO THE LENGTH OF ITS LEGS.
MINIATURE SCHNAUZER
M
FRENCH BULLDOG
SHIBA
L
WELSH CORGI
BORDER COLLIE
2L
...AND CORGIS ARE SHORT IN HEIGHT, BUT HAVE A LARGE CHEST AND A BODY AS LONG AS A MIDSIZE DOG.
LABRADOR RETRIEVER
3L

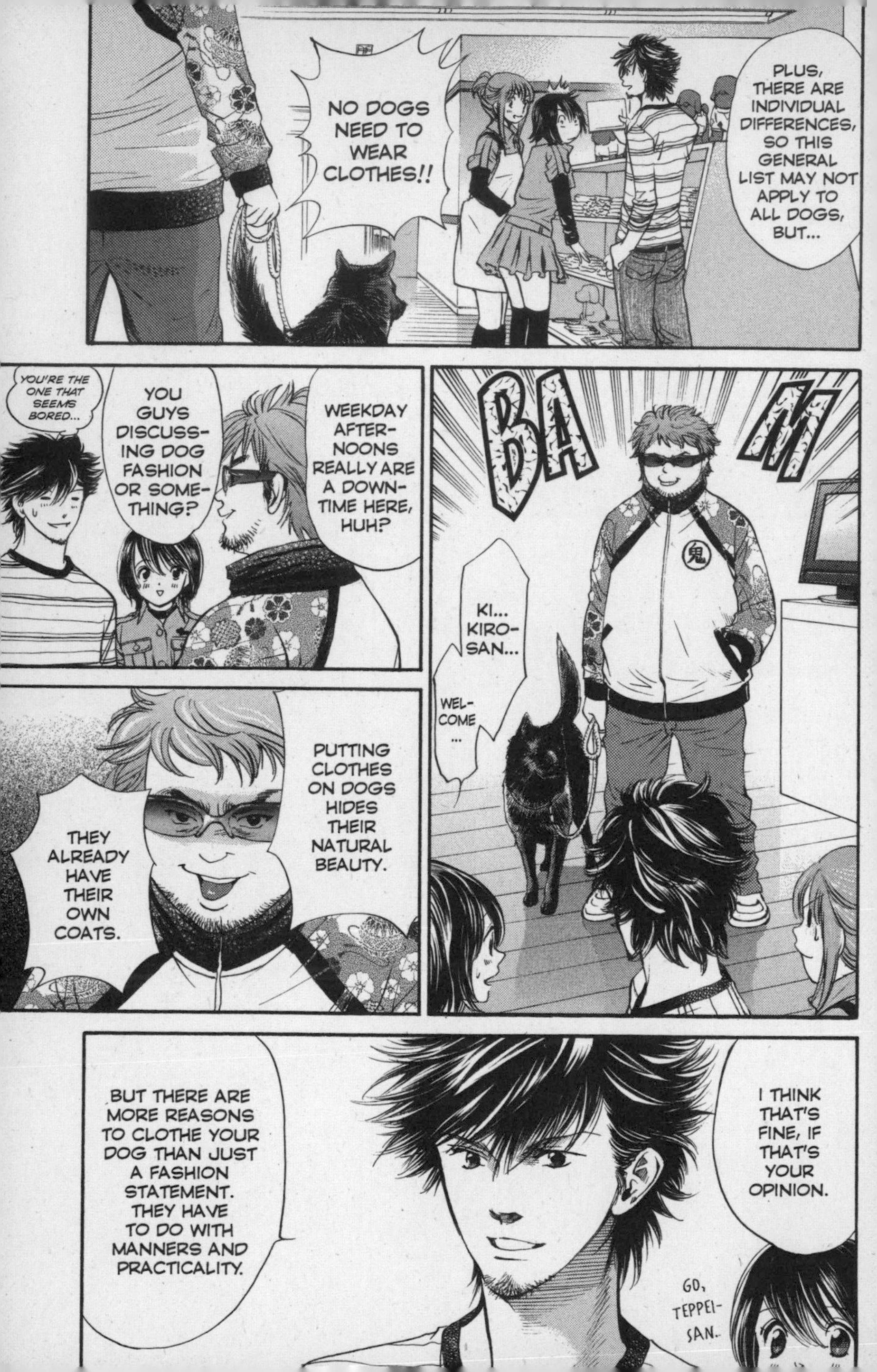
PLUS, THERE ARE INDIVIDUAL DIFFERENCES, SO THIS GENERAL LIST MAY NOT APPLY TO ALL DOGS, BUT...
NO DOGS NEED TO WEAR CLOTHES!!
BAM
KI... KIRO-SAN...
WEL-COME...
WEEKDAY AFTER-NOONS REALLY ARE A DOWN-TIME HERE, HUH?
YOU GUYS DISCUSS-ING DOG FASHION OR SOME-THING?
YOU'RE THE ONE THAT SEEMS BORED...
PUTTING CLOTHES ON DOGS HIDES THEIR NATURAL BEAUTY.
THEY ALREADY HAVE THEIR OWN COATS.
I THINK THAT'S FINE, IF THAT'S YOUR OPINION.
BUT THERE ARE MORE REASONS TO CLOTHE YOUR DOG THAN JUST A FASHION STATEMENT. THEY HAVE TO DO WITH MANNERS AND PRACTICALITY.
GO, TEPPEI-SAN..

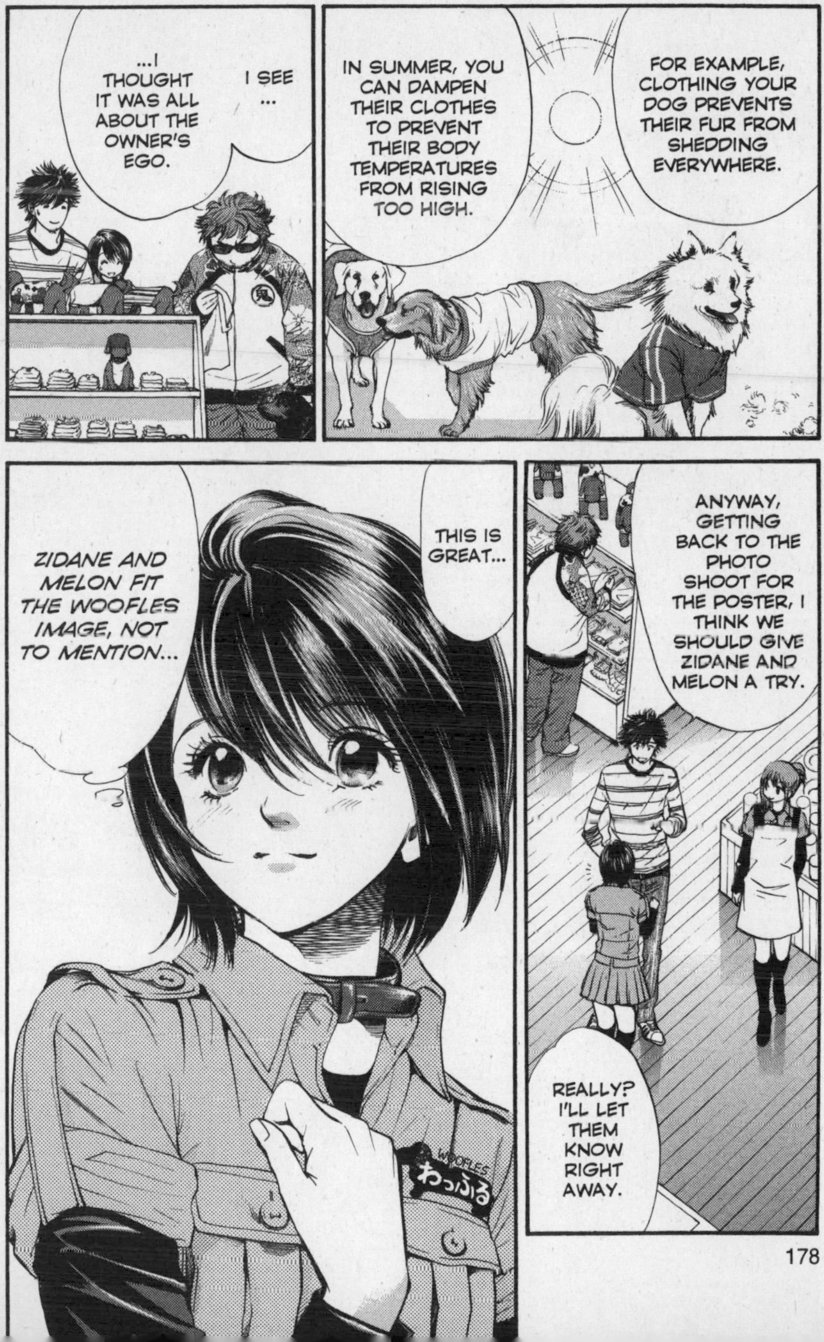
FOR EXAMPLE, CLOTHING YOUR DOG PREVENTS THEIR FUR FROM SHEDDING EVERYWHERE.
IN SUMMER, YOU CAN DAMPEN THEIR CLOTHES TO PREVENT THEIR BODY TEMPERATURES FROM RISING TOO HIGH.
I SEE ...
...I THOUGHT IT WAS ALL ABOUT THE OWNER'S EGO.
ANYWAY, GETTING BACK TO THE PHOTO SHOOT FOR THE POSTER, I THINK WE SHOULD GIVE ZIDANE AND MELON A TRY.
REALLY? I'LL LET THEM KNOW RIGHT AWAY.
THIS IS GREAT...
ZIDANE AND MELON FIT THE WOOFLES IMAGE, NOT TO MENTION...
WOOFLES
わっぷる

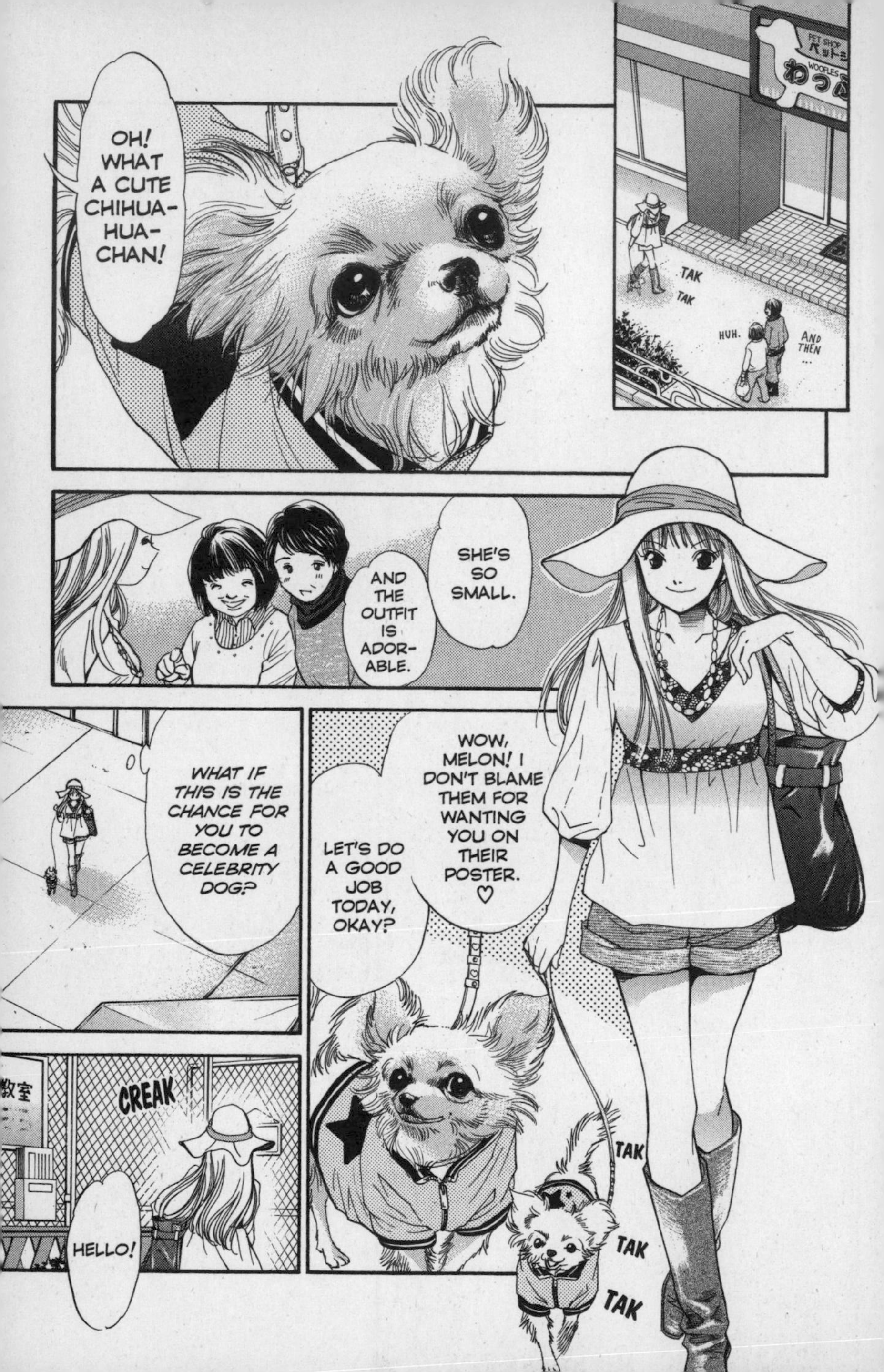
PET SHOP
WOOFLES
TAK
TAK
HUH.
AND THEN ...
OH! WHAT A CUTE CHIHUA-HUA-CHAN!
SHE'S SO SMALL.
AND THE OUTFIT IS ADORABLE.
WOW, MELON! I DON'T BLAME THEM FOR WANTING YOU ON THEIR POSTER. ♡
LET'S DO A GOOD JOB TODAY, OKAY?
TAK
TAK
TAK
WHAT IF THIS IS THE CHANCE FOR YOU TO BECOME A CELEBRITY DOG?
CREAK
HELLO!

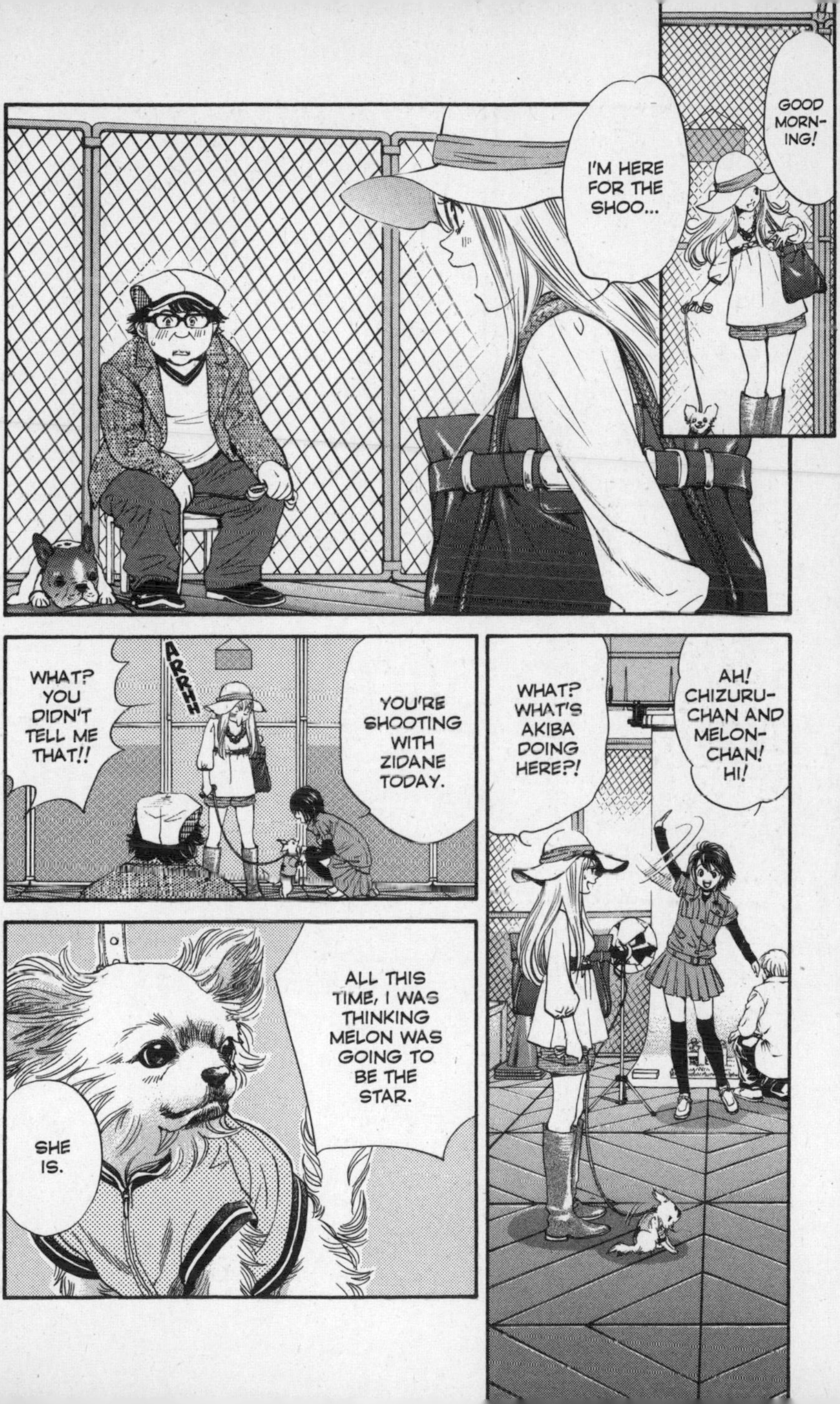
GOOD MORNING!
I'M HERE FOR THE SHOO...
AH! CHIZURU-CHAN AND MELON-CHAN! HI!
WHAT? WHAT'S AKIBA DOING HERE?!
YOU'RE SHOOTING WITH ZIDANE TODAY.
ARRHH
WHAT? YOU DIDN'T TELL ME THAT!!
ALL THIS TIME, I WAS THINKING MELON WAS GOING TO BE THE STAR.
SHE IS.

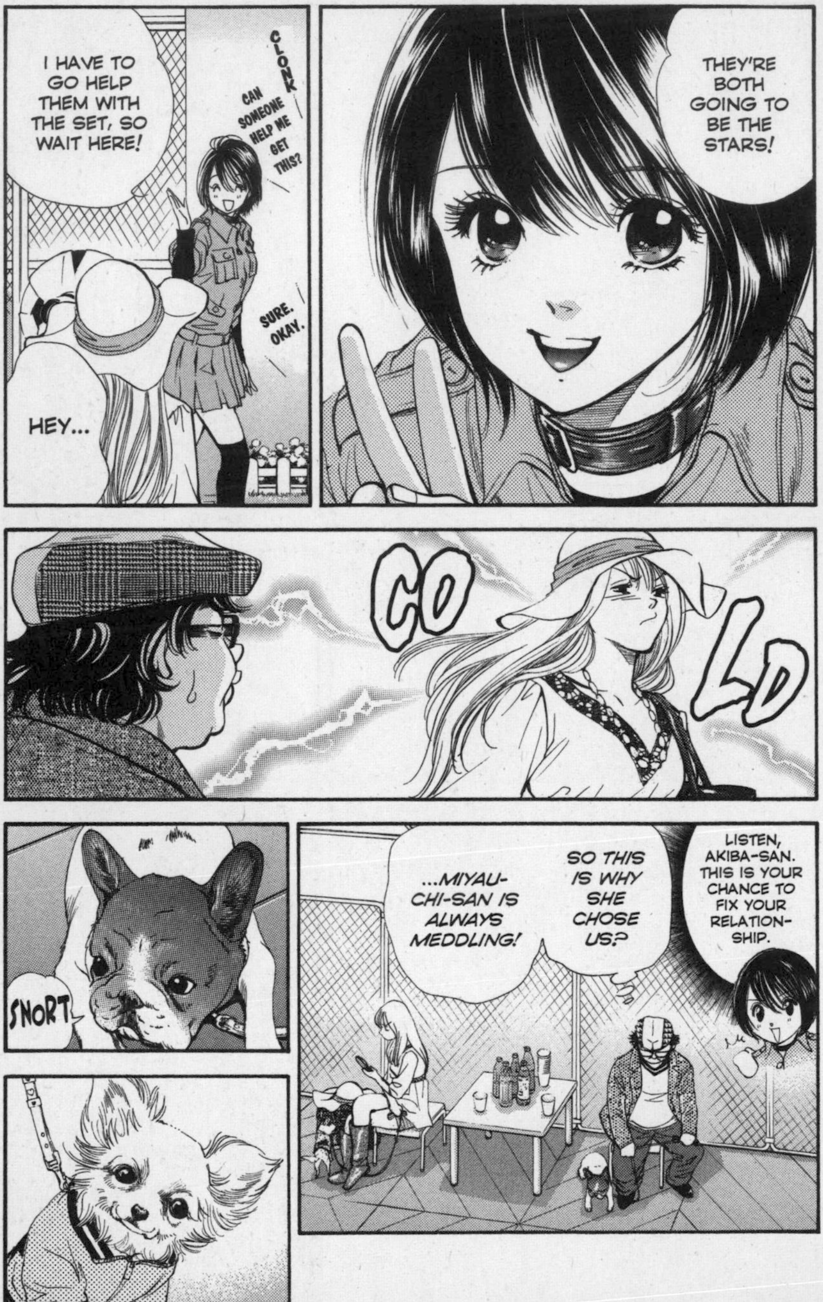
THEY'RE BOTH GOING TO BE THE STARS!
CLONK
CAN SOMEONE HELP ME GET THIS?
I HAVE TO GO HELP THEM WITH THE SET, SO WAIT HERE!
SURE. OKAY.
HEY...
COLD
LISTEN, AKIBA-SAN. THIS IS YOUR CHANCE TO FIX YOUR RELATION-SHIP.
SO THIS IS WHY SHE CHOSE US?
...MIYAU-CHI-SAN IS ALWAYS MEDDLING!
SNORT

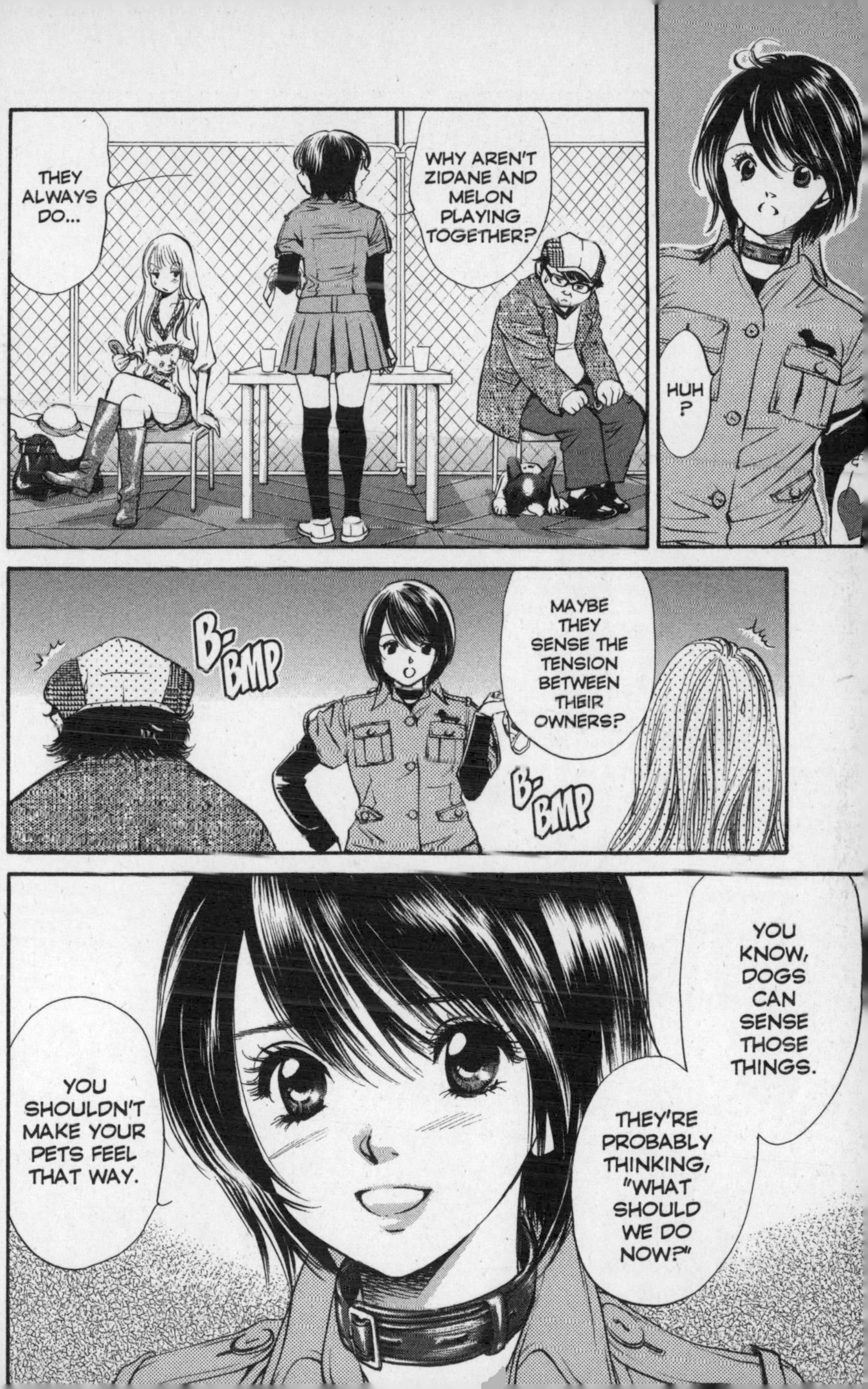

HUH?
WHY AREN'T ZIDANE AND MELON PLAYING TOGETHER?
THEY ALWAYS DO...
MAYBE THEY SENSE THE TENSION BETWEEN THEIR OWNERS?
B-BMP
B-BMP
YOU KNOW, DOGS CAN SENSE THOSE THINGS.
THEY'RE PROBABLY THINKING, "WHAT SHOULD WE DO NOW?"
YOU SHOULDN'T MAKE YOUR PETS FEEL THAT WAY.

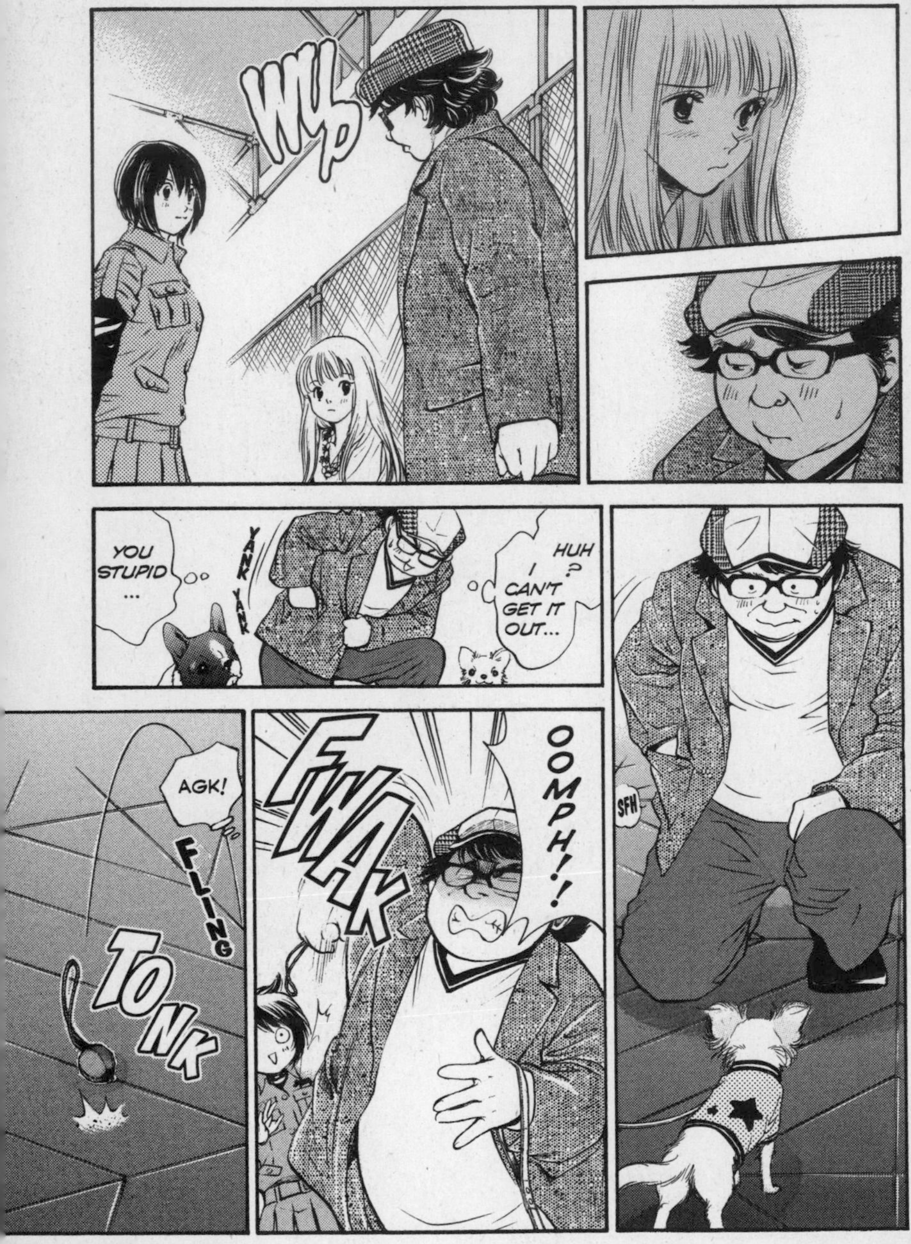
WUP
SFH
HUH? I CAN'T GET IT OUT...
YANK YANK
YOU STUPID...
OOMPH!!
FWAK
AGK!
FLING
TONK

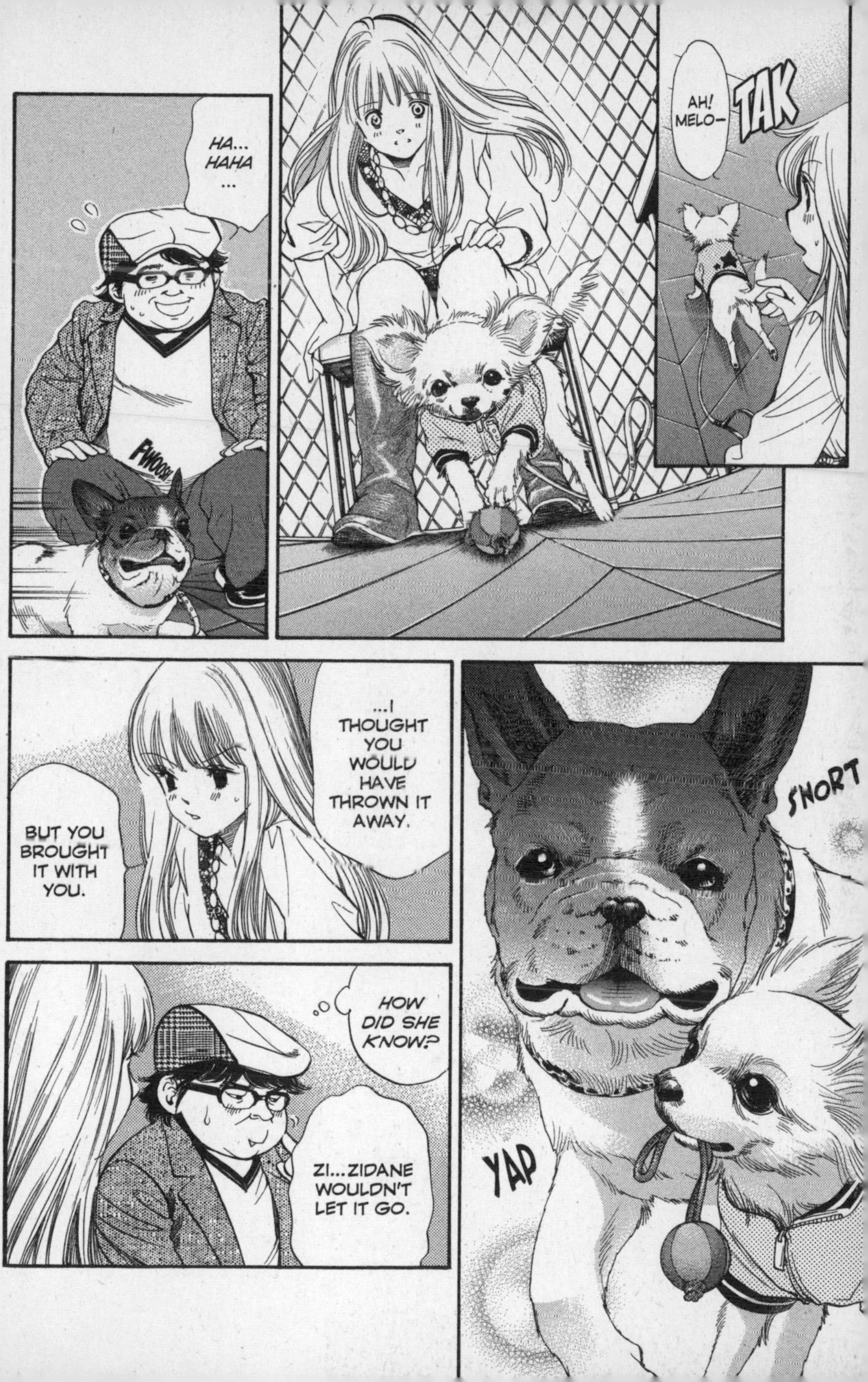

AH! MELO—
TAK
HA... HAHA ...
PWOOSH
S'NORT
YAP
...I THOUGHT YOU WOULD HAVE THROWN IT AWAY.
BUT YOU BROUGHT IT WITH YOU.
HOW DID SHE KNOW?
ZI...ZIDANE WOULDN'T LET IT GO.

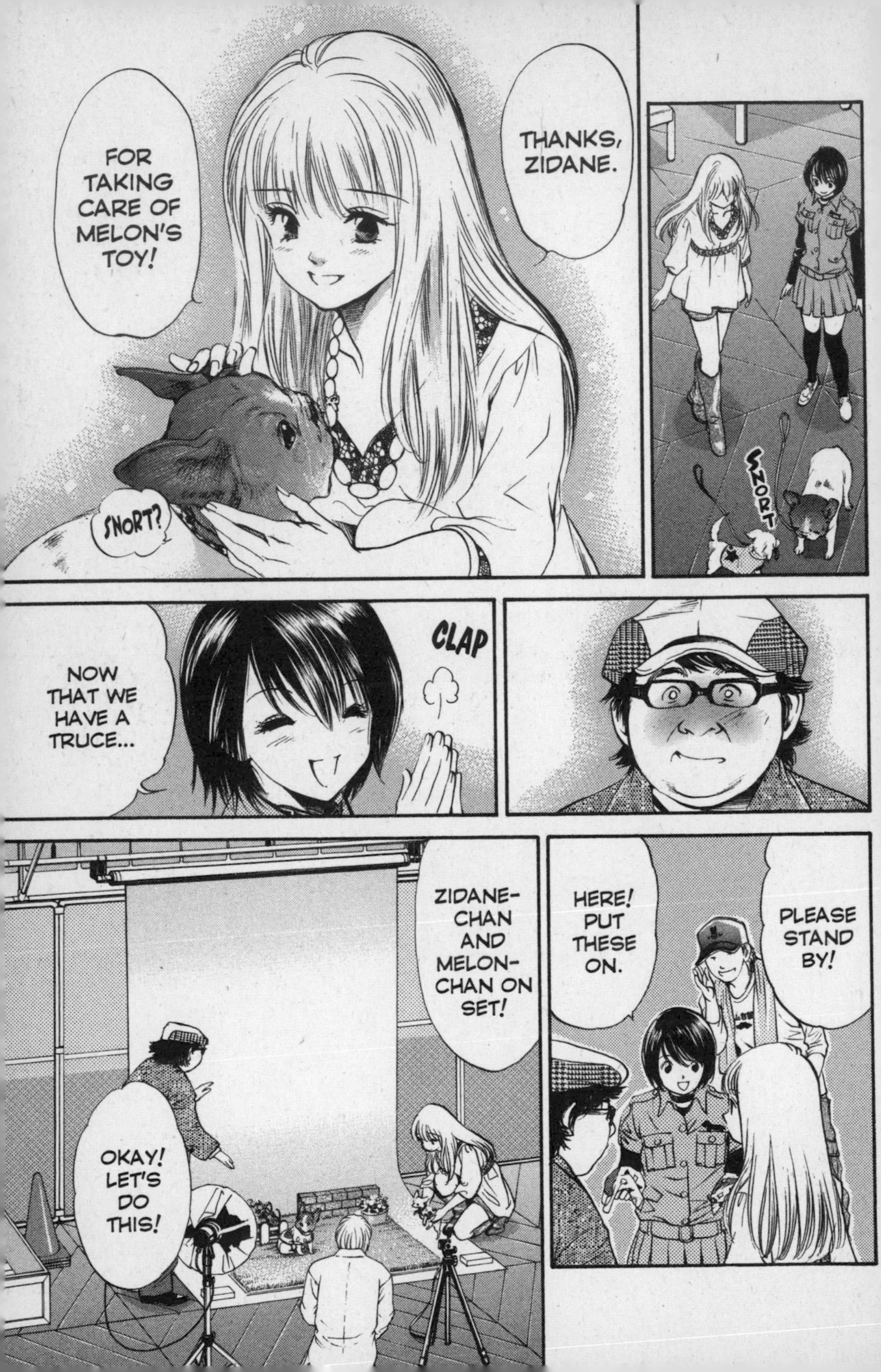
SNORT
THANKS, ZIDANE.
FOR TAKING CARE OF MELON'S TOY!
SNORT?
CLAP
NOW THAT WE HAVE A TRUCE...
PLEASE STAND BY!
HERE! PUT THESE ON.
ZIDANE-CHAN AND MELON-CHAN ON SET!
OKAY! LET'S DO THIS!

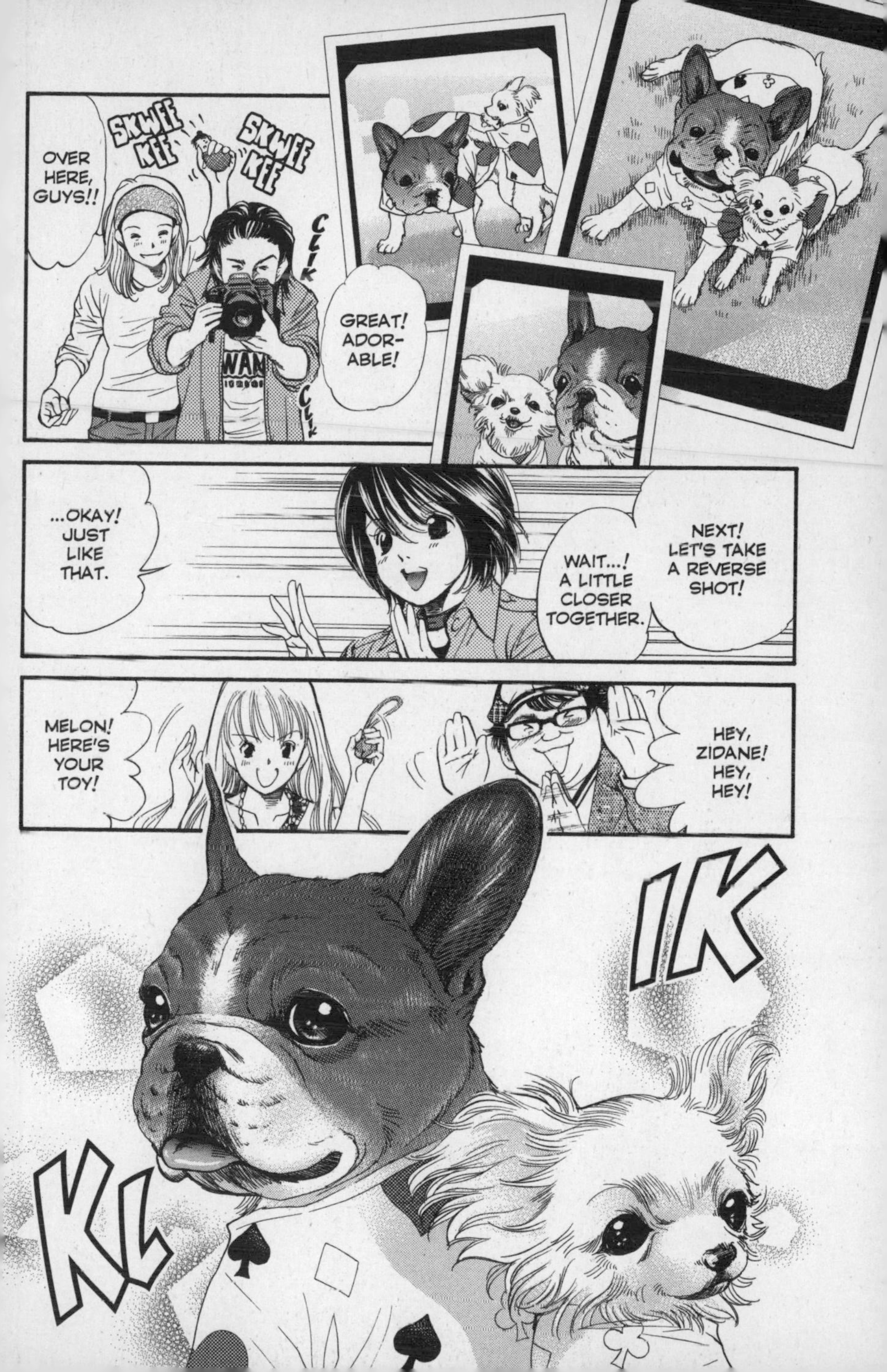
GREAT! ADOR-ABLE!
SKWEE KEE
SKWEE KEE
OVER HERE, GUYS!!
CLIK
CLIK
NEXT! LET'S TAKE A REVERSE SHOT!
WAIT...! A LITTLE CLOSER TOGETHER.
...OKAY! JUST LIKE THAT.
HEY, ZIDANE! HEY, HEY!
MELON! HERE'S YOUR TOY!
IK
KL

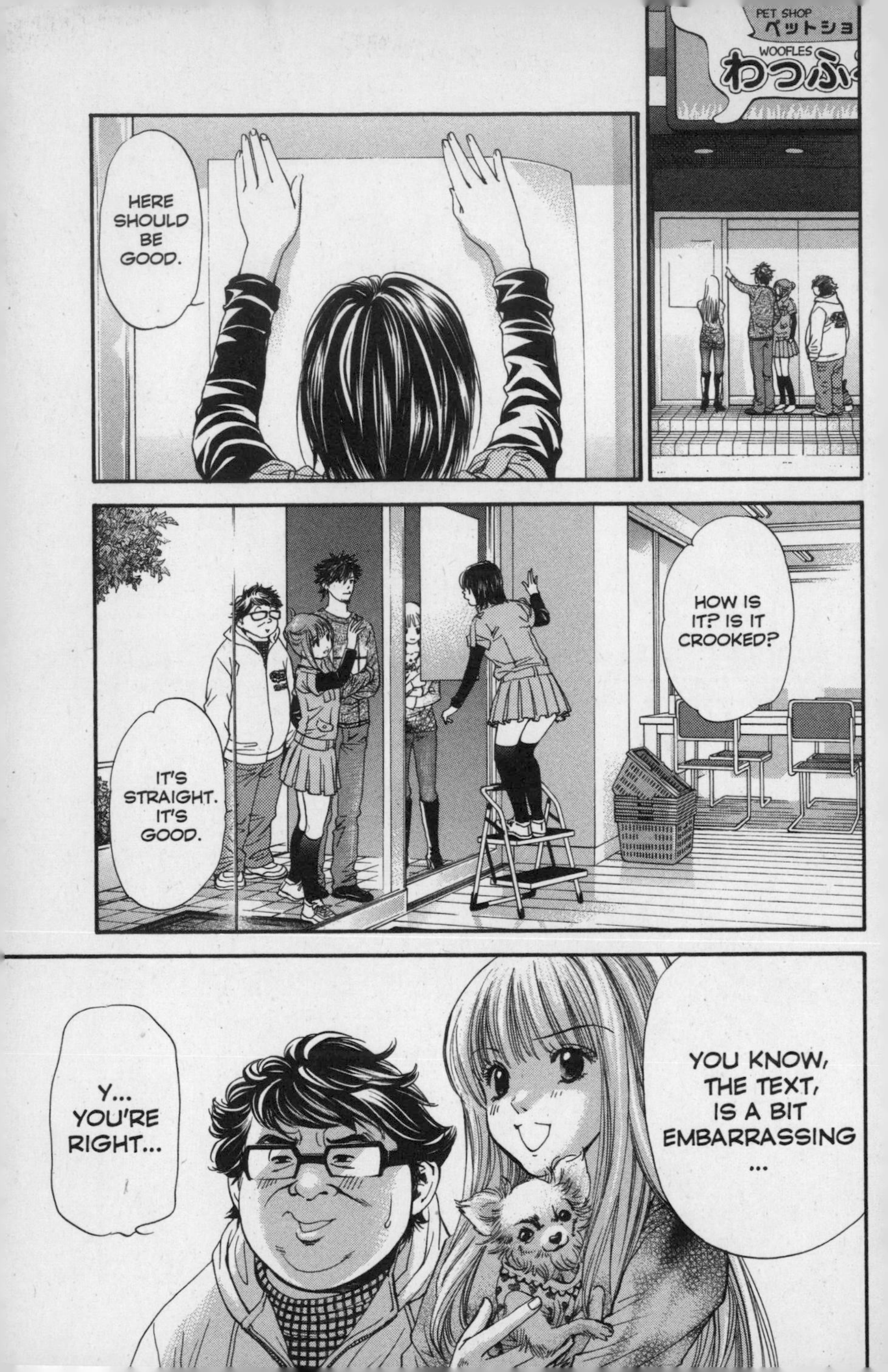
PET SHOP
ペットショ
WOOFLES
わつふ
HERE SHOULD BE GOOD.
HOW IS IT? IS IT CROOKED?
IT'S STRAIGHT. IT'S GOOD.
YOU KNOW, THE TEXT, IS A BIT EMBARRASSING ...
Y... YOU'RE RIGHT...

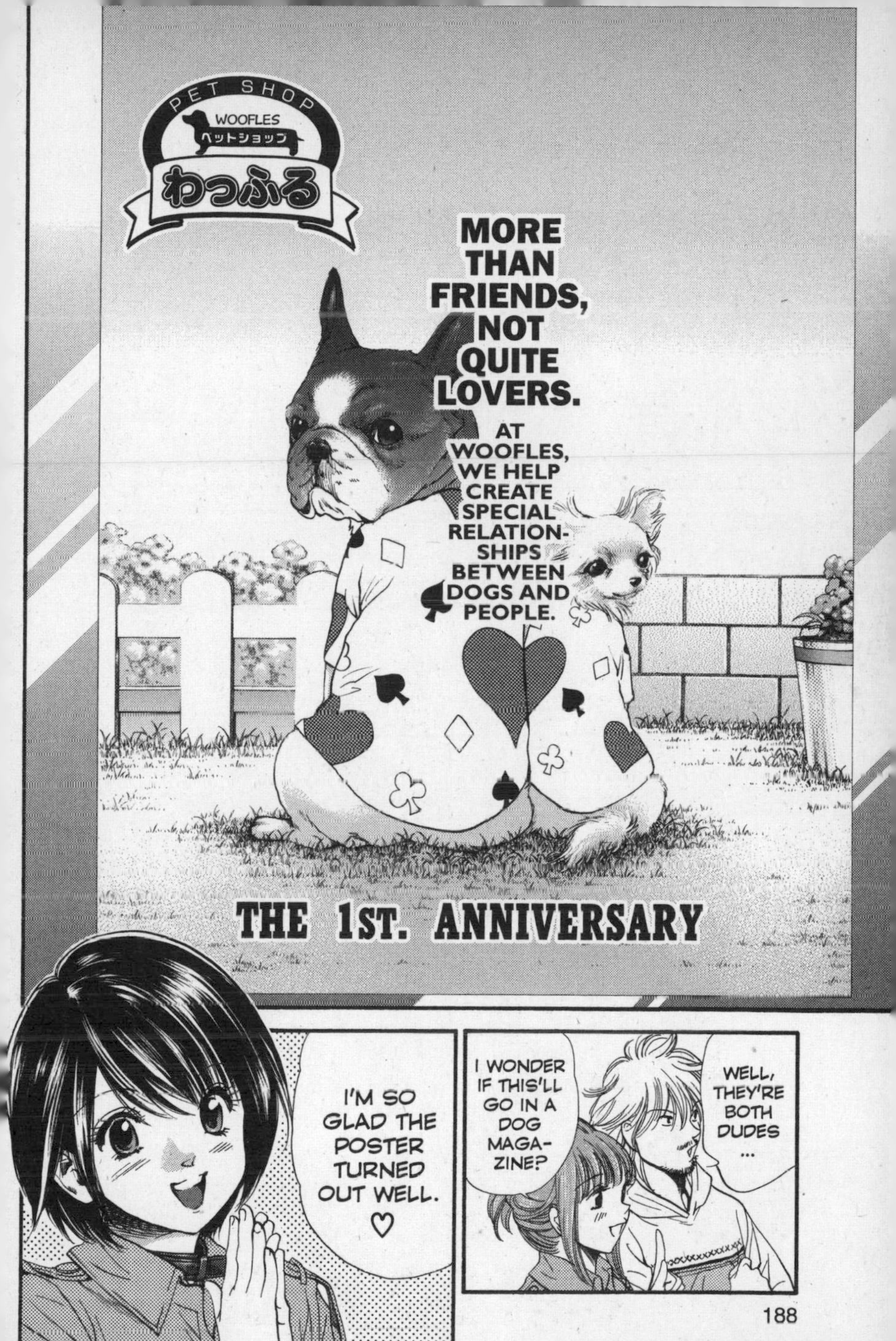
PET SHOP
WOOFLES
ペットショップ
わっふる
MORE THAN FRIENDS, NOT QUITE LOVERS.
AT WOOFLES, WE HELP CREATE SPECIAL RELATION-SHIPS BETWEEN DOGS AND PEOPLE.
THE 1ST. ANNIVERSARY
I WONDER IF THIS'LL GO IN A DOG MAGA-ZINE?
WELL, THEY'RE BOTH DUDES ...
I'M SO GLAD THE POSTER TURNED OUT WELL. ♡

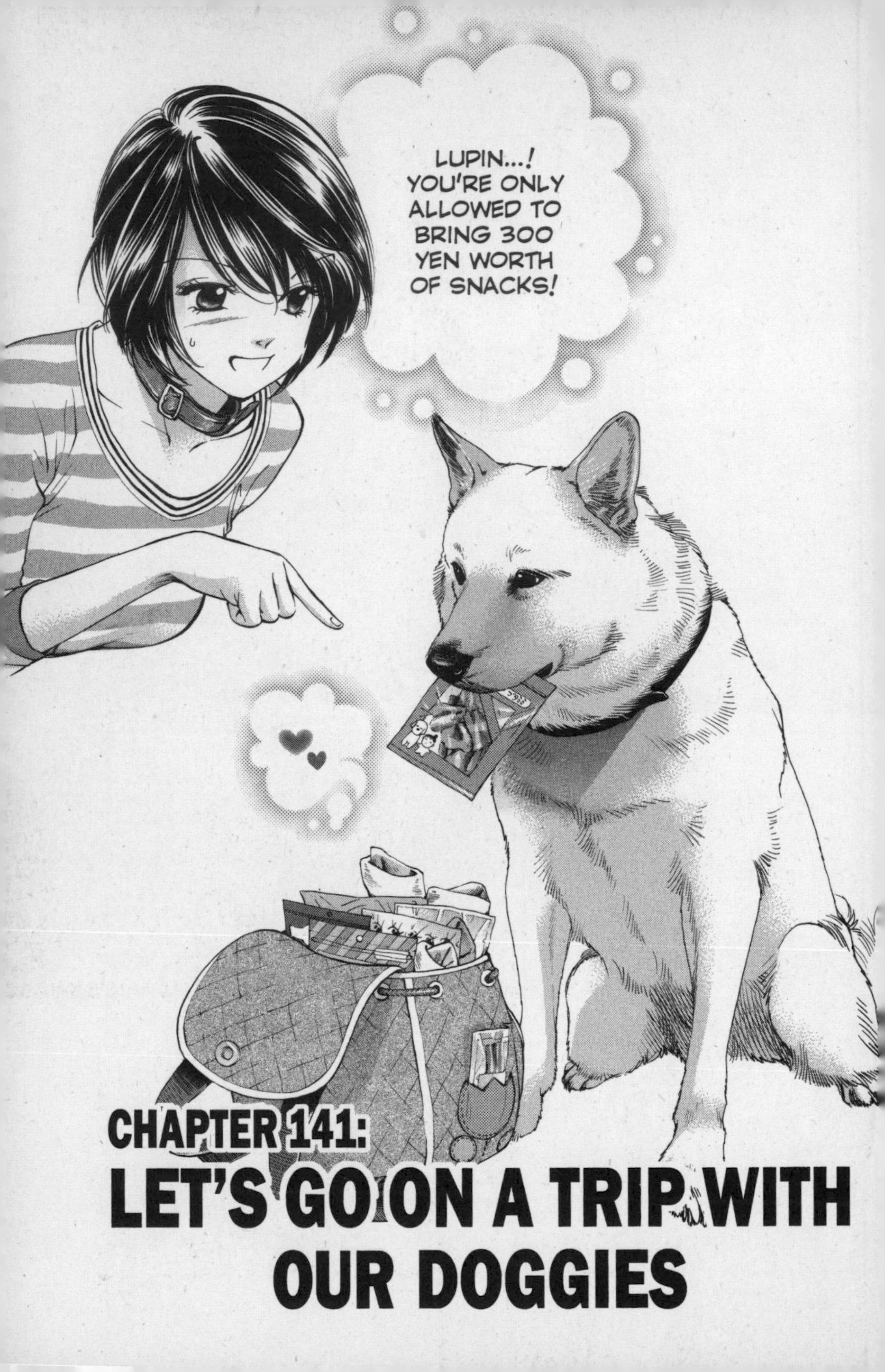
LUPIN...! YOU'RE ONLY ALLOWED TO BRING 300 YEN WORTH OF SNACKS!

CHAPTER 141: LET'S GO ON A TRIP WITH OUR DOGGIES

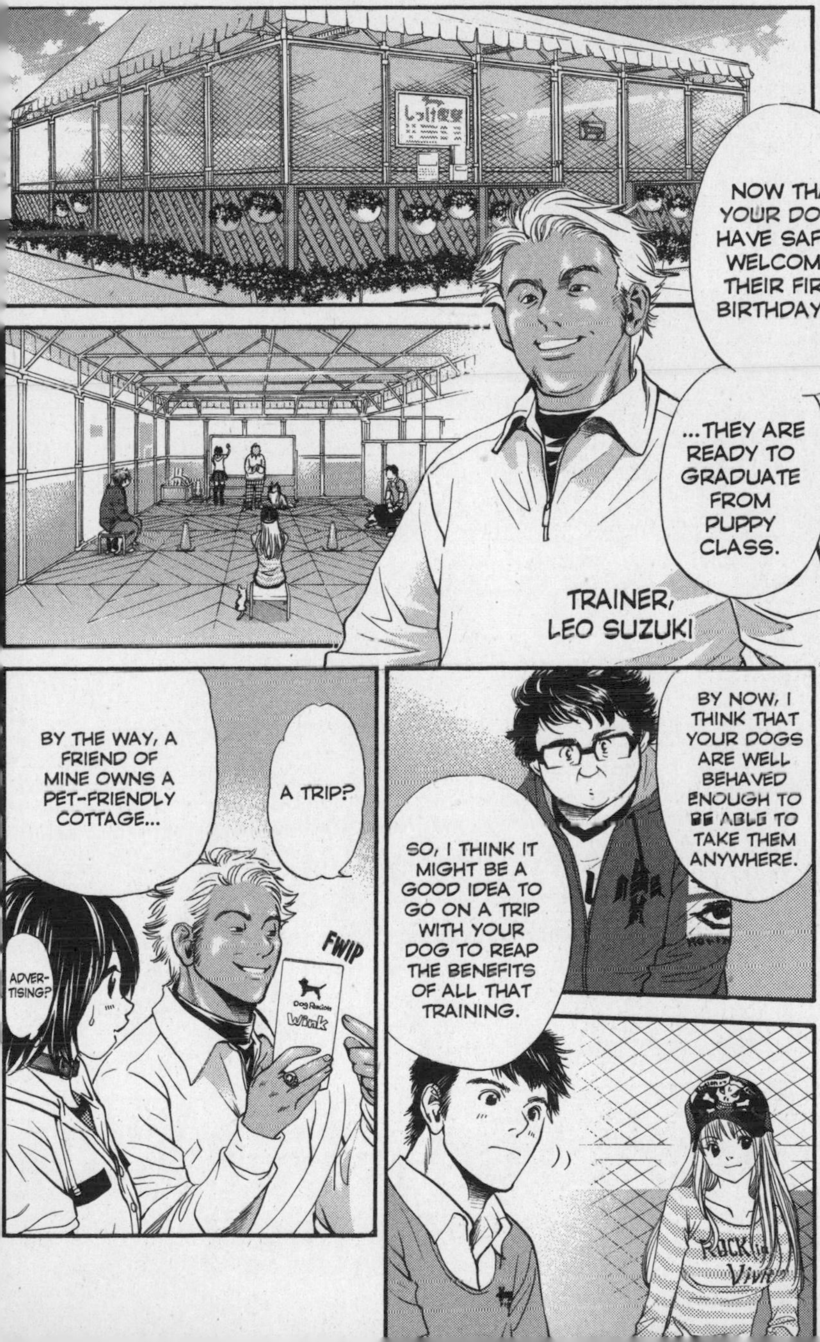
NOW THAT YOUR DOGS HAVE SAFELY WELCOMED THEIR FIRST BIRTHDAYS...
...THEY ARE READY TO GRADUATE FROM PUPPY CLASS.
TRAINER, LEO SUZUKI
BY NOW, I THINK THAT YOUR DOGS ARE WELL BEHAVED ENOUGH TO BE ABLE TO TAKE THEM ANYWHERE.
SO, I THINK IT MIGHT BE A GOOD IDEA TO GO ON A TRIP WITH YOUR DOG TO REAP THE BENEFITS OF ALL THAT TRAINING.
A TRIP?
BY THE WAY, A FRIEND OF MINE OWNS A PET-FRIENDLY COTTAGE...
FWIP
Dog Resort Wink
ADVER-TISING?

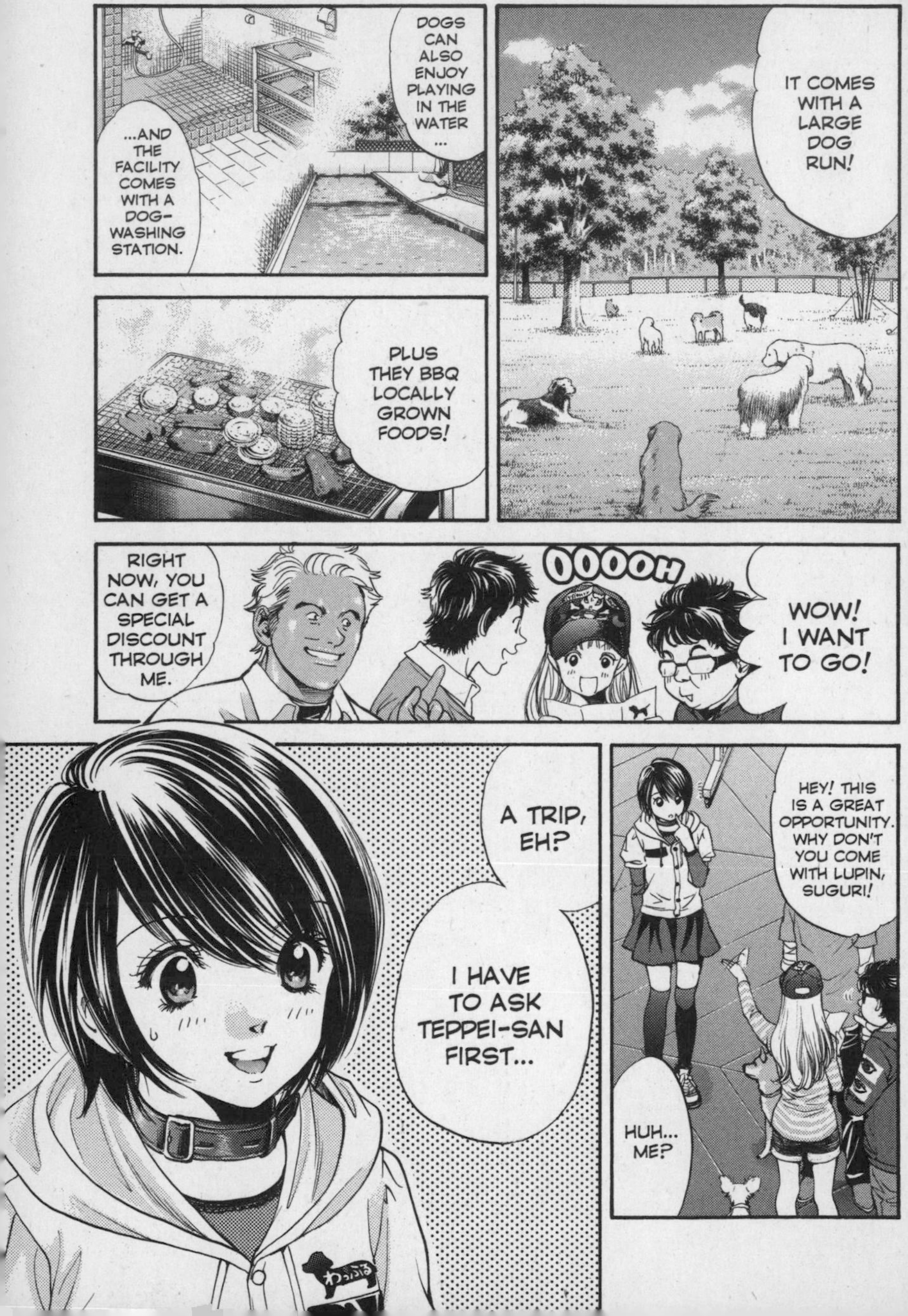
IT COMES WITH A LARGE DOG RUN!
DOGS CAN ALSO ENJOY PLAYING IN THE WATER...
...AND THE FACILITY COMES WITH A DOG-WASHING STATION.
PLUS THEY BBQ LOCALLY GROWN FOODS!
WOW! I WANT TO GO!
OOOOH
RIGHT NOW, YOU CAN GET A SPECIAL DISCOUNT THROUGH ME.
HEY! THIS IS A GREAT OPPORTUNITY. WHY DON'T YOU COME WITH LUPIN, SUGURI!
HUH... ME?
A TRIP, EH?
I HAVE TO ASK TEPPEI-SAN FIRST...

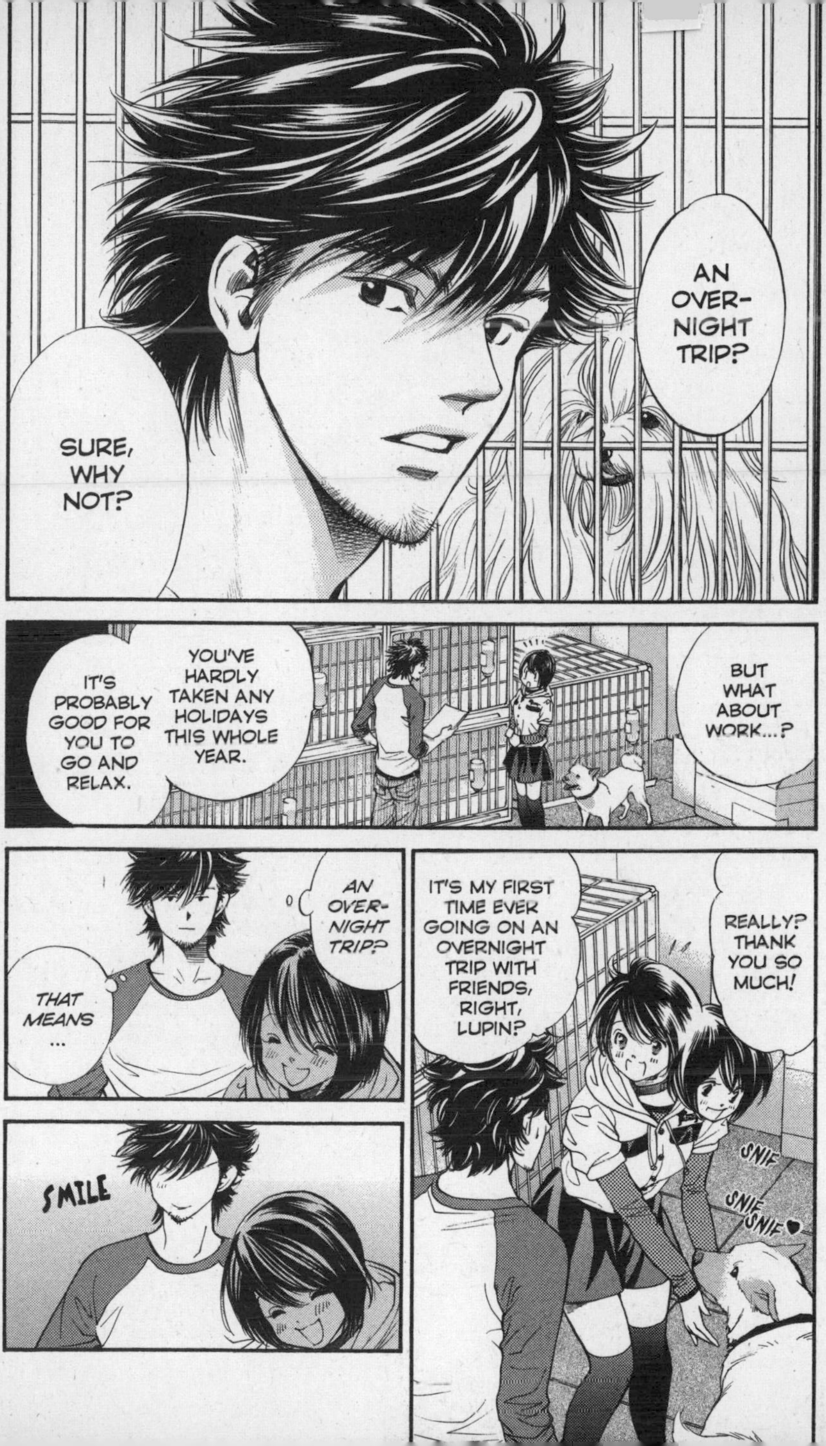
AN OVER-NIGHT TRIP?
SURE, WHY NOT?
BUT WHAT ABOUT WORK...?
YOU'VE HARDLY TAKEN ANY HOLIDAYS THIS WHOLE YEAR.
IT'S PROBABLY GOOD FOR YOU TO GO AND RELAX.
REALLY? THANK YOU SO MUCH!
IT'S MY FIRST TIME EVER GOING ON AN OVERNIGHT TRIP WITH FRIENDS, RIGHT, LUPIN?
SNIF
SNIF SNIF♥
AN OVER-NIGHT TRIP?
THAT MEANS ...
SMILE

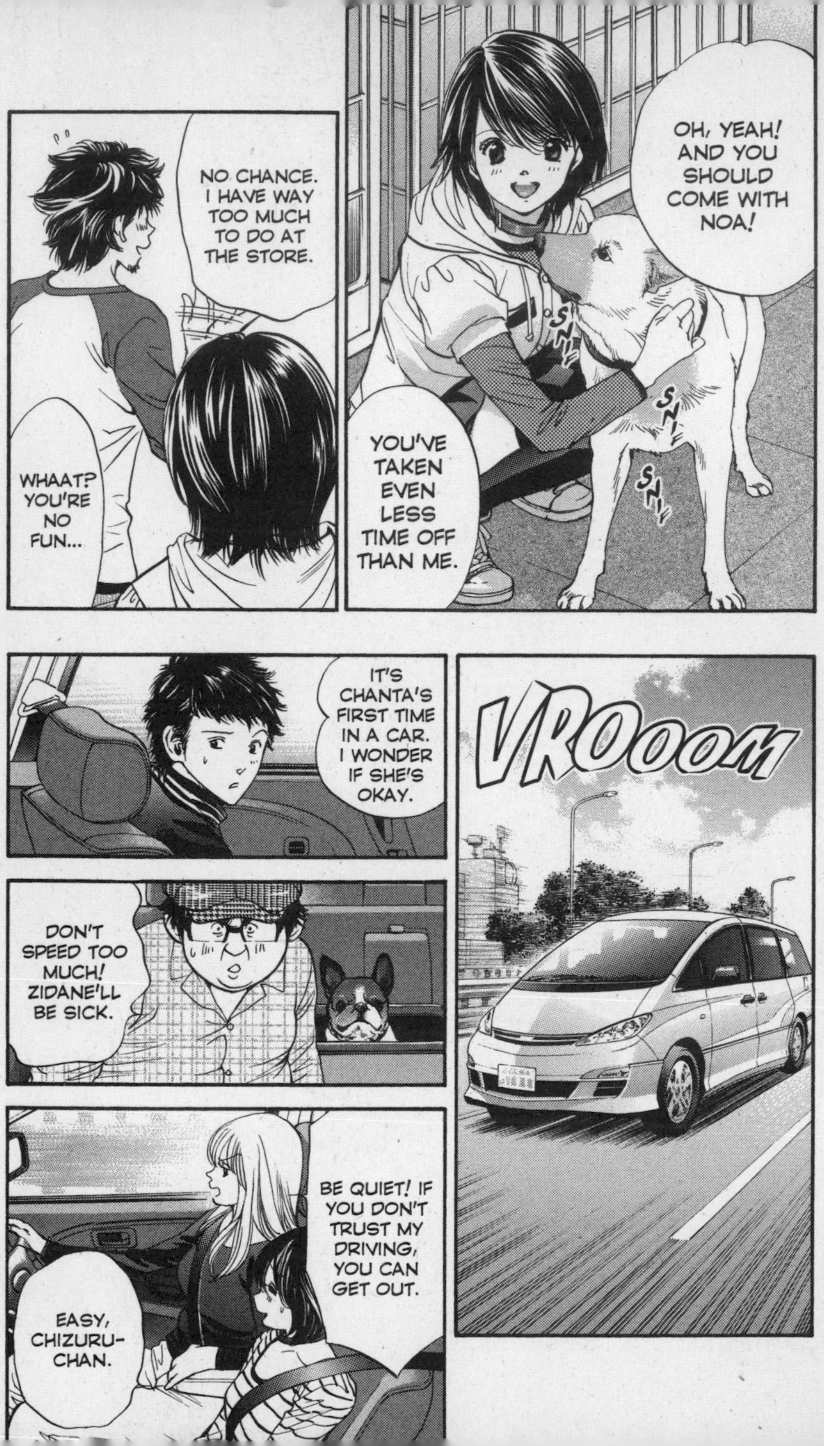
OH, YEAH! AND YOU SHOULD COME WITH NOA!
YOU'VE TAKEN EVEN LESS TIME OFF THAN ME.
NO CHANCE. I HAVE WAY TOO MUCH TO DO AT THE STORE.
WHAAT? YOU'RE NO FUN...
VROOOM
IT'S CHANTA'S FIRST TIME IN A CAR. I WONDER IF SHE'S OKAY.
DON'T SPEED TOO MUCH! ZIDANE'LL BE SICK.
BE QUIET! IF YOU DON'T TRUST MY DRIVING, YOU CAN GET OUT.
EASY, CHIZURU-CHAN.

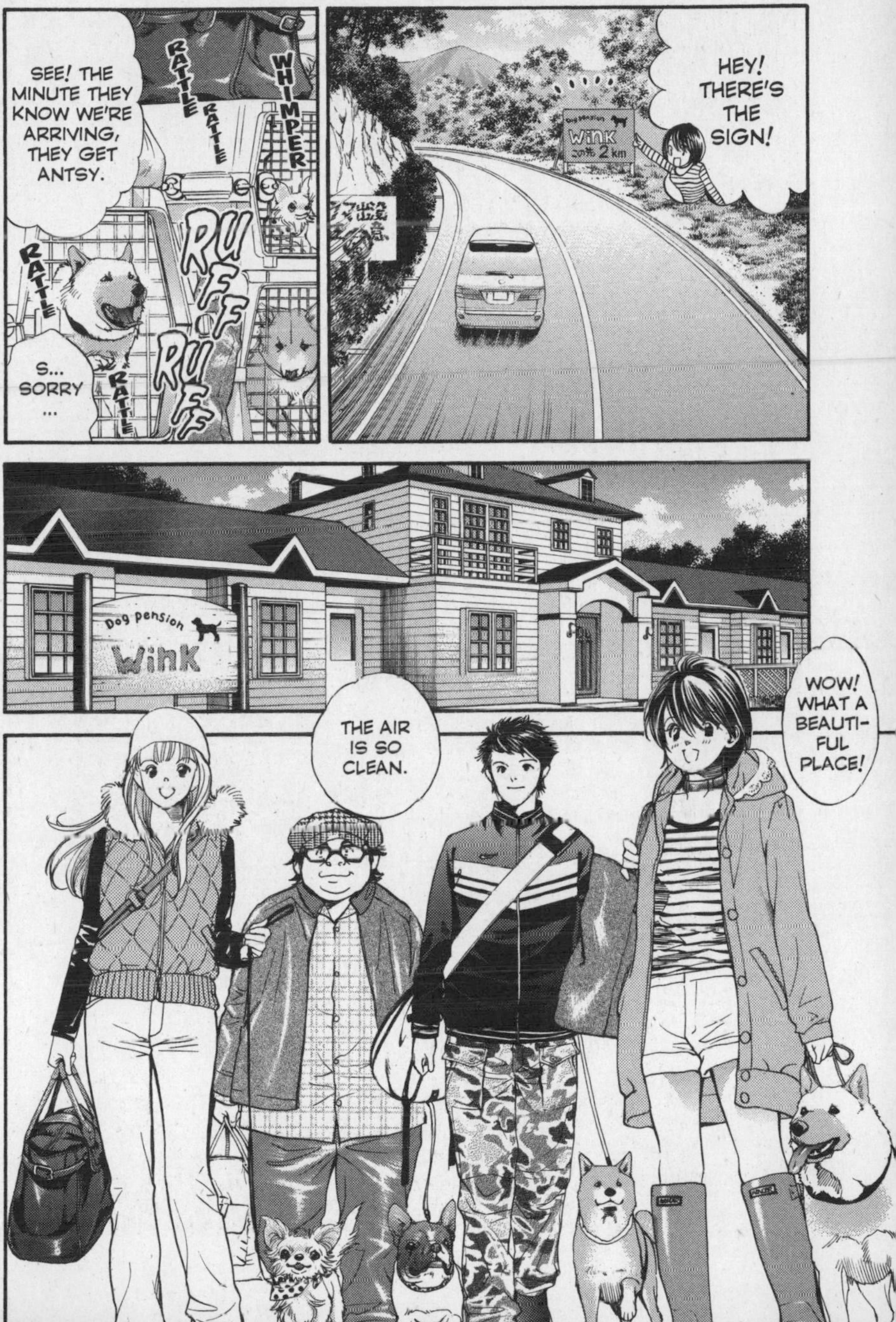
HEY! THERE'S THE SIGN!
Dog pension Wink 2 km
WHIMPER
RATTLE RATTLE
SEE! THE MINUTE THEY KNOW WE'RE ARRIVING, THEY GET ANTSY.
RUFF RUFF
RATTLE
RATTLE
S... SORRY ...
Dog pension Wink
WOW! WHAT A BEAUTIFUL PLACE!
THE AIR IS SO CLEAN.

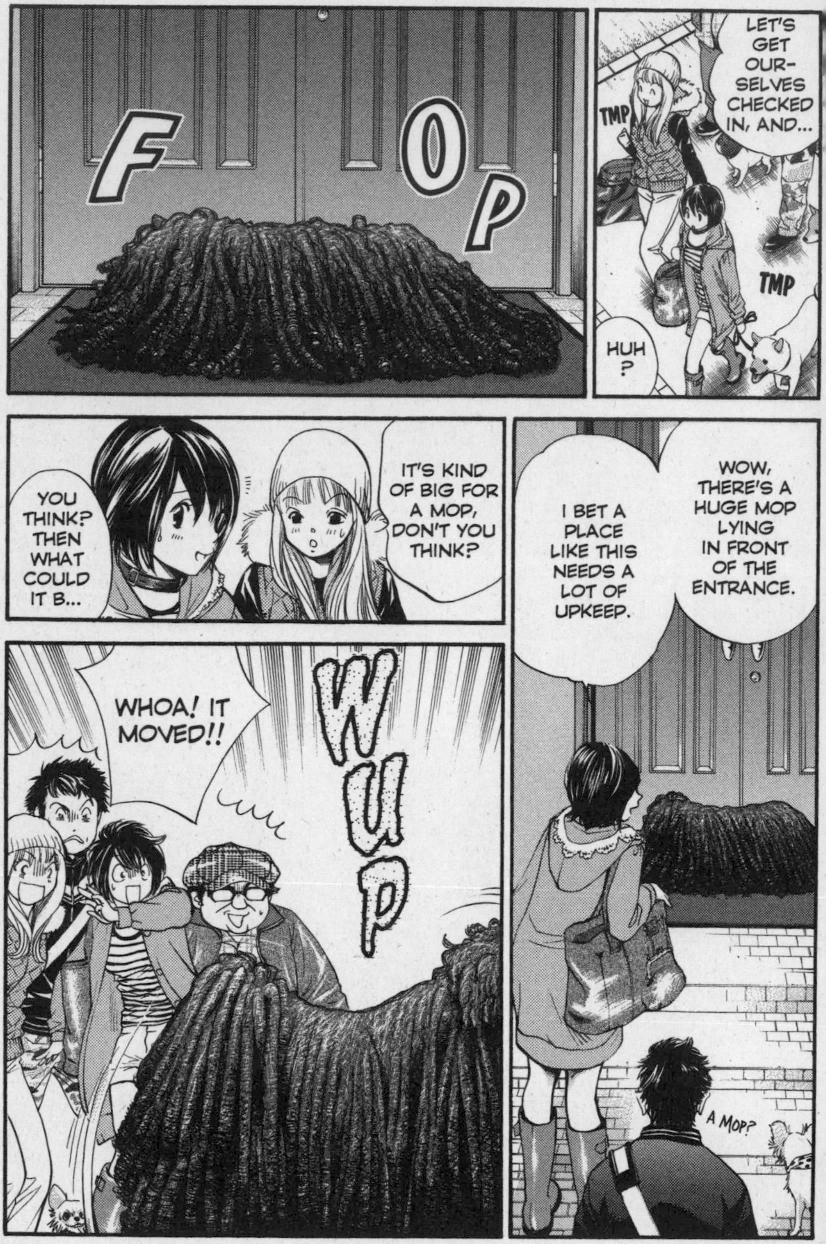
LET'S GET OUR-SELVES CHECKED IN, AND...
TMP
TMP
HUH?
FOP
WOW, THERE'S A HUGE MOP LYING IN FRONT OF THE ENTRANCE.
I BET A PLACE LIKE THIS NEEDS A LOT OF UPKEEP.
A MOP?
IT'S KIND OF BIG FOR A MOP, DON'T YOU THINK?
YOU THINK? THEN WHAT COULD IT B...
WUP
WHOA! IT MOVED!!

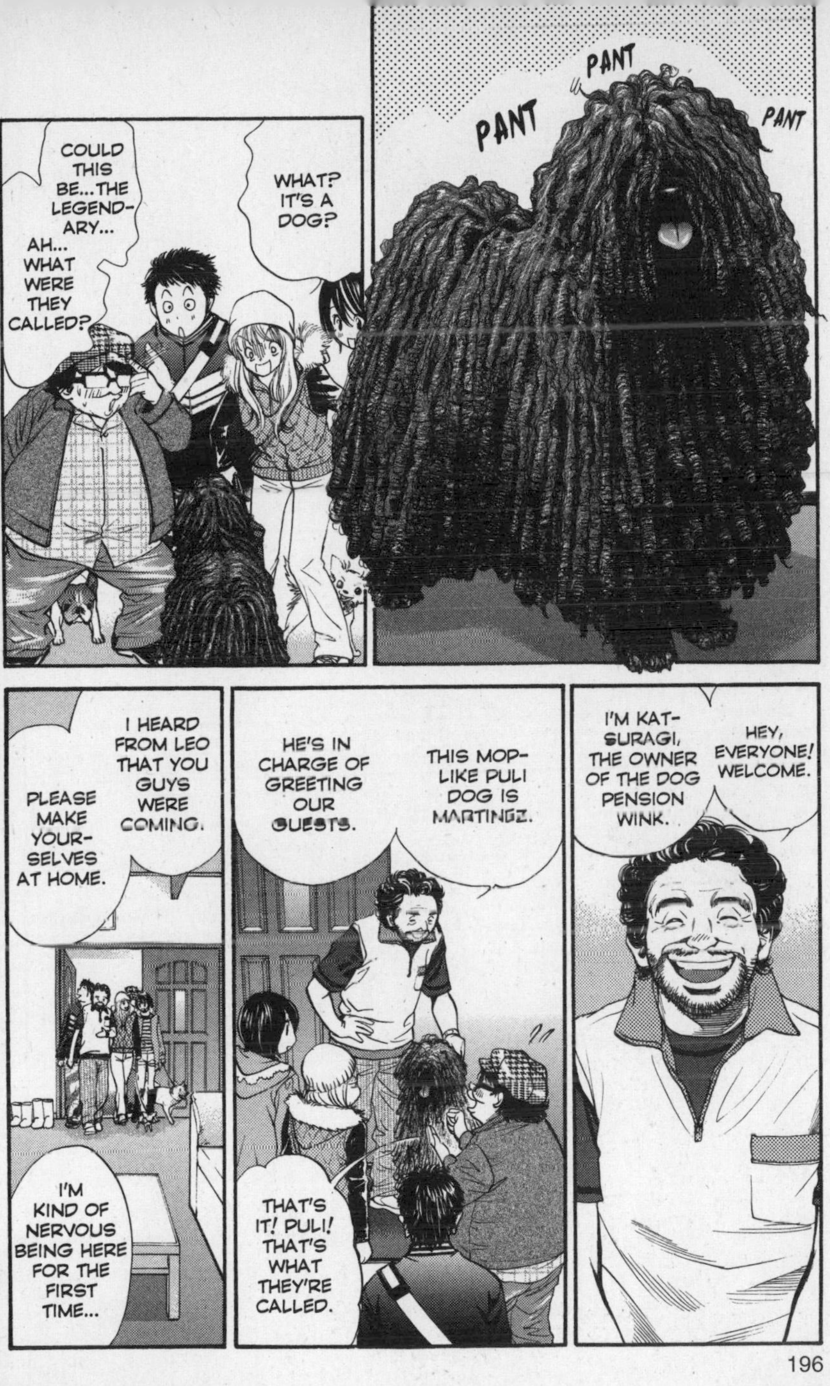
PANT
PANT
PANT
WHAT? IT'S A DOG?
COULD THIS BE...THE LEGENDARY...
AH... WHAT WERE THEY CALLED?
HEY, EVERYONE! WELCOME.
I'M KATSURAGI, THE OWNER OF THE DOG PENSION WINK.
THIS MOP-LIKE PULI DOG IS MARTINEZ.
HE'S IN CHARGE OF GREETING OUR GUESTS.
THAT'S IT! PULI! THAT'S WHAT THEY'RE CALLED.
I HEARD FROM LEO THAT YOU GUYS WERE COMING.
PLEASE MAKE YOURSELVES AT HOME.
I'M KIND OF NERVOUS BEING HERE FOR THE FIRST TIME...

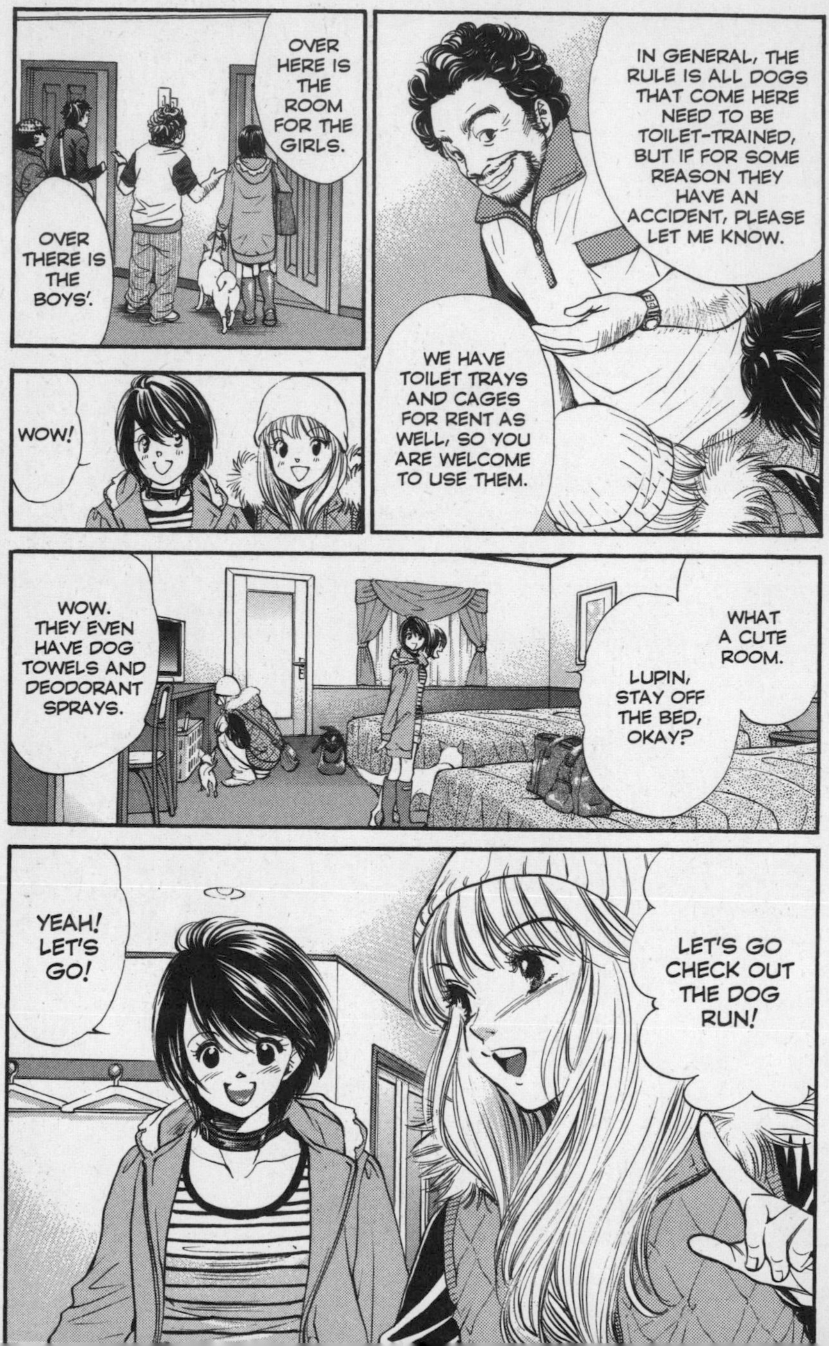
IN GENERAL, THE RULE IS ALL DOGS THAT COME HERE NEED TO BE TOILET-TRAINED, BUT IF FOR SOME REASON THEY HAVE AN ACCIDENT, PLEASE LET ME KNOW.
WE HAVE TOILET TRAYS AND CAGES FOR RENT AS WELL, SO YOU ARE WELCOME TO USE THEM.
OVER HERE IS THE ROOM FOR THE GIRLS.
OVER THERE IS THE BOYS'.
WOW!
WHAT A CUTE ROOM.
LUPIN, STAY OFF THE BED, OKAY?
WOW. THEY EVEN HAVE DOG TOWELS AND DEODORANT SPRAYS.
LET'S GO CHECK OUT THE DOG RUN!
YEAH! LET'S GO!

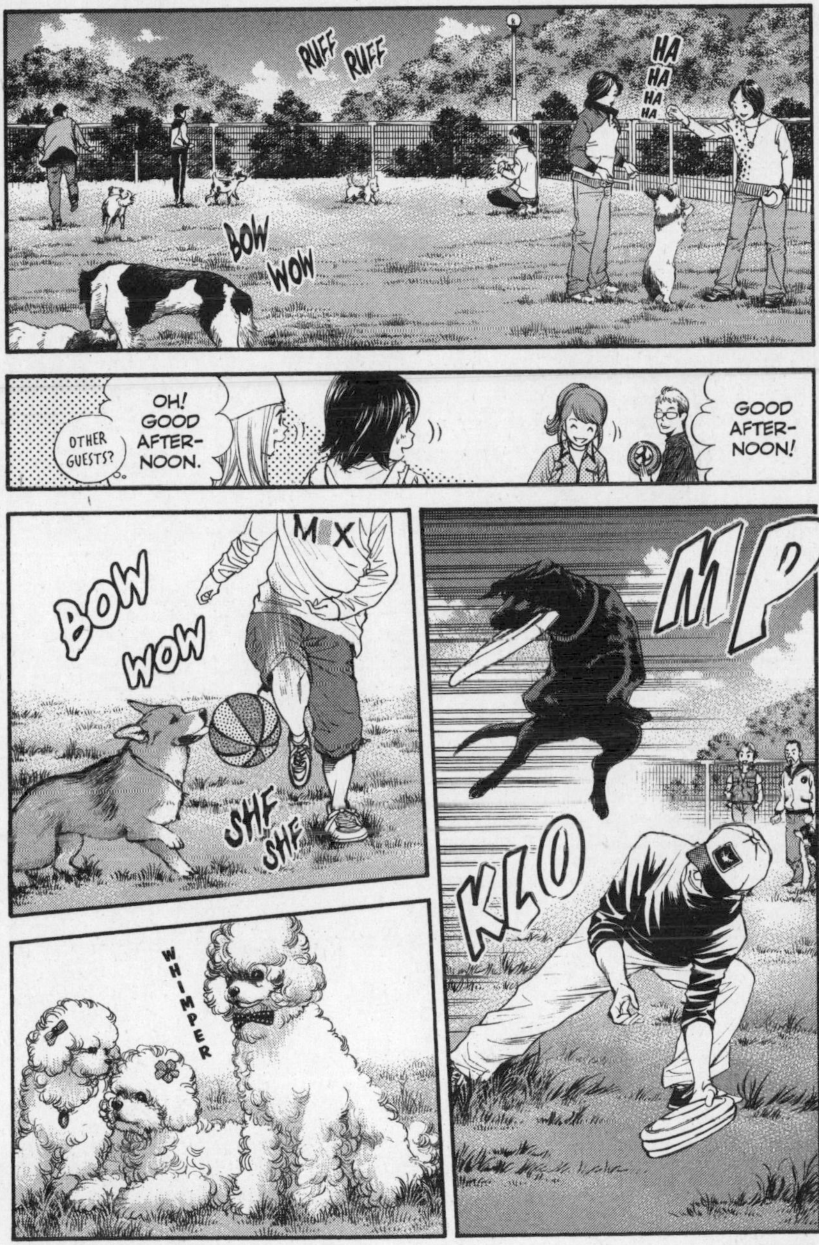
HA HA HA HA
RUFF RUFF
BOW WOW
GOOD AFTER-NOON!
OH! GOOD AFTER-NOON.
OTHER GUESTS?
MP
KLO
BOW WOW
SHF SHF
WHIMPER

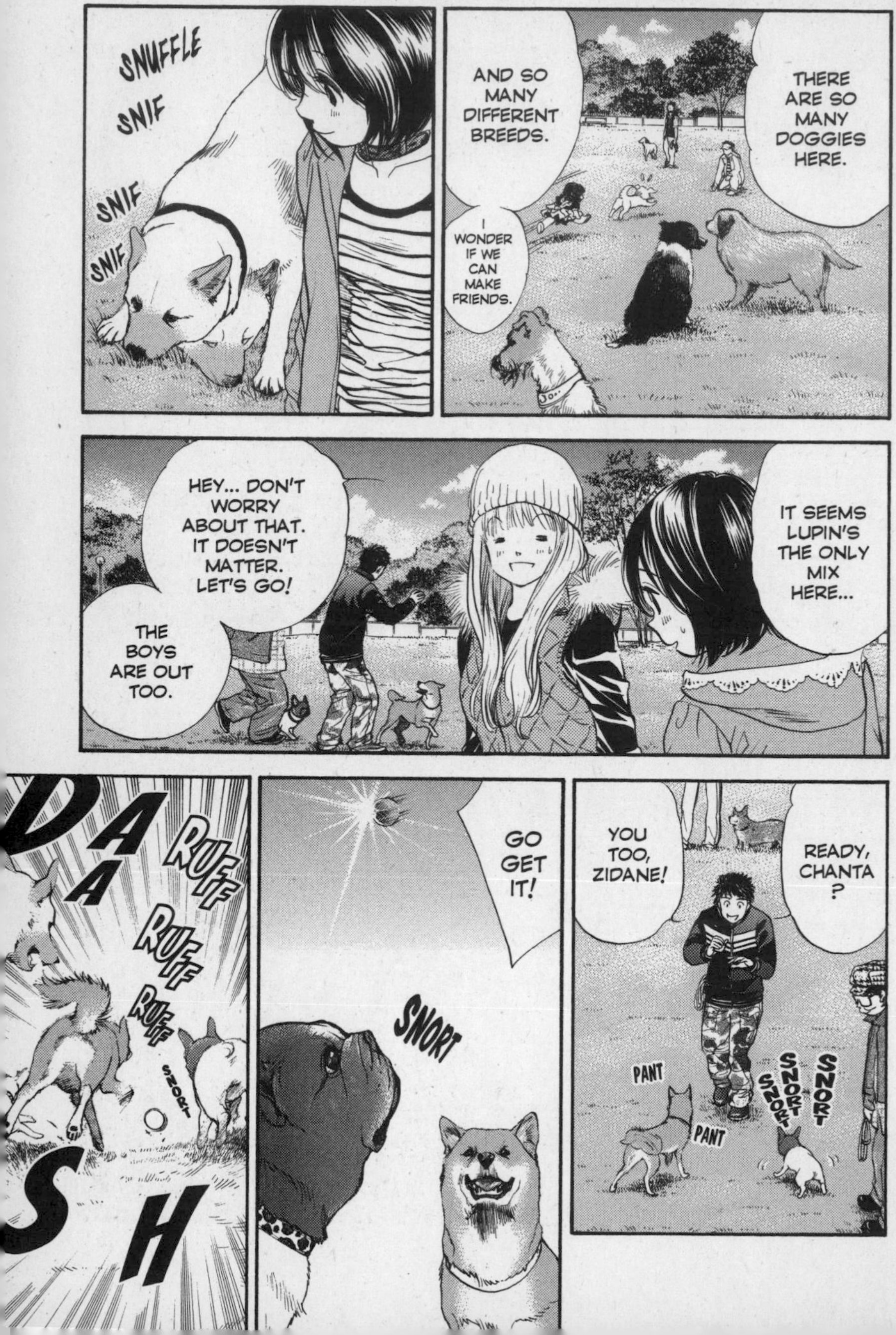
THERE ARE SO MANY DOGGIES HERE.
AND SO MANY DIFFERENT BREEDS.
I WONDER IF WE CAN MAKE FRIENDS.
SNUFFLE
SNIF
SNIF
SNIF
IT SEEMS LUPIN'S THE ONLY MIX HERE...
HEY... DON'T WORRY ABOUT THAT. IT DOESN'T MATTER. LET'S GO!
THE BOYS ARE OUT TOO.
READY, CHANTA?
YOU TOO, ZIDANE!
SNORT SNORT SNORT
PANT
PANT
GO GET IT!
SNORT
DAASH
RUFF RUFF RUFF
SNORT

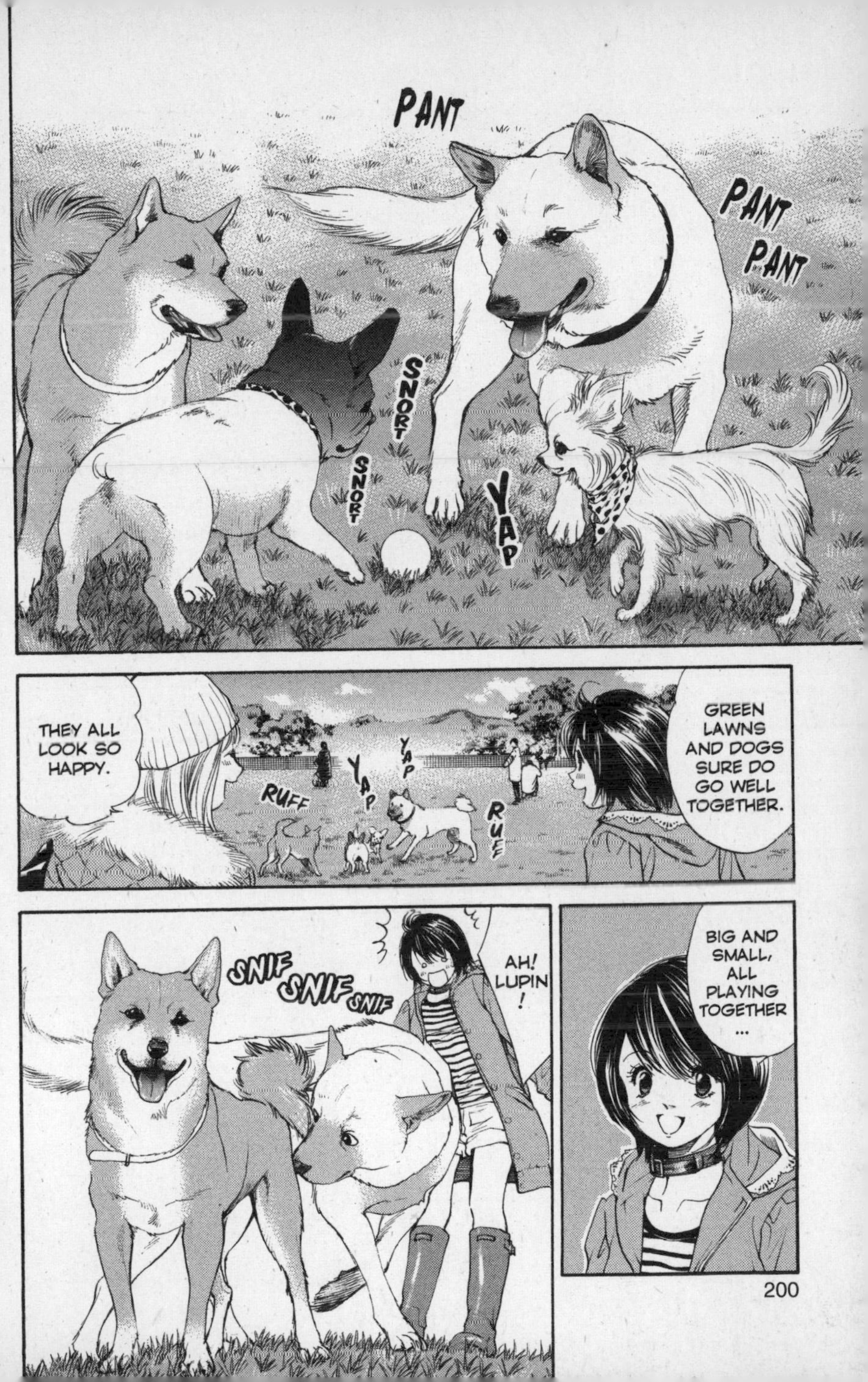
PANT
PANT PANT
YAP
SNORT
SNORT
GREEN LAWNS AND DOGS SURE DO GO WELL TOGETHER.
RUFF
YAP
YAP
RUFF
THEY ALL LOOK SO HAPPY.
BIG AND SMALL, ALL PLAYING TOGETHER ...
AH! LUPIN!
SNIF SNIF SNIF

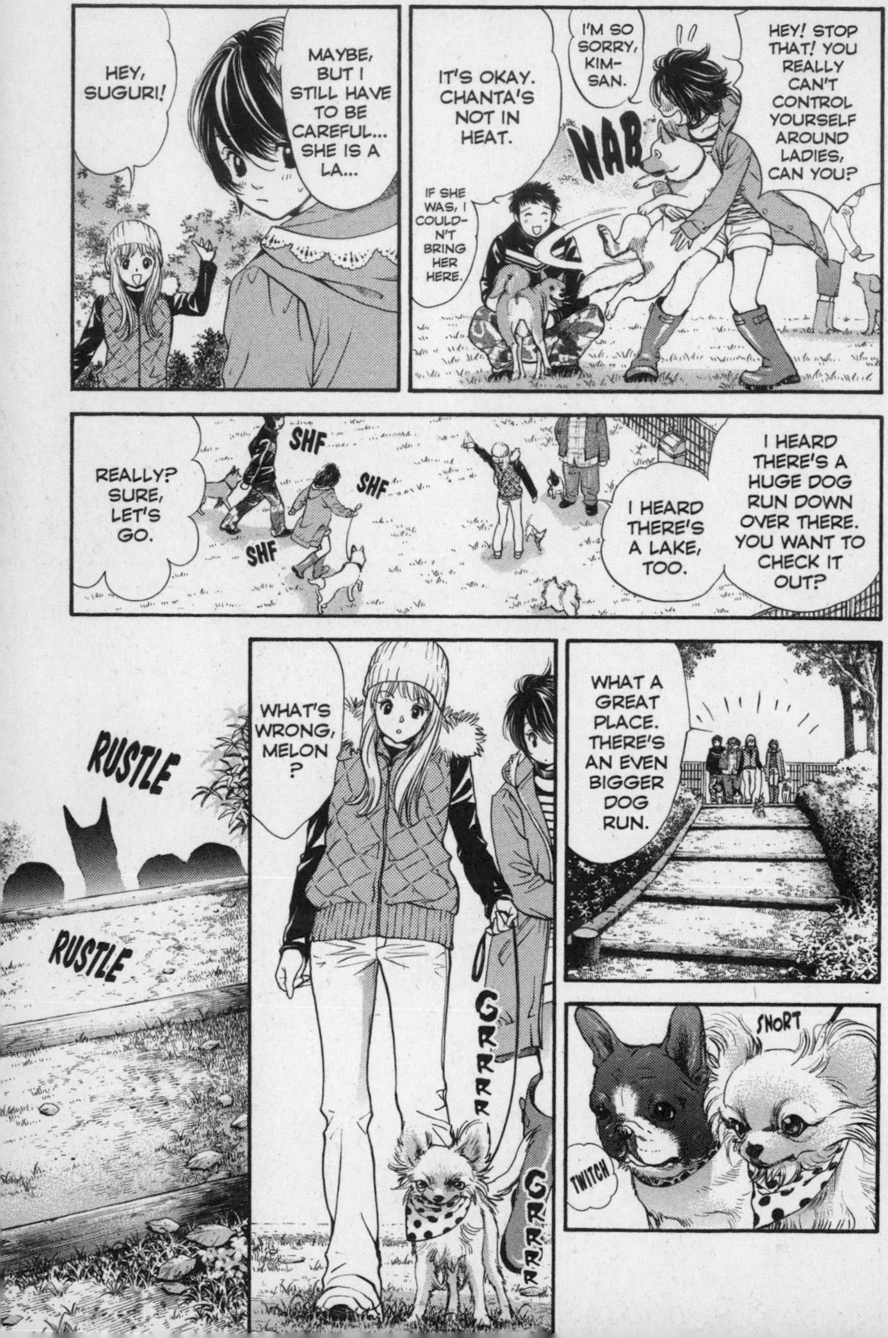
HEY! STOP THAT! YOU REALLY CAN'T CONTROL YOURSELF AROUND LADIES, CAN YOU?
I'M SO SORRY, KIM-SAN.
NAB
IT'S OKAY. CHANTA'S NOT IN HEAT.
IF SHE WAS, I COULDN'T BRING HER HERE.
MAYBE, BUT I STILL HAVE TO BE CAREFUL... SHE IS A LA...
HEY, SUGURI!
I HEARD THERE'S A HUGE DOG RUN DOWN OVER THERE. YOU WANT TO CHECK IT OUT?
I HEARD THERE'S A LAKE, TOO.
SHF
SHF
SHF
REALLY? SURE, LET'S GO.
WHAT A GREAT PLACE. THERE'S AN EVEN BIGGER DOG RUN.
SNORT
TWITCH
WHAT'S WRONG, MELON?
GRRRR
GRRRR
RUSTLE
RUSTLE

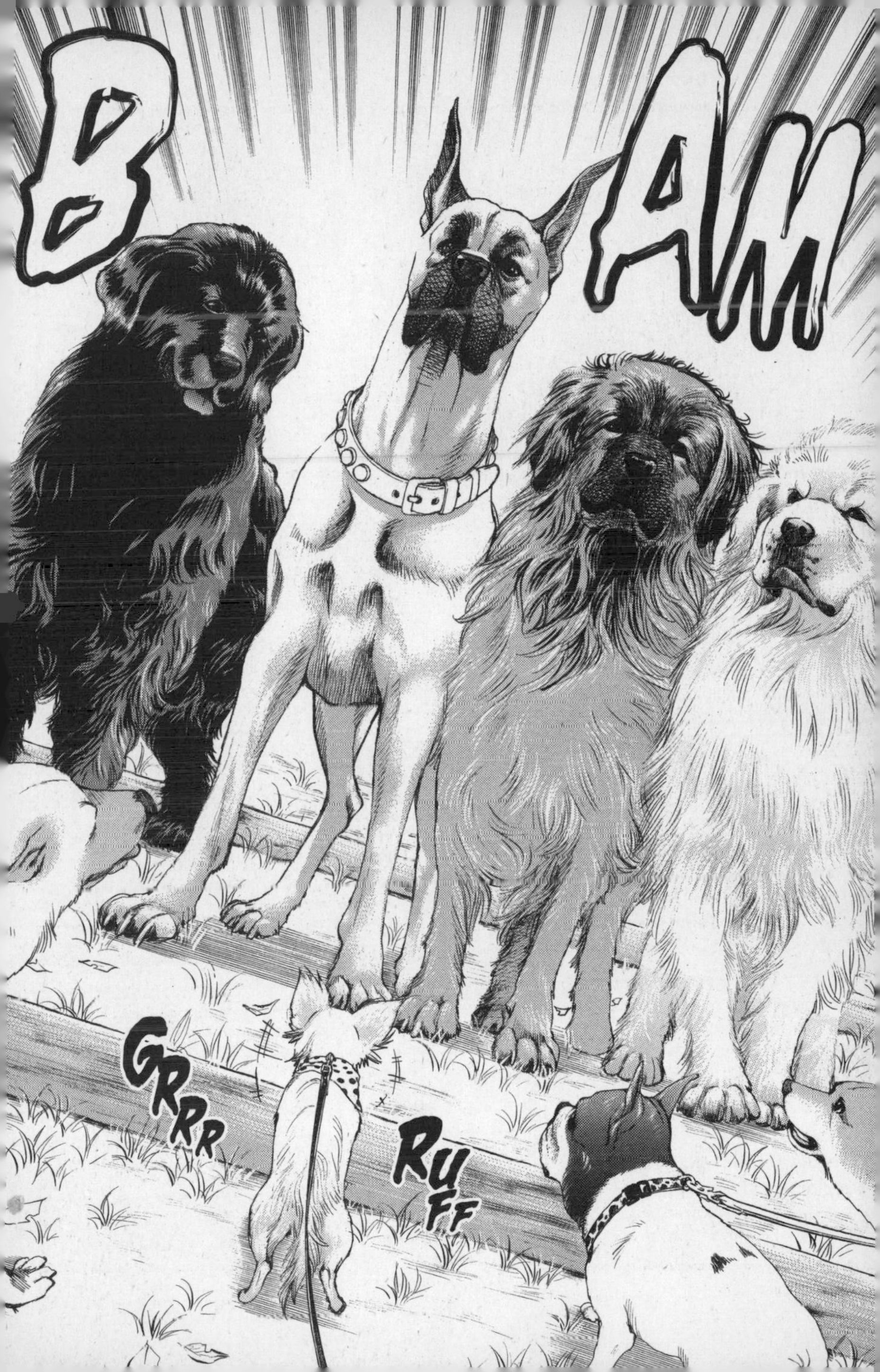
BAM
GRRR
RUFF

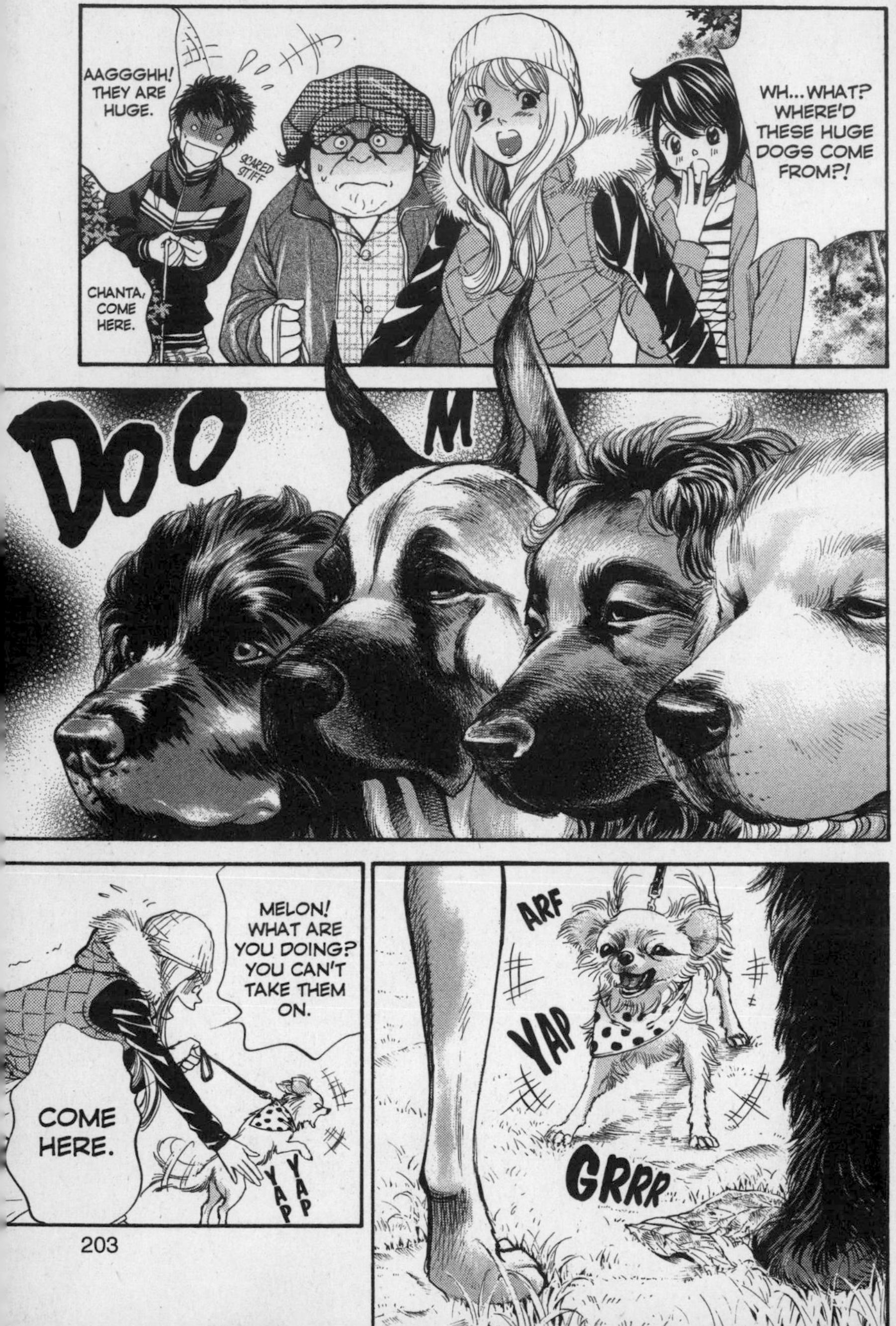
WH...WHAT? WHERE'D THESE HUGE DOGS COME FROM?!
AAGGGHH! THEY ARE HUGE.
SCARED STIFF
CHANTA, COME HERE.
DOO
M
ARF
YAP
GRRR
MELON! WHAT ARE YOU DOING? YOU CAN'T TAKE THEM ON.
COME HERE.
YAP
YAP

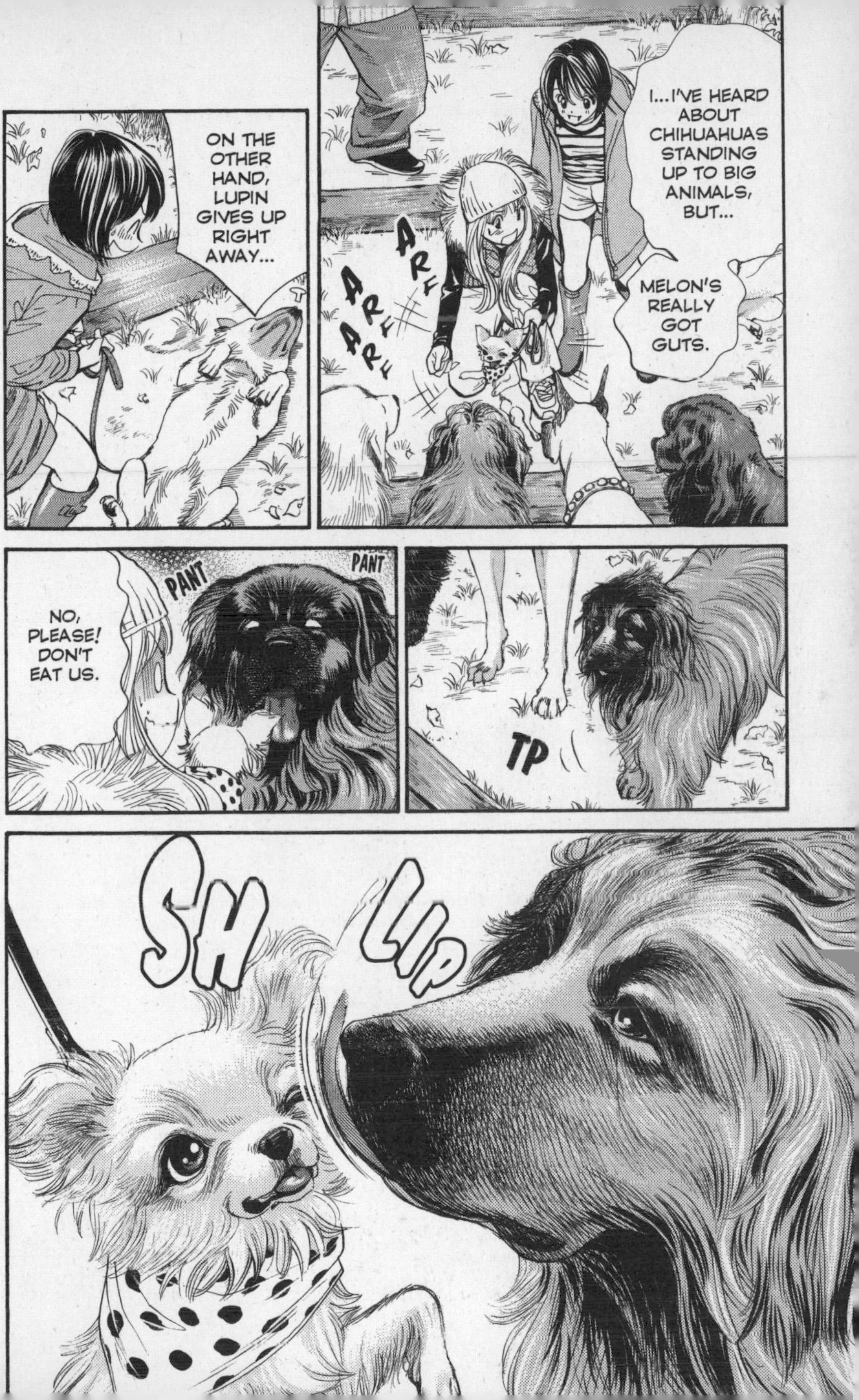
I...I'VE HEARD ABOUT CHIHUAHUAS STANDING UP TO BIG ANIMALS, BUT...
MELON'S REALLY GOT GUTS.
ARF
ARF
ARF
ARF
ON THE OTHER HAND, LUPIN GIVES UP RIGHT AWAY...
TP
PANT
PANT
NO, PLEASE! DON'T EAT US.
SH
LIP

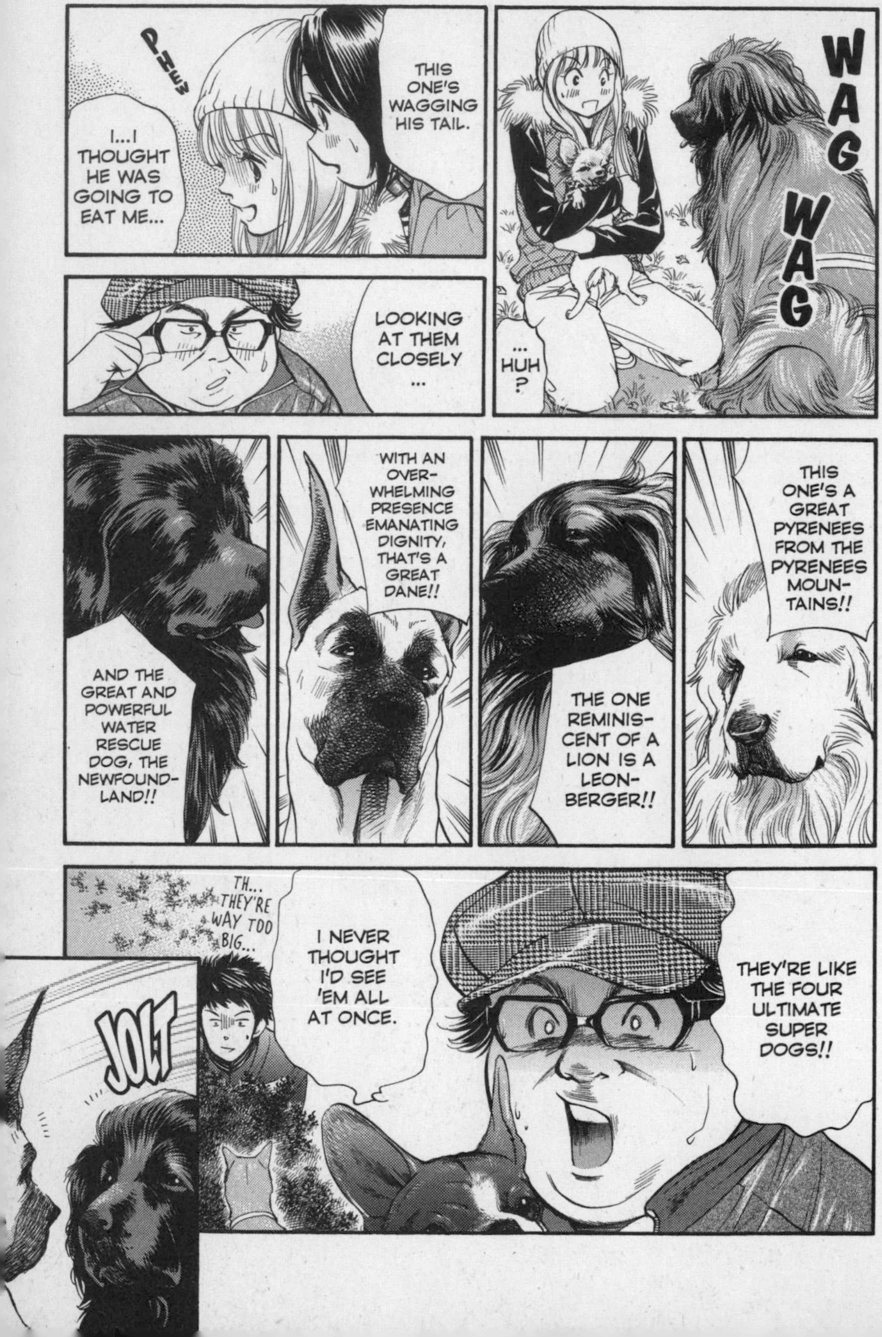
WAG WAG WAG
... HUH?
THIS ONE'S WAGGING HIS TAIL.
PHEW
I...I THOUGHT HE WAS GOING TO EAT ME...
LOOKING AT THEM CLOSELY ...
THIS ONE'S A GREAT PYRENEES FROM THE PYRENEES MOUNTAINS!!
THE ONE REMINISCENT OF A LION IS A LEONBERGER!!
WITH AN OVERWHELMING PRESENCE EMANATING DIGNITY, THAT'S A GREAT DANE!!
AND THE GREAT AND POWERFUL WATER RESCUE DOG, THE NEWFOUNDLAND!!
THEY'RE LIKE THE FOUR ULTIMATE SUPER DOGS!!
I NEVER THOUGHT I'D SEE 'EM ALL AT ONCE.
TH... THEY'RE WAY TOO BIG...
JOLT

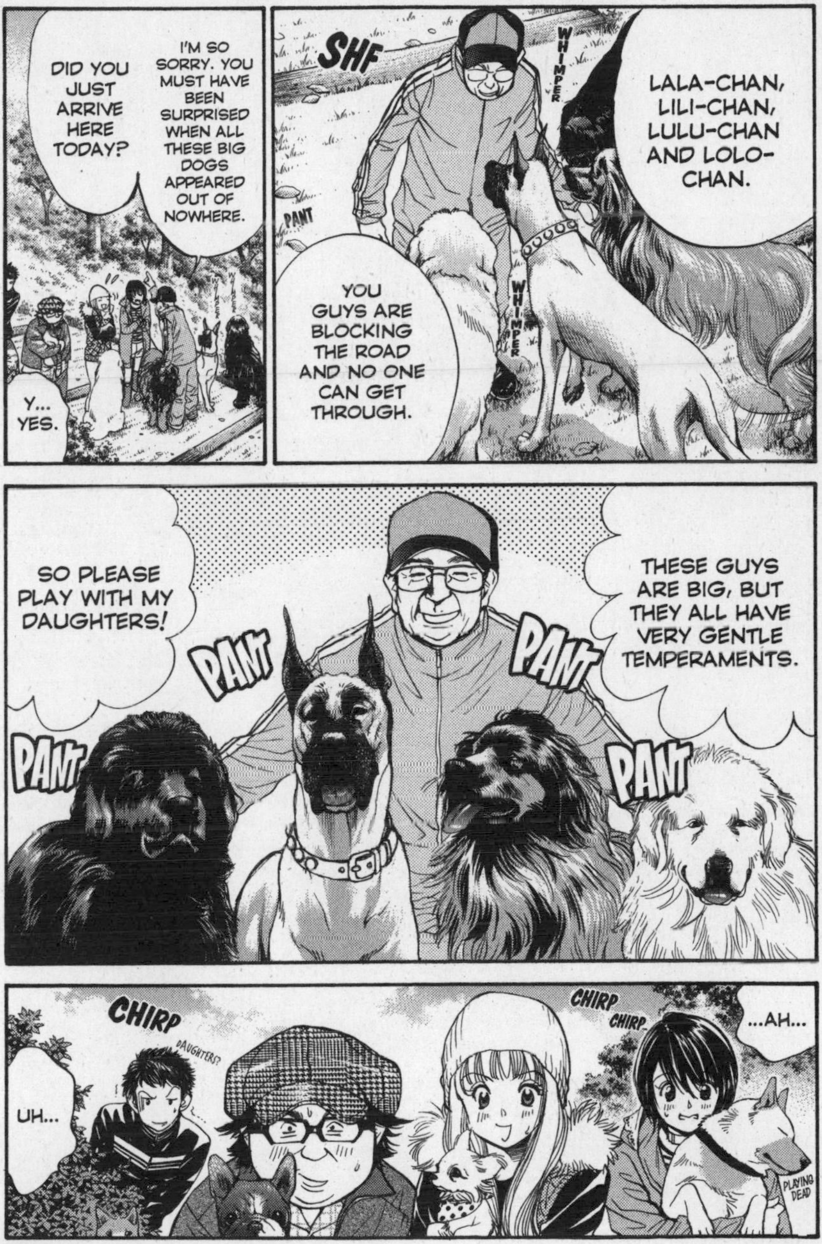
SHF
WHIMPER
LALA-CHAN, LILI-CHAN, LULU-CHAN AND LOLO-CHAN.
PANT
YOU GUYS ARE BLOCKING THE ROAD AND NO ONE CAN GET THROUGH.
WHIMPER
I'M SO SORRY. YOU MUST HAVE BEEN SURPRISED WHEN ALL THESE BIG DOGS APPEARED OUT OF NOWHERE.
DID YOU JUST ARRIVE HERE TODAY?
Y... YES.
THESE GUYS ARE BIG, BUT THEY ALL HAVE VERY GENTLE TEMPERAMENTS.
PANT
SO PLEASE PLAY WITH MY DAUGHTERS!
PANT
PANT
PANT
...AH...
CHIRP
CHIRP
PLAYING DEAD
CHIRP
DAUGHTERS?
UH...

13 THANK YOU/THE END

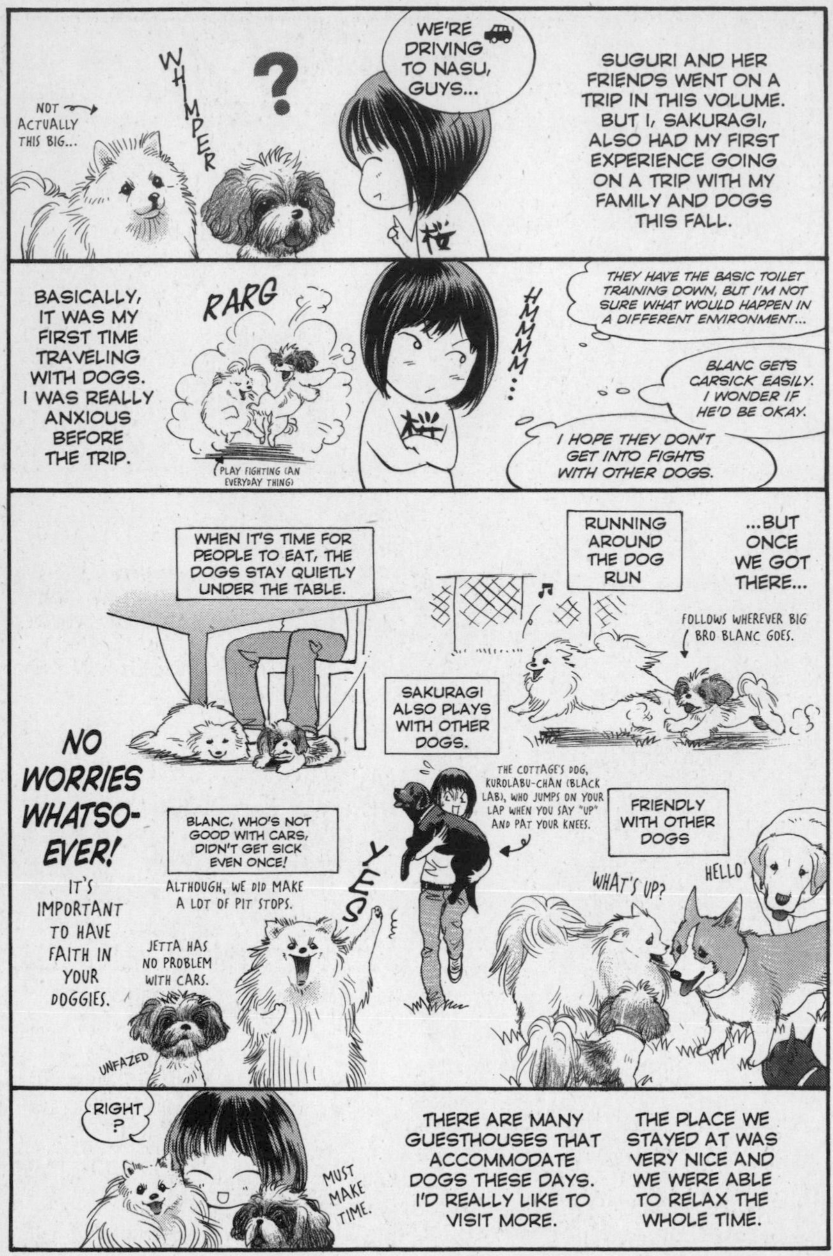
SUGURI AND HER FRIENDS WENT ON A TRIP IN THIS VOLUME. BUT I, SAKURAGI, ALSO HAD MY FIRST EXPERIENCE GOING ON A TRIP WITH MY FAMILY AND DOGS THIS FALL.
WE'RE DRIVING TO NASU, GUYS...
?
WHIMPER
NOT ACTUALLY THIS BIG...
桜
THEY HAVE THE BASIC TOILET TRAINING DOWN, BUT I'M NOT SURE WHAT WOULD HAPPEN IN A DIFFERENT ENVIRONMENT...
BLANC GETS CARSICK EASILY. I WONDER IF HE'D BE OKAY.
I HOPE THEY DON'T GET INTO FIGHTS WITH OTHER DOGS.
HMMMM...
桜
RARG
PLAY FIGHTING (AN EVERYDAY THING)
BASICALLY, IT WAS MY FIRST TIME TRAVELING WITH DOGS. I WAS REALLY ANXIOUS BEFORE THE TRIP.
...BUT ONCE WE GOT THERE...
RUNNING AROUND THE DOG RUN
FOLLOWS WHEREVER BIG BRO BLANC GOES.
WHEN IT'S TIME FOR PEOPLE TO EAT, THE DOGS STAY QUIETLY UNDER THE TABLE.
SAKURAGI ALSO PLAYS WITH OTHER DOGS.
FRIENDLY WITH OTHER DOGS
HELLO
WHAT'S UP?
THE COTTAGE'S DOG, KUROLABU-CHAN (BLACK LAB), WHO JUMPS ON YOUR LAP WHEN YOU SAY "UP" AND PAT YOUR KNEES.
NO WORRIES WHATSO-EVER!
BLANC, WHO'S NOT GOOD WITH CARS, DIDN'T GET SICK EVEN ONCE!
ALTHOUGH, WE DID MAKE A LOT OF PIT STOPS.
YES
IT'S IMPORTANT TO HAVE FAITH IN YOUR DOGGIES.
JETTA HAS NO PROBLEM WITH CARS.
UNFAZED
THE PLACE WE STAYED AT WAS VERY NICE AND WE WERE ABLE TO RELAX THE WHOLE TIME.
THERE ARE MANY GUESTHOUSES THAT ACCOMMODATE DOGS THESE DAYS. I'D REALLY LIKE TO VISIT MORE.
MUST MAKE TIME.
RIGHT?

INUBAKA

Everybody's Crazy for Dogs!

From Yokokura Moomin-san in Miyagi Prefecture

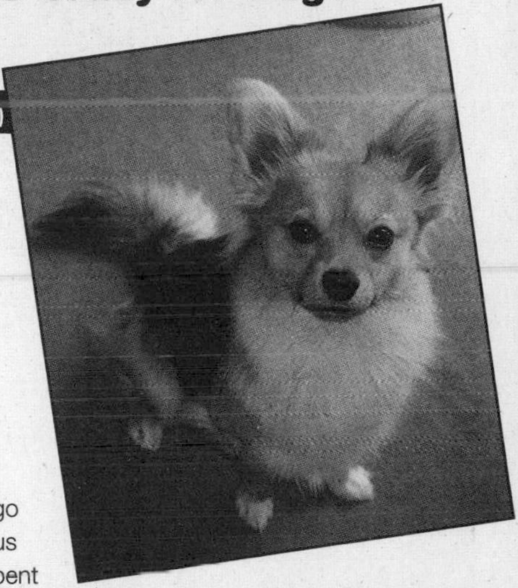

Lou-kun (Papillon and Pomeranian mix)

Last year (2007) Lou went to heaven. Thanks for leaving behind so many wonderful memories. Right now he's probably running around in heaven with Czerny-chan, and watching over his mommy. Right, Lou-kun?

Yukiya Sakuragi

It's unfortunate that they often have to go before we do, but our dogs leave with us the countless hours of happiness we spent together with them. After writing Czerny's story, I was able to engrave in my heart that losing a pet is not just about grief. Lou-kun, I hope you are resting peacefully up there…

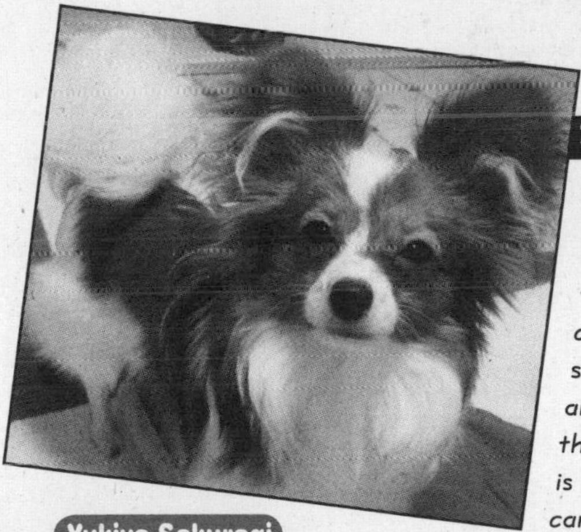

From Arai-san in Osaka

Rei-chan (Papillon)

Rei is such a baby, but loves everyone. She wags her squirrel-like tail so much that you might think it would come off! Apparently, she stares right into your eyes, and will not look away. From this picture, you can see she is looking straight into the camera lens. So cute!

Yukiya Sakuragi

The white hair coming out of her butterfly ears is adorable! It's like an accessory. They say she's a real baby when she's at home, but with these eyes, you probably can't help but spoil her… Dangerous! (lol)

From Katahira-san in Yamaguchi Prefecture

🐾 Papi-chan (Papillon)

She knows many commands, including the basics like "shake hands," "shake other hand," "sit," "down," and "stay," as well as more advanced ones like "beg" and "crawl." What a smart dog! But when it comes to sleepy time, she has to have her favorite blanky. Maybe she feels she's not spoiled enough?

Yukiya Sakuragi

She curls up in a blanket to sleep? It's adorable just picturing it. She seems very talented. She's beautiful and seems to have a good relationship with her owner. I hope she stays strong and healthy.

From Dainari-san in Hokkaido

🐾 (Left) Ucchi-chan (right) Komame-chan (Chihuahua and pug)

The owner says Ucchi is a real wimp. But as long as she's playing with her sister Komame, she's happy. ☆ Komame on the other hand is always peppy. In fact, so much so that it is almost impossible to even take a picture of her. It is nice that the girls get along so well.

Yukiya Sakuragi

A 7kg Chihuahua?! My Jetta (shih tzu) is about 7kg. That's a big Chihuahua. But she's a wimp, right? That's adorable. The pug on the other hand is 5kg. Maybe it's because she moves so much that she's still small for a big eater. What a cute duo.

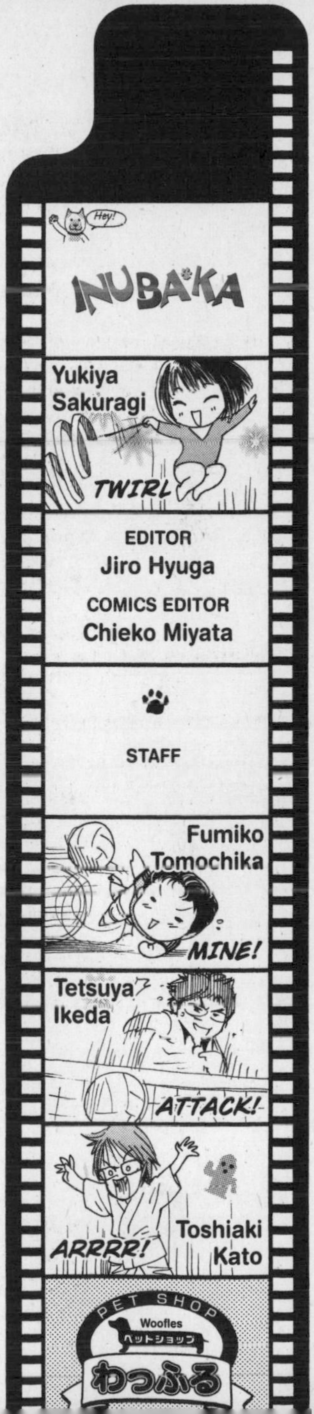
Hey!
INUBAKA
Yukiya Sakuragi
TWIRL
EDITOR
Jiro Hyuga
COMICS EDITOR
Chieko Miyata
STAFF
Fumiko Tomochika
MINE!
Tetsuya Ikeda
ATTACK!
Toshiaki Kato
ARRRR!
PET SHOP
Woofles
ペットショップ
わっふる

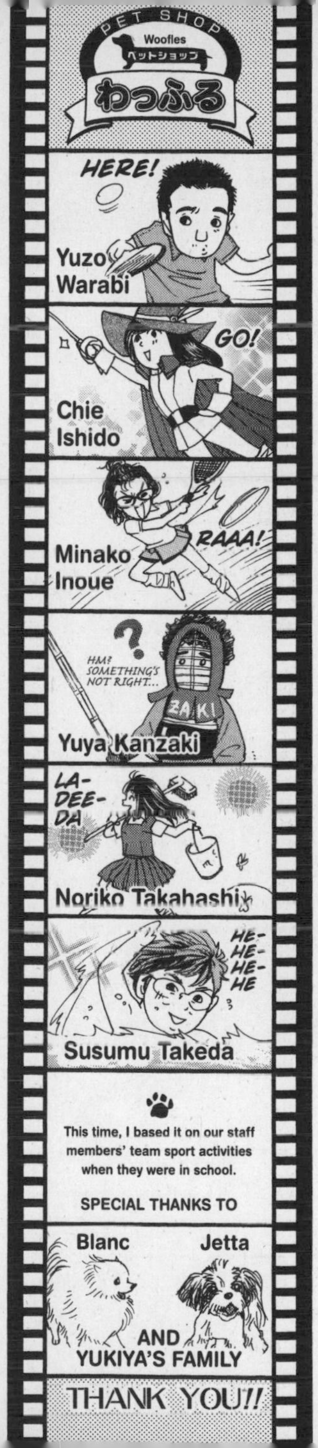
PET SHOP
Woofles
ペットショップ
わっふる
HERE!
Yuzo Warabi
GO!
Chie Ishido
RAAA!
Minako Inoue
HM? SOMETHING'S NOT RIGHT...
ZAKI
Yuya Kanzaki
LA-DEE-DA
Noriko Takahashi
HE-HE-HE-HE
Susumu Takeda
This time, I based it on our staff members' team sport activities when they were in school.
SPECIAL THANKS TO
Jetta
Blanc
AND YUKIYA'S FAMILY
THANK YOU!!

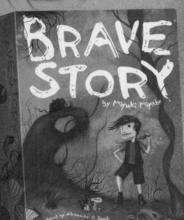

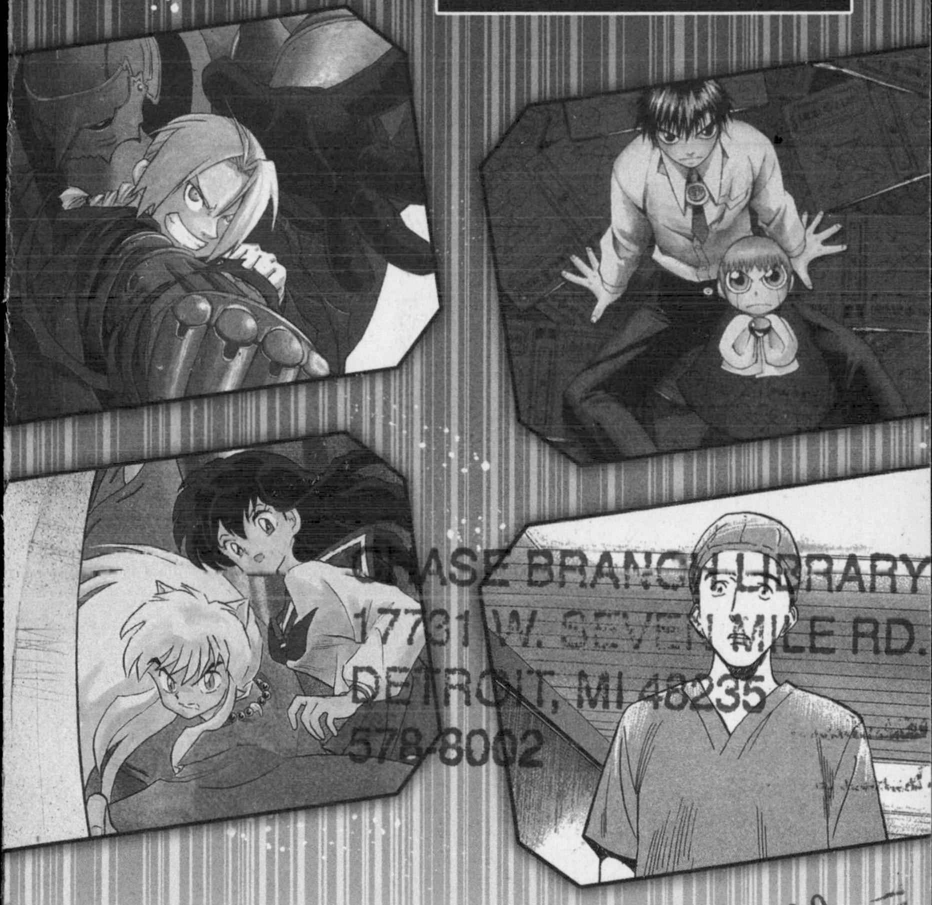